Representations of Classical Greece in Theme Parks

Imagines – Classical Receptions in the Visual and Performing Arts

Series Editors: Filippo Carlà-Uhink and Martin Lindner

Other titles in this series

Art Nouveau and the Classical Tradition, by Richard Warren
Classical Antiquity in Heavy Metal Music, edited by K. F. B. Fletcher
and Osman Umurhan
Classical Antiquity in Video Games, edited by Christian Rollinger
A Homeric Catalogue of Shapes, by Charlayn von Solms
Orientalism and the Reception of Powerful Women from the Ancient World,
edited by Filippo Carlà-Uhink and Anja Wieber
The Ancient Mediterranean Sea in Modern Visual and Performing Arts,
edited by Rosario Rovira Guardiola

Representations of Classical Greece in Theme Parks

Filippo Carlà-Uhink

BLOOMSBURY ACADEMIC
LONDON • NEW YORK • OXFORD • NEW DELHI • SYDNEY

BLOOMSBURY ACADEMIC
Bloomsbury Publishing Plc
50 Bedford Square, London, WC1B 3DP, UK
1385 Broadway, New York, NY 10018, USA
29 Earlsfort Terrace, Dublin 2, Ireland

BLOOMSBURY, BLOOMSBURY ACADEMIC and the Diana logo are trademarks of
Bloomsbury Publishing Plc

First published in Great Britain 2020
This paperback edition published in 2021

Copyright © Filippo Carlà-Uhink, 2020

Filippo Carlà-Uhink has asserted his right under the Copyright, Designs and Patents Act, 1988, to be identified as Author of this work.

For legal purposes the Acknowledgements on p. ix constitute an extension of this copyright page.

Cover design: Clare Turner
Logo design: Ainize González and Nacho García
Cover image © Frédéric VIELCANET / Alamy Stock Photo

All rights reserved. No part of this publication may be reproduced or transmitted in any form or by any means, electronic or mechanical, including photocopying, recording, or any information storage or retrieval system, without prior permission in writing from the publishers.

Bloomsbury Publishing Plc does not have any control over, or responsibility for, any third-party websites referred to or in this book. All internet addresses given in this book were correct at the time of going to press. The author and publisher regret any inconvenience caused if addresses have changed or sites have ceased to exist, but can accept no responsibility for any such changes.

A catalogue record for this book is available from the British Library.

A catalog record for this book is available from the Library of Congress.

ISBN: HB: 978-1-4742-9784-4
PB: 978-1-3501-9447-2
ePDF: 978-1-4742-9786-8
eBook: 978-1-4742-9785-1

Series: IMAGINES – Classical Receptions in the Visual and Performing Arts

Typeset by RefineCatch Limited, Bungay, Suffolk

To find out more about our authors and books visit www.bloomsbury.com and sign up for our newsletters.

Contents

List of Figures		vii
Acknowledgements		ix
1	Representing History in the Theme Park: The Case of Ancient Greece	1
	'It's a Small World' after all – and it includes Greece	1
	Historical theme parks and their uses of the past	3
	Theme parks, representations of the past and historical culture	11
	Postmodern aesthetics and the (ancient) past: Affective turn and pastness	20
	Ancient Greece in reception	26
	Ancient Greece in the theme park	36
2	German Philhellenism in the Theme Park	39
	The position of ancient Greece in German culture	39
	'Griechenland', *Europa-Park*, Rust	44
	'Strand der Götter', *Belantis*, Leipzig	61
3	Spain, Ancient Greece and the Land of Myths	75
	Ancient Greece in Spanish popular culture	75
	Terra Mítica, Benidorm	80
4	Ancient Greece, the United States of America and the Theme Park	105
	The presence of ancient Greece in US American (popular) culture	105
	Glimpses of ancient Greece in US parks	110
	Mount Olympus, Wisconsin Dells, Wisconsin	117
5	The Far East, Ancient Greece and the Theme Park	129
	Ancient Greece in Eastern Asia	129
	Happy Valley Beijing, People's Republic of China	132
	E-Da, Kaohsiung, Republic of China	149
6	Ancient Greece in France: The World of a Gallic Warrior	167
	Re-mediatization and the theme park	167
	Ancient Greece in France	168

	Ancient Greece in the Astérix world	171
	Parc Astérix	177
7	Greece – In the Form of a Conclusion	189
	Notes	197
	Bibliography	229
	Index	249

Figures

1	'Templo de Kinetos', *Terra Mítica*, Benidorm, Spain: The Temple of Zeus at Olympia	19
2	The entrance to the dark ride 'Happy World', *Happy Valley Beijing*, People's Republic of China	25
3	Pontius Pilate's *praetorium* in *Tierra Santa*, Buenos Aires, Argentina	27
4	Statue of Poseidon, *Europa-Park*, Rust, Germany	48
5	The loading station of the water coaster 'Poseidon', *Europa-Park*, Rust, Germany	51
6	The madhouse 'Cassandra', *Europa-Park*, Rust, Germany	59
7	'Die Fahrt des Odysseus', *Belantis*, Leipzig, Germany: The Trojan Horse	66
8	'Die Fahrt des Odysseus', *Belantis*, Leipzig, Germany: Charybdis	67
9	Detail of the restaurant 'Acropolis', *Terra Mítica*, Benidorm, Spain: The Porch of the Caryatids	86
10	'Los Ícaros', *Terra Mítica*, Benidorm, Spain	96
11	'Auditorio de Pandora', *Terra Mítica*, Benidorm, Spain	97
12	'Poseidon's Fury. Escape from the Lost City', *Universal Studios*, Orlando, USA	116
13	The Trojan Horse in *Mt. Olympus*, Wisconsin Dells, USA	119
14	The Entrance to *Mt. Olympus*, Wisconsin Dells, USA	120
15	The roller coaster 'Hades 360', Wisconsin Dells, USA	127
16	The themed area 'Aegean Harbour' in *Happy Valley Beijing*, People's Republic of China	134
17	*Happy Valley Beijing*: Greek warriors	138
18	Statue next to 'Trojan Horse', *Happy Valley Beijing*	141
19	'Trojan Horse', *Happy Valley Beijing*	142
20	Trojan Horse on the 'Trojan Plaza', *E-Da Theme Park*, Kaohsiung, Taiwan	156
21	The Cyclops from 'Big Air', *E-Da Theme Park*, Kaohsiung, Taiwan	163
22	The 'Vase of Heracles', *Parc Astérix*, Plailly, France	176
23	'Discobélix', *Parc Astérix*, Plailly, France	185
24	Loading station of 'Tonnerre de Zeus', *Parc Astérix*, Plailly, France	187

Acknowledgements

The project of this book began through a chance encounter and some shared interests with Florian Freitag, with whom I began to discuss theme parks and how we might be able to make them the object of our research in 2012. The first common trip to *Terra Mítica* was the outcome of those discussions, after which we not only started publishing together, but were also able to secure a generous research grant from the German Research Foundation (DFG) for a project on 'Time and Temporality in Theme Parks', which we directed together from 2014 to 2017. Sabrina Mittermeier and Ariane Schwarz cooperated on the project and thus participated in the 'research trips' organized in that context. To them, and to all the people I visited theme parks with, goes my gratitude. Special thanks go to Nicolas Zorzin, who was essentially the victim of a trap I set: as he lives in Taipei, and is an archaeologist researching in the field of cultural heritage and uses of the past, I invited him to join me for a couple of days in Kaohsiung. Little did he know what was expected of him. I am very glad that we are still friends, and that he has found interesting material for his own research; surely, I profited immensely from his knowledge during our visit to *E-Da World*.

It is rather obvious that a research project such as that which Florian and I led cannot imply visiting only the seven parks investigated here, nor meeting only the people I spent time in these parks with: many other parks needed to be seen, and I met leading researchers in theme park studies, together developing crucial discussions on theory and methodology at conferences, at dinner, or in the parks themselves. I am particularly grateful to Scott A. Lukas, who came to Mainz in 2013 as a guest professor on invitation from Florian and me, and with whom we visited, among others, the *Disneyland Resort* and *Universal Studios* in Los Angeles. His knowledge of the theme park world and his insights are unique, and without him this book would not only look very different; it would not exist. Gordon Grice was also with us in Anaheim, and on other occasions. His perspective as an architect and designer of theme parks was at times invaluable in moving me on from strange theoretical reflections, bringing my attention back to practical issues. In Germany, I found a colleague and a friend in Jan-Erik Steinkrüger: no one knows the park of *Phantasialand* as well as he does, and his impulses, once again deriving from another discipline (geography), have set my chain of thought into motion many times. Céline Molter has opened my mind to the ethnological approach to theme parks, and to a world I had never really considered before: that of religious theme parks. In this same field, I was able to have a dialogue with Crispin Paine, who also allowed me to read his monograph before it was published. I also would like to thank people I did not meet in person, but who answered my questions via email, providing me with information, pictures and videos that I could use for my study. All of them work for companies that construct theme park attractions, and they have been crucial sources of information for many points dealt with in this volume. I thank them in alphabetical order: George Dobler (Sunkid), Menno Draaisma (Mondial Rides), Charlotte van Etten (Vekoma), Kathrin Siegert (Huss) and Peter Ziegler (BeAR). Last but not least, the anonymous reviewers at Bloomsbury contributed with their precious advice to make this book more reader-friendly.

If there is one thing I learned while working on this book, and more generally while working on theme parks, it is how challenging and difficult, yet at the same time wonderfully exciting, interdisciplinarity is. I had the great fortune of being able to interact with excellent scholars from a hugely broad spectrum of other disciplines, but always in a very relaxed climate based on mutual respect, a desire to learn from each other, as well as on humour and good spirits. Research on theme parks continuously built and reinforced a strong friendship with Florian, and no visit to a theme park – even when beset by weather, nuisances, technical problems or whatever came to pass – ever finished without having laughed most of the time. For this reason, this book is dedicated to him.

1

Representing History in the Theme Park: The Case of Ancient Greece

'It's a Small World' after all – and it includes Greece

'It's a Small World', located in the 'Fantasyland' area of all Disney *Magic Kingdoms* (with the sole exception of *Shanghai Disneyland*), is one of the most popular theme park rides worldwide.[1] Originally developed for the New York World's Fair of 1964 and then relocated to *Disneyland* in Anaheim, California in 1966, it quickly became one of the most recognizable trademarks and a true staple of the *Magic Kingdoms*, opening in 1971 in Orlando, in 1983 in Tokyo, in 1992 in Paris and in 2008 in Hong Kong. The riders, accompanied by a highly recognizable song which might be the most-played song in musical history,[2] sail on boats on a ride through the world ('the happiest cruise that ever sailed'), in which the different countries and peoples are embodied by dolls representing children in traditional costumes.[3] As can be expected, each country is represented in a highly stereotyped way, with the costumes, monuments, and at times the traditions which are considered most typical and recognizable.[4] This means that countries and peoples are generally represented in a historical way, in reference to the most famous phases of their histories, those which left the most recognizable monuments. By being represented in this way – each country as a small diorama – anachronisms may ensue, which bring together different recognizable phases of the country's history: Italy, for instance, is represented in *Disneyland Paris* by a Roman chariot race, next to a representation of Venice, an opera singer, and many other details.[5] This does not apply to Greece, which is perceived only through its ancient phase, immediately recognizable by the international public.[6]

In Anaheim, the original ride caters to the worldview of the public that was expected when the ride was developed – mostly US Americans.[7] The façade of the attraction is a collage of representations of several famous monuments – the choice is definitely Western-centric, and the Parthenon, included next to the Eiffel Tower,

Big Ben and others, is thus raised to the level of icon for one of the crucial phases of world history.[8] The representation of Greece within the ride, though, is so small that it is extremely easy to overlook. Interestingly, it is not located in the European section, but after the clearly marked passage to Asia, between Russia and the Middle East. A lone doll represents Greece: a shepherd, wearing furs and a red cap, evoking the red scarf which is a component of female traditional dress in many regions of Greece or a fez, who plays the Pan flute (referencing Greek mythology in its very name) to a lamb. The shepherd sits on the capital of an Ionic column, placed on an architrave held by two further white columns. It is rather easy to identify the components of this representation: the ruins of classical antiquity leave space to the 'naturalistic' idea of Greece as a wild landscape (never again touched by civilization), in which shepherds play music while tending to sheep or goats. The costume evokes the Ottoman and modern clothing, with a clear reference to the fustanella (known in the United States through the Greek communities),[9] while the geographical positioning reveals an Orientalizing gaze which locates Greece among the post-Ottoman countries, thus attributing it to Asia.

Moving on to Orlando, Greece is still located in Asia, but it is the first country the riders meet in this section, in direct contiguity to Europe. The scene is much bigger, and while the main element remains the same Pan flute-playing shepherd with lambs, he is located in a broader landscape of ruins. The idea of Greece as pristine and uncontaminated landscape has disappeared in favour of a more 'symbolic' representation, dominated by the colours of the Greek flag: the white of the ancient buildings and the blue of the hills, mountains, and even of the sunflowers. The columns are more stylized and abstract but still recognizable as Ionic; the number of columns and pediments is greater, and in the background a mountain with a temple on the top is likely a visual reference to the Parthenon, here meant to signify Mount Olympus. Classical culture is thus highlighted over 'natural' Greece, even if the latter does not disappear (life in Greece after the classical period is still represented as playing music to lambs), and Greece in general seems to attract more attention.

The ride in Tokyo reproduces that of Orlando;[10] indeed, Greece seems to be understood in Japan as the 'starting point' of Western trips to the Orient: in this way, 'Oriental Trip' in *New Reoma World*, Marugame, Japan, moves, exactly as 'It's a Small World', from Greece, represented by 'a Greek church, a few houses and a white-washed terrace', to then display the Middle and Far East (all seen from a projected Western perspective).[11] Yet this was impossible in Paris: not only as Greece is nearer and better known in France, but also because Greece had joined the European Economic Community in 1981. Catering to the knowledge and expectations of this different public implies a crucial difference: shifting Greece into the European section.¹² The main – and only – human character remains the shepherd, who is still playing his Pan flute to the lambs. Away from the 'abstract' representation in Orlando, the hills are again green, and the landscape is naturalized through the insertion of tall trees, making the representation similar to that in Anaheim: ruins evoking a far-away past and a pastoral (or bucolic) present. Yet this is presented here in a more positive way, as a sign of closeness to 'Nature', within an Arcadian landscape that is different from that in California. The ruins are represented in much more detail; a group of three columns with an architrave is round in shape, something which breaks the most usual and conventional representations of ancient Greek architecture but has a clear direct referent: the tholos of the sanctuary of Athena Pronaia in Delphi. In Europe, the number of available 'images' of Greek antiquity is larger, also because the country is a much closer and cheaper tourist destination. Finally, there is a further reference to classical mythology: above the shepherd flies a winged horse, Pegasus, revealing that this idyllic, Arcadian vision of Greece is actually the stuff that myths (and dreams) are made of. The attribution of Greece to Europe could not be undone in Hong Kong, where the Greek scene is positioned between Italy and Switzerland. Yet the scene is the same as in Anaheim, with only a slightly more modern, more 'abstract' design. From Hong Kong, Greece is again very far away, almost lost between better-known countries.

Why was Greece represented in these slightly, yet significantly different ways in the different Disney parks? Starting from this question, and moving beyond the world of Disney parks, this book will investigate and explain the ways in which classical Greece is represented and reproduced in theme parks throughout the world. In order to proceed to such analysis, though, it is necessary to provide first a theoretical framework about theme parks and representations of history and historical cultures within them. This first chapter aims to elaborate and present such framework, which will be deployed in the following sections of the book for the analysis of the single theme parks taken into consideration.

Historical theme parks and their uses of the past

Theme parks and their antecedents

Conventionally, the inauguration of *Disneyland* in Anaheim, California in 1955 is considered the 'birth' of theme parks. Indeed, it was through *Disneyland* that the form 'theme park' came to mean a specific kind of themed environment, or themed space,[13] within which a set of defined characteristics emerged:[14] theme parks are artificially created (generally in their entirety); they are closed, unmovable; and they consist of a 'collection' of different forms of attractions, games and entertainment offers. Above all, they are characterized by a thematic consistency, meaning that either the entire park or individual parts of it (clearly identified and themselves closed off from the rest) are inspired by a specific theme:[15] 'theme parks are cultural mind maps – symbolic landscapes of psychological narratives. They are the multidimensional descendant of the book, film, and epic rather than the offshoot of the roller coaster and tilt-o-whirl.'[16]

However, scholarship is ever more certain of the genealogy of antecedents that brought us to the 'postmodern' theme park;[17] this genealogy also explains why cultural and historical themes are so important within theme parks. Most – and the most popular – antecedent forms of the theme parks were conceived, often also with a didactic component, as instruments to bring the visitors to landscapes, animals, traditions from cultures far away in space or time. World's fairs, zoos and human zoos are perfect examples: in the nineteenth century, zoological gardens had already begun to develop immersive strategies, for instance through architectural forms which imitated the animals' region of origin,[18] thus enhancing the visitors' sense of seeing something 'exotic'; ethnological exhibitions, with a colonial gaze, displayed the cultures of exotic populations perceived as 'primitive'.[19] The aim was to reinforce the sense of identity (and superiority) of the visitors, displaying an alterity which was represented as exotic, 'inferior' and 'archaic'.[20] As a consequence, the exotic other is almost always represented as 'stuck in the past', implying a connection between the idea of a geographical distance (of the exotic culture) and a temporal one.[21]

Open-air museums moved in the same direction, starting with *Skansen* in Stockholm, which opened in 1891 and collected and reproduced the traditional architecture and lifestyle of various parts of Sweden (and the animals representing Swedish wildlife) at a moment when they were perceived as endangered by industrialization and ever-stronger migration to the cities.[22] Such structures, distinct from the 'exotic shows', represent one's own (historical) culture, both for insiders (in the sense of continuity and identification) and outsiders (to highlight the national pride for visitors from other countries).[23] By 'freezing' this culture in time, be it in the form of a reproduction of one specific moment or the fusion of different time periods (represented by different buildings, in one imagined paradigmatic moment of the traditional lifestyle), such representations also always end up reifying an idealized version of the culture represented as being anchored in a previous time – as past.

This occurs in *Disneyland*, too: the complete separation from the outside world, which *Disneyland* made much clearer and more radical,[24] as well as the act of paying for a ticket and moving through the gates of the parks (a ritual-dynamic action that highlights the separation between Inside and Outside),[25] are both central instruments in creating an immersion that is not only functional to entertainment, but also to the development of a 'patriotic' historical consciousness.[26] The pedagogical aspect was in this sense very clear to Walt Disney, who proposed to his visitors (originally mostly US Americans) the reified utopia of the small American town at the beginning of the twentieth century, materialized in the entrance area of the park, 'Main Street U.S.A.', the only one that each visitor cannot avoid crossing.[27]

It so happens that most themes represented in theme parks are 'historical' or 'cultural' – what Scott Lukas calls theming based on 'place and culture'.[28] As formulated by King and O'Boyle, the theme park is more correctly a 'time park'.[29] We see this beginning with the classification of possible theme park themes developed by Fichtner and Michna in 1987.[30] Excluding their category number 5, 'Play worlds, as water parks, circus' (these are not theme parks in the narrower sense, as they are not characterized by a consistent theme applied either to the entire park or to single sections of it), the other four categories are defined as follows:

1. 'Foreign worlds in the dimension of time'
   a) Past and nostalgia
   b) Future
2. 'Foreign worlds in the dimension of space'
   a) Foreign people, regions
   b) Wild nature
3. 'Foreign worlds in the social dimension': foreign cultures, folklore
4. Unreal worlds, such as miniatures, ghosts, fairy tales.

As with all classifications, the limits are clearly visible: the difference between 2a and 3 is disputable to say the least, as well as the definition of miniatures as being unreal. Miniature parks, representing the main monuments of a country in a miniaturized form and thus displaying the unity of the nation and its 'spirit' in a clear and easily transmissible form, are relevant instruments of nation building for the creation of a feeling of belonging to the national identity, as deployed in countries such as Israel, Indonesia, Italy, etc.[31] Their 'reality' – their perception as real – is demonstrated by acts of dissidence, resistance, and even destruction practised by visitors upon them as a symbol and a form of ersatz for the civic body.[32]

However, independent of this, one can see how all the categories identified are deeply historical: there is no need to discuss this for section 1, as it is sufficient to note that imaginations and visualizations of the future are also historical and dependent on the specific culture of the moment in which they have been developed (and thus they can also be represented as 'past visualisations of the future', as in the case of steampunk).[33] But nor can foreign cultures, folklore, wild nature, or other regions be represented in the form of an evolution or of change. What is represented is always 'frozen in time', in a way reifying this frozen moment as the paradigmatic and archetypical representation of that specific culture, region, or ecosystem. As summarized by Schlehe and Hochbruck, this either represents 'the creation of a history of a nation, region, or ethnic group, as an offer to the visitor for imaginative identification, or it is the creation of a seemingly timeless exotic Other, juxtaposed to the Self and serving to stabilize and position it in the global world'.[34] 'Time' is thus proposed by Bryman as one of the 'ingredients' of theming, which generally do not come alone, but in association, alongside space, literature, cinema, music, sport, architecture, fashion, etc.[35]

Finally, unreal worlds need to be visualized, too, and this happens in ways which are necessarily inspired by historical phases and their symbolic association with values in the culture of reference. In the Western imagination, for instance, the world of magic (and associated images of witches and fairies) is deeply entrenched in the imaginary of the Middle Ages. This is strengthened by the fact that fairy tales, as extremely old and traditional components of folk culture, are often also associated with this historical phase and with the images of realms, kings, princes and princesses, etc. As put by Marcus Folch, 'a false medievalism' is 'the normative ecology for fantastic literature', even if 'classical structures often subtend fantasy's medievalizing edifice'.[36] As a consequence, themed environments dedicated to these worlds take inspiration from medieval architecture, or from what is imagined to be a visualization of the Middle Ages. The world of Harry Potter, as represented in the movies and then in the corresponding themed areas in the *Universal Orlando Resort*, is thus characterized by architectural forms associated with the Middle Ages.

'Historical' and 'cultural' theme parks, stereotypes and authenticity

How can one thus define what is a 'historical' or a 'cultural' theme park? Beyond the apparently simple statement that 'cultural theme parks are parks that use cultures as their themes',[37] there is much less clarity than one might think. Not only is the concept of 'culture' an extremely problematic one, widely discussed in literature; such a definition also does not help us to see how specific cultures (such as the European Middle Ages) influence the representation of themes which cannot be considered 'cultural', nor how the representation of specific cultures is re-mediatized from other popular media (we will see a clear example of this later in *Parc Astérix*). This is crucial, because previous and popular visualizations have a strong influence on determining how later decisions in the representation of a world, a character, or a culture are taken. In this sense, any representation of the world of fairy tales, or of Harry Potter, for instance, that shifted away from a stereotypical 'medieval' setting would be unexpected and disturbing. This complication is further demonstrated by the case of a 'cultural theme park' entirely based on popular knowledge and revolving around a painting which might not actually be authentic, as analysed by Ong and Jin.[38] It is thus better to replace the concept of 'cultural' with that of 'historical', which allows the inclusion of all forms of re-mediatization, the chains of reception, and the influence of historical phases on the representation of fantastic worlds, leaving us 'only' with the problem of defining what is history – or better, from what moment the past can be considered 'history'.[39] I have suggested elsewhere a conventional, and rather drastic, answer, proposing to identify as 'historical' every theme representing a culture, a society, an event, a character, for which there are no living witnesses left.[40] I will leave this problem aside for now, however, as the focus of this book, on the representation of the ancient world and more specifically of classical Greece, means this question is of secondary importance here.

The representation of the chosen themes must therefore make use of existing stereotypes: the public has foreknowledge about a theme (it does not matter whether right or wrong) and has pre-built visualizations of it, deriving from movies, paintings, postcards, comics, video games etc.: 'the historical theme park will content itself with rearranging those things the visitors knew before into forms that appear simultaneously new and familiar',[41] generating what Chapman has called 'historical resonance'.[42] The condition for a successful immersion in the theme is, in this sense, its recognizability:[43] the individuation and recognition of images and concepts which are already known about a foreign culture or a historical period gives a sense of satisfaction and the feeling of 'having learnt' through seeing and touching,[44] while being confronted with representations that are perhaps more historically correct, yet unrecognizable, risks causing a sense of alienation which can lead, in the end, to a lack of amusement and therefore a commercial failure.[45] It is therefore no surprise if these forms of reception continue and perpetuate ideas which, from a scientific perspective, should be classified as 'mistakes'.[46] This is why representations in theme parks are inherently conservative,[47] and follow an approach to history that basically essentializes and naturalizes contemporary expectations and social structures: 'this nostalgic approach to history assumes the nuclear family unit as the central social organising system, that the individual is a transhistorical construct, and most importantly, that encounters with the physical reality and material culture of a given period will sufficiently stimulate the total experience of that period'.[48]

In this sense, while a scholarly correct representation may be considered 'authentic' in the sense that authenticity is perceived as a property of the object ('museological authenticity'),[49] it risks failing to create any feeling of 'authenticity', here meaning an attribute of the experience of the public confronted with the object ('existential authenticity').[50] Li Yang has called this 'a tourist's perception of authenticity' and defined it as being composed of two parts: 'tourists' preconceptions of the visited culture' and 'tourists' perceptions of the actual manifestation of the culture in the attraction',[51] the latter clearly linking to MacCannell's concept of 'staged authenticity' in tourism which began, during the 1970s, the scholarly debate on the very concept at stake,[52] and led to a reversal of the focus from the 'offer' to the 'demand'. Both aspects, the 'museological' and the 'existential', have been partially integrated through the concept of 'performative authenticity', which insists on how the bodily practices of the visitors contribute to the authentication of the places.[53] This terminological tension is clearly visible in scholarship from the 1980s, as in Orvell, who came to define the nineteenth century as a 'culture of imitation', the twentieth as a 'culture of authenticity' and our world, after the Second World War and the development of mass popular culture since the 1960s, as the 'culture of the factitious', in which 'we have a hunger for something like authenticity but we are easily satisfied by an ersatz facsimile'.[54]

Umberto Eco (wrongly) considered this cultural movement to be exclusively American, and tried to sociologically explain it as deriving from wealth without history: 'the past must be preserved and celebrated in full-scale authentic copy', up to the point that the entirely real becomes identified with the entirely fake, and the sign 'aims to be the thing, to abolish the distinction of the reference, the mechanism of replacement'.[55] This is what he defined as 'hyperreality', while Lash and Urry tried to define the postmodern economy as an 'economy of sign and space', in which 'what is increasingly produced are not material objects, but signs'.[56] All this is particularly important when dealing with the past, as a lived experience cannot, of course, be 'authentic' in any museological sense, and thus must be a 'staged authenticity', albeit one that is experienced as deeply authentic.[57]

An episode from the era of human zoos is particularly meaningful. Carl Hagenbeck, the 'inventor' of these ethnological exhibitions, organized the presentation of a group of Native Americans called Bella Coola. Their costumes and large traditional masks attracted much praise from the scholarly community, as the presentation was considered to be ethnologically well-conceived and precise; it ended in a financial catastrophe, as the public could not connect this appearance with the image of the Native Americans from the prairies which they knew from novels, drawings, paintings, and shows in the style of Buffalo Bill. Journal articles defined the Bella Coola as 'not Indian enough' or 'false Indians'; their 'museological authenticity' was, for the visitors, simply 'not authentic'.[58] 'heritage fabricated by the media often seems more real because it is more familiar than the original'.[59] This issue has been explored in connection with *Colonial Williamsburg*: when the living history museum decided to integrate dirt, garbage and dung to transmit a less sanitized idea of the past – which would appear more authentic[60] – it attracted criticism from some visitors, who complained about the choice.[61] What's more, considering dirt as a quantifiable sign of authenticity, the management made the site even 'dirtier' than it was, thus falling into another stereotype, that of the past as being simply a more primitive version of the present.[62]

In theme park studies it is almost compulsory to quote Jean Baudrillard in reference to such questions of representation and authenticity, who in *Simulacra and Simulation* (1981) dealt with the evolution of systems of sign. According to Baudrillard, there are three kinds of simulacrum, associated with different historical stages: in the premodern world, the first order is that in which the originals are impossible to replace, and copies are just placeholders (natural simulacra). With the Industrial Revolution, the second order brought, through mechanical reproduction, the impossibility of distinguishing original from copy, transforming all of them into commodities (productive simulacra). Finally, in postmodernism, the third order inverts the traditional concepts: the simulacrum precedes the original and originality loses any significance (simulacra of simulation).[63] While this resembles Eco's argument, I would argue that this actually has only a limited significance for immersive environments with a historical and/or cultural theme, which break the traditional, museological, concept of authenticity but have an external referent without which they would completely lose their meaning.[64]

Indeed, Baudrillard's idea of the simulation of third order, specifically used to explain *Disneyland* and connected to the assumption that 'we need a visible past, a visible continuum, a visible myth of origin, which reassures us about our end',[65] should instead be framed in terms of a radical change in the perception of time and temporality characteristic of the last quarter of the twentieth century, which we will argue in more detail later. What Baudrillard considers to be a simulation of third order, arguing for instance that a perfect copy of the caves of Lascaux makes the original artificial,[66] is rather a process of presentification, which 'flattens' various time layers onto a broad present.[67] The hyperreal is, for Baudrillard, surely 'more true than the true, more real than the real', but this is connected to a strong conviction that 'there is not even the possibility of simultaneity in the order of time';[68] on the contrary, as we will see, it is precisely the possibility of simultaneity and of 'time travel' that allows immersive historical environments to function.[69] This also allows us to overcome a major difficulty in Baudrillard's theory: the fact that 'it is not evident that simulation and representation are mutually exclusive'.[70]

Far more important is Baudrillard's classification, in the same work, of the four different stages of the sign-order: the faithful copy; the perversion of reality (the assumption that the copy is not faithful); the pretence of reality, in which the sign pretends to be a copy, but has no original; and finally, the simulacrum, which has absolutely no contact with reality.[71] The forms of representation encountered in historical theme parks do not thus move within the sign-order of the simulacrum, but within that of the pretence of reality, in which images assemble to hint at and reference a reality that is not hidden behind them. As formulated by Adey, 'simulations and models can be comprehended not merely as copies or referents, but as mediators'.[72]

With few exceptions, theme parks are first and foremost commercial enterprises, as were most of their antecedents.[73] In this sense, their political and ideological aspects should not be underestimated, but they also are presented to the public in a way that makes them 'enjoyable' and guarantees the economic success of the park. They do not represent the main aim of the park, nor the condition for its survival. In this sense, 'visitors to amusement parks seek to maximise their enjoyment by preferring rides and attractions linked to historic themes that are easy to recognise, simple to grasp, and fun to join'.[74] Even parks with a didactic or political aim, such as the miniature park *Taman Mini Indonesia Indah* that is dedicated to creating a sense of Indonesian national identity (and to which admission is free),[75] cannot afford to unsettle visitors nor confront them with unknown and unrecognizable images; they also work with the stereotypes available, combining them to their specific aims. Even religious theme parks, which have a substantially different aim and should not necessarily be connected with sanitized versions of history, end up deploying the same representation mechanisms: 'one visitor to the *Holy Land Experience* [a religious theme park in Orlando] suggested that it was better that the real thing, not as "smelly" as butcher's alley (suq el-lahham) in Jerusalem's Old City – and much less crowded'[76] (and representing, again, a historical past: Judaea in the time of Roman rule).

Theme parks, representations of the past and historical culture

Externality, Disneyfication and Disneyization

To investigate the forms through which 'history' is represented in theme parks, it is necessary to discuss two concepts recurrently used in scholarship: externality and Disneyfication/Disneyization. The former, 'externality', has been introduced to highlight that a themed environment, and therefore a theme park, must represent something different from what is already available there, where the representation is created.[77] Theme parks are not bound by rules of place or availability: 'they generally stand in an arbitrary relation to the sites where they are built, since fantasy has no fixed geographic relation'.[78] The passage is marked by the closed boundary of the theme park, which could not exist if it represented what is available outside the gates. As Lowenthal puts it: 'our theme parks, no less than the themed gardens of the Middle Ages, are Other: They come into being and thrive only by *opposing* the chaos or ruin of the untamed and untidy mess beyond'.[79] The central point is a form of deterritorialization, which leads the visitor not just to look upon an exterior zone as an observer, but to occupy it and experience it directly, to internalize it and make it domestic. This was very clear to Walt Disney already when *Disneyland* was established, in 1955, as a sign at the entrance of the park famously claims that 'Here you leave today and enter the world of Yesterday, Tomorrow, and Fantasy'.[80]

But as this plaque makes clear, externality cannot be taken only in a cultural and geographical sense, it can also be understood in a temporal sense; it does not exclude representations of genealogy and continuity to imply only representations of otherness and exoticism. Indeed, while theme parks can represent cultures and historical phases which are extraneous to the location of the park, they can also represent the past of that very same region. Theme parks can 'assert their localness by celebrating their local nationalistic identity either in the actual attractions offered, in the mascots they use, or in the programme of activities they run (e.g. festivities)'.[81] This can be primarily aimed at visitors from abroad, for whom the discovery of the 'traditional cultures' of a place that is already 'exotic' merely reinforces the feeling of exoticism (as in the *Polynesian Cultural Center* in Hawaii);[82] yet many parks are directly aimed at local visitors, and in general both the 'local' and the 'exotic' gaze are active and productive in the construction of identity at the same time.[83]

Temporal externality – the opportunity, through immersion, to 'visit' the past of that same region – is enough to mark the boundary of the themed environment. At the same time, it constructs identity, not through the forms of opposition described by Lowenthal, but through the identification of a continuity, the construction of a historical narrative which allows us to identify 'our ancestors':[84] one example (a 'real' theme park with roller coasters) is *Six Flags over Texas*, which celebrates Texan history and its different phases.[85] While representations of ancient Greece in China, for instance, are surely very exotic, ancient Greece can be activated in Western Europe, and not only in Greece, as the 'cradle' of Western civilization, and thus represented as temporally other, but deeply 'ours',[86] as this in particular is how ancient Greece is presented within schools and school books throughout Europe.[87] In spite of the fact that few Western (and even European) countries have a direct connection with Greek antiquity and Greek ruins on their territory, most would still represent ancient Greece as being a part of their own history and identity. The choice of themes within the theme park thus depends strongly on the structures of identity available where the park is built; at the same time, the forms of representation deployed in the theme park produce, or rather confirm and reinforce, these identity structures through the forms of historical narrations deployed there. This implies that the same historical culture can be represented in different contexts and assume different meanings in these contexts: this will be a red thread that runs throughout the entire book.

Theme parks are thus deeply ideological: using the different approaches to history as defined by Cornelius Holtorf, they can (1) be 'evolutionary', stressing the continuity and sequencing of historical periods and 'facts'; they can (2) be 'political', stressing the construction and representation of different pasts in different presents; or they can (3) adopt the mechanisms of 'time travel'.[88] It is important to stress the concept of travel, as the rite of passage at the entrance of the park allows visitors to experience a 'departure', 'a limited breaking with established routines and practices of everyday life and allowing one's senses to engage with a set of stimuli that contrast with the everyday and the mundane'.[89] Importantly, indeed, the 'traveller' is all the time aware of the fact that he is actually not moving to the past at all.[90] Theme parks and themed spaces are not 'frauds' and do not aim to truly convince their visitors that they are entering a new time or a new dimension;[91] they work through the constant awareness that the immersion they provide is a temporary separation from the reality outside, which is not forgotten at any moment. Indeed, 'if we were totally to become Mississippi steamboat passengers or Star Wars characters, immersed in their concerns and goals and fears and anxieties, we would not have the concomitant awareness that the experience was "fun" and "different" ... A theme park is an attraction, not a conversion to a new identity.'[92] The visitors thus look at what surrounds them with a 'tourist gaze', 'directed to features of landscape and townscape which separate them from everyday experience' (the principle of externality) and based on anticipation, 'constructed and sustained through a variety of non-tourist technologies' which create structures of expectation.[93] In this sense, the process of immersion cannot work if the visitors are not 'willing' to enjoy it and bring to the theme park the 'correct' predisposition.[94]

Nonetheless, when they have a historical theme, theme parks provide information about the past, even if 'time travel' generates an experience of the past that is not intellectual-argumentative in nature: to use Graburn's adaption to museum studies of Lévi-Strauss's vocabulary, the knowledge derived is 'mythic' and not 'scientific'.[95] The results are extremely powerful historical images: powerful because they are interiorized by the visitors through their sensorial experience (in the same way tableaux vivants are 'offered as a form of shared experience', to follow Samuel),[96] and not 'learnt' argumentatively, as occurs with a reading of historiography; they are also powerful due to the sheer number of people reached.[97] Even rather unsuccessful theme parks have visitor numbers on a scale entirely different from those who read history books, and sometimes even from the audience of historical documentaries on TV, which are considered the main channel through which people come into contact with history in our society.[98] The only reasonable comparison would be the number of people reached by historical video games.[99]

These aspects have been perceived by some as worrying, and one consequence has been the development of the concepts of 'Disneyization' and 'Disneyfication'. The first concept, introduced by Bryman, defines 'the process by which the principles of the Disney theme parks are coming to dominate more and more sectors of American society as well as the rest of the world'.[100] According to Bryman, while Disney cannot be considered solely responsible for this evolution, but rather as emblematic of these dynamics ('structural Disneyization'), its success has also made it influential in accelerating and perpetuating such a trend ('transferred Disneyization'). This consists of the ever more widespread use of theming as a way of attracting customers, but also hybrid consumption, the development of merchandising and the use of performative labour, and entails a strong control over and thus surveillance within the themed area:[101] 'without a specific social and material context' – writes Zukin, who describes this phenomenon and locates it within the complicated relationship between market and place, even if he does not use the concept of Disneyization – 'the organising principle in these landscapes is simply a visual theme'.[102]

Disneyfication, on the other hand, is used to indicate in an exclusively pejorative way the adoption of a 'Disney approach' to different areas and fields of action, mostly literature and history.[103] It was originally used to signify how literary and cultural products from different origins, when 're-elaborated' by Disney, became distorted, undoubtedly Disneyan products, obscuring the previous life of these works. However, the concept was later applied to urban planning and eventually to representations of history, to define a process through which contents and objects are rendered in a superficial, simplistic and whitewashed way. In this sense, the concept of Disneyfication has been adopted in many situations to refer to representations of heritage and of history perceived to be produced 'as in the theme park', in a too simple, undifferentiated, commercial, untroubling way.[104] Beyond that, the concept is also pejorative in a second sense (a criticism often raised against reconstructions and immersive historical environments): that they place the spectators in a purely passive role, taking away from them the possibility of reconstructing and rebuilding the past in individual forms and giving them 'no role other than the consumption of kitsch'.[105] And yet, if we define kitsch as 'the attempt to repossess the experience of intensity and immediacy through an object',[106] it becomes clear that 'historical theme parks' are indeed kitsch, but in a more positive fashion, as they allow people to experience with intensity and immediacy a different time and culture through the objects which compose their theming.

Disney's America

The discussion about the appropriateness of theme park representations of history, their opportunity and dangers reached a peak when in 1993 Disney announced the project of a theme park, *Disney's America*, to be built near Haymarket, Virginia, in an area dense with historical memories, not far from *Colonial Williamsburg*.[107] The park would have opened in 1998, consisting of nine themed areas representing American history, from a Native American village to a Civil War fort and the two World Wars. There were two main criticisms of the project: the impact on the area, as well as on the 'real' historical sites surrounding the park; and the ways in which Disney would have represented American history and its contested issues, from the massacre of Native Americans to slavery. In a context marked by the Culture wars,[108] a general fear was that the park would have provided a sanitized, whitewashed vision of history which would have ultimately, due to the popularity of Disney and the immersive, sensorial approach to history provided, been impossible to correct. The concept of 'Disneyfication of history' thus evolved into the concept of 'Distory', intentionally playing with both the name Disney and the prefix 'dis-' ('opposite or absence of'). Introduced by Fjellman, this concept defines a postmodern form of presentation of the past which is based on spectacle, decontextualizes stories from the past and constructs authoritative narratives.[109] This was not the stance of all scholars and historians: some argued that the project could be positive, provided Disney were ready to involve professional historians, and David Lowenthal even claimed that the park could have helped to generate a stronger interest in the past: 'so might Disney's Historyland generate interest in actual historic places and themes'.[110] Nonetheless, the project was abandoned, after having revealed the strength of the tensions surrounding the past and history and its interpretation, and the clash of interests between professional historians and a commercial enterprise such as Disney. Yet it is important to highlight that theme parks have also developed, over the past few decades, special didactic programmes and offers that are generally reserved for schools: *Terra Mítica* in Benidorm, Spain, for instance, offers materials to visit the park while learning about the ancient world.[111] As formulated by Huyssen,

> we cannot simply pit the serious Holocaust museum against some Disneyfied theme parks. For this would only reproduce the old high/low dichotomy of modernist culture in a new guise ... For once we acknowledge the constitutive gap between reality and its representation in language or image, we must in principle be open to many different possibilities of representing the real and its memories.[112]

Theme parks and historical culture

Theme parks are, in the end, an important means of visualization, of transmission, of popularization of history and historical knowledge, as their images and narratives are incorporated 'into the discursive body of mutualized knowledge'.[113] In this sense, they are a crucial part of what German scholarship calls the *Geschichtskultur*, the 'historical culture' of the communities where they exist, and those of their visitors. The concept includes all the forms and ways in which a chosen society or community deals with its history, including academic research, school teaching, popular culture, and so on;[114] theme parks must therefore be analysed in terms of their connections and relations to the other components of the relevant 'historical cultures', in order to explain how their figurations of history work within the specific contexts in which they have been created. Rüsen recognized three main dimensions of the 'historical culture': an aesthetic, a political, and a cognitive, which he later broadened to five, adding a moral and a religious dimension.[115] While admitting that all are present in any representation of history, Rüsen considers them to be separate from each other; in his opinion, a strongly aesthetic approach reduces both the argumentative side of the cognitive dimension and the political dimension.[116] Yet, if it is true that theme parks, acting mostly on the aesthetic side, do transmit images of history in a non-argumentative way, this in no way makes such images less political.[117] In the theme park, the past is a 'present past', which is activated and functionalized to make sense of one own's experience, to create and reinforce identities and orient action.[118] It is not only narratives that perform this function: images, recognizable as symbols, can also assume a semaphoric value, activating the memory processes, historical knowledge, and values connected to them.[119]

According to Rüsen, there are four approaches through which meaning and sense are given to history:[120] the first is the traditional approach, which constructs a sense of identity between the past and the present, in the sense of 'we were always the same'; the second, the critical approach, instead highlights the superiority of the present by arguing that the past was characterized by mistakes, cruelty, a lack of democracy, etc. Through the third approach, the genetic, a continuity is constructed between past and present, while also stressing the evolutionary process which makes the present a better, improved version of the past. Finally, the exemplary approach sees in the past a repository of positive and negative examples, which can be considered helpful to orient our actions. These approaches must be considered as ideal types, as they do not necessarily exclude each other, but can coexist within one and the same representation of history.

Still, they are also useful for understanding how history 'works' in the theme park: the representation of the small American town of the early twentieth century in 'Main Street U.S.A.' in *Disneyland*, for instance, is traditional as it appeals to what, in the ideology underlying the representation, lies at the 'core' of American values. It is genetic, as it stresses the evolutionary continuity from that world to the America of today, and it is exemplary, as it expresses the model of the ideal Americanness as conceived by Walt Disney.[121] The critical approach is harder to find in the theme park, as it would require the representation of negative aspects which are generally filtered out, and can thus appear only in the form of 'dark theming', that is, the intentional choice of a scary, uncanny, unsettling, troubling theme.[122] The other three approaches are easily visible and conform to very widespread mechanisms of the popularization of history: moralization, as the easiest way to 'give sense' to historical narration,[123] intrinsic in the exemplary approach; and the 'teleologisation' that constructs a continuative narration, which is reassuring in its inevitability, providing an easy frame for us to 'understand' history and to found and reinforce identity. As the 'revelation of mortality is of no use for group identity – it is precisely what has to be suspended',[124] such teleological plots are particularly successful in the construction of collective identities and are not by chance the background for most nationalistic interpretations of history. Transmitted within society and through schoolbooks, these also provide the bulk of stereotypes with which the theme parks operate, thus constantly reinforcing such teleological narratives further. Archaeological reconstructions – an antecedent of these immersive environments – were already being used in the first half of the twentieth century 'to give people a dramatised sense of being part of the state, "with a share in its future"'.[125]

The 'domestication' of history in the theme park

In this way, theme parks are, when they represent history, a form of modern 'heritage', according to Lowenthal's definition, for whom 'heritage' is the past activated and functionalized for group identity, a 'possessive' or 'partisan' past: 'History is for all, heritage for us alone.'[126] According to the geographer, heritage 'domesticates' history in three ways, by updating (making actual), upgrading (making better) and by excluding.[127] These three dynamics are put into practice through a series of representational strategies; in particular, theme parks operate, as Florian Freitag and I argued a few years ago, through four specific strategies to represent history.[128] These should not be understood as sequential, but rather as a theoretical model which defines different aspects of the mechanisms of the 'translation' and 'transformation' of history within theme parks, which operationally occurs through a creative process not so neatly ordered in distinct phases. The first strategy is that of 'selection'. As in any form of historical narration, it is impossible to reproduce the entirety of the past. A selection is, in this sense, necessary, and the selection that occurs in the theme park is specific to the characteristics and needs of this medium. As most theme parks attempt not to have only one specific target age, but generally try to include and attract families as a consistent part of their public (the Disney parks are in this sense, once again, paradigmatic examples), there is a tendency to avoid any family-hostile themes.[129] War, death, poverty, sickness, executions and slavery are all themes that are generally avoided, if one excludes the already mentioned specific cases of 'dark theming', which follow specific rules and are addressed to specific groups of the public. This is not exclusive to theme parks, and is generally an important criterion in the development of touristic offerings: as highlighted by Duke, archaeological sites that are open to visitors (in the case of his study, the Minoan sites on Crete) have no reference to the lives of poor people, nor traces of 'squalor and disease', nor do they mention human sacrifice or cannibalism, instead presenting an image of Minoan Crete as a rich and opulent society, dedicated to technological progress and prosperity, untouched by war.[130] If death and destruction are evoked, it is only in the sense of explaining how this society came to an end – just as they are present (and would be impossible to omit), for instance, in Pompeii.

The second strategy is abstraction: the selected, stereotypical 'themes' are translated into typical visualizations, which can be recognized by the greatest number of observers possible. This implies not only, as Lowenthal highlights, vagueness and generalization, as well as mixing places,[131] but also the creation of pictograms which can directly evoke a period, a culture, a place.[132] This means (as so often happens in the reconstruction of ancient environments) that architectural elements can be completely de-functionalized: a bunch of white columns can signify antiquity, even if they just stand there, not holding any roof.[133] By creating such pictograms, the process of abstraction also corresponds to what Winnerling has called, in a study of historicizing video games, 'reduction':[134] the forms thus transformed maintain their shape but are emptied of content. The Greek temple in the theme park is not necessarily a temple; it can be a restaurant, a shop, the loading station of a roller coaster, a prop, etc. A Greek temple, to continue with this example, can be a reconstruction of a real ancient temple (as in *Terra Mítica*, see Fig. 1) or an imaginary one (as in *Europa-Park*, see Fig. 5), but as long as we see a white structure with six or eight columns on the front, generally Doric or Ionic, and a pediment with sculptures, we have evoked through abstraction the Greek temple; it can be 'antique Greekness'.[135] Such abstractions can be in contradiction to what is known by scholars: the polychromy of Greek temples is not only certain (since the first half of the nineteenth century), but also widely known at a popular level;[136] still, with very few exceptions (we will see one in *Parc Astérix*: Fig. 23), this has in no way modified

Fig. 1 'Templo de Kinetos', *Terra Mítica*, Benidorm, Spain: The Temple of Zeus at Olympia © Pau Garcia Solbes (elPachinko.com).

the generally recognized pictogram of the Greek temple – if it is not white, it is not easily recognizable. This whiteness was central to philhellenic aesthetics, 'in tune with the ideals of austerity and simplicity associated with classical Greek art and life',[137] and its acceptance was therefore relatively slow even among scholars.[138] Its symbolic importance even today, as a symbol of purity, but also of unstainable and indestructible strength, in connection with the ideal value of Greece as the cradle of the modern world and of democracy, makes it somehow impossible to renounce: it is 'the tone of clarity and remoteness'.[139] This is why even the 'performance' of ancient Greek statues in the opening ceremony of the Olympic Games of Athens in 2004 represented them as white: 'it projected a Europeanised, whitewashed version of the Greek ideal to audiences around the world'.[140]

The third strategy is immersion, the kind of detachment from daily life that allows 'time travel': 'the mechanism of themeing makes it possible to transmute time into physical space'.[141] Immersion is what places the visitor in the situation of 'losing oneself by indulging in an eternalized moment of joyful consciousness, never-ending in its timelessness'.[142] This is the very essence of 'living history',[143] the fact that another time and another culture are not only represented in fragmentary ways, which imply the deployment of one sense at a time (as in the traditional museum), but by activating most or even all of them at the same time, in a holistic, 'reconstructionist' effort: 'the more sensory a themed space, the more it can communicate to the visitor and the more that it can demarcate itself from other themed or non-themed spaces'.[144] Immersion is therefore constructed not only through visual devices, but also through music, language, voices, the smell and taste of food (which is often specific to each single themed area), through the vegetation chosen for the specific area and its smell, and so on,[145] in an integrated use of the senses often defined as 'ambiance'.[146] This in general also implies a clear separation of each themed area from those surrounding it and from whatever is outside the park, to avoid any intrusion that might break into the immersive experience.

Finally, the fourth strategy is transmediality: the theme park deploys a series of different, more or less immersive media, such as architecture, film, music, sculpture, painting, arranged so as to fuse into one coherent intermedial construction. The evolution towards the direct experience of living history is embedded in the evolution of immersive media, such as movies, which have created in the public an expectation of 'participation in the past',[147] and the sense of a direct, personal, emotional involvement with it, as in the concept of 'thrill history', originally developed in the 1950s in connection with historical films.[148] Not by chance have intellectuals complained that the success of these historical movies was not due to a desire to know the past, but rather nostalgia (on which, see below).[149] The presentification operated by the movies and similar media may be enhanced through the development of the specific inter- and transmedial strategies of theme parks.

Postmodern aesthetics and the (ancient) past: Affective turn and pastness

History, postmodernism and the theme park

Immersive and themed environments deal with history and its representation within a specific cultural context, at least within the Western world:[150] in relation to the reproduction of previously available stereotypical knowledge, Lowenthal has made clear that these kinds of representations of history, as in theme parks, provide 'no surprises, just postmodern ha-has'.[151] But what exactly is the connection between history and postmodernism in the theme park? It has been noted from many different sides and perspectives that the 'postmodern world' has experienced a clearly recognizable 'history boom' – a growing interest in history, occurring through very diverse social and cultural groups. Indeed, in postmodern culture, even history becomes hyperreal.[152] However, this 'new passion' for the past has almost no connection with the work and research by professional historians; it provides approaches to the past that can be enjoyed during free time, and are thus generally of a leisurely nature.[153] The postmodern disappearance of clear boundaries between high and popular culture also applies to the popularization of history:[154] meanwhile, claims that professional historians have no specific monopoly or prerogative in dealing with the past are over twenty years old, and Raphael Samuel has highlighted the role of the 'theaters of memory' built around the 'unofficial knowledge' of the past.[155] One consequence of this is that the past has also become 'a resource that could be utilised for widening the profit margin for various endeavours'[156] (theme parks among them), as well as raising a number of debates about the 'commodification' of the past, of history, and of cultural heritage, which escape the scope of this book.[157]

Baudrillard noted this, claiming that history represented the 'lost referential, that is to say our myth',[158] although he considered this phenomenon a mere 'fossilisation', the transformation of history into a musealized narrative, thus completely misunderstanding the main aspects of this new historical interest: presentification and immersion. Such a 'history boom', indeed, is intrinsically connected to the aesthetic and cultural phenomena that are typical of postmodernism and must be read in the context of the shifting perception and understanding of time and temporality, as well as within the development of the so-called 'experience society'. The former has been investigated in the past few years by scholars such as Aleida Assmann, Andreas Huyssen, Hans-Ulrich Gumbrecht and Lucian Hölscher.[159] Building on the work of Reinhard Koselleck, who has shown that the perception of time as linear, moving through the three different layers constituted by past, present and future, is not 'natural', due to fundamental physical underpinnings, but is a cultural construct that emerged in Europe in the time of the Enlightenment,[160] these scholars have argued that this 'modern' perception of time started collapsing in the second half of the twentieth century, giving space to a 'new', postmodern temporality in which the different time levels conflate into a 'broader present' (to use Gumbrecht's definition), or a 'present past' (following Huyssen).[161] In this sense, master narratives connecting the past, present and future disappear in favour of concurrent narratives.[162]

It is not important to linger here on the causes of such a shift, on which the aforementioned scholars have no agreement: an idealized past in which community values were stronger, growing pessimism about the future, the development of apocalyptic scenarios, mostly connected to ecological catastrophes, have all been repeatedly identified as the central factors,[163] together with a reaction to the complete detachment from the materiality of presence (and of the body) caused by digital communication and digitalization,[164] or anxiety connected to the speed of technological change,[165] as well as post-anthropocentric and post-human 'configurations of knowledge'.[166] More important here is to highlight certain specific characteristics, which are relevant to the appearance of historical themes in the theme parks. First, the 'history boom' is connected to a general loss of trust in the future, seen as problematic and apocalyptic. As Paradis puts it, 'a redirected focus on the past, rather than on the future, remains a central component of postmodern theme development'.[167] This is the core of 'nostalgia': a feeling of loss in which a utopian dimension is oriented not towards the future, but towards the past or, sometimes, 'sideways. The nostalgic feels stifled within the conventional confines of time and space'.[168] Gumbrecht speaks in this sense of a boundary between present and past which has become 'porous' and of 'a present of simultaneities which expands always more'.[169]

Nostalgia and popular culture thus conflate into a new historic style,[170] and in particular into those forms of living history which constitute the bulk of the 'leisurely approach' to history (with a strong impact on the didactic of history and on museology, too, as living history becomes one of the most popular forms of historical teaching and education).[171] As Svetlana Boym has put it, 'the nostalgic desires to obliterate history and turn it into private or collective mythology, to revisit time like space, refusing to surrender to the irreversibility of time that plagues human condition'.[172] This is the product of what has been defined as the 'affective turn':[173] the new interest in the past is not based on a desire for scholarly knowledge and forms of argumentative, discursive appropriation of knowledge, but on the search for a direct, sensorial experience of other times and other cultures. What derives from it is, according to Winnerling, an 'affective historicity', 'the attempt to create representations that convey the feeling of (representations of) the past', which therefore 'follows mainly aesthetic and imaginative procedures to arrive at its results'.[174] This is the same approach to history that Anderson and later Holtorf defined as 'time travel', which the latter presents as typical only of society during the last few decades.[175] Gumbrecht hints at the same phenomenon, calling it, in a less optimistic way, 'historical entropy'.[176]

Of the two kinds of nostalgia identified by Boym – the 'restorative nostalgia', which 'attempts a transhistorical reconstruction of the lost home', as expressed in total reconstructions of the monuments from the past; and the 'reflective nostalgia', which lingers on the longing itself and does not reconstruct, rather developing an aesthetics of ruins[177] – it is thus the first which dominates in themed environments and theme parks. According to Olalquiaga,

> nostalgia and melancholy represent two radically opposite perceptions of experiences and cultural sensibilities. One, traditional, symbolic and totalizing, uses memories to conceptually complete the partiality of events, protecting them with a frozen wreath from the decomposition of time; the other, modern, allegorical and fragmentary, glorifies the perishable aspect of events, seeking in their partial and decaying memory the confirmation of its own temporal dislocation.[178]

In this sense, theme parks are also nostalgic and therefore, in Olalquiaga's terminology, an expression of a nostalgic kitsch and a melancholic kitsch, which revel in a feeling of loss.[179]

The 'experience society' and 'time travel'

This way of relating to history is further embedded in what has been defined in sociological literature as the 'experience society' (*Erlebnisgesellschaft*), a term created in 1995 by Gerhard Schulze to describe Western (and particularly German) society in the second half of the twentieth century. According to this model, the essentially certain fulfilment of primary needs has reoriented this opulent society towards a quest for 'experience'. As such experiences become the aim of action, a 'market of experiences' comes into existence, characterized by a demand and a supply of experience. In a similar way, Pine and Gilmore have described as 'experience economy' a context in which services and products, in order to be sold, must be presented as 'experiences' (which dovetails perfectly with Wolf's definition of 'entertainment economy' for the economy after the Cold War).[180] In connection with history and archaeology, the 'experiential' nature of (post-)modern tourism has been explained so: 'whereas a well-read museum visitor used to be satisfied with a typology of flints in a glass case, reinforcing contemporary notions of linear progress, the modern visitor prefers to see the flint in use, with a brush shelter and a column of smoke from a wood fire as a backdrop – or at least a three-dimensional image of some such scenes'.[181] Themed environments thus make history experienceable, in spite of it being physically irretrievable;[182] in this sense, time travelling is indeed made possible. All this applies quite obviously to a Western cultural context, and can therefore explain the 'historical theme parks' in this area of the world – Baudrillard (and Eco) have been correctly criticized for 'universalizing'

Western concepts and values,[183] and their mistake should not be carelessly repeated.

Yet this form of time travel leads visitors to experience not the past, but pastness. What matters (and this leads us back to the discussion on authenticity) is not the 'being-old' of what is experienced.[184] What is actually old is, on the contrary, often problematic for immersion, because of its ruined status, its reworking and continuous use in following periods, because of its embeddedness in modern structures; immersion needs something that 'looks ancient', but is nonetheless in pristine condition, as it would have looked when it was first constructed. In this sense, according to Jameson, 'the time-travel evocation is misleading', as what is at stake is 'praxis' and 'reconstruction', 'a present reality which has been transformed into a simulacrum by the process of wrapping, or quotation, and has thereby become not historical, but historicist – an allusion to a present out of real history which might just as well be a past removed from real history ... the past as fashion plate and glossy image'.[185]

This does not mean that ruins cannot be represented in the theme park: we will see many examples of this. Their presence, still, is due to the specific choices of theme. A themed area can subsume different historical phases in one abstraction, and thus show as new (and not ruined) buildings that belong to different periods (we will see that in the Greek area of *Europa-Park*, for instance, antiquity coexists with modern Greece; in a similar way, the Chinese area of *Phantasialand*, Germany, conflates the Qing and Ming dynasties). But on other occasions, the choice of a specific temporal layer as a theme implies representing previous phases and buildings as already 'past'. They thus materialize a 'double pastness', becoming 'past for the past'. We will find examples in *Terra Mítica*; in *Phantasialand*, again, the Mexican area is themed around Mexico directly after the Revolution: the Maya and the Aztec cultures are present, but in the form of ruins, and the water coaster 'Chiapas', which brings the visitors through a Maya pyramid, has the waiting area themed to the archaeological museum of Palenque, where riders have to walk through large boxes and archaeological material piled up within a depot.[186]

This applies even though classical ruins have, at least in Western culture, a different status, since the idealization of classical antiquity as the cradle of civilization makes them be 'not so much leftovers of bygone eras as their testimony. In looking at classical ruins, we see past them into the tradition they stood for, ignoring their present state for the sake of the symbolic glory and universal value attributed to them'.[187] For this reason, very often, in countries moulded by Western culture, any representation of ruins is Graeco-Roman in style, even when the narrative underlying speaks of a nomadic population from northern Africa moving south and founding a city later destroyed by an earthquake, as in South Africa's *Lost City*.[188] And yet, in spite of this different value of Graeco-Roman ruins, it is difficult to make them compatible with the necessities of immersion – unless, as just described, they are inserted as the past of the temporal layer to which we are supposed to move.

The Greek temple will be much more often shown as a new, functioning temple, with its cult statue within. This also explains why, as we will see, theme parks all over the world do represent Greek temples, but none of them hosts a replica of the Parthenon: the most famous Greek temple of the world is so iconic in its ruined form on top of the Acropolis[189] that its reproduction in a pristine status would be much more disturbing than that of the much less iconic Temple of Zeus at Olympia. Of this, little remains of the terrain, but its reconstruction (and the reconstructions of the cult statue of Zeus by Phidias) are very well-known, also in popular culture: temple and statue appeared prominently, for example, in the Disney movie *Hercules* (1997). It is therefore no surprise if this temple and its famous statue are the ones chosen to represent 'the Greek temple' in both *Terra Mítica* in Benidorm, Spain and in *Happy Valley Beijing* in China [see Fig. 1; 2].

Fig. 2 The entrance to the dark ride 'Happy World', *Happy Valley Beijing*, People's Republic of China © Jeremy Thompson (Creative Commons license).

Ancient Greece in reception

What has been stated above concerning selection, abstraction, foreknowledge and stereotypes leads us to consider what aspects and images of ancient Greece are particularly present in popular culture, and with what meaning. Despite the 'boom' in the study of classical receptions in the past two decades, representations of the ancient world in theme parks have been surprisingly neglected, as only a few scholars had given any attention to this before Florian Freitag and I published our first articles on the topic in 2015.[190] It is true that Mark Gottdiener had indicated 'classical civilisations' as a common theme of built environments, but he did so in terms of its reduced importance when compared to previous times and its continued relevance as a symbolic referent for state and institutional buildings.[191] Maria Wyke noted in 1995 the presence of the ride 'Escape from Pompeii' in *Busch Gardens Williamsburg*; Marxiano Melotti attracted attention to theme parks in his Italian monograph on archaeological tourism; and Stephanie Malia Hom dealt with a representation of ancient Rome in the Italian theme park *Rainbow Magic Land*, Rome;[192] but this was all. Yet antiquity (and classical antiquity) are very present in the theme park, and not only in *Busch Gardens*. The attention shown to theme park studies is now growing, but this is still, as far as I know, the first attempt at a systematic study of the representation of antiquity in theme parks globally. Throughout this volume, I will compare the ways in which classical Greece has been represented in theme parks all over the world, that is, in different cultural contexts and historical cultures. Greece offers an important case study, since ancient Greek culture is popular (and loaded with symbolic meaning) almost everywhere.[193]

Yet Greece seems to have been much less fortunate than Rome in modern reception, in terms of the sheer quantity of reception products that recall classical Greece, that is, the number of themes which were reproduced, actualized and represented (this is also valid for theme parks, as representations of Rome are more frequent).[194] Reception works in chains, and precedent re-elaborations and their success are extremely important in defining visual elements which will be used and redeployed, and thus reinforced, made stronger and made available again for further acts of reception.[195] This is not just a feature of the last few decades, as in the Victorian age a much smaller amount of novels and plays were set in ancient Greece than in Rome, and this has influenced the presence of both ancient cultures also in later stages of reception.[196] All this also has consequences on the development of a clearly recognizable 'Greek' visual language: the pictogram 'Greek temple' discussed above, for example, is very often also used to visualize Rome (for instance, in the representation of Pontius Pilate's *praetorium* in the religious theme park *Tierra Santa* in Buenos Aires, which is, once again, an abstraction of the Greek temple, here meant to be evocative of 'paganism': Fig. 3), and visualizations of Greece very often deploy 'abstracted' Roman pictograms (for instance, in the representations of ancient soldiers, or in any structure with arches, which were essentially unknown within Greek architecture).[197]

Nonetheless, Greece has remained present in representations of the past. Among the antecedents of the theme parks we must count the panoramas, paintings and later photographical reproductions which, thanks to their huge dimensions, served to 'immerse' the observer in the landscape represented.[198] One of the most famous panoramas, by Robert Barker and Robert Burford,

Fig. 3 Pontius Pilate's *praetorium* in *Tierra Santa*, Buenos Aires, Argentina © Danita Delimont / Alamy Stock Photo.

bought by the University of Harvard in 1819, was *The Panorama of Athens*, a gigantic representation of Athenian archaeological remains, stretching from the Parthenon to the Temple of Theseus, which created the illusion of 'looking at ancient Athens from a nearby hill'.[199] In this early immersive representation of ancient Greece, the motives and the stereotypes which still characterize popular knowledge of it are already present: first of all, the association with high culture, or rather with the birth of high culture – of literature, philosophy, democracy and Western thought – here embodied by its position at Harvard and its use for the instruction and gratification of students and the public, who were supposed to identify with the picture and realize the connection between the modern, democratic United States and the cradle of all democracies.

Greece is then Athens: while other parts of ancient and modern Greece are popularly known, none is so visually present as today's capital,[200] because of its connection with democracy and almost the entirety of Greek literature which has survived the centuries. As Lowenthal has highlighted, history is represented as being shaped by cultures, but these are seen as monolithic blocks, essentially unchangeable and without a historical evolution.[201] This is also reinforced by the ways in which ancient history is taught in schools across Europe and the world, that is, through an approach that considers different peoples and cultures as closed boxes – the Greeks, the Romans, the Phoenicians.[202] And thus, 'tradition conflates Greek classical culture to a single entity from Homer through Aristotle and beyond';[203] this is essentially the same mechanism that underlies the 'abstraction' within theme parks. As Holtorf states, 'in an insecure and constantly changing world, people desire peace of mind and reassurance in relation to their livelihoods, ways of life and values. They seek answers rather than more questions. They like romanticising the past and trust established brands more than new products'; one example is 'the world of Classical Greece featuring shining temples with Doric columns and philosophers immersed in discussion on the market square'.[204]

Greece is also generally presented through its ancient phases: in popular representations, there are no traces of later periods of Greek history, nor of the current inhabitants of the country; the ruins of its glorious past are the dominant motif. This is hardly surprising, considering how Western Europe 'rediscovered' Greece in terms of its ancient past, and especially how Western philhellenism considered ancient Greece as a 'world heritage', while often despising contemporary Greeks as 'unworthy' of their ancestors:[205] 'to most Europeans before the sixteenth century – but also later – Greece possessed an identity focused entirely on its past'.[206] Philhellenism expressed itself politically in strong solidarity with the Greek independentist movement against the

Ottomans, basing on the Orientalist stereotype of the Ottomans as ur-otherness, thus reinforcing the idea of Greece as ur-Western.²⁰⁷ Greek cultural memory is constructed along similar lines (not surprisingly, considering the Western contribution to the foundation of the independent state), presenting the modern state as being in direct contact with and a continuation of the greatness of classical antiquity (the self-definition 'Hellenes' replaced that of *Rhomaioi*, 'Romans', during the nineteenth century),²⁰⁸ with a sense of identity and continuity that eventually might also include Byzantine Orthodoxy, but obliterates the Ottoman centuries.²⁰⁹

After independence was achieved, the relationship between Western Europe and Greece deteriorated quickly, leading to even further Western disdain of contemporary Greece and a stronger idealization of ancient Greece, which is somehow valid still today, as 'in a European tradition that takes its classical heritage for granted, the neglect of Greek ethnography is both surprising and significant. It emphasizes the besetting ambivalence of a country that falls disconcertingly between the exotic and the familiar. Modern Greece does not fit comfortably into the duality of Europeans and Others'.²¹⁰ And yet, the end of the nineteenth century brought an additional twist: the idea of Greece as a land wherein to relax and escape daily stress: 'if the early nineteenth century artists had portrayed a Greece that was a timeless, rarefied, intellectual world, the Classicists of the late nineteenth century presented a spectacular realm of perpetual holidays'.²¹¹ The development of mass tourism, the explosion of which particularly took place after the Second World War,²¹² saw an ever-growing number of visitors every year, and the 'realm of perpetual holidays' became the second face of Greece. Advertisements for holidays in Greece leave no doubt about this: 'the website of the Greek National Tourist Organisation (GNTO), for example, as well as the myriad marketing tools used by private-enterprise tourist packages, all prominently display ancient ruins or statues (clothed and naked), which occupy the pole position with sun and beaches for alluring tourists'.²¹³ The Greece of popular culture is thus defined by its ancient past and its touristic present, with an almost complete obliteration of all that is in between – the Roman, Byzantine and Ottoman periods. These two poles are further simplified, focusing purely on a set of recurring images, topics and stereotypes. The 'eternalized' image of ancient Greece remains centred, as noted above, mostly on Athens (and at times Olympia), while touristic Greece is generally framed around the image of the Aegean islands, particularly Santorini and Mykonos – the abstraction at work consists of a set of small white buildings with blue domes, facing the sea.

Alongside these images of Greece, a third one has developed since the time of philhellenism – that of the Greek landscape as being 'eternal' and 'natural', and thus dehistoricized and reified. 'To imbue the Greek landscape with the qualities they upheld as ideal and harmonise it with its literature, French and English painters massively misread that landscape.'[214] So developed the image of the Greek Arcadia, made of green meadows, mountains, goats and sheep, and populated by shepherds (human or mythological), nymphs and satyrs. This is the popular picture of 'non-coastal' Greece, which also removes it completely from history and from the passage of time, delivering it to a mythological realm and thus making it into the perfect stage for the narratives and characters of classical myth. Once again, this imagination has lost neither force nor actuality, even among scholars of classical archaeology, as is demonstrated by formulations such as this: 'Truly, the power of the landscape – the mountains, the empty sky, the sea and its wine-dark blueness – is felt nearly everywhere in Greece, but in certain spots the triangulation is crisper, purer, and the lines of sight seem to rivet the beholder as if in stone.'[215]

The Western engagement with Greece has, since the nineteenth century, been strongly material: the ruins, the architectures, the landscapes, have been described and highlighted in each and every description of Greece.[216] These therefore provide the visual repertoire for the strategies of representation. Selection and abstraction, as previously mentioned, operate quite clearly: Athens is at the very centre, most of all its most iconic symbol,[217] the Parthenon, whose presence, in its iconic aspect as ruins, seems unavoidable every time that 'Greece' needs to be evoked. This is nothing new, and derives from the obsession with the Acropolis of Athens which characterized philhellenism: 'no object was more likely to awaken a train of reflections connected with what they had seen or read about Greece than the image of the Acropolis of Athens'.[218] Its connection with Periclean Athens transformed the temple in the nineteenth century into not only an aesthetic model, but also a symbol of freedom and democracy, one connected to Greece's struggle for independence, but also, on a pan-European level, in opposition to the 'Roman' inspiration of Napoleon's Empire.[219] In 1983, and again in 2017, the Argentinian artist Marta Minujín made the productivity of this connection clear with her 'Parthenon of books', a replica of the Athenian temple built with books that had been forbidden – by the Argentinian junta in the first version, and more generally in the second, when the replica was also built on a spot in Kassel where Nazi sympathisers burned books in 1933. As Nisbet formulates it, 'throw us an establishing shot of the Acropolis, and we think Philosophy, Art, Democracy – and switch off'.[220] In the mid-1990s, a professor of archaeology and classical art still thought it necessary to attempt to explain the 'objective reasons' which make the Parthenon into 'the monument of all monuments',[221] considering the connection of the Western world with classical antiquity 'deep, intuitive', and attributing to Greek architecture 'the uncanny ability ... to express ... universal human concerns in a universally meaningful fashion'.[222]

Indeed, in 1834 the restoration of this temple was one of the first interventions of the independent kingdom of Greece into the cultural sphere (after having taken the then not so automatic decision of establishing the capital of the kingdom in Athens), with the removal of all traces of post-classical occupation from the Acropolis accomplished by 1874.[223] The iconic value of the Parthenon is strong throughout the world: in 1955, for instance, the movie *Cinerama Holiday*, which showed a US couple visiting Europe and a European couple visiting the United States, presented it as one of the wonders of Europe, which must be visited when travelling across the Old World. As mentioned above when dealing with abstraction, the Parthenon can be replaced by 'any' Greek temple, and this constitutes one of the main elements of the representation of Greece, as demonstrated for example by school books throughout Europe: none of them lacks an image of a Greek temple or the Acropolis (as a picture or a reconstruction), often accompanied by an illustration of the architectonic orders.[224]

Next to Athens is Sparta, whose reception is decidedly more ambiguous and less abundant, essentially connected only to the Persian Wars and the Battle of Thermopylae. This is not only dependent on the fact that, as Thucydides already highlighted in the fifth century BCE, this much less monumental polis did not leave behind such archaeological material to affect the perception and the memory of the general public. This depends far more on the image of Sparta as a militaristic and totalitarian society,[225] which causes it to be represented, in European school books, as essentially the counterimage to Athens,[226] as well as on the consequent idealization of Sparta in the Third Reich, which negatively loaded the reception of this polis. Only Thermopylae – which in the wider frame of the Persian Wars fall into the easy category of the 'Western origins' fighting against the Orientalized other – have a place in reception, yet one that is not exempt from discussions and ideological readings, as demonstrated by the huge discussions about Frank Miller's *300* and the movie derived from it (Zack Snyder, 2006). Alongside Thermopylae, only one other 'plot' from the history of ancient Greece is popular: the life and conquests of Alexander the Great.[227] The rest of ancient Greek history is essentially absent from reception: this is due to the existence of hundreds of poleis during the classical period, as well as the confusing relationships of the Hellenistic kingdoms, which are simply too complicated to be accessible to a broad public. This is distinct from the simple (and easy to render as a moral narrative) plot of conquest, enlargement, decadence and decline provided by the Roman Empire.[228]

But history is not what ancient Greece offers most to modern reception, beyond the vistas and the ruins. Indeed, much more popular and well-known than history throughout the world is Greek mythology (this is markedly different from the reception of Rome, which is almost exclusively historical). Surely, the mythological narratives are at times no less complicated than the historical, but with their elements of heroism, of supernatural intervention, with the passions they describe and generate, they maintain an incredible appeal to a very broad public; indeed, as has recently been underlined, already in the Roman Empire, Greek myths were an important component of popular culture: they were continuously reproduced in different media as theatrical shows, and represented 'a collective store of wisdom in the same way as fables and proverbs. And for those in the crowd that did not know the myths, then the pantomime also provided an education in them.'[229]

It is hard to pin down the reasons for the success of mythology, but Florian Freitag and I tried to list certain aspects that are of particular relevance to its success in theme parks.[230] First, after classical antiquity, myths have remained an important staple of Western culture. They have been deployed as moral narratives, as exempla, and, after Freud and Jung, as transhistorical and transcultural expressions of the subconscious; this has played an important role in transmission of their knowledge as well as their acceptance as paradigms of human feelings and behaviours.[231] As a consequence, myths have also become increasingly popular outside the Western world; that they have been adapted to different geographical and cultural contexts further strengthens the belief in their value as archetypes. In this function, myths are 'de-historicized' (and returned to a pre-historic and almost fantastic past); this contributes to a de-semantization of the contents of their narrative, so that war, death, revenge and violence in myth are less troubling and less 'real' than their historical counterparts. This makes them possible to represent in the theme park, in spite of their 'negative' content.

In antiquity, myths were already flexible narratives, existing across a very broad range of forms; in modernity, this flexibility still holds, and novels, comics, movies, video games – as well as theme parks – can act freely upon the mythical material, creating new narratives which are more apt to the specific necessities of each product. We will see many different variations of the myth of Odysseus, for instance, as it has been 'translated' in *Europa-Park* and *Belantis* in Germany, in *Terra Mítica* in Spain, and in *Happy World Beijing* in China. Finally, the very nature of myths, as action-packed narratives involving human beings, monsters, heroes, magic and supernatural elements, makes them particularly apt for translation and adaptation across a wide variety of media, especially immersive media such as movies, video games and theme parks. This action strongly contributes to their incorporation – often with ease – into the narrative of rides (including thrill rides).

Greek mythology (and Greek religion, as mythology mostly consists of narratives including the gods and their intervention into human affairs) is central to all facets of reception of classical Greece: in school books,[232] as well as comics, movies and advertisements. The religious content of myths also reinforces the centrality of the Greek temple in the visual imagination of classical Greece, with the Parthenon as the intersection of the two major themes: mythology/religion and Athens.[233] The Homeric cycle (and in particular, in the twentieth century, the adventures of Odysseus) is by far the most popular set of narratives. Achilles and the Trojan War were more successful in the nineteenth century and in historical paintings,[234] but it is rather easy to understand that shifting perceptions of masculinity, heroism, war and psychology during the following century led to a displacement of the warrior hero by the travelling and cunning hero. The latter's adventures are not only well known and thrilling, but particularly apt to postmodern aesthetics, as they perfectly express the core of nostalgia, with the homecoming and longing, but also the deep fear – or rather, anticipation – that the homecoming might be not satisfactory.[235] The Trojan War and the ensuing adventures of Odysseus are also 'abstracted' with a symbol every bit as iconic as the Parthenon, which we will meet in almost all the theme parks analysed in this volume: the Trojan horse. A theme that was already common in ancient art,[236] the wooden horse that brought an end to the war is a pictogram evoking the entire complex of narratives connected to the Trojan cycle and the beginning of Odysseus' troubles. The Homeric cycle is followed in popularity by the Argonauts, and then by Heracles.[237] The latter, in spite of his fame as the paradigmatic Greek hero[238] (mostly in connection to the twelve labours), is less present in reception than Achilles or Odysseus, perhaps because of the more fragmented nature of the narratives surrounding him and certain problematic issues connected to his life (and death).

The prevalence of mythology causes the selection and abstraction of a further part of the Greek archaeological heritage: Bronze Age, and particularly Minoan, architecture. The association of Bronze Age Crete with classical mythology is not new, and not only because the ancient Greeks themselves dated their myths to a period corresponding, in modern chronologies, to the Bronze Age (famously, Eratosthenes dated the fall of Troy to 1184 BCE). The archaeological excavations of the nineteenth century (particularly Schliemann's) led to the popular assumption that the 'places of the myth' could be materially identified and visualized in the archaeological record: Mycenae thus became Agamemnon's reign, and Troy was 'found'. On Crete, an island associated with a series of myths – from Zeus' childhood to the more popular ones of Minos, the Minotaur, Daedalus and Icarus – the same happened after Evans transformed the Palace of Knossos into a popular visual reference. Even school books, although they do not present such a direct (and wrong) connection, tendentially locate the sections on Greek religion and myth towards the beginning of the Greek chapters, before the emergence of the poleis.[239] Minoan Crete has been frequently understood as 'pre-Greece' and therefore, for the Western world, as an antecedent, not a form of alterity: it is 'European',[240] 'a memorial to the origins of the West, the ideological construct that has for better or worse guided much of Europe and the study of its prehistory'.[241] The 'Cretomania' of the early twentieth century was a central contribution to the diffusion of these images and associations, as with that between the complex architecture of the Palace of Knossos and the mythical Labyrinth.[242] The rest of the work has been done by tourism: myth is strongly associated with Crete in the touristic offerings on the island, and particularly in Knossos.[243] The association is thus strong throughout reception products: the movie *Helen of Troy* (1956) set the age of myth in the archaeological facies of the Bronze Age, equating the Achaeans with Mycenaean culture, and the Trojans with the Minoan;[244] twenty-five years later, *Clash of the Titans* (1981) deployed ample Minoan architecture to visualize the 'age of myth'. This was 'abstracted' in a few selected stereotypes: the red columns, broader on the top than at the bottom; the merlons in the shape of bull horns; a few well-known frescoes, such as that of the Tauromachy; and in terms of buildings, the north portico of the Palace of Knossos, generally represented alone, without the rest of the palace, as 'a summarised image of the palace', which 'combines the ruined with the deceptively impressive element of a well-preserved monument, inviting the visitor to admire an allegedly very old but still standing structure'.[245]

Another set of recurrent stereotypes in the reception of ancient Greece is connected to the role attributed to it, and particularly to classical Athens, as being the cradle of the modern Western world.[246] In Europe there is a strong and constant insistence on the importance of Greece and the Greek heritage to define the very concept of the continent itself, its boundaries and its identity;[247] Europa is, after all, a figure from Greek mythology. There is, therefore, a search for continuity, for a 'traditional' and 'genetic' way of attributing sense, which leads to viewing classical Greece as the 'origin' of modern interests, rites and approaches, while simultaneously highlighting how much better our world is.[248] Two topics are of particular relevance here: sports and intellectual achievements. Starting with the latter, one of the most stereotypical images connected to ancient Greece is that of the ancient philosophers founding the entire intellectual world of the West, spending their time discussing elevated topics.[249] In this sense, Greece is also presented as being the cradle of our civilization, to which it is genetically connected. In this sense – as is also the case in the teaching of history within European schools – the ancient Greeks are often presented as the founders of science, as the first humans to interrogate themselves about nature and try to discover natural laws.[250]

As for sports, the assumption is that the ancient Greeks were particularly fond of physical activity and great athletes. The Olympic Games and their related symbols are highly relevant here, as they trace a direct line from the most important sports event of the modern world to their ideal ancient roots. This connection has been materialized since 1936 in the ceremony of lighting the Olympic flame in the ruins of the sanctuary of Zeus at Olympia.[251] It is therefore no surprise if the modern Olympic Games are considered part of the Greek cultural heritage,[252] nor that their fortieth anniversary was celebrated (in 1936, the same year that the torch started moving from Greece) with a huge feast in Athens, which evoked the Minoan, the classical, the Byzantine and finally contemporary Greek cultures (again skipping all the centuries in between).[253]

This connection between the ancient Greeks and sports also has strong repercussions on the reception of Greek art, especially sculpture. Greek sculpture has been considered to be highly realistic since the nineteenth century (and at a popular level still is), but at the same time to represent 'Platonic' ideals to which reality should tend. The representation of bodies (mostly male) in iconic Greek classical statues has thus been considered to represent the '"transcendental" anatomical type of man', while at the same time any variation from it could be considered deformity.[254] In 1886, Charles Rochet wrote that Greek art shows the archetypes of the human body;[255] in the late nineteenth century, in connection with Darwinism, the idea was developed that physical activity leading to attaining that type of body would guarantee survival;[256] the realistic nature of Greek art guaranteed the attainability of that ideal physical shape. This was the cultural context in which, in 1896, the modern Olympic Games were founded.[257] Sports thus not only represent one of the most recurrent aspects of ancient Greek society to be highlighted in popular history, as well as in school books, but their illustration is generally also accompanied by a photograph of an ancient Greek sculpture to represent such an ideal athletic body, in most cases either Myron's *Discobolus* or Polykleitos' *Doryphoros*.[258] The former, in particular, is often considered paradigmatic of beauty, health, sport and vitality.[259] As we will see, these sculptures also regularly appear, in copy or as a reference, in theme parks.

The popular motifs and stereotypes discussed up to this point can be confirmed by looking at companies that offer Greek theming and props for parties. The London company *Theme Traders Creative Event Production*, for instance, offers as Greek props images of ruins, paintings reproducing life in antiquity, columns and classicizing architectural decoration, statues of ancient deities such as Poseidon, 'Greek pots and urns', and – to cover the holiday side – fishing boats.[260] *Event Prop Hire*, based in Wetherby, UK, offers classical busts, Roman helmets, and classicizing architectures with arches (confirming the general lack of separation between Greek and Roman antiquity), urns, plinths and columns. They also offer mules and goats accompanied by fig and olive trees – evoking the idea of a 'natural' Greece, far from any kind of progress – a beach bar, a beach sunset, and furniture in the unmistakable colours of white and blue, evoking both the Aegean islands and the colours of the Greek flag.[261] A further example is offered by the Romanian airline *Blue Air*, and the special offer with which it decided to celebrate the opening of a new route connecting Turin and Athens on 4 June 2016: the first fifty passengers to appear at Turin Airport at 11.00 am that day dressed as Greek deities would fly to Athens for free. (Modern) Athens as a tourist destination was thus again directly connected to antiquity, and more directly to mythology; one look at the pictures of the 'winners', mostly wearing togas, reveals once again how the iconography of ancient Greece is actually, in modern Western popular culture, often a 'derivative' of the filmic image of ancient Rome.[262]

Ancient Greece in the theme park

Yet, as revealed by the example of the different 'It's a Small World' rides presented at the beginning of this chapter, the repertoire of signs connected to ancient Greece can be deployed in different ways. The cultural contexts are different, indeed, as are the time periods in which the theme parks were constructed, and the 'historical cultures' in which ancient Greece has been represented, reproduced, re-functionalized and 'used' (to different aims and with different backgrounds) are thus different. Nonetheless, the repertoire of selected and abstracted motifs, architectural styles, decorations and narratives is in itself extremely stable and consistent throughout the world: the Acropolis, the Greek temple, the Palace of Knossos, sports, democracy and the predominance of myth will be shown in Germany as in the People's Republic of China, in the United States as well as in Taiwan. This is the reason for the organization of the book, which is divided into chapters according to the geographical distribution of the theme parks and not, for instance, according to their chronology. Each chapter will begin with a presentation of the presence and the specific forms of the perceptions, representations and 'uses' of Greece within the countries and areas in which the theme parks are located, before then proceeding against this background to describe the theme parks in general – their history, characters and ideological underpinnings – in order to better understand the specific forms assumed by the representations of classical Greece in each of them.

Seven parks have been chosen, on three continents, so as to provide a meaningful set of examples and case studies, and to reach reasonable conclusions on the ways in which 'immersive Greece' is represented in the theme park. The main focus of the book, though, is on Europe: four of the seven parks are located here. This has some specific reasons: not only is the ancient Greek culture perceived as being part of the Western European identity, but the connection is, even at popular level, also more direct, thus explaining why more parks with a Greek theme can be found in this part of the world. The specific competences and studies of the author also allow a much more in-depth analysis of European cultural contexts than of the American or Eastern Asian ones. While I hope I have managed to represent the role of Greece on these other continents in a meaningful and reasonable way, expanding these sections to include finer distinctions and more precise ways of embedding classical antiquity into the local popular culture is something which lies beyond my knowledge and expertise. Finally, it was important to include one park in which classical Greece is not represented 'directly', but in a re-mediatized form: this was made possible by *Parc Astérix*, while also increasing the number of European parks considered.

As the book proceeds geographically, the analysis begins with the European parks, in the next chapter dealing with the two German parks, *Europa-Park* and *Belantis*, before moving on to the Spanish *Terra Mítica* in Chapter 3. In the section that follows I will deal with the United States, predominantly with the *Mt. Olympus Water and Theme Park*, before moving on to the Far East in a chapter analysing *Happy Valley Beijing* in the People's Republic of China and *E-Da World* in Kaohsiung, Taiwan. The last chapter is dedicated to *Parc Astérix*, as the specific characters within this park (and their connection to re-mediatization) make it

Table 1 Chronology and team of the field trips

Name of the park	Dates of visit	Companions
Europa-Park	11–12 July 2014	Florian Freitag
	27 July 2016	Florian Freitag, Ariane Schwarz and a group of students from the University of Mainz, campus Germersheim
Belantis	11 August 2015	
Terra Mítica	1–3 November 2012	Florian Freitag
Mt. Olympus	12–14 May 2016	Florian Freitag
Happy Valley Beijing	11–12 March 2017	Florian Freitag
E-Da World	17–19 March 2017	Nicolas Zorzin
Parc Astérix	16–17 August 2013	Florian Freitag
	14–15 April 2015	Florian Freitag, Sabrina Mittermeier, Ariane Schwarz

more reasonable to deal with it at the end, thereby breaking with the geographical scheme that ran though the book until that point.

I conducted field research in all seven parks, in some of them more than once. During most of the visits, I was accompanied by friends and colleagues who, as experts in theme parks or in the local culture, could help me to deploy the mechanisms and criteria of what has been defined, in specific reference to this field of studies, 'creative research'.[263] I therefore consider it relevant to show here, in the form of a table [Table 1], both with whom I visited the park and when I visited. This last point is important, considering the fact that some of the parks changed radically after my visit, built new attractions, etc., but also because the season of the visit – as well as the weather – most certainly influences how the park works, how crowded it is, as well as how it is perceived and visited. Yet this book reflects a much longer history of reception of ancient Greece in different regions of the world, and a much longer history of the theme park as a medium and its representations and receptions of (ancient) history. In this sense, I am confident that the arguments proposed over the next chapters remain valid despite the sometimes very fast alteration, or even disappearance, of single rides and entire parks.

2

German Philhellenism in the Theme Park

The position of ancient Greece in German culture

The 'love story' between Greece and Germany is both long-lasting and well-known. Beginning with the Enlightenment, the cultural movement known as philhellenism (clearly visible already in Hölderlin's *Hyperion*, for example) grew, consolidated and was eventually institutionalized in association with the Greek War of Independence (1821–32). A German, Otto I of Bavaria (whose father, Ludwig I, was responsible for the construction of the Walhalla, a national monument celebrating the victory over Napoleon and which took the form of the Athenian Acropolis),[1] was chosen to become the first king of the new state.[2] Philhellenism, the German 'alternative to Rome-centred cultural history',[3] shaped the German intellectual elites, infiltrated all social strata and deeply influenced German nationalism, constructing a proximity and a continuity between ancient Greece and the German Empire.[4] This cultural movement was strongly based on visual and material culture: it was Greek art, rather than philosophy or literature, that was at the very core of this 'passion' for ancient Greece.[5]

German 'Graecomania' owes much to Johann Joachim Winckelmann and developed in a normative way, through the constitution of recognized canons, mostly of artworks.[6] This implied the swift and widespread popularization of images of famous Greek statues, temples and vases, which constituted (and to a large degree still constitutes) the horizon of expectation and the basis of recognition of classical Greece for the German public. As for the rest of the Western world, antiquity constituted the main attraction and therefore the main reason to visit and write about Greece, while 'contemporary life' within the region was of secondary importance, or none at all.[7]

This did not change during the twentieth century. When publishing her 1935 study on 'the influence exercised by Greek art and poetry over the great German writers of the eighteenth, nineteenth and twentieth centuries' (as the subtitle states), Eliza Marian Butler called it *The Tyranny of Greece over Germany*. As in other countries, the first decades of the twentieth century were a time of crisis for traditional, elitist education, and therefore also the role of Classics as the academic discipline of the elites, but the German Graecomania revealed itself to be highly resilient.[8] The Greek model, faithful to its visual nature, lost its character of an educational ideal, transforming instead into an aesthetic (mostly corporal) ideal.[9] In the second half of the nineteenth century, the cult of the Greek body had become a central staple of many nationalisms,[10] and German nationalism also adopted the ideal of the Greek body as the goal of training;[11] the beauty of the Greek body was thus exalted as an ideal, a model of inspiration and a paradigm of strength.[12]

This tendency reached a peak in the cult of the ancient body developed within the Third Reich,[13] and its most visible form was the organization of the XI modern Olympic Games in Berlin in 1936. Leni Riefenstahl's propaganda film *Olympia – Fest der Völker* (1938) begins among Greek ruins and Greek sculptures and shows the 'ancient sports' (discus and javelin, shot put, gymnastics), before switching to the journey of the Olympic flame to Germany (the first torch relay in history) and Hitler opening the games.[14] In 1938, the volume *Unsterbliches Hellas* (Immortal Greece), edited by Charilaos Kriekoukis, the press officer at the Royal Greek legation in Berlin, and Karl Böhmer, the Reich Head at the Foreign Political Office of the National Socialist Party, aimed to demonstrate, with text and pictures, the deep connection between Greece and the Third Reich. Such a connection also played an important role in the propaganda connected to the German occupation of Greece (1941–4).[15] During the Third Reich, while the 'disdain for non-utilitarian education hastened the demise of the classical schools',[16] Greece still played a major role;[17] the Greek body was also a means of celebrating the supposed common Aryan descent of the Dorians (and therefore the Greeks)[18] and the Germans.[19] Constructed in this way, the direct continuity between ancient Greeks and Germans thus excluded the modern Greeks, who were despised as a mixture of Albanians, Slavs and Turks who did not preserve the 'racial purity' of their ancestors. Sparta, rather than Athens, was viewed as the model, deeply influencing, for example, the Napolas – the Nazi elite schools. The Spartan model, particularly the ideal of Spartan education, as described by Xenophon, was already strongly present in the Prussian Cadet schools and was now transferred to the Third Reich's military education system. This is relevant as it explains why, after the Second World War, Sparta became a sort of taboo and essentially disappeared from German popular perceptions of ancient Greece, at least until the US American movie *300* (Zack Snyder, 2006) was marketed in the country. Yet even Thermopylae risks recalling how the battle was used on 30 January 1943 by Göring as a parallel to the German defeat in Stalingrad.[20] Indeed, due to both the problematic associations of Sparta and the visual nature of German philhellenism, even in Germany, 'ancient Greece' means after the Second World War only Athens,[21] in direct opposition to Sparta and its use by the Third Reich, and as an archetype of Western democracy.[22] Sparta was now presented as the 'opposite' of Athens, 'less Greek' than the 'perfect Greekness' of Athens.[23] Alexander the Great is also less present here than elsewhere: Alexander's image as the 'conqueror of the East' again risks evoking a hyper-militaristic and aggressive image which cannot be adopted in post-Nazi Germany, and Alexander is surprisingly under-represented in German school history programmes,[24] which provide an important point of access for the past into modern popular culture.

While philhellenism in the narrower sense declined and disappeared after the Second World War,[25] Germany did not lose its interest in, or its passion for, Greece. In fact, since the 1960s it has been strengthened, principally due to two factors: the large community of Greek immigrants in (Western) Germany and the ensuing daily presence of Greek culture, music, food; and the growing touristic industry, which has seen Greece become one of the main and most beloved holiday destinations for Germans. Greek migration to Germany has steadily increased since the war: during the Greek Civil War (1946–9) and its immediate aftermath, many Greek communist families found refuge in the DDR, but it was in the BDR that Greeks started to be present in huge numbers as *Gastarbeiter*, especially during the years of the military junta (1967–74). The peak was reached in 1973, when according to the *Statistisches Bundesamt*, 407,614 Greeks lived in Western Germany. From that moment on, the number increased and decreased at various times, but with 283,684 recorded members in 2012, Greeks nonetheless represent the fourth-largest community of immigrants in the country.[26] This explains why some specific aspects of modern Greek culture are better known in Germany than in other European countries: Nana Mouskouri and Melina Merkouri were (and remain) very popular in the country; Nikos Kazantzakis' novel *Zorba the Greek* (1946) has sold over a million copies there and has been printed in over 60 different editions; the movie adaptation (Michael Cacoyannis, 1964) is also very popular and its soundtrack, 'Zorbas's Dance', immediately evokes 'Greekness' in Germany, as in most of the Western world. The magazine *Zeit* defined the Greeks in 2010 as the 'most beloved' foreigners in Germany, recalling how a Greek was the first foreigner to appear on the very popular TV show *Lindenstraße*:[27] the character, Panaiotis Sarikakis, who was in the show from 1985 to 1996, was, not by chance, an innkeeper.

A very visible component of the Greek presence is indeed represented by Greek restaurants; according to a study from 2003, Greek cuisine was the third most-loved in Germany, with a particularly strong following in the eastern parts of the country, in which Greek cuisine took second place, a very close second to the winner, Italian food.[28] Greek restaurants are for the most part heavily themed, and thus present the majority of Germans with 'images of Greece' that have become widely known, highly recognizable and highly stereotypical. The names of these restaurants are drawn from three main sources: ancient Greek culture (mostly classical mythology), with many instances of Aphrodite, Dionysus, Heracles; touristic destinations (the number of Athens, Knossos and Mykonos is uncountable); or from other, specific and recognizable aspects of modern Greek culture, Taverna and Sirtaki being the most prominent. Inside, the decoration follows two main styles: one is the classical element, represented by columns, pictures or reproductions of the Parthenon, or the Athenian Acropolis, the Palace of Knossos, etc.; the other is the 'holiday destination', with white beaches, sunny skies, small islands, white buildings and blue domes. Blue and white, the colours of the Greek flag, are also the colours immediately associated with traditional Aegean buildings, with the beaches and the sea/sky, and are therefore a staple in every representation of Greece. It is enough to look at *Dekochef.de*, an internet page selling decorations for themed parties: their 'Greek offer' consists of nothing more than the usual party objects, but in white and blue.[29] Other German internet pages containing advice for a Greek evening suggest the blue and white next to costumes that derive from classical mythology, such as Aphrodite or Heracles,[30] or add 'terracotta tones' to the blue and white and suggest the insertion of classical sculptures, vases and amphorae.[31] These images are purely stereotypical: most of the Greeks that live in Germany (and who own the restaurants) actually come from the northern and internal parts of the country, especially from Macedonia and Thrace,[32] thus from areas which are distinctly different from the popular perceptions of their country of origin.

In terms of tourism, Germans represent the largest nationality group to visit Greece, with 2.5 million visitors in 2014.[33] Touristic images of Greece represent thus a highly recognizable visual set, also used in the restaurants; this in turn, just as in the theme parks, reinforces and consolidates this highly stereotypical repertoire. In tourism, Greece reveals the same 'double set' of signifiers identified above: the 'intellectual', archaeological holiday, graphically symbolized by the Athenian Acropolis;[34] and the 'sea' holiday, visualized by the beaches and small, sun-kissed villages inhabited by friendly cats. A brief look at the pictures on the introductory page for the Greek holiday destinations of a famous German tour operator is illuminating: the banner picture is of the Athenian Acropolis, with the Parthenon in a frontal, dominating position; beneath, the list of possible destinations is accompanied by pictures that generally represent just a beach, with the exception of Santorini – represented by prominent white houses and blue domes – and Mykonos and Paros, which also feature villages with their small white buildings centre stage.[35]

In addition to the images and stereotypes that exist worldwide, within Germany these philhellenic roots create a particular focus on the artistic achievements of the ancient Greeks, their love of beauty, manifestations of their 'genius', and the 'humanistic' nature of their civilization.[36] On the other hand, very little attention is paid to sport as an achievement of ancient Greece: while the Olympic Games are considered a good way to motivate the pupils and show them connections to the modern world, and are thus are highly present in school books,[37] the relation of the corresponding body culture with the Nazi regime makes it impossible to celebrate the athletic aspects of ancient Greece in the same way as elsewhere. Even certain highly famous and well-recognized artworks, such as the *Discobolus*,[38] tend to be less present than in other countries, for the same reason. Indeed, Myron's sculpture was the object of a real obsession for Hitler, who in 1938 bought the Roman copy that now sits in the Museo Nazionale Romano; not by chance, this was the statue that, in the opening scene of Riefenstahl's *Olympia – Fest der Völker*, 'transforms' classical antiquity, its art and its bodies, into the modern German, Aryan body.[39] There are thus no reproductions in German theme parks of this sculpture, popular otherwise in other parks, such as *Terra Mítica* and *Parc Astérix*. While topics that are popular elsewhere, such as sports, as well as almost the entirety of Greek history and politics (as shown above) are thus quite absent from German popular culture, mythology has a dominant role. Myths are often interpreted as having universal value, as a reflection on mankind, its achievements, its struggles. Once again, the school system provides a good explanation of this presence – while in German school programmes, ancient history (and particularly Greek history) is only a marginal subject, with just a few basic concepts being transmitted,[40] Greek mythology is still quite present, both in history classes as well as in literature and art classes.[41]

The Greek government's debt crisis (2009–18) has brought another consequence of philhellenism to the fore in Germany: an underlying prejudice against modern Greeks as Orientalized and 'unworthy of their ancestors'. While this is not so relevant to the themes within this book – as we have noted, theme parks avoid 'negative' and complicated themes – it is nonetheless relevant to highlight how such 'Greek-bashing' has been presented alongside the same images and stereotypes as the 'positive' messages. A 2011 article in the *Berliner Zeitung*, which foresaw a substantial migration from Greece to Germany (which did not occur), was significantly titled 'Schöne Strände sind nicht genug' ('Beautiful beaches are not enough');[42] during 2010, the weekly *Focus* twice used the Venus de Milo as their cover image. In February (8/2010),[43] the statue showed the readers the middle finger, beneath the title 'Betrüger in der Euro-Familie!' ('Traitors in the Euro-Family').[44] Ten weeks later (18/2010),[45] the title 'Griechenland – und unser Geld!' ('Greece – and our money') was accompanied by the same statue, this time stretching out her hand as a beggar. In a not so different way, the title of a weekly *Der Spiegel* from May 2012 (20/2012) 'Akropolis Adieu! Warum Griechenland jetzt den Euro verlassen muss' ('Acropolis, Goodbye! Why Greece must now leave the Euro') showed a picture of ruins (a hint both to Greece and its crisis, and to economic 'decline'); on the front was an Ionic column that held a Euro coin, now broken and partially fallen to the ground. In July of the same year (29/2012), the same weekly had the title 'Unsere Griechen. Annäherung an ein seltsames Volk' ('Our Greeks. Approach to a peculiar people').[46] Emphasizing the alterity (and thus the exotic nature) of the Greeks, as well as the heterotopic nature of their country (which is 'just' an Other Place, good for holidays and a break from daily life), we see a drawing of an Aegean island (Santorini or Mykonos), the blue sea and Alexis Sorbas. Cigarette in mouth and glass of ouzo in hand, he is dragging a German tourist, full of money and holding a copy of the book *Socrates for Dummies*, a symbol of the fascination that ancient Greek culture and philosophy still holds for Germans.

'Griechenland', *Europa-Park*, Rust

History of the park

With 5.7 million visitors in 2017, *Europa-Park* in Rust, Germany is the second most visited theme park in Europe (after *Disneyland Paris*), and the 21st most visited worldwide;[47] it has twice received the Golden Ticket Award as 'Best Amusement Park' in the world (2014 and 2015). *Europa-Park* has developed over the years but did not follow a plan with a pre-conceived number of themed areas. The park was born as an exhibition area for the company Mack GmbH & Co., which produces roller coasters and amusement rides. After travelling to the

United States in 1972, Franz Mack, who had controlled the family company since 1958, along with his son Roland decided to create a theme park to showcase the firm's creations.[48] The family thus bought the park of Schloss Balthasar, a Renaissance building dating to 1442 (which today hosts a restaurant),[49] as well as a neighbouring amusement park, and in 1975 opened *Europa-Park*.[50] The name did not originally come from the theme – at that time there was none – but from the neighbouring lake, Europaweiher.[51] *Europa-Park* is a unique example of a theme park that did not take its name from the theme, but rather assumed its theme based on the already existing name when the Mack family decided to adopt one. This occurred in the early 1980s, when the park already had over a million visitors a year. From that moment on, the theme was adopted in a consistent way, promoting the ideal of a theme park which, located within a border area, allowed a freedom of movement between European countries many years before the Schengen Treaty.[52] Indeed,

> the Europe staged in the park is an ideal place, beautiful and harmonious – a place far beyond actual political contention and conflict where a united Europe is alive in people's hearts. This is central to the park's construction of its corporate image and is continuously stressed by the Mack family who cultivate their social and political commitment promoting the European ideal.[53]

The first themed area, Italy, opened in 1982, followed by the Netherlands (1984), Great Britain (1988), France (1989), Austria and Scandinavia (both 1992), Switzerland (1993), Spain (1994), Germany (1996), Russia (1998), Greece, inaugurated in 2000, Portugal (2005), Iceland (2009) and finally Ireland (2016). Apart from these themed areas, there are three more: 'Adventureland', situated around the lake in the centre of the complex, which represents – with a rather strongly colonialist perspective – an exotic African continent; 'Grimms Märchenwald', an area for small children with attractions themed along the lines of the Grimm brothers' folk tales; and an area dedicated to 'Arthur and the Minimoys', developed around the franchise of the successful series of movies (Luc Besson, 2006, 2009, 2010). The five hotels follow more or less the same logic, each recalling a specific European building or destination – a Spanish *finca* on the Mediterranean (*El Andaluz*, 1995), a Spanish medieval palace (*Castillo Alcazar*, 1999), the Colosseum mixed with an Italian *piazza* (*Colosseo*, 2004), and a Portuguese monastery (*Santa Isabel*, 2007); the lone exception is *Bell Rock* (the most recent, opened 2012), which recreates a New England village. The history of *Europa-Park* explains its rather chaotic plan, which reveals how it has grown by buying up adjacent parcels of land, without a pre-planned development strategy. Since its opening in 1996, the German area ('Deutschland'), composed of a street with antique cars (and a statue of Frank Mack) and directly inspired by 'Main Street U.S.A', as with its Disney model, constitutes the entrance to the park, through which all visitors must walk. In this sense, by walking through the entrance gate, visitors exit the 'real' Germany, have a sort of 'acclimation' in *ersatz*-Germany, then move onwards towards the other European countries, which do not follow any recognizable pattern, but are arranged according to their opening year and the parcels available for sale at that moment.

The park has thus consistently developed the theme derived from its name, following a logic of progressive expansion according to commercial success, with every new themed area dedicated to a new European country. The only exception was Scandinavia, which is often perceived in Western Europe as a single block, and not easily differentiated within its constituent countries. Each country is represented as a village and more or less follows the same scheme: in each section there is a main attraction, around which the shops, restaurants etc. are built in the form of the 'typical architecture' of the country (as well as offering 'typical' food and products). These are often animated by events representing the culture of the country.[54] To heighten the sense of authenticity, 'musealized' objects (such as a piece of the Berlin Wall in the German area, or the MIR space station within the Russian area) have been inserted throughout the park. Original architectural elements have also been imported from the country (in Greece, for instance, these include wooden doors, ceiling beams and tiles),[55] as well as exhibitions and performances of traditional handicrafts in the style of living history museums.[56]

This focus on countries and their cultures shows an inspiration borrowed from World Fairs and Universal Expositions; but while at these fairs, as also at *Epcot*'s 'World Showcase', the countries represented were involved in the planning and were able to influence or determine how they were to be seen by the visitors, in *Europa-Park* it is the German stereotypical view of each European country that predominates (as, once again, Scandinavia makes clear).[57] The stereotypes to address are also quite homogeneous, as the visitors, in spite of their high numbers, mainly come from a limited number of nations, namely those that surround the park. The most numerous are from Germany (in 2013, almost half the total), followed by the French and the Swiss. These three nationalities together make up well over 90 per cent of the park's visitors. Considering the development of tourism within Europe since the end of the Second World War, the park aims not so much to show the visitors unknown or exotic localities, but rather places they might already have visited in person.

They thus aim for an effect of recognition and reactivation, not only of something that is already known, but also of something they might have already experienced in person.[58] This is 'sublimated' by its distilled, abstract form: not one Italian beach, but a pictogram of Italy; not one Greek island, but a summary of all Greece. Each country is thus presented as a monolithic block in which, through the strategy of abstraction, single elements are posed as symbolical representatives of national culture.[59] In this sense, the park places each country in a specific historical phase, perceived as the most recognizable and/or offering the most opportunities for the development of the attractions: the Netherlands are thus presented in colonial times, France in the nineteenth century, Spain during the fifteenth, etc.[60]

'Griechenland' in Rust

The description of the Greek area ('Griechenland') on the *Europa-Park* webpage starts with a simple sentence, perfectly revealing the two fields of stereotyping of Greece: 'Wo die Götter Urlaub machen: Willkommen in Mykonos!' ('Where the gods go on holiday: Welcome to Mykonos!').[61] Classical mythology as a symbol of ancient Greek culture, alongside the famous holiday destination with its picturesque village and sandy beaches, are thus presented together in just a few evocative words. A bronze statue, placed in front of a souvenir shop, represents Poseidon, holding a horn and a spear, standing on the waves and trampling a fish with his right foot [Fig. 4]: the ancient god of the sea, to whom the main attraction of the area is dedicated, represents both 'souls' of theme park Greece.[62] The references to antiquity are scattered everywhere: the trash bins of the area are decorated with a motif of blue waves, or with a Greek fret design and the reproduction of a *pinax* from the Athenian Acropolis, representing a warrior holding a shield with the representation of a satyr.[63] Next to these, the maritime element is highlighted once again: the centre of the area is a body of water, which forms the basin of the water coaster 'Poseidon', but also a mimicry of the Mediterranean Sea; visitors can walk along a path decorated with dolphins beside this 'lake'.[64]

Mykonos, as the webpage explicitly states, provides the strongest source of inspiration for 'Griechenland': the entrance gate to the area is a simple white arch, which appears old and in need of restoration (following the stereotype of the modern Greeks, unable to take care of their heritage), and bears the blue indication MYKONOS. This reduction of the Republic of Greece to the twin aspects of antiquity and tourism reveals once more how ancient Greece, even

Fig. 4 Statue of Poseidon, *Europa-Park*, Rust, Germany © Thomas Pusch (GNU Free Documentation License).

while perceived as the cradle of Western civilization (and in spite of the presence of ancient Greek settlements throughout the Mediterranean, from Spain to Turkey, from Italy to North Africa), is perceived as having a direct territorial and genetic connection with modern Greece. It has also been noted how schoolbooks about ancient Greece generally reproduce maps of modern Greece, only marginally hinting at the much larger area of Greek settlement.[65]

As previously noted, 'Griechenland' is not a copy, but a retelling of history: visitors feel the sense of confidence that derives from having already seen it all, given the familiarity of famous European tourist destinations.[66] It is thus not ancient Greece but the Greece of today, in the twenty-first century, filtered through German stereotypes: there are remains from the classical times, archaeological excavations, a windmill (one of the souvenir shops) – a typical feature of the Aegean islands and Mykonos in particular – donkeys, a wine press (with the metal parts painted in blue), an olive press, and a giant oil jar. References to the Greek Orthodox church also appeal to touristic and commercial images, for instance in the form of wall paintings inspired by Greek icons. Small fountains complete the decoration, while the Greek language (a characteristic identifier) is visible everywhere: on the signs with fictitious street names, on the trash bins, etc. Often the words are modern Greek words, sometimes transliterations of German and English, only comprehensible to visitors who know the Greek alphabet: in the 'Taverna Mykonos', for instance, one can read above the cash machines 'ΦΡΙΣΧΗΕ ΜΥΣΧΗΕΛΝ / ΛΥΝΧΗ ΔΙΝΝΕΡ', 'Frische Muscheln (fresh mussels) / Lunch dinner'. Using a device that is typical to 'represent Greece', the Latin alphabet is also reshaped to resemble the Greek, for instance using the Greek sigma (Σ) or csi (Ξ) in place of E, or drawing the letters in an 'angular' way. Throughout the area typical Mediterranean flora has been planted: laurel, pines, wine, olive and fig trees.[67]

The main attraction of the area, around which 'Griechenland' is constructed, is 'Poseidon', a water coaster inspired by the myth of Odysseus. 'Fluch der Kassandra' is hosted in an Orthodox church, and 'Pegasus' is a coaster set in an archaeological excavation (archaeology within Europe is quite automatically Greek). The latter name shows once again the importance of mythology in the reception of ancient Greece:[68] the local station of the EP-Express, the monorail which travels around the park, is called 'Olymp', and a further attraction is 'Der Flug des Ikarus' ('The Flight of Icarus'). In the local space for shows, ice skaters perform in 'Surpr'Ice with the Gods of Greece', in which Medusa tries to disrupt the festivities. The Greek area hosts a relevant theatre for shows; however, this is no explicit homage to the ancient (and well-known) tradition of Greek theatre. The building, a circus tent, shows no traces of theming (much less than the 'Globe Theatre' in the English sector, for instance) and pre-exists 'Griechenland'; since its construction in 1992 and until 2000, it belonged to Switzerland. Its role as an ice arena, hosting skating shows, is better explained by this early phase than by its actual location. Nonetheless, 'Surpr'Ice with the Gods of Greece' (summer seasons 2015–16), is the first show that attempts to fit in with the Greek theme through its plot; 'Helenas Traum' ('Helen's Dream', summer season 2007) evoked the ancient mythological character – but only in name, as it was an acrobatic skating show. All the other shows hosted here in other years, as in the winter seasons, are totally unrelated to Greece.[69] The reference to the sea, and to what is perceived in popular culture as 'mythology', is reinforced once again in 'Abenteuer Atlantis' ('Adventure Atlantis'). The local restaurant, the 'Taverna Mykonos', serves gyros, moussaka, squid, Greek wine, ouzo and Metaxa,[70] while 'Atlantissnack' provides refreshing fruit and Greek yoghurt, and drinks can be purchased at the 'Troja Kiosk'. To round up, the sweets shop is called 'Penelope Glykos', the souvenir shop 'Helena Souvenirs' and a basketball fair attraction stand is called 'Olympia Basketball', thus bluntly recalling the connection between Greece and sports. The objects sold in the souvenir shops (displayed in cabinets sometimes shaped as ancient columns) are specific to the themed area, and once again reinforce the image of Greece presented here: alongside copies of ancient works of art and broken vases are ceramics decorated with motives inspired by the proto-Geometric and Geometric styles, stone owls, paintings and pictures of the Greek islands, and objects that generally recall the sea (such as models of lighthouses and life buoys). The plush animals on sale are tortoises, dolphins, seals and octopuses. Ruins and the sea are impossible to divide.

'Poseidon'

'Poseidon' is the main and largest attraction of the area, around which the entire sector 'Griechenland' was planned and developed. It is not surprising, considering once again the 'maritime' image of Greece as the land of sun and sea, that this role would go to a water coaster.[71] At the same time, the ride category is the source of inspiration for the name: 'Poseidon', the Greek god of the seas. Poseidon's most famous role in ancient myth is the enemy of Odysseus, as he tries to lead the hero astray and prevent him from reaching Ithaca. In the Homeric tradition, this hostility was caused by Odysseus blinding the Cyclops Polyphemus, Poseidon's son. The water coaster in *Europa-Park* starts from the role of Poseidon as god of the seas (and the storms) who tries to obstruct Odysseus' travel, but constructs it around a quite different narrative, which is presented to the visitors in the waiting area. Odysseus, as visitors learn from a film, is a rather arrogant fellow, and has provoked the gods by conquering Troy against their will, thus inviting their anger. The gods protest this lack of respect, but Odysseus claims he will be able to march on the Olympus and put an end to their power; this provokes Poseidon's rage. The visitors are thus placed in the role of Odysseus' companions, as they endure the god's wrath in boats. The relationship to myth is quite free – nothing like this can be found in the ancient tradition. Nonetheless, this is a 'faithful' way of dealing with ancient mythology, which was always open to variants and variations.[72]

The main visual marker of the coaster, and the entire themed area, is the ride's loading station, which is in the form of a Greek temple [Fig. 5]. This is accessed

Fig. 5 The loading station of the water coaster 'Poseidon', *Europa-Park*, Rust, Germany © Jürgen Ehrler Hobby-Fotografie.

from the rear: when riding the coaster, the façade of the temple is the last thing one sees, when the vehicles go back into the loading station. Yet for every park visitor coming to the Greek area, the temple is the most prominent visual element within the area, and through its position on the lake shore it serves as a 'weenie', a visual icon attracting visitors to a specific direction. In order to reach the entrance from the back, every visitor must walk along the lake and see the building. The Greek temple thus becomes, following the mechanism of abstraction, the pictographic synthesis and most evocative symbol of Greece as a whole.[73] By conforming to people's expectations, as described above, as well as with the chronotope of the themed area, and thus the representation of a temple as it could be seen by visitors today (the Parthenon once again playing the role of a model), the temple is predictably white. The shape is quite standard: a hexastyle, peripteral Doric temple, as with the Temple of Zeus at Olympia, although the central columns have a much broader inter-columnal space than would be acceptable in an ancient temple, as they have to allow space for the ride vehicles to pass through them. As is to be expected from an ancient Greek temple, the pediment is decorated with sculptures; however, they are no reproductions or reconstructions of ancient artworks, but purely inventions. In the centre is Poseidon, the tutelary deity of the ride, sitting on a throne; a very unusual iconography, never met in pediments, but perfectly explicable given the name and story of the ride. Next to him is Athena, perhaps to hint at the legendary fight between the two deities for the control of Attica, which was represented on the Western pediment of the Parthenon. The sculptures show a huge mixture of styles, from the more archaizing (reproducing the 'severe style') to the more classicizing, or even post-classical; all iconographies are inspired by ancient motifs, even if not from genuine architectonical sculpture: the gryphon on the right is a motif which, in Greek art, appears instead in ceramic paintings and reliefs. This is not a contradiction of the principles of immersion and of 'authenticity': this building has everything that a visitor can expect from a 'Greek temple' and creates an immersive 'Greek atmosphere'.

As mentioned, those who wish to ride must first walk beside the central lake; from here, they can already see the two drops of the coaster, and get soaked by the ride vehicles falling into the water.[74] But they can also soak the passengers of the ride vehicles with water pistols in the shape of dolphins that are installed along the path, an 'interactive' scenario that increases the theatricality of the scene.[75] At the end of the path, they pass through a reproduction of the Lion Gate from Mycenae, which represents the entrance to both 'Poseidon' and 'Pegasus'. Here, the paths to the two rides separate, and those aiming for 'Poseidon' see a building topped with the typical crenellation in the shape of ox horns known from the Palace of Knossos. Through the legs of a large wooden horse, whose head is directed towards the building, the visitors enter a queuing area inspired by Minoan architecture, decorated with amphorae, paintings copied or inspired by Minoan art (for example the frescoes from Akrotiri), as well as by archaic and Orientalizing art.[76] This is no surprise: as explained, the Bronze Age is a visualization of the age of myth, and particularly of the Homeric myth, associated with it by Schliemann's archaeological activity.[77] As we approach Odysseus' myth (in popular culture his name is connected to the stratagem of the horse at the end of the Trojan War), it is clear why a Minoan building, already 'conquered', with a wooden horse at its gate (and already in ruins: visitors can also see a sunken ship), represents the entrance point of the ride. In the first courtyard, a Greek inscription relates, in 'correct' ancient Greek, that it is forbidden to move or damage the 'antiquities', to take away even the smallest part as a souvenir, to take pictures or make videos, as well as to take babies or animals on the ride. The idea of ancient Greece as a culture in which much was written on stone and exposed to the public, which derives from democratic Athens, is here brought to the fore, demonstrating once again the perception of ancient Greece as a 'monolith', without much attention to chronological detail. Through a last 'Minoan' door, decorated with the painting of a bull, visitors now enter a series of rooms in which they find a statue of Atlas holding the world on his shoulders, and a digital projection of a speaking Agamemnon mask (again Bronze Age, Mycenae, Schliemann, Homeric epos), before entering a cave in which, against the background of the noise of the waves, they see the short introductory movie.

Now the visitors access the temple; however, internally this is no temple, but rather the docks of a fishing village. Here, Poseidon's rage has become evident: a huge trident is stuck in the building. After entering the vehicle, a small coloured boat like those you would expect to find on a Mediterranean beach, visitors exit the temple through a huge opening in the wall 'caused' by the trident. Next to this is the shield of Athena, decorated with the Medusa: the goddess tried to help the hero, and Poseidon fought her, too.[78] From here riders pass through a few segues, scenes of destruction and ruin, which partially coincide with the elements seen from the queuing area.[79] At this point, Poseidon definitively catches the boat, brings it up the lift-hill and then, via some convolutions, down two plunges in the lake; after this, riders are brought back into the temple, this time through the colonnade on the main façade. Odysseus has not been killed, and fortunately nor have his companions; still, he has learnt not to provoke divine authority and to be respectful of those who are bigger than him. He also has cooled down a little during the German summer.[80]

'Pegasus'

The Youngstar coaster 'Pegasus', which shares the entrance with 'Poseidon', was opened in 2006; in 2016 it was implemented with virtual reality (Coastiality) and transformed into a VR coaster,[81] without changing the decoration of the ride;[82] in 2017, 'Pegasus' was returned to its original format, and the virtual reality part was removed. The choices for its name and symbol are connected to the pre-existing water coaster: as Pegasus is, in mythology, generated by Poseidon and Medusa, its birth is essentially evoked by the trident and the head of the Gorgon inside the loading station of 'Poseidon'.

The theming is not directly from Greece, but rather archaeology; the waiting area represents an archaeological excavation from the early twentieth century, that is, from the time of the great discoveries: the Palace of Knossos, discovered in 1878, was excavated between 1900 and 1935; the German archaeological mission at Olympia began in 1875 and went on for decades; the Altar of Pergamon was brought to Berlin in 1879, where it was reconstructed between 1897 and 1899 and opened to the public in 1901, etc. Walking through the waiting area, visitors see an archaeological excavation, with material partially placed in wooden boxes. The chief archaeologist, unsurprisingly dressed in a colonial style, snores under a tent, while a young assistant tries to wake him: this is an ironic reversal of the popular theme of the 'archaeologist as adventurer', most often problematically connected to colonial and imperial undertones.[83] Scattered throughout the area are a diverse mixture of objects – part archaeological material, part garden sculptures.[84]

Archaeology is a very widespread subject in popular culture, which attracts a great deal of attention due to its elements of exploration, mystery and discovery.[85] In a theme park dedicated to European countries, the ride and themed sector dedicated to archaeology are located in Greece – the country's identity is strongly tied to its ancient past. This is far more the case than in Italy, for instance, for which the discontinuities and differences between the Roman Empire and the modern state are more strongly anchored in popular knowledge. Greece is antiquity and tourism, therefore ruins and archaeology, especially lazy archaeology in the sun, which not only parodies the archaeologist conceived as 'a mixture of Schliemann, Carter and Indiana Jones',[86] but also insists on the sunny, holiday atmosphere in Greece, as well as on the relaxing value of a day at the theme park and the adventure value of the roller coaster ride.

True to its chronotope, the ride has recognizably steampunk aesthetics: it is one of the tropes of nostalgia to mix a longing for the past with an interest in technological progress, both in the sense of inventing and idealizing past inventions and technologies (as is the case here), or in 'technonostalgia', the idea that the most modern techniques can help us to rejoin the past (in the style of *Jurassic Park*).[87] The loading station, in a sort of evocative parallel to 'Poseidon', is thus again a Greek temple, but one which has been found and reconstructed by archaeologists using materials which are also evocative of the steampunk style: mainly tin. In the same sense, the vehicle of the coaster that represents Pegasus, the winged horse from Greek mythology, brings the riders to a bumpy flight in steampunk style.[88] This evokes images of technology and advancement from the twentieth century, thus simultaneously representing a typical trope of postmodern nostalgia,[89] here connected to a yearning for the warmth of Greece and the Mediterranean.

'Flug des Ikarus'

Classical mythology is such a powerful repertoire of stories and symbols that it can at times function through nothing more than the imposition of a name, without any further specific references to the narrative or the ancient world. This is clear in the case of 'Flug des Ikarus'. As will become evident, many of the theme parks analysed in this book have an attraction dedicated to the myth of Daedalus and Icarus; however, this seldom goes beyond the name. Given the popularity of the myth, and the context of a themed area dedicated to Greece, the reference is sufficiently recognizable and understood as an element in the chain of receptions for this specific myth.[90] In this sense, the name has also been attributed to rides outside the world of theme parks: the itinerant condor ride 'Ikarus der Mythos', for instance, travelled across Europe until 2007, and was seen again in Berlin during the festival Neuköllner Maientage in 2009. It has gondolas representing falcon-like birds and decorations in a classicizing style representing mythological scenes, while the stylized image of a young man, wearing a short white gown (often associated with antiquity, and mostly with Egypt) and bearing wings, surmounts the entire attraction.[91] An identical ride, 'Ikarus', with the same figure on top, was featured from 1989 to 2011 in the medieval area of the Italian theme park *Gardaland*. The myth of Icarus can thus be a label, evoking flight even with a very unspecific (or different) theme.

This is also the case in *Europa-Park*: the 'Flight of Icarus' is a balloon race. A dominant blue colour is the only other element that fits within the Greek theme. The attraction opened in 1996, when the Greek sector did not yet exist; it was located in the Swiss area and was simply called 'Ballon-Fahrt' ('Balloon Trip'). This is nothing strange or unique to *Europa-Park*, and is significant only in relation to the power of Greek mythology: a 'generic' attraction that could be placed anywhere, the theming ultimately depending only on the name (as well as the main colour, although this can be changed), adopts, to fit into a Greek area, a mythological name, as this is much more recognizable to a general public than any other elements of Greek culture. This is what Younger defines as 'associative theming', in which 'decoration is simply attached to an element which has no intrinsic link with the theme it is being associated with'.[92] If there is anything connected to flight and air travel, Icarus is an immediate connection, in spite of the rather negative connotation this should generate. In the myth, Icarus is supposed to fly with wings held together by wax invented by his father Daedalus but, as he flies too close to the Sun, the wax melts and he falls into the sea, drowning.[93] That such a myth is evoked in the park would seem to conflict with the basic rule that theme parks generally exclude problematic aspects such as death from their representation policies. Ultimately, however, this is not a contradiction: first, the 'sad' finale of the story is not evoked in attractions such as this that relate to Icarus; only the act of flying is presented. Second, the myth is not only widely known to the public, it also represents a very 'far-away' and unreal sphere, a realm of archetypes. Because of this, death, pain, and war within mythology can be represented in the theme park, as they appear with an archetypal value, as episodes that 'did not really happen', thus appearing much less dramatic and problematic than 'historical' wars and deaths.[94]

'Abenteuer Atlantis'

A 'mythological' theme of a very particular nature characterizes the shooter 'Abenteuer Atlantis' ('Adventure Atlantis'), inaugurated in 2007.[95] There are many possible reasons for its existence: 'Poseidon', constructed by Mack, is based on the model of a very similar coaster they had delivered two years before to *Sea World Orlando*, 'Journey to Atlantis' (also with ancient referents, as we will see).[96] A connection between the Greek area and Atlantis could thus have been present within the Mack company due to these rides; more generally though, Atlantis is consistently seen as being connected with ancient Greece.[97] The connection with the sea and sea travels would already be sufficient to explain why an Atlantis ride would be in a Greek area, but there is much more: when the theme moves beyond being simply 'beneath the Ocean' and becomes a 'lost city', its connection to Greek antiquity is unavoidable, be it in classical style or in reference to the Bronze Age, and particularly Minoan architecture, given its general connection to the 'mythical'.[98] This is also due to the most popular and widespread theory about the 'identification of Atlantis' since the 1970s, which argues that Plato, who invented the island and its city during the fourth century,[99] had some indirect memory of a great volcanic eruption which destroyed the island of Santorini.[100] Atlantis would thus be a Platonic reinterpretation of Minoan culture. As this is visualized as 'the time of myth', Atlantis can be located next to the Labyrinth, the Minotaur and Icarus.

The connection between Atlantis and ancient Greece (and in particular Athens) is indeed genetic, as Plato presented it as a dystopic kingdom, which in extremely ancient times (in literary fiction, nine thousand years before Solon, i.e. before the early sixth century BCE) would have occupied an island behind the Pillars of Heracles and fought against Athens.[101] The reception of Atlantis began immediately after Plato:[102] the 'lost city' was transformed from a dystopia into a utopia, with frequent debates about its eventual existence, by the end of antiquity.[103] All this lies outside the scope of this book: it is enough to note here the 'boom' that Atlantis has experienced since the nineteenth century and the special relation of this myth to melancholy and nostalgia.[104] In this sense, the classicism of Atlantis is integral to the myth and its success: 'it is not hard to see how Atlantis, in its anecdotal condensation of both the Greco-Roman Empire – the pillars, temples and togas – and the mysteries of divine (however catastrophic) intervention, could easily come to represent the golden age of Western civilization, as well as its apocalyptic demise'.[105]

Since the nineteenth century, the success of Atlantis has depended not only on Plato, but also on Jules Verne. In *Twenty Thousand Leagues Under the Sea* (1869–70), captain Nemo and the Nautilus visit, among many other places, the Lost City. Verne's work is deeply conditioned by classical culture, starting with the name Nemo, which evokes the Polyphemus episode from the *Odyssey*. His references to Atlantis also demonstrate a deep knowledge of ancient sources, such as Aelian and Theopompus. The description of Atlantis in the novel thus leaves no doubts how the city, which in Verne's novel is abandoned, should be visualized:

> Right there in front of my eyes – ruined, broken, collapsed – appeared a city destroyed, its roofs fallen, its temples flattened, its arches broken, its columns lying on the ground, but with the solid proportions of a type of Tuscan architecture still discernible. Further on lay a few remains of a gigantic aqueduct; here, the silted bulge of an acropolis, with the floating forms of a Parthenon; there a few traces of a quayside, as if some antique port had once sheltered the merchant vessels and war triremes on the shores of a long-lost ocean; further still, the long lines of broken-down walls and broad deserted streets: a whole Pompeii sunk beneath the waters, that Captain Nemo was bringing back to life before my very eyes![106]

Following this, according to the comic Brick Bradford ('The Time Top', 1935), Atlantideans speak ancient Greek,[107] while the movie *Atlantis, The Lost Continent* (George Pal, 1961), set at the time of ancient Greece, shows Atlantis as a sort of hyper-technological, steampunk Athens. Disney transformed Verne's novel first into a movie (Richard Fleischer, 1954), and then a series of theme park rides: a walkthrough in *Disneyland* in California (1955–66), which was then replicated in *Disneyland Paris* ('Les mystères du Nautilus', opened 1994); a submarine ride in the *Magic Kingdom*, Orlando (1971–94); and a further one in *Tokyo DisneySea* (opened 2001, the same year in which Disney released the motion picture

Atlantis: The Lost Empire).¹⁰⁸ These Disney rides do not represent the Atlantis section of Nemo's adventures, but they have certainly transformed them into an important referent for theme parks. *Europa-Park*'s 'Abenteuer Atlantis' has built upon this set of references (and those offered by 'Atlantis' at *Sea World*) and was developed in a clearly 'Vernean' genealogy, in the context of the popular association of the Lost City with classical antiquity.

Within the ride, visitors meet the 'Professor' and his helper, a turtle, in the waiting area. The mission is to find the legendary city of Atlantis, which lies at the bottom of the Ocean, along with its treasure. Embarking on their vehicles, which represent submarines, visitors are carried throughout the Ocean's depths while shooting at targets such as sea monsters and dangerous fish.¹⁰⁹ Visiting wrecks and caves, diving to always greater depths (as revealed by the depth-fish, the sea dragons, and the shifting soundtrack), the visitors reach the Lost City and its treasure chest (already opened by the Professor and the turtle). The Lost City itself appears to be a classical city, mixing Greek and Roman elements: whole and broken marble columns and capitals, arches with marble intarsia, decorative elements such as racemes. Such a representation of Atlantis, in the form of ruins rather than as a reconstructed visualization of the Lost Continent, is consistent with both the Vernean tradition and the theming: the riders do not travel back in time (nor do they discover that Atlantis still exists), but rather use their steampunk technological knowledge to find the remnants of an extremely ancient civilization.

'Fluch der Kassandra'

When the Greek area opened in 2000, it hosted only three attractions: 'Poseidon', 'Flug des Ikarus' and the madhouse 'Fluch der Kassandra' ('Cassandra's Curse').¹¹⁰ In the queuing area, visitors are presented with a particular version of the myth of Cassandra:¹¹¹ the Trojan priestess of Athena foresaw the destruction of the city in the war but was not believed – not because of divine punishment, but because the Trojans were too proud. Dragged to Greece, she was killed alongside Agamemnon and, while dying, cursed those responsible with eternal restlessness. In order to avoid this, when her body was cremated, her soul was captured in an amphora, which remained closed for centuries. But when restoration works were made on a church on the island of Mykonos, the amphora was rediscovered and opened in an act of curiosity. The soul of Cassandra, finally freed, started spinning around time and space, and her curse falls on the spinning riders. The story confirms once again, through a cross-contamination with the myth of Pandora, the flexibility of ancient myth and the freedom with which it can be changed, as well as the fact that myth allows the representation of war and death, which would otherwise be unacceptable in a theme park. The madhouse, a rather simple yet highly widespread staple attraction, here receives a narrative background, anchored in a well-known narrative. The story of the priestess who could foresee the future but was not believed is indeed popular throughout the Western world, but enjoys a particular popularity in Germany. Here it is a strong component of 'popular knowledge', present not only in novels like Christa Wolf's *Kassandra* (1983), but also in Lotto TV ads, where she represents a symbol of negativity and pessimism, an always black vision of the future.[112] This is not entirely coincidental to the role attributed to Cassandra in the ride, but there is a clear overlapping in the negative characterization of the figure.

The building hosting the ride, the church in which the amphora was found, is the village's Orthodox church [Fig. 6]. In the same way as the temple of 'Poseidon', it represents a pictographic and abstract representation of recognizable architecture: the churches from the Aegean islands. The main inspiration seems to be the church of Agios Nikolaos on Mykonos, but the ride's building is very different from this church. The dome is placed on a higher and thinner cylinder,

Fig. 6 The madhouse 'Cassandra', *Europa-Park*, Rust, Germany © Thomas Pusch (GNU Free Documentation License).

which somewhat evokes the very well-known images of Oia, Santorini. Whereas Agios Nikolaos is characterized by triangular pediments, the church in *Europa-Park* shows only round forms, which again appear to be inspired by Oia, perhaps the most popular building of this kind.

Once they have entered, visitors wait in a first room, a dark library surmounted by a monk entirely covered by a dark cloak and holding scrolls, evoking medieval monasteries, who tells the story of Cassandra and the ride. Here, with dim light and surrounded by fragmented elements of the classical world (the torso of the Venus de Milo, broken amphorae, etc.) and by 'Byzantine' reliefs, the visitors wait their turn to enter the madhouse. This is decorated with a mixture of the most diverse visual reminders of the different epochs of Greek history: Classical black vase paintings and Byzantine mosaics, with a dominant gold colour representing Odysseus and the Sirens; fragmented marble intarsia and an archaizing metope representing Pegasus; weapons (spears, shields) and a black and white mosaic with the portrait of a bearded, long-haired figure.[113] The experience of the visitors, spinning in the madhouse, is underscored by the music, and by Cassandra's curse. The latter contributes to the immersion, even if it does not necessarily help to understand the plot, as it is spoken in modern Greek, thus once again confirming how ancient and modern Greece are barely distinguished. In this way, while the curse contributes to the immersion (the voice pronouncing it is certainly not friendly, and it is evident to everybody that it is Cassandra, as the first two words, *Ego Cassandra*, are probably understandable to many people), it does not appear to be too scary or violent; indeed, the text is not presented in a language that would be understandable, for instance, to most children visiting the park:[114]

> I am Cassandra, priestess from Troy
> They took me away from the sacred spaces of Athena,
> Cursed shall you all be ... cursed!
> Cursed for eternity, you shall burn, you shall burn,
> And in no direction ever find calm.
> Cursed, you shall burn!
> Cursed shall you all be,
> Beneath the hands of your children,
> In the middle of the fire of Hell
> You shall burn for eternity.
> I am Cassandra, cursed
> Shall you all be, cursed!

The accompanying music, which creates a clear climax accompanying the spinning of the room, is an elaboration of a track called 'Oceania', which opens and closes the album of the same name by Didier Orieux and Agnes Portal (Koka Media, 1999). The idea that Greece evokes the sea even in 'darker aspects', and needs music inspired by (and which in turn evokes) the sea, has thus also found its way into the madhouse. In this sense, 'Fluch der Kassandra' is a perfect synthesis of the system of symbols that represent Greece in *Europa-Park*: the cultures of ancient and modern Greece are impossible to distinguish, together forming a picture, dominated by antiquity (with a preponderance of mythology) and the idea of a sea vacation on an Aegean island.

'Strand der Götter', *Belantis*, Leipzig

History of the park

Belantis, the biggest theme park in Eastern Germany, was developed relatively soon after the reunification of the country. As all the country's important and successful theme and amusement parks – *Europa-Park, Phantasialand, Holiday Park, Hansa-Park* – were in the former Western Federal Republic of Germany, it was decided to build an 'Eastern' park, which could attract the population of the new federal states, especially Saxony, with its large, populous cities such as Dresden or Leipzig; the park was also partially funded by the state of Saxony and the European Union.[115] Following the model of other successful parks, particularly that of *Europa-Park*, it was decided not to build a very large park, which would have required huge numbers of visitors to be successful, but rather to start with a smaller investment and enlarge in the subsequent years. The park was built between 2002 and 2003, and opened in 2003, attracting 500,000 visitors in the first year – a number that has steadily grown year by year, to over 600,000 visitors in 2016.[116] Following the initial plans, new investments are being made every year. These, in contrast to *Europa-Park*, do not consist of opening new themed areas, but of buying new rides to be placed within various spots in the park (some themed areas are still rather 'empty').[117] In order to save money, however, the park has invested little in thrill rides, and has correspondingly developed a profile as a theme park for families, in which grandparents and grandchildren can ride together.[118] The project thus became an important part of the process of requalification for a large area south of Leipzig, characterized by open-air excavations to extract lignite. This area was (and is still being) progressively transformed into a lake region, as the previous mines are filled in with water. The park thus belongs to a fairly substantial series of theme parks built as parts of projects to reuse land on which the previous use could not be continued and which would not be appropriate for other private initiatives,[119] at the same time integrating them within a larger public initiative to rescue an economically depressed area. The mascot of the park, Buddel, recalls the verb *buddeln* – 'to dig, to excavate' – and directly connects to this environmental intervention.

Buddel is a bear loosely dressed up as an explorer, consistent with the main theme of the park: *Belantis* presents itself as the 'AbenteuerReich', the 'Realm of Adventure', with overarching themes of travel and geographical exploration, while the architecture and decorative style is broadly inspired by the garden and landscape architecture of the eighteenth century.[120] The name of the park seeks to evoke the dominant myth of exploration, mystery and civilization which is, as already noted, Atlantis: *Belantis* is a mixture of the name of the Lost Continent and the Italian word 'bello' ('beautiful'), which is widely known and understood in Germany.[121] The park is built on a 'loop pattern':[122] the general map is a reproduction of a world map, around a central lake loosely shaped in the form of the Mediterranean Sea and the Atlantic Ocean. As noted by Francaviglia, theme parks 'embody visions of places ... and are thus maps',[123] and are in this sense very often inspired by the geography relative to the cultures represented, in this case the world (or, to be more precise, Europe, North Africa and America). The entrance area, Schloss *Belantis*, is the smallest; it consists of a German Baroque palace and of 'Buddels Jahrmarkt', a fair with traditional fairground attractions such as a carousel. These represent a 'starting point' for exploration. From here, visitors should move counter-clockwise, as this direction gives to the visit also a chronological sequence. The first area the visitor meets, the 'Tal der Pharaonen' ('Valley of the Pharaohs') is dedicated to ancient Egypt; moving on, they encounter ancient Greece, 'Strand der Götter' ('Beach of the Gods'). Two more areas follow, which evoke the Middle Ages, the German 'Land der Grafen' ('Land of the Counts') and the British 'Insel der Ritter' ('Island of the Knights'). Approaching the Atlantic, 'Küste der Entdecker' ('Coast of the Discoverers') recalls the great exploratory journeys of the sixteenth century, while the final two themed areas are dedicated to the 'discovered' pre-Columbian societies: 'Prairie der Indianer' ('Prairie of the Indians') for North America, and 'Reich der Sonnentempel' ('Empire of the Temples of the Sun') for South America.[124]

Ancient Greece in Belantis' world

The very name of the Greek area shows, in a way that is highly consistent with what has been said until now, how ancient Greece is presented to the German public: the 'beach' evokes the maritime holiday destination, while the 'gods' show that mythology occupies centre stage. The dominant colours of the Greek area are, unsurprisingly, white and blue; while *Belantis* renounces any use of the Greek alphabet (in contrast to *Europa-Park*), it still adopts an edgy font for the signs in the Greek area, which seeks to evoke both antiquity and inscriptions on stone. Around the themed area are small, white, Ionic columns holding bronze basins. The biggest part of the themed area, hosting the attractions 'Säule der Athene' and 'Götterflug', as well as the embarking station of 'Flug des Ikarus', is also on a hill, which could be evocative of the Acropolis, or better of the generalized perception (based on the case of Athens), that a Greek polis should have had its 'centre' on a hill. As a final touch, the area is characterized by music which resembles sirtaki and evokes 'Greekness'. However, the overall level of theming is quite low, far lower than in most of the other parks analysed in this volume (but also lower than in other themed areas of *Belantis*),[125] and the area has no actual buildings. This surely derives from the history of the park itself and future interventions will perhaps correct it – the Egyptian area has already seen a strong improvement in its theming with the construction of the family roller coaster 'Cobra des Amun Ra' (2015). Nonetheless, before its construction, the Egyptian section already had a much stronger theme, through a 38-metre-high pyramid, through which the water coaster 'Fluch des Pharaos' ('The Pharaoh's Curse') moves. It must be noted, however, that while a huge pyramid is sufficient to evoke Egypt, white Ionic columns also evoke Greekness but are betrayed by their dimensions, which are much less impressive and thus less immersive. In this sense, there seems to have been less attention paid to the theming of 'Strand der Götter' than to other thematic areas.

As in *Europa-Park*, and perhaps in connection with the popular association of ancient Greece and the theatre, the Greek area hosts the main structure for shows, the 'Arena des Zeus' ('Zeus' Arena'), opened in 2008. Once again, it is only very lightly themed: it is a sort of circus tent, and the only connection to Greece is the white and blue colouring. The shows held inside do not have any thematic connection to Greece.[126] Aside from mythology, and the stylized Ionic capital that symbolizes the themed area on the signs across the park, the park builds upon the widespread idea that the ancient Greeks 'invented' science (in particular, physics). This is another popular stereotype surrounding classical Greece, represented here by a rather well-known fair attraction device, which produces 'astonishing' effects through basic physical phenomena: the 'Schalen des Pythagoras', or 'Pythagoras' Bowls' are two large, vertical basins that are placed at some distance from each other, but in such a position as to resonate with each other.[127] So, if one visitor whispers something in one basin, another standing next to the second basin can clearly hear what was said, even if it is inaudible to everyone in between. The physics is elementary, but it has a great effect on children and can be realized at a very low cost. The theming is almost non-existent: a mouth and an ear are painted in the two basins to indicate that one must speak and the other listen. All the theming thus derives from its location in the Greek area and its namesake, widely recognized as an ancient sage, philosopher, scientist and mathematician (as everybody learns the Pythagorean Theorem in school, for instance).

The ancient Greeks were no strangers to dazzling people with technology: famously, Heron of Alexandria developed a way to open the doors of a temple 'automatically' thanks to steam power, and he invented the 'aeolipile', but also the first vending machine of the world (which dispensed water), as well as a mechanical theatre. Despite the 'modernity' of such inventions, and thus their great potential to 'update' (to use Lowenthal's concept) and make antiquity more contemporary, they are not widely known at a popular level, nor offer clear recognizability, and thus do not belong to the set of 'stereotypes' useful to a theme park. It is thus improbable that the park is hinting at this specific tradition with such devices. It seems much more probable that such 'scientific' attractions are here (besides potential reasons of space) because ancient Greece, the land of philosophy and mathematics, of Pythagoras and Archimedes, but also of Euclides, seemed much more apt to host them than pharaonic Egypt or medieval England, which are surely less famous at the level of popular culture for their intellectual achievements. Egypt is much more celebrated in popular reception for its funerary culture and 'mysterious aspects' than, for instance, for their agricultural techniques (with the concurrent mathematical knowledge) or their expertise in medicine.

'Fahrt des Odysseus'

The main attraction in the Greek area of *Belantis* is, as in *Europa-Park*, dedicated to the myth of Odysseus. The ride by the Swiss company BeAR Rides, built in 2003 and strongly re-thematized in 2009, is nonetheless very different: it is a pleasant 15-minute-long tow-boat ride.[128] Nonetheless, it is clear that the connection between Odysseus (and more generally ancient Greece) and seafaring is the productive popular association that explains the centrality of both rides. At the entrance, marked by a broken white column and the inscription 'Odyssee' ('Odyssey'), the visitors embark in boats which lead them to travel, in a much less adventurous way, through seven selected adventures of Odysseus.[129] These are presented and explained in every boat by an annotated map. The boats, realized in fibreglass and polyester according to a pre-made design,[130] are painted in blue and decorated with stereotypical Greek motives: meanders, waves and dolphins, but the bow is shaped like the neck and head of a swan. There is no connection between swans and the adventures of Odysseus, but they play an important role in medieval German mythology: the Swan Knight (*Schwanritter*) travels on a boat shaped in the form of a swan, or drawn by swans. This myth has an important reception history in German culture (its most famous 'transformation' is Wagner's *Lohengrin* from 1850, in which the hero arrives to Brabant on a swan-drawn boat, and leaves at the end on a dove-drawn boat, after the swan transforms into Gottfried, Duke of Brabant). So, while the swan is extraneous to the Odyssean tradition, the concept of a swan-boat as a vehicle for the hero is present in German culture, which could explain this choice.

The riders sail across the section of the park's lake that represents the Eastern Mediterranean, along the coasts reproducing Greece and Italy. The latter has no themed area of its own in *Belantis*, but is integrated into the Greek sector, particularly this ride. It has been customary since antiquity to identify various places described in the Homeric Odyssey with geographical places around Italy and Sicily. During the twentieth century (and even into the twenty-first), there was a research tradition of trying to search for the 'real places' of Odysseus' adventures (forgetting that a myth, as such, is not real), locating the individual episodes at specific spots: this was the endeavour, for instance, of Ernle Bradford, author in 1963 of *Ulysses Found*, as well as Jean Cuisinier's in 2003. Circe's island is thus often placed in Italy (and Circe was in antiquity, as with Bradford, already connected with Cape Circeo),[131] while Scylla and Charibdis are located in the Strait of Messina (as in Thuc. 4.24; Verg., *Aen.* 3.429–432); the land of the Cyclopes was, according to Thucydides (6.2.1), in Sicily, with Bradford placing it around Trapani. The boat ride does not act systematically on such identifications, but generically locates Odysseus' travels in the Mediterranean between the Italian and the Anatolian peninsulas.

When the boat detaches from the dock, it moves directly towards the huge, blue (for Greece) wooden horse on the shore representing the Trojan horse [Fig. 7]. Visitors can read in the boats Odysseus' stratagem and remember that this was how the Greeks won the war and conquered Troy (*Od.* 8.499–520; Verg., *Aen.* 2.13–317). The horse is located, on the 'world map' of the park, at the north-eastern edge of the lake representing the Mediterranean, in a place corresponding

Fig. 7 'Die Fahrt des Odysseus', *Belantis*, Leipzig, Germany: The Trojan Horse © Uwe Dörnbrack.

to Hissarlik, the site which, since Schliemann's discoveries (1870), is identified in popular imagination (and certain parts of scholarship) with ancient Troy. Without entering into the details of a huge scholarly discussion (German Classicists were engaged with the possibility of 'finding Troy' exactly in the years in which *Belantis* was built, during the early 2000s),[132] it is nonetheless important to highlight here that theories giving a historical background and a historical location to the Homeric poems have always held great fascination for the public. These led to the general conviction that Troy, a historical city, was indeed the site of a major war during the Bronze Age.[133]

The second scene, 'Der Strudel des Charybdis' ('Charybdis' vortex'), introduces visitors to the two sea monsters Scylla and Charybdis, who live on two rocks in front of each other; Charybdis would have sucked up and then spit out the sea water three times per day, thus generating a vortex (*Od.* 12.105–106). These two monsters (with Scylla enjoying the greater popularity, as it represents the true danger and eats six companions of the hero, while Charybdis is easily avoided: *Od.* 12.235–259) have traditionally been located, since antiquity, within the Strait of Messina.[134] But here, Charybdis is placed in Egypt: the vortex is that which the vehicles of the water ride 'Fluch des Pharao' descend after falling off the pyramid

Fig. 8 'Die Fahrt des Odysseus', *Belantis*, Leipzig, Germany: Charybdis © Uwe Dörnbrack.

[Fig. 8].¹³⁵ While in this way the park could make one built environment relevant to two rides, with a consequent financial gain, this also means that visitors can, at the right moment, look at each other while they sit on two entirely different kinds of ride: the quiet lulling of Odysseus' boats is confronted by the soaked and screaming passengers of the water coaster, and their reciprocal gaze increases the sense of interaction and complicity among visitors to the park. This unusual concentration on Charybdis is thus due to its visualization as a vortex, which allows the construction of such a double gaze.¹³⁶ Moving further towards the northern shore of the lake, the boats approach an island, which in shape and position corresponds to Crete, but here represents Aeaea, the island of Circe. The explanation, 'Circe and the Island of the Swine' ('Circe und die Insel der Schweine'), recalls how Circe transformed Odysseus' companions into pigs and held the hero captive for a year, insisting on her magical abilities (*Od.* 10.203–574). This corresponds to the modern reception of Circe, a divine figure within the *Odyssey* and Greek culture, later understood as an evil and dangerous magician.¹³⁷ On the island, a female figure (Circe), dressed in a white toga with bronze stripes and a blue helmet (again colour-coding for Greece), is surrounded by boars. The statues are set among quite luxuriant vegetation, which should recall that, according to the explanations on the boat, Circe lived surrounded by flowers and magical herbs. The helmet is atypical for Circe but recalls the most famous iconography of a female figure from Greek myth: Athena.[138]

In the reproduction of the Tyrrhenian sea, the riders encounter the god Poseidon, surprisingly not represented here as the angry deity who caused all of Odysseus' troubles, in spite of the popularity of this narrative, which we encountered in *Europa-Park*. The description in the boat informs us that he is a very powerful god, who rules over the sea. If he is in a good mood, the sea is calm and not dangerous; if he is in a bad mood, he can cause earthquakes and flooding. The reason must be found in the genre of the ride: this is not a coaster, but a very quiet tow-boat ride; even 'dangerous encounters', as with Circe or later Polyphemus, lose any sort of adventurous character. In this sense, a direct reference to Poseidon's rage would have been extraneous to the spirit of the attraction. The visual representation of Poseidon as a god of adventure and storms here once again represents an effective way of connecting the visitor's gaze across two different rides. While sitting on the boat, the riders see both aspects of Poseidon: the statue of the god, a rather conventional naked male torso emerging from the waters, with hair moved by the wind and holding a trident, decoratively marks both this ride and the water carousel 'Poseidons Flotte', clearly representing troubled navigation. Once again, the passengers of the tow-boats can hear the screams of those caught in Poseidon's storm, and once again a prop is used, with the added financial convenience, for two rides. But Poseidon's bad mood is on the other side and does not apply to Odysseus' travels.

The boats then turn right and enter a cave that lies under Italy, more precisely under the volcano of 'Flug des Ikarus'. While the episode of the Cyclops is more often located in Sicily, there is a tradition, starting with Thucydides, which situates Polyphemus on a small island in front of Campania, between Naples and Cumae, and which seems to have been used as inspiration here.[139] Crossing this tunnel, which brings them from the 'Tyrrhenian' to the 'Adriatic Sea', the boats pass next to an eye on the wall. Cyclopes, as everybody knows, have only one eye: the one eye on the cave's wall is therefore a perfect and easily understandable pictogram to represent the popular episode of Polyphemus. When the boat approaches, the eye is closed, and the visitors can clearly hear snoring sounds; but when they get directly in front of the eye, it awakens and asks: 'Who is there?'. Other voices, Odysseus and his companions, reply, as popularly known, 'Nobody'; the voice of the Cyclops then growls in a menacing way, while the boat exits the tunnel from the opposite side. The explanation on the boat states that the Cyclops kept Odysseus and his companions as prisoners in their cave for one year, blocking the entrance with a giant rock. Only by blinding Polyphemus could Odysseus find his way out. The myth has been quite radically changed here: the Odyssean episode does not imply any lengthy period of captivity (one year is the time Odysseus spends with Circe, while Polyphemus is blinded on the second day, and on the following day Odysseus and companions can escape: *Od.* 9, 116–460); the reason for the change might here simply be an increase in drama, or a mistake connected to Circe's episode. While the Odyssean episode takes place on 'a flat island' (*Od.* 9.116), the entrance to the 'cave' shows, on the lintel, a drawing of five snakes in the shape of a star and the inscription, in Greek letters, 'Tataros' (ΤΑΤΑΡΩΣ). This is clearly a misspelling of Tartaros, ΤΑΡΤΑΡΟΣ, a part of the Underworld: the episode of Polyphemus has thus been 'mixed' (similar to that of Cassandra and Pandora in *Europa-Park*) here with that of the *Nekyia*, Odysseus' encounter with the souls of the dead (*Od.* 11.23–626). While this is no journey to the Underworld, it has often been remembered and received as such – and the episode has been traditionally located, once again, in Campania.[140] If the designers of the ride knew of both theories that located Polyphemus and the encounter with the souls here, this may have been the reason to conflate the two episodes. Interestingly, both theories are present in Victor Bérard's work (four volumes on *Les navigations d'Ulysse*, published between 1927 and 1929), which might thus be recognized as the inspiration for this Odyssean geography. The cave is quite dark, and the walls are decorated with images of wrecks, more consistent with a submarine journey (perhaps one to the Underworld) than to the island of the Cyclops.

The scene that follows, the 'Snakes of Heracles' is not connected to the myth of Odysseus. It might be tempting to think that those who designed the ride, through a rereading of the *Nekyia*, took inspiration from the fact that Heracles is the last soul that Odysseus meets and to whom he speaks (*Od.* 11.601–626), but in the Homeric verses there is no reference to this specific part of Heracles' legend. At the same time, the scene can also be derived from the Pillars of Heracles, traditionally located since antiquity at the Strait of Gibraltar. In German, 'Schlangen des Herkules' can sound like a pun on 'Säulen des Herkules', the Pillars, even if they are not correctly positioned within the '*Belantis* geography' (they are at the head of the Adriatic Sea, around Aquileia, more or less). Here are the two enormous snakes which, according to the myth, Hera sent to kill Heracles when he was a baby; the demigod, showing his supernatural strength, strangled them. This explanation refers to Heracles' strength, but avoids mentioning that they had been sent by Hera: this would imply having to explain why, thus telling how Zeus betrayed his wife with a mortal, Alcmene (incidentally, by appearing to the latter in the shape of her husband). As such stories of sex, betrayal and jealousy are not appropriate to the theme park, they are simply left aside. The decoration is also rather 'pictographic', as it represents two intertwined snakes, with no sign of Heracles.

The last scene is on the island of the Sirens. Before arriving there, the boats travel beneath the ropeway of 'Flug des Ikarus', resulting in a third (and final) reciprocal look between the two sets of visitors on different attractions; this time, though, there does not seem to be a justification within the narrative of the ride (nor the other). The Sirens are located on an imaginary island just south of Salento (where there is, in reality, no island),[141] decorated with a wreck and skeletons, who still wear their helmets and shields. These, as well as the oars of the wreck, are blue; the Sirens are not visible, and the music is a quiet, New Age-style melody. The boat's explanation is clear: the Sirens' song could drive mariners crazy so that their boats would crash onto the rocks, but Odysseus' crew closed their ears with wax, and could sail past the Sirens without any trouble. Nothing is related of the very famous Odyssean narration, according to which Odysseus, bound to the mast, listened to the Sirens' song, while his crew with closed ears heard nothing of how he screamed to be let go (*Od.* 12.166–200). This episode has a sexual connotation in popular perception (in reception the Sirens had been, in late antique and medieval Christianity, understood as the temptation of the flesh) and introduces troubling aspects such as seduction, bondage, insanity, suicidal drive, which likely seemed inappropriate to the ride's planners.[142]

The riders can now sail back to the loading station having recognized well-known episodes of the *Odyssey*, refreshed their knowledge of the myth and activated their stereotypical knowledge of ancient Greece. The designers of the ride used what is probably the most famous ancient myth and worked with it freely; they were also informed on the possible geographical identifications of the places of the Homeric poem, following them at some stages (as well as being inspired by them for the conflation of two different Homeric episodes), but leaving them aside when the requirements of the ride would have made their implementation less effective or impossible (as is the case with Charybdis, as well as the Sirens, for the opposite side of 'Italy' would not have had space for their island).

'Flug des Ikarus'

As in *Europa-Park*, the ride 'Flug des Ikarus' ('Icarus' Flight') in *Belantis*, a skydive constructed by Sunkid (2003), has no real connection with the myth and shows an extremely low level of theming, thus confirming the observations above on the 'theming power' of names from classical mythology. Having climbed the hill that constitutes the 'acropolis' of the Greek area, visitors sit on gondolas shaped like parachutes, and with two parallel ropes, 'fly' at a height of 12 metres over the 'Adriatic Sea' and the boats of the 'Fahrt des Odysseus' until they reach 'Italy', or rather a huge volcano occupying half of the peninsula. Once their gondola has arrived, the volcano emits some smoke and the visitors are dragged back to the starting point.

The ride allows visitors to move relatively slowly over a portion of the park, and as mentioned, the interaction initiates a reciprocal look between two different attractions. It has a very simple structure, with an almost complete absence of any theming to ancient Greece, aside from its name. The skydive is the standard model offered by the company, and is their bestselling product.[143] The volcano, through its position, seems reminiscent of Vesuvius; this might recall, in the general association of Greece and Rome, the eruption of 79 CE, which destroyed Pompeii and Herculaneum. There does not seem to be any connection with the myth of Daedalus and Icarus, aside from the very general idea of approaching in flight something glowing and hot.

'Götterflug'

At the top of the hill that forms most of the Greek area is the sky roller 'Götterflug' ('The flight of the gods'), constructed in 2009 by Gerstlauer Amusement Rides GmbH. As explained in the flyer by the company,[144] this is a new evolution for this type of ride. The passengers enter the vehicles on the ground, leaving their legs to dangle free. Each vehicle has two wings, which can be moved by the passengers with handles. This makes the seats rotate, giving each passenger an individual 'flight experience', varying from the more scenic to the more thrilling, when the seats spin at a height of 22 metres at around 50 km/h.[145] The main body of the ride is not themed, but simply a structure that holds together the seats and makes them rotate; the theming is limited to the entrance and the wings. The former is marked by a statue base with the name of the ride (written in blue), surmounted by what resembles an ancient Greek statue of a god (in a caricatured way), crossed with the iconography of the philosopher: the statue shows an elderly man, whose body does not correspond to any classical ideals, with a long beard and an angry expression. He wears a sort of gown around the waist; another cloth hangs from his left shoulder, in what is probably a reproduction of a *himation* (perhaps with a *chlamys*). The right hand holds a very long staff, surmounted by a small sphere, which recalls a sceptre. There are very few models of this in ancient sculpture, and one cannot go beyond a vague similarity with representations of artists and philosophers, as in the statue of the Cynical Philosopher in the Musei Capitolini in Rome, or the lyre player by Pythagoras of Rhegion (a Roman copy of which is in the Louvre). The face resembles 'funny' divinities, such as the Egyptian Bes. Additionally, the figure has wings, which are curiously set very low, at the waist; this is the height at which visitors have the wings when they ride the sky roller, and likely the reason for the iconographic choice.

Flight is not something one immediately attributes to divine figures in popular perceptions of ancient Greece, and the 'Flight of the Gods' is a strange construct: such an attraction could have been much more efficiently themed on the myth of Daedalus and Icarus, but at the time it was built, 'Icarus' Flight' already existed and could not be renamed (or removed). This impression is confirmed when one looks at the decoration on the wings, which are painted as rows of bird feathers, a decoration that would apply perfectly to the myth of Icarus, as his wings were shaped by Daedalus precisely by attaching feathers to his arms with wax. All in all, the sky roller is a thrill ride inserted into an area that is otherwise characterized by very quiet attractions; its level of theming is, as in most of the 'Strand der Götter', low, and seems to have been additionally hindered by the fact that the most automatic and obvious referent for this kind of attraction had already been taken, thus forcing a more generic and less recognizable theme.

'Poseidons Flotte'

A stronger theming characterizes 'Poseidons Flotte' ('Poseidon's Fleet'), a water carousel opened in 2007 which, as mentioned, is positioned at the western extremity of the Greek area and shares a statue of the god with 'Fahrt des Odysseus'. As already noted, this ride represents the 'wild' side of the god, and thus the stormy sea, compared to the lulling navigation of the tow-boat ride. Poseidon had no fleet in Greek mythology, but the reference is clearly to his power, as god of the seas, to create storms and/or help ships in difficulty. The ride, realized by a cooperation between Immo Heege GmbH and Zierer GmbH,[146] is composed of nine boats and a central island. The latter spins, and the boats tend to be pushed out by centrifugal force, becoming perpendicular to the centre. The boats also have rudders, which can be used to orientate the ship's axis and therefore its grade of resistance to the centrifugal force and the water streams.[147] The vehicles are shaped in the form of ancient Greek boats, or at least how they are imagined to have been: they are painted so as to appear wooden, decorated by a stripe with a blue meander-like geometrical motive, with an eye painted on the bow, a series of holes recalling the presence of oars and rowers, and three circular symbols which simply 'look Greek': a letter lambda; a blue reversed S against a white background; a trident, Poseidon's symbol. The control station is shaped like a Greek temple, with white columns and lintel (but without capitals), and above these a frieze and pediment; interestingly, the frieze and pediment are painted red and blue: the building thus contradicts the generalized image of white, marble Greek temples in favour of a more animated, vivid (and more accurate) representation of a colourful structure. While this might play with the fact that, as already mentioned, it is fairly widely known that Greek temples were not white,[148] it also allows it to have colours that better fit in with the surroundings: the bridge and spinning centre are brown, as are the boats; nearby is the green statue of the god, imitating oxidized bronze, while the boats from 'Fahrt des Odysseus' are blue and white. A purely white structure would have not been able to visually attract the attention of the visitor, who must walk towards it to board the boats.

'Säule der Athene'

'Säule der Athene', or 'Athena's Column', is a tower constructed by Sunkid in 2003. The visitors sit on chairs placed on the four sides of the column, and by pulling a rope in front of them, can raise their chair around 8 metres to the top.[149] As with the 'Flug des Ikarus', Sunkid delivered their standard tower, and the theming was made by the park,[150] again at a rather low level. The name likely refers to the position of the tower on the 'hill' of the area: as this recalls the Acropolis, it also recalls the presence of the statue of Athena Promachos and of the Parthenon, dedicated to Athena. The entrance is marked by a rectangular white stone, evoking Athenian inscriptions, on which the name of the ride and practical information are written in blue. The tower has the form of a stylized column: it is white with a sort of capital, and surrounding it are low fragments of columns, which also function as places to sit.

The 'Säule der Athena' is consistent with the rest of 'Strand der Götter' – the Greek section of *Belantis* is a good example of a low level of theming, displaying staple theme park attractions, with the sole exception of 'Fahrt des Odysseus'. They are loosely decorated and made to evoke ancient Greece almost exclusively through their names, recalling deities and mythological figures. The power of ancient myth in popular knowledge is once again the main lesson that we can draw from *Belantis*, considering how, among all the cultures present in the park, Greece is the only one not presented through its 'historical' manifestation, but exclusively through references to mythology.

3

Spain, Ancient Greece and the Land of Myths

Ancient Greece in Spanish popular culture

While a genealogical relationship with Greece was constructed in Germany, based on an elitist view of classical antiquity and a radical neglect of Ottoman and modern Greece, Spanish popular culture has taken a different approach to the ancient Greek culture. The main reasons for this are twofold: the presence of Greek archaeological remains on Spanish territory, and the development, particularly in the last three decades, of a 'Mediterranean' identity. Following the end of Franco's dictatorship, several factors – the development of democracy, Spain's adhesion to the European Union, Spanish cultural memory in relationship to antiquity, and the way in which antiquity is presented in school programmes (which, as always, is a principal point of entry into historical knowledge in society) – have all shifted away from the previous autochthonist interpretations, which claimed a genetic continuity between the original inhabitants of the Iberian Peninsula and modern Spaniards. From the perspective of Francoism, antiquity was an interesting 'prequel', although far from a central or crucial experience of the Spanish nation. The main point of reference was considered to be the *siglo de oro* (sixteenth century), and the 'unity' of the peninsula realized by the Visigoths and their conversion to Catholicism were presented as the 'starting point' for national history, following Herder's model of the 'rejuvenation' brought to Europe by the Germanic invasions.[1] Nonetheless, Franco's regime had insisted on projecting the national identity into a prehistoric past, with a sense of greatness and most of all unity (in the political, geographical, and racial sense)[2] against the challenges that came at the regime from the separatism of certain regions (notably Catalonia). Scholars thus tried to identify the moment in which one could speak of a *homo hispanicus*, considering it native to the region or as being generated by the Celtic invasions and their mixing with the local substrate – the only permissible influence. Francoism did not invent such a vision of the Spanish past, which had already been widespread since the nineteenth century, but it did make it into the official and only permitted orthodoxy.³

Franco's autochthonism lived alongside an ambiguous evaluation of the Roman Empire. The positive view coalesced around the early integration of Spain into the empire, and its role as the homeland of Emperors (Trajan, Hadrian) and intellectuals (Seneca),⁴ who 'regenerated' the Roman Empire when it needed it.⁵ Rome was thus presented as an 'organizing power' which brought political and cultural skills and 'unified' the peninsula for the first time,⁶ but at the same time the Iberian resistance to Rome was celebrated as national heroism. The most famous example is the national myth, already very popular in the nineteenth century,⁷ of the inhabitants of Numantia, dying rather than surrendering to the Romans; Spanish nationalism also shared with the Portuguese one the tradition of the Lusitanian leader Viriatus, who rebelled against Rome.⁸ The Roman times have also been more present in popular culture than prehistory, which was only the subject of academic discussions.⁹ The comic *El Jabato*, for example, published from 1958 to 1966, tells the story of an Iberian who, considered terribly dangerous by the Romans, must live in exile and is continuously harassed by the Roman armies. This comic would enjoy some success even after the end of the dictatorship, leading to the publication of two new episodes in 2008 and 2010. Nationalistic expressions of Spanish pride of this kind do indeed still exist, also in popular culture: an example is the comic *Thurrakos el Celtíbero*, a copycat of Astérix, in which a village of brave Spanish people resist the Roman invaders (even the graphic elements, from the legions to the woods with boars, are derived from the French model).¹⁰

Yet against this autochthonist perspective, another nationalistic historical narrative has developed around the idea of Spain as a territory at the crossroads of civilization, whose specific value is a mixture of cultures and peoples which could meet there, attracted by the beauty of the land, its climate and its resources. The greatness of the Spanish people is thus presented as the logical consequence of such a melting pot. This, as will be shown in discussing *Terra Mítica*, does not mean that inclusiveness is presented as a value: the representation of mobility in past centuries, and especially in the ancient world, is still functional to a nationalistic agenda stressing the superiority of the Spanish nation. Such a narrative is the evolution of historical models which had been developed during Francoism and even before: the idea that different peoples, who appeared on the Iberic stage at various moments, contributed to the cultural evolution of Spain. While this was used during the dictatorship to argue that their contribution was merely cultural and did not change the ethnicity of the Spanish people,¹¹ these elements of diffusionism could be developed into a narrative of cultural impulses that shaped Spain's peculiarity. It is in this context that Greece plays a specific role in Spanish cultural history.

The Greeks had been presented as a positive and relevant contribution to Spanish civilization since the end of the nineteenth century, when 'they had the best reputation because they were apparently not motivated by selfish interests', as opposed to the Carthaginians or the Romans.[12] Yet under Franco, Greece was neglected. The most important archaeological journal of the dictatorship was called *Ampurias* (1939–82): the name, that of the most important archaeological site in Catalonia, symbolically denied the existence of a separate Catalan identity.[13] Emporion had been used since the late nineteenth century to argue for the distinctness and specificity of Catalonia, also through its early contact – and thus greater proximity – to Greece (and to the Greek and Cretan independence movements, generally supported by most European nations).[14] The meaning of this site was reactivated after the end of the dictatorship: in 1992, the Olympic flame did not travel to Barcelona, where the Summer Olympic Games took place, but to Emporion, to once again stress this original connection between Catalonia and Hellas.[15] The appropriation of Ampurias to the Francoist, centralist model of Spanish history and identity therefore also implied a radical reduction of the 'Greek' element: in the editorial opening the first issue, the city was defined as 'the most Western Greek colony', and immediately afterwards as the 'point of entrance' of the Romans to Spain.[16] This changed after the end of Francoism, when scholars of Ancient History started dedicating more attention to the Greek presence in Spain,[17] thus making the Greeks more relevant in historical culture and in the popular perception of the archaeological past of the peninsula. A clear sign of such a change can be found in an advertisement for the national airline Iberia from 1987: with the slogan 'get ready for a vacation that's destined to go down in history' (and following the narrative of invasions caused by the beauty of the country), the ad argued that everybody wanted to go to Spain: the Phoenicians, Greeks, Romans and Visigoths above all.[18]

The Greeks thus became a crucial component of this multivocal Spanish identity, for many reasons: their colonial foundations on the peninsula (though in fact only two – Emporion/Ampurias and Rhode/Rosas); their trade activities there (which included the settlement of Greeks within local towns, for instance); Greek artefacts, such as coins, found in Spain; the Hellenic influence on Iberian art (along with the idea that Greek influence would have helped Iberian culture to improve its artistic standards, as revealed by the 'Dama de Elche', for example); the numerous mentions within Greek literary sources of towns and peoples in

Iberia.¹⁹ The most famous example of the latter is Tartessos, the city of king Arganthonios, of the battle between Heracles and Geryon, and of deadly ferrets.²⁰ Sometimes considered an Aegean colony, in the twentieth century the city became a symbol of the antiquity of Spanish civilization, a pre-Spanish monarchy and an example of the resistance of the indigenous Spanish population against foreign invaders.²¹ Although in recent years references to a direct contact of the territory with the Greek civilization have tended to be reduced in school books, which show a process of homologation at the European level,²² the idea of a direct connection between Greece and Spain is still strong at a popular level and reinforced by the archaeological remains that show the Greek presence in and influence on the Iberic peninsula.

At the beginning of the twentieth century, it was believed that the pre-Roman population of Spain was composed of two archaeologically recognizable groups, the Celts and the Iberians;²³ their meetings and fusion would have created, especially in the central parts of the peninsula, the Celtiberian people and culture. During Francoism, it was a central part of the historical orthodoxy to stress that Spanish ethnicity and culture were of northern and European origin, not southern or African. It was a staple of Francoism to play down any contribution to Spanish society and culture by Carthage (classified as a Semitic culture), as well as by the Arabs in the Middle Ages,²⁴ and to exalt the Celtic component of the pre-Roman populations of Spain.²⁵ This occurred during the period of the general 'Celtomania' at that time in Europe, but also allowed the nation to project back into the past a Spanish 'connection' to central Europe which was appealing to Franco. This element was thus – and to a greater extent than earlier – far more highly praised than the 'Iberian' one.²⁶ The Celts were also highlighted through their Indo-European ethnicity: they would have arrived to Spain and oriented it towards Europe, or even 'Aryanised' it.²⁷ The Iberians, sometimes identified as ancestors of the Basques or the Catalans, were now seen as a substratum which was completely Celticized, and the 'Celtiberians' thus became the ancestors of modern Spain.²⁸ This changed after democratization: in the last part of Franco's dictatorship, from the 1960s onwards, the 'Iberian' element was already brought to the fore more often, as opposed to the 'Celtic'; the creation of the Autonomous Communities made the search for a common, centralized and unique 'Spanish' antiquity much less palatable in a nation which began to stress the specificities of the single regions in discourse far more strongly.²⁹

The presentation of ancient Greece in Spanish school books is not radically different from that of the rest of Western Europe: the focus is mostly on Athens (followed by Sparta) and on the polis as a specific political and social institution of the ancient Greek world; much less space is dedicated to the kingdoms, even the Hellenistic ones. Religion and art are presented as the greatest achievements of the Greeks. The illustrations are also the usual: the Palace of Knossos, the Acropolis of Athens and the Parthenon, maps representing the Greek mainland and the colonized regions.[30] Indeed, the Royal Decree of 1991 indicated, for Greek history, that the following elements should be transmitted: 'foundation of European culture. The polis. Greek democracy. Hellenism. Art and Culture'.[31] This was reduced in 2006 to just one point – democracy – as the 'minimal teaching' to be delivered on ancient Greece.[32] The general insistence on the national cultural patrimony and on the possibility of teaching ancient history *in situ* within archaeological excavations also implies a substantial reduction of the Greek part in favour of the Roman; it is thus no surprise if the didactic book series 'Biblioteca de la Clase', published in Catalan, contains only three books dedicated to ancient Greece, more precisely to Greek mythology, the Olympic Games, and daily life in the colony of Emporion.[33]

Yet as in the other southern European countries, there exists a specific character in how school books communicate ancient history: they insist on the Mediterranean Sea as the unifying factor, as the connecting element for the different topics of (ancient) history, as a vector of civilization through which culture was developed and transmitted.[34] Democratic Spain has been ever more embedded in initiatives and groups that stress a common Mediterranean belonging. Since the 1970s, for instance, the southern countries of the EEC, then the EU, have been involved in a dialogue on the definition of a common agenda with countries on the other shores of the Mediterranean through the 'Global Mediterranean Policy' (1972–92). This began when Spain was not yet an EEC member State, prior to the 'Renovated Mediterranean Policy' (1992–5), the Euro-Mediterranean Partnership ('Barcelona Process', 1995), the Euromediterranean Summit of 2005 in Barcelona, and finally the 'Union for the Mediterranean', founded in 2008 at the Paris Summit for the Mediterranean. In this context, archaeology and history were not left to one side: in 1998 the first Euromed Heritage Programme began, intended to incentivize cooperation between the two sides of the Sea in the field of cultural heritage. There were, in total, four Euromed Heritage Programmes, with the last finishing in 2013. All this was communicated intensively to a broad section of the public: national radio broadcasts, for example, have featured the programme 'Mediterráneo' every Sunday since 2008, concerning the culture of both sides of the Sea.[35] While the Celts have often been 'used' to create the sense of a pan-European identity,[36] in

Spain and other southern European countries, the Mediterranean Sea became the unifying factor to a 'Mediterranean identity', which combines Spain, southern France, Italy and Greece, and eventually North Africa; in relation to antiquity, this focuses more on the connections and exchanges of the Iberian peninsula with the Romans and the Greeks, but also with the Egyptians, Phoenicians and Etruscans. This 'Mediterranean identity' also has its representations in the theme park: the largest and most visited resort in Spain, *PortAventura World* (in Vila-Seca) has a themed area called 'Mediterránea' within the theme park *PortAventura Park* (inaugurated in 1995). This is the entrance area which, as with 'Main Street U.S.A.' in *Disneyland*, greets the visitors with a reference to their 'own' history, represented by a traditional Catalonian fishing village; we will see that *Terra Mítica* develops similar strategies of identification and recognition.

Terra Mítica, Benidorm

History of the park

Terra Mítica has changed rather dramatically over time, and its complicated history has influenced how its theming operates. The area where the park is located had been declared of special natural interest; when a huge fire swept away the forest in the summer of 1992, however, it became a building area. A few years later, in 1996, it was decided to build a theme park there; the public company Sociedad Parque Temático de Alicante S.A. was founded, giving the concession for the realization of the theme park to Terra Mítica SA, owned by the Generalidat Valenciana, the Foundation Bancaja and the Caja de Ahorros del Mediterráneo. Building the park involved a huge investment and a great deal of effort: it was considered the most ambitious building project of its kind in Europe. Its location – on the outskirts of Benidorm, one of the most important tourist destinations in Spain, near the international airport of Alicante-Elche, not far from the city of Valencia, and where the water park *Aqualandia* and the marine animal park *Mundomar* were already attracting tourists since respectively 1985 and 1996 – was expected to provide a sufficient base of visitors to guarantee at least three million entrances in the first year of activity. This was not the case, and even if the park did score an impressive two million visitors/year at the very beginning of its activity, it was not enough to cover the expenses of a project that was far too big from its conception.

Terra Mítica opened in 2000 and consisted of five themed areas in a loop structure,[37] each connected to Mediterranean civilizations: 'Egípto' (Ancient Egypt), 'Grécia' (Greece), 'Las Islas' (The Islands), 'Roma' (Rome) and 'Iberia'. The focus on antiquity was evident from the three mascots: Cuca, a frog representing Greece (perhaps a reference to Plato's famous statement that the Greeks inhabit the shores of the Mediterranean as frogs sitting around a pond);[38] Mític, a hippo dressed as a Roman legionary; and Babá, a camel (for Egypt). In 2001, a strategic agreement for four years was made with Paramount Parks, which branded the park starting in 2002.[39] When things did not get any better, in 2004 the park began to operate only from March to November (it was previously open all year), and the payment of salaries was suspended. As the Paramount brand did not improve the situation and the park wanted to break the contract with them, Paramount filed for bankruptcy protection from its creditors. The park became independent once again, and in 2006 produced a profit for the first time in its history. However, one of the reasons for this was the sale of 139,000 square metres of land.[40] This implied a break in the original loop: 'Roma' and 'Iberia' were no longer connected. At this point, the park went through a period in which the consistency of theming was sacrificed for a need to increase attractiveness and popularity. In 2008, two new thematic areas that had nothing to do with the park's conception were added: 'Ocionía' (an area with pay-as-you-go attractions, placed in the Egyptian sector) and 'Atalaya' (an outdoor adventure park, also positioned in the Egyptian area, near the entrance). Both closed in 2010. In the same year, the three mascots of the park had to make space for popular characters from cartoons: Heidi, Vicky the Viking and Maya the Bee. As 2009 had incurred a loss of almost €17 billion, in 2010 the management of the park was given for ten years to the company who owned *Aqualandia* and *Mundomar*.[41] Aqualandia-Mundomar finally bought the park from its previous holders in 2012.[42] It is at this stage, in October 2012, that I visited *Terra Mítica*, and most of the material within this chapter derives from that field trip (my visit took place during the Halloween season, which caused a strong overlay in the theming, mostly consisting of pumpkins and spider webs, and a change in some of the shows, which were themed to witches, zombies and other monsters). The situation was still far from optimal, with many attractions closed and no indication of when they might be reopened; many restaurants and shops were out of business and there had been a clear relocation of some attractions (for example 'Titanide', previously located in the closed area which had connected 'Roma' and 'Iberia'). The Roman arch of triumph, which once led onto a road flanked by imperial statues and then to the Iberian area, was now closed, and the statues in the abandoned area could only be seen through the planks that closed this section of the park. An important intervention occurred in 2013, leading to a reopening of all the attractions and a division of the park into two parts: Egypt, Greece and Rome remained in *Terra Mítica*, while 'Las Islas' and 'Iberia' (which was annexed to a part of Egypt) went on to form *Iberia Park*. This was now open to the public and the attractions were, as with 'Ocionía', charged on a pay-as-you-go basis. On this occasion, the 'Mediterranean Village', which was originally part of 'Iberia' and had been closed since 2005, was also reopened.[43] This section, now called 'Iberia Village', could be booked for private parties and celebrations such as weddings.[44] As this again did not work particularly well, since 2014 *Iberia Park* has been gated once more, and a ticket required to enter. However, the two parks were not reunited, and were still divided in the 2018 season.

The next major challenge to the existence of the park came on 7 July 2014, when an 18-year-old visitor from Iceland, on holiday with family and friends, died in a tragic accident in 'Roma', as a harness failed and he fell from the roller coaster 'Inferno'.[45] However, in 2016 *Terra Mítica* gained in strength with the construction of a hotel, the 'Grand Luxor Hotel', which guarantees free access to this park (but not *Iberia Park*) to its guests;[46] the opening season was nonetheless further reduced, to lower costs. *Terra Mítica* is now open three months a year, from June to August, plus additional days in September and for Halloween; *Iberia Park* is only open in July and August.

The general structure of the park and its use of the past

As previously mentioned, the park was conceived as a sort of loop structure in which the five thematic areas, each representing a Mediterranean civilization, are positioned around a central lake mimicking the Mediterranean Sea. Their location is at the same time broadly geographical and historical. At the entrance of the park, in the south-eastern corner, stand five statues that represent the themed areas: the Dama Oferente del Cerro de los Santos ('Iberia'); the Discobolus ('Grécia'); one of the goddesses protecting Tutankhamun's canopic shrine ('Egipto'); the Poseidon of Cape Artemision ('Las Islas'); and the Augustus of Prima Porta ('Roma'). The visitors first pass to 'Egipto', which is also chronologically the first civilization represented. They are then led through the throng of attractions and, at the time of our field trip, through a system of differentiated opening times for each themed area, to move counter-clockwise, thus visiting 'Grécia' in the north-eastern corner next. From there, they could proceed to the north-western area, occupied by 'Roma', or to the central area which represented 'Las Islas', the islands of the Mediterranean Sea, the second section themed to ancient Greece. At the end of the loop, in the south-western corner of the park, is 'Iberia', the only area not based on an ancient civilization. The theme here is 'transhistorical' Spain, with a special focus on the Middle Ages and the early modern period: the only reference to antiquity is a bumper cars ride called 'Jabato' after the hero from the comics, but also from Team Jabato, a company that produces cars.

Visiting the park is thus a teleological process of progressively approaching Spain and Spanish culture as the final point of the evolution of civilization around the Mediterranean basin. The underlying narrative is clear, and follows a rather widespread model: predecessors and ancestors are acknowledged and praised in their role of highlighting how their successors ('We') progressed, becoming ever better (and impossible to improve upon further).[47] In this sense, Egypt is represented as the cradle of Mediterranean and Western civilization; Greece, visualized both as an Aegean, 'mythological' civilization ('Las Islas') and as the white, marble polis of classical times ('Grécia'), is the cradle of democracy and of Western culture. The relationship with Rome is more ambiguous and contested: 'Roma', strongly inspired by Tuscany and generally by the Italian style, clearly shows an admiration for the Roman Empire and its achievements, referring to the importance of Spain in Roman times, while also highlighting local resistance. For example, while the show 'Imperium' (2013) was a circus show about three explorers discovering all the different cultures integrated into the Roman Empire, the show 'Hispania' (2011–12) focused on a group of brave Iberian women who attacked the Roman legions to free their men, while the Romans were represented as a cowardly, ineptly imperialistic and abusive power.[48] 'Espartaco' (2013–16) also negatively represented the Romans as cruel lords: a fat senator and his young wife abuse the gladiators and force them to fight for their lives, until the gladiators rebel, led by Spartacus, for a better society and their freedom.[49] Finally, the show 'Nerón', (2014–16) draws on the popularity of a 'bad' Roman emperor and the story of him burning down the city.

'Iberia' was originally mostly composed of a 'Mediterranean Village', rather similar to that of *PortAventura*, hosting no rides, only shops and restaurants (and therefore somehow following the example of 'Main Street U.S.A.', even if not positioned at the entrance of the park). This section occupies a promontory in the central lake and was positioned in such a way as to be easily (and almost unavoidably) accessed by all visitors who came to 'Iberia', whether they arrived from 'Roma' or from 'Las Islas'. When this part was closed, 'Iberia' remained a very small section with few rides. Still, as long as the park was undivided, 'Iberia' maintained its clear teleological function thanks to the large arena located there (with 2,000 seats). The show 'Barbarroja' – which began in 2000 with the opening of the park, was suspended for a very short time and subsequently reintroduced – is held there daily.[50] The show takes place in the late afternoon (now at 7.00 pm), and thus constitutes a sort of high point to a visit to the park, with the additional function of controlling visitor flows by leading them back to Egypt and to the gates once the show has finished. The story is fairly simple: in a typical Spanish village, such as the 'Mediterranean Village', an 'Edenic couple' – a brave and virtuous Spanish boy and girl – singlehandedly oppose the invasion of the Ottoman pirates led by Baba Aruj, a historical figure (1473–1518) who plays an important role in Spanish cultural memory. The couple are then engaged and live happily ever after.[51] The message is clear: confronted with the absolute otherness represented by the Ottoman pirate (who conforms to every Orientalist stereotype), the Spanish couple triumphs due to their virtue and the strength of their feelings, saving civilization and moving it forward. This message is further reinforced by the recurring representation of the Spanish people as being 'static' throughout the centuries as well as autochthonous, from the Dama Oferente at the entrance, to the 'Hispania' and 'Barbarroja' shows; the contributions by Egypt, Greece and Rome have enriched Spanish culture, according to the narrative explained above, bringing it to its 'perfect' state.

It is interesting to highlight that *Terra Mítica* not only proposes this clear vision of history but has also aimed from the very beginning to become an educational structure, both for individual visitors and for schools. The educational provisioning for general visitors consists of a number of explanatory tables in four different languages (Spanish, English, French and German) located next to the reproductions of ancient monuments. The offering for schools is varied and rather unique. Not only is there a reduction of the entrance price for school classes,[52] the park also realized four didactic guides (for 'Egípto', 'Grécia', 'Las Islas' and 'Roma') which can still be downloaded from the internet (even if the park has changed, as we have seen, and the guides have not been updated)[53] and should help to prepare visitors and transform their trip into an occasion for learning 'art and history'.[54] Each guide starts with a simple, schematic representation of the ancient society at stake: in the case of Egypt, for instance, information is provided on agriculture in the Nile Valley, on the existence of slaves, on the three kinds of writing, on basic religious ideas (polytheism, life after death, judgement after death) and the most recognizable products of Egyptian art. After this, the guide moves on to show what has been represented in the theme park (within the part named 'urban setting'), explaining the reproductions of ancient monuments visible in the park and the sources of inspiration for settings which do not correspond to any archaeological reality (such as the 'Obelisk square', which is inspired by the harbours of the Nile Delta and hosts an obelisk inspired by 'Cleopatra's Needles'). In the next section the rides are presented, with a short description of their theming and its inspiration, before eventually describing the building which hosts them, as with the Pyramid of Cheops. Finally, the buildings are described one by one, with illustrations showing the reconstruction in the theme park next to the original building as it is now. Finally, 'representación y simbología' (representation and symbolism) presents the decorative elements which can be found in the area: for Egypt, these are representations of the gods, identified by their attributes, pharaonic symbols (the different shapes of headdress), and the various types of columns from Egyptian architecture used in the park. The guides should provide, as is the intention of the park, information which allows the pupils to recognize what they have learned during their visit, thus enhancing their capacity for immersion and identification and transforming their visit to the theme park into a 'time travel' with didactic potential.

'Grécia'

'Grécia' is located on the north-eastern corner of the lake that mimics the Mediterranean, thus evoking the geographical position of the Greek mainland, once again directly identified with 'ancient Greece'. The first sentence of the guide for schools immediately activates the importance of Greece for Spanish identity: it reminds the reader that the Greeks lived all over the Mediterranean, including in Spain, where they founded Ampurias; directly afterwards the text indicates important elements of our modern life which we owe to the Greeks: theatre, logics/philosophy/physics, sports, in specific reference to the Olympic Games, and democracy. The theme of the area is, consistent with this, the classical Greek polis; although Athens is referenced, as this is the most popular ancient polis, and its monuments are the best-known, what is represented here is no specific polis, but an abstracted and pictographic representation of 'the' Greek polis. In this section are reproduced monuments from various parts and various periods of ancient Greece; their arrangement within the area also follows a chronological order, bringing the visitors from the earliest phases of ancient Greece to the Hellenistic period, and then to the Roman world. The entrance to this section, coming from Egypt, is a reproduction of the Lion Gate from Mycenae. The explanatory table and the booklet for schools explicitly identify Mycenae as the city of Agamemnon, thus sticking with Schliemann's identification, and more generally to the historicization and geographical anchoring of the Homeric poems. Immediately behind the entrance is the reproduction of the other best-known monument from Bronze Age Greece, the Palace of Knossos, which hosts the dark ride 'El Labirinto del Minotauro'.

The path then continues uphill: the core of 'Grécia' is set on top of a small hill, evoking the image of the Acropolis. Indeed, there is a reconstruction of Phidias' Athena Lemnia on a tall pedestal (the statue was originally on the Athenian Acropolis), along with the restaurant 'Acropolis', a 'Greek temple' with Ionic columns (but closed intercolumnar space), with a copy of the Porch of the Caryatids from the Athenian Erechtheion on one side [Fig. 9]. The visitors thus walk from the 'prehistory' of Greece to its classical manifestation, as on the top is a square, with the rides 'Synkope', 'Titánide', 'La Furia de Tritón' and the 'Templo de Kinetos'; the latter is a reproduction of the Temple of Zeus at Olympia [Fig. 1]. On the square we encounter also the 'Fountain of Hera' (a platform whose corners are decorated with four tortoises holding a small naos with the statue of a female figure holding a spear, modelled on the Hera Barberini), and a relief with a Greek inscription. This is a reproduction of the heading of an inscription from 403–402 BCE containing the text of three decrees legally defining the

Fig. 9 Detail of the restaurant 'Acropolis', *Terra Mítica*, Benidorm, Spain: The Porch of the Caryatids © Pau Garcia Solbes (elPachinko.com).

relationship between Athens and Samos; the relief, showing Hera and Athena holding hands, is rather typical of this kind of document. Beneath the relief the first part of the inscription, written with larger letters than the rest, has been copied.[55] The fact that this relief is a precise copy of a part of an existing inscription is a clear sign of how precise and detailed the theming of *Terra Mítica* has been at the beginning. On the square there is also the 'Olympic Exedra', a photo opportunity evoking the popularity of ancient Greek sports. The explanatory table (and the material for schools) refers to the ancient Olympic Games and the popularity of their winners, who would receive statues in their cities of origin. The structure is a semi-circular exedra faced by a fountain; at the centre of the exedra, which is raised and can be reached via a short set of stairs, is a podium decorated with Roman numbers. Podiums did not exist in antiquity, nor (obviously) did the Greeks use Roman numbers, but this is irrelevant: while the podium immediately creates the connection between ancient sport and modern Olympic Games, the Roman numbers give an aura of 'antiquity'.[56] Within the exedra are nine statues, in part reproductions of ancient Greek sculptures (or more accurately of the Roman marble copies which have survived), in part simply inspired by classical sculpture. Some of these are directly connected to sports: this is the case with Polykleitos' *Diadumenos*, which represented a winning athlete, or of Lysippos' *Apoxyomenos*, the athlete scraping himself with a strigil. In other cases, the connection is less certain, and if certain sculptures have – at least sometimes – been interpreted as related to sports (such as Polyclitus' *Doryphoros*), they are relevant here in connection with the idealization of the Greek body.

The next area is another square, dominated by a huge wooden horse: it is here where most of the Greek area shows take place, such as 'Troya, la conquista' (see below), or the dance show 'El Sueño de las Nayades', in which girls dance to Greek-sounding music.[57] Yet there is also a large structure with Ionic columns hosting a reproduction of the Boy with Thorn (and thus including the Hellenistic period).[58] Another building, the front decorated by Corinthian columns, inspired by the Stoa of Zeus from the Athenian Agora, originally hosted the shop 'Pórtico del Ágora', now 'Isla Golosina'. A portico with a wooden roof on Corinthian pillars and benches on the side faces the sea. This once again creates an opportunity for immersion, as well as to stress the 'Mediterranean identity' binding Spain and Greece: from here and from the Athenian Acropolis, one can see the same sea.[59] In spite of the presence of the Trojan horse, there is nonetheless a sort of temporal implication of moving from the classical acropolis to Hellenistic sculpture and to a dominating Corinthian style: in popular history, the three architectural styles – Doric, Ionic and Corinthian – are often understood as a chronological sequence. Even the toilets here are built with a temple-like front and Corinthian columns, decorated with a fresco representing a chariot race. This is a copy of a famous fresco from Paestum, in Italy (tomb 10 of the necropolis of Andriuolo-Laghetto); what is important here is not the geographical location of the original, but the chronological context (fourth century BCE, consistent with the rest of this section), and the reference to 'sports', here in the form of chariot races. Doric columns again dominate the courtyard, alongside tables from the restaurant 'Plaka' (the name of the central borough of Athens, just beneath the Acropolis), which should recall the Stoa of Attalus from the Athenian Agora; by 2012 this had closed and transformed into an area with vending machines. With the entrance to 'Alucinakis' the space opens onto the monumental gate of the Roman area; here there are still reproductions of Lysippos' *Eros Stringing His Bow* and the Venus of Arles, which complete the impressive collection of copies of ancient Greek artworks. The vegetation consists of predominantly 'Mediterranean plants', especially olive trees[60] and cypresses. As ancient music is unknown beyond certain tentative reconstructions, which are surely not well known, the soundtrack is the very predictable sirtaki.

The theming revolves around the most recognizable aspects of ancient Greece: sports, temples and column styles, which occupy the last page of the booklet for schools. Mythology is substantially neglected, but this is due, as we will see, to the existence of 'Las Islas': the historical Greece is in 'Grécia'. Yet 'Grécia' shows a very high level of theming; the precise details reveal a systematic focus on ancient Greek art and culture by the park's designers. While it has been argued that a higher level of theming is generally an economic advantage for the park, as a higher investment in this area is compensated by greater visitor numbers and visitor fidelity, *Terra Mítica* not only does not conform to this model, but seems to reveal that it has an upper limit. Above a certain amount of detail in theming, the process of recognition stops: the Parthenon has already signalled Greece, so the addition of a relief from an Attic decree does not provide any element which the average visitor can grasp to activate mechanisms of identification. In this sense, the extremely high level of theming of *Terra Mítica* may have even increased the costs of the park and contributed to its financial unsustainability.

The shows

What has been observed until now is also confirmed by an analysis of the shows hosted in this area throughout the years. Leaving aside street shows as

'Arquéologos', it is worth concentrating on two shows in particular, which clearly reveal the image of ancient Greece proposed in the park: 'Troya la conquista' and 'Hércules'. 'Troya la conquista' was staged until 2013 alongside the Trojan horse, which was an important stage feature. The flexibility inherent to classical myths applies here even to one of the best-known narratives from ancient mythology and epics, as in *Terra Mítica*, the Trojans win the war. The show begins with the horse: Paris and Helen, deeply in love, are convinced that the war is over. This is not the case: the Greeks, led by Achilles (who in the Homeric tradition is already dead by now; Odysseus is absent from the show), emerge from the horse and engage the Trojans in stunt duels. The Greeks appear to win, but in the final duel Paris defeats Achilles (who has slaughtered Hector), kills him, and saves Troy. What is represented in this show is not entirely original, and is once again embedded within chains of reception and transformations of meaning: the movie *Helen of Troy* (2003) already depicted Paris as a 'romantic hero', 'hopelessly devoted to a virtuous Helen', while Achilles 'becomes a sadistic and seemingly unstoppable villain'.[61] The movie could thus have been a source of inspiration for the show. The story is even more understandable when read against the general ideology of the park and the other shows, especially 'Barbarroja'. Only the Adam–Eve couple, Paris and Helen, survives: the strength of their affection turns them into the true heroes and the founders of a 'new world'. Any other representation of their relationship 'more faithful' to the ancient mythical versions would have had to portray either Paris as a kidnapper, or Helen as an adulteress, or both, and these are somewhat inappropriate topics for the theme park. Additionally, the show transmits clear values which, projected onto the ancient Greek period, appear to be objectified and naturalized, contributing to the creation of the teleological model that is intrinsic to the park. The representation is highly gendered: Helena does not fight, yet she is the one to defeat Achilles, as she distracts him long enough for Paris to grab a weapon and kill him. In this way she represents the (stereotypical) cunning woman helping her partner with her feminine wiles. Achilles lacks any form of piety or respect towards the divine, explicitly challenging the gods and considering himself above them and their power; therefore, he must die. Pride and impiety are defeated by love and religiosity, and so values which are thus represented as being 'universally positive' can, in 'Barbaroja', become 'Spanish'.

Since 2015, the 'Grécia' area has hosted another show, 'Hércules', which takes place in front of the 'Templo de Kinetos' and the 'Fountain of Hera'. This may be significant, as the former is a temple of Zeus, Heracles' father (and in the historical model, the Temple of Olympia, Heracles' labours were the subject of the sculptural decoration), and Hera, Zeus' wife, is Heracles' bitter enemy.[62] The voice introducing the show recalls this hostility against the son of Zeus and Alcmene, and how Hera forced Heracles to commit 'terrible deeds', after which Heracles needed to seek the pardon of the Delphic oracle. Such deeds are not mentioned here: according to the myth, Heracles, driven crazy by Hera, killed his own children, again a topic not suitable for a theme park. As Heracles had come through the oracle's sentence into the service of Eurystheus, the latter forced him to undertake the twelve labours. The first of them, the Nemean Lion, inspires the show. Once again using the existing structures of the park as a stage, the actors positioned themselves in front of the temple. The first message which the show transmits is, as with the Trojan show, a strong sense of respect for the divine and the exaltation of piety. Not only is the sense of sin and redemption (which is also present in the ancient myth) particularly highlighted in the introduction; the show also opens with a Nemean priest praying for Zeus to finally eliminate this terrible curse from the town of Nemea, while a young lady is offered in sacrifice to the lion, hinting at the myth of Andromeda.[63] The lion is a construction held by five warriors, who act in a stunt show against two 'Nemeans' [Fig. 1]. After the latter are defeated, the priest says that the Olympus had forgotten Nemea, but now Zeus has sent his own son Heracles. He arrives on a chariot, kills the lion and becomes king of Nemea (although not before getting really angry when his friend and companion is killed, in a cross-reference to the myth of Achilles and Patroclus). Both shows are barely more than a costume narrative around a stunt show; nonetheless both not only take well known episodes and characters from classical mythology, revealing what it is expected to be available as foreknowledge among the public, but they also insist on piety and religiosity as positive values that ensure ultimate victory. Read against Spanish Catholicism and the fight against the Ottoman pirates in 'Barbarroja', this assumes a specific meaning in the construction of an ancient Greece of shareable, recognizable values.

'El Laberinto del Minotauro'

The shooting ride 'El laberinto del Minotauro', by Sally Corporation, is hosted in a structure inspired by (although not a replica of) the Palace of Knossos.[64] The attraction is thus placed directly after the entrance to the Greek area, in the 'prehistory' section of the Greek polis. The Palace of Knossos, popularly (and sometimes even in scholarship) identified with the palace of Minos, and therefore with the place of the Labyrinth, is the perfect location for a ride inspired by the myth of the Minotaur. The popular location of the age of myth in the Greek Bronze Age and the widespread knowledge of the Palace of Knossos as probably the most famous architecture of that period, reinforces the sense of authenticity inspired by the theming. The queuing area and the pre-show are characterized by reproductions of Minoan art: the Tauromachy Fresco from Knossos, the Akrotiri Boxer Fresco, the Prince of Lilies, the Charging Bull and the Hagia Triada sarcophagus. In the pre-show area, visitors are invited to form groups of six. This is a 'technical' requirement, as the vehicles have six seats, but may also be an allusion to Theseus' group of companions in the ancient tradition. Sitting on the vehicles, while shooting at targets, the visitors are then brought through twelve scenes, at times divided by segues without shooting targets; in this sense, the booklet for schools lists twenty 'scenes'.[65]

Most of the scenes derive from classical mythology, and not only from the corpus of myths related to Crete. Actually, the only element which seems to hold the scenes and segues together is the popularity of the narration and/or of the forms of its visualization: the Hydra is thus next to a lion (possibly that of Nemea) and the Centaurs, but also Cerberus, a dragon, and even pterodactyls, a princess captured by a sea monster (Andromeda?), and bandits with monstrous bodies, before riders reach the Minotaur's cave and kill the monster. Originally, not all visitors would be able to reach the Minotaur, as a device sent certain participants (those who had not reached a certain score by scenes five and eight) directly to the exit; in 2012, during a visit to the park, this function had been deactivated, however. The ride deploys a broad set of known stories and recognizable iconographies (the princess evokes Disney princesses, archaeological ruins are placed in a forest environment, reminiscent of the Indiana Jones films) around the narrative of Theseus and the Minotaur, which provides the majority of and the starting point for the narrative, but is also freely altered. The adventurous side of many Greek myths of travel and exploration and the bravery of challenging and defeating a dangerous monster are thus deployed to create an entertaining ride which connects classical mythology with movies and video games and their imagery. In order to achieve this, the detail in the theming is very high, especially in the waiting and pre-show area.

'Titánide'

'Titánide' is a suspended looping coaster realized by Vekoma Rides in 2003. Originally, the coaster was placed in 'Iberia' and called 'Tizona': in the park's narration, this was the name of the new sword of El Cid, which frantically swirled to strike its enemies. The theming included a Medieval tower, while from the coaster it was possible to enjoy a view of the 'Mediterranean Village'. When the entire section beyond the Roman triumphal arch was closed, however, 'Tizona' was closed and relocated, placed in a previously empty spot on one side of the 'Acropolis square', right next to the 'Templo de Kinetos' and reopened in 2010 with the name 'Titánide'. The change in name was essential to the re-theming; the new name evokes the myth of the fight of the Titans against the gods and the 'titanic' experience provided by the roller coaster itself. However, as this happened at a rather dark moment in the history of the park, little attention seems to have been paid to the re-theming; this is, beyond the name, almost non-existent. The new logo, for example, depicts a purple female bust, from whose head roller coaster tracks spread in the shape of horns, with big earrings and a sci-fi look, all against a background evoking the roller coaster. 'Titánide' is therefore a further example of 'associative theming'; yet this kind of theming was extraneous to the original intentions of the park, only becoming widespread through its financial difficulties, which imposed a series of substantial interventions and changes which did not, and likely could not, maintain the very high level of attention to detail and precision within the theming of the original plan.

'Templo de Kinetos'

When visitors reach the centre of 'Grécia', the Acropolis, they are confronted with a reconstruction of the Temple of Zeus at Olympia, one of the most important and famous works of classical Greek architecture [Fig. 1]. The temple has been realized by the Spanish company Animala with a metallic structure, fiberglass reinforced polyester and thixotropic mortars.[66] While it is curious that *Terra Mítica* contains no reproduction of the Parthenon (but again, its iconic status in ruins might have dissuaded from offering its reconstruction in a pristine status),[67] the presence of the statue of Athena and the Erechtheion already constitutes a clear visual references to Athens, and the insertion of this temple allows the polis of *Terra Mítica* to become a more generic, abstract Greek polis. More importantly, the attention to detail in the park would have implied hosting another statue of Athena within the temple, while in this way the father of the gods, Zeus, can also attract some attention, as he is not represented in any other sculpture in the themed area. The attraction, earlier called 'Teatro de Olimpia' is a 5D movie-based ride hosted within the temple: 3D movies are accompanied by movements of the seats, but also by the possibility of games with odours and water.[68] The movies can be changed frequently, with many different films often being shown within the same day. These were, in earlier years, thematically more fitting: in the beginning, 'Secrets of the Lost Temple', an archaeological adventure, was shown in the temple;[69] in 2006, 'El guerrero del amanecer' was shown, in which ancient deities with a futuristic look asked a hero of pure heart to fight with magical weapons against Chaos and Hades to bring the Sun back to Olympus.[70] In the following years, such a connection was neglected: during our field visit in 2012, the temple showed 'Crashendo', a movie in which a piano player, along with their piano, moved frantically along streets and paths. 'Templo de Kinetos' is thus a paradigmatic example of an attraction which has no connection at all to the theme but is nonetheless inserted into an architectural structure, disguising this extraneity by wrapping it within a very high detail of theming. The Temple of Zeus from Olympia is, after the Parthenon, the second most famous ancient Greek temple, whose architectural form can thus be used as a pictogram. The temple is reconstructed with some liberty: the architectural forms are accompanied by the eastern pediment featuring the chariot race of Pelops and Oenomaus, but the metopes are missing and the entrance area is enriched by a frieze representing a sacrifice scene. Inside the temple is a 9-metre-tall reconstruction of the cult statue of Zeus which was hosted in the Olympic temple, realized by Phidias and considered one of the seven wonders of the ancient world. Its colours, white and gold, are also a reconstruction of the original statue, which had visible surfaces in gold and ivory. The black colouring of the throne is also faithful to ancient sources, as the original was in ebony. Some details are realized with great precision, such as the dancing women (Victories, according to Pausanias) at the feet of the throne, or the animals and lilies adorning the golden robe of Zeus, the three Graces and the three Seasons on top of the throne; other elements known from ancient descriptions are missing, however, in particular those which would not be appropriate in theme parks: the front feet of the throne of Phidias, for instance, showed two young boys being devoured by sphinxes, and below the sphinxes were Apollo and Artemis shooting down Niobe's children. Passing next to the statue and moving to the cinema's waiting area, visitors encounter another statue, which has absolutely no connection with the temple of Zeus at Olympia: the Farnese Hercules. The statue could be here to provide more theming to the interior of the temple, which would otherwise be empty (the walls simply show a decoration with meanders). Heracles, as the son of Zeus, is in any case connected to the cult statue: the metopes of the temple of Olympia, not reproduced here, represented his labours.

'La Furia de Tritón'

The ride, located next to the 'main square' of the Greek sector, is a splash water coaster of the Spillwater type made by the Swiss firm Intamin AG.[71] The association between water rides and Greece is an easy one, considering the general idea of Greece as a maritime nation and the numerous, very famous ancient myths connected to navigation. Additionally, a park such as *Terra Mítica*, where temperatures can become very high during summer, has a special interest in investing in water rides, which provide welcome refreshment from the Costa Blanca sun. The strongest focus on water, as will be highlighted, is in the area 'Las Islas', which occupies the centre of the lake that mimics the Mediterranean, but there is also a water coaster in the Egyptian area ('Cataratas del Nilo'), a themed area which is less automatically connected to water and sailing in popular knowledge (and rather to the sands of the desert). This desire to have many water rides throughout the park must coexist, however, with the fact that the myths regarding adventurous sailing are located in 'Las Islas', and that 'Grécia' thus has a lack of strong, recognizable referents that could be deployed; as a consequence, 'Furia de Tritón' has a low level of theming, rather uncommon for the first generation of rides in *Terra Mítica*. However, the location of the ride, as well as the fact that the splashes occur while looking directly into the façade of Acropolis and next to the temple of Olympia, both indirectly generate a strong level of theming and immersion, albeit due to the surrounding architecture rather than the ride itself. The visitors board the boats, cross a cave and an installation in which they see statues of tritons before arriving to the first lift. As in *Europa-Park*'s 'Poseidon', the two lifts are followed by two splashes,[72] both of which involve the boat landing in front of other visitors walking on the 'acropolis', also activating mechanisms of 'double gaze'.[73]

Further rides

Despite the high level of theming that *Terra Mítica* shows, 'Furia del Tritón' is not the only ride whose theming is 'indirect', that is, generated by the generally high level of detail within the area and not by any particular theming of the ride itself. The financial problems of the park consistently diminished the attention to theming for the rides added during following years. This applies to 'Synkope', a giant swing ride of the model Revolution by Mondial Rides,[74] built in 2003 and opened in 2004. Mondial Rides provided the park with the steel structure and the operating accessories in the colour requested by *Terra Mítica* (orange), without any element of theming,[75] nor were further elements added after the installation. The name is the only theming: *synkope* is an ancient Greek word meaning 'cutting into small pieces', 'stoppage', or 'sudden loss of strength'. A syncope, in Spanish a *síncope*, is indeed a fainting causing a short loss of consciousness and muscle strength. As a syncope can be generated by situations of fear, and in this sense it is also popularly used to refer to stressful or scary situations, the name with its Greek-sounding connotation is used to refer to the thrill component of the ride. At the entrance, the name is accompanied by a logo representing a muscular man throwing the discus. The reference to the Discobolus of Myron (as well as to the extremely famous ancient Greek sport) is evident, while also alluding to the spinning which will be experienced on the ride, where the visitors sit around a swinging round form, which recalls a discus. The connection to sports is also consistently reinforced by the blunt Olympic theming of the waiting area. However, visitors sitting on the ride and swinging across once again enjoy the indirect theming: 'Synkope' is located in front of 'Templo de Kinetos', and this is a strong visual reference for the ride. As the riders spin and are lifted up, they also see the exedra, the Fountain of Hera, the Palace of Knossos and the restaurant 'Acropolis' many times (as well as the Egyptian pyramid from the nearby Egyptian area).

Moving in the direction of Roma, in front of the Trojan horse, is 'Los Ícaros' [Fig. 10], a traditional swing ride placed on the side of the hill facing the sea, which is visible at all times during the ride (the presentation of the ride on *Terra Mítica*'s internet page insists on the views from it).[76] The entrance to the ride has a simple, classicizing architectonic form: the sign with the name of the ride upon two pillars is flanked by two winged figures, above which is a very simple pediment with a sun in the centre. The reference is clearly to the myth of Icarus, perfectly recognizable due to its great popularity, as well as its general connection with 'flight'; while the representation of the Sun evokes the tragic end of the classical narrative, this is once again 'desemantised' because of its mythical character.[77] The swing ride is decorated with images of ancient Greeks with wings, accompanied by many faces of the god Aeolus blowing his winds; the light blue colour and the general style of the illustration is evocative of the Art Nouveau swing rides from early amusement parks and from the fairground, thus following an aesthetic of nostalgia.

The last attraction of 'Grécia', just before the gate of 'Roma', is the small junior coaster 'Alucinakis', built by Zamperla in 2000. In the original planning, all major attractions had a smaller version for children; 'Alucinakis' is thus the family variant of the big wooden coaster 'Magnus Colossus', located in 'Roma'. The ride is in the Greek area, however, and the entrance is correspondingly themed through

Fig. 10 'Los Ícaros', *Terra Mítica*, Benidorm, Spain © Pau Garcia Solbes (elPachinko.com).

a small porticus with three Corinthian columns. The name, through the suffix *-akis*, is also meant to 'sound Greek' while added to the Spanish word 'alucinante', which means hallucinatory, but also mind-bending, fantastic, awesome. The level of theming is extremely low: the indirect theming is once again very relevant, but the position of the ride makes this rather more 'Roman' than 'Greek'. The temple of Zeus is not visible, nor is the other Greek architecture, while the big Roman limes wall and the Colosseum are always clearly recognizable. This is not necessarily a problem or a mistake, as 'Alucinakis' connects to the larger coaster in the Roman area and is positioned only a few metres within the Greek area.

'Las Islas'

'Las Islas', the second Greek area of *Terra Mítica*, is located in the centre of the park, occupying the area of the 'islands' (actually one island) of the ersatz Mediterranean, in reference to the Greek islands of the Aegean. It is the smallest area of the park and could be accessed (before the division of the park) from 'Egípto', 'Roma' and 'Iberia'. The daily opening of 'Las Islas' was set at a later time, thus making a visit there, for visitors who arrived early in the morning, only possible after Egypt and Greece. The area is themed around the Greek myths, in particular the heroic myths connected to travels by sea, most prominently the myth of Odysseus and that of the Argonauts, which constitute the narrative of the two main attractions of the area. Indeed, according to the didactic material, this area is also called 'El Gran Viaje', the Great Voyage. The age of myth is generally connected, in popular imagination, to the Greek Bronze Age, and the area is generally themed around Minoan culture. The booklet for the schools reinforces this by explicitly connecting the mythical narratives with the civilizations discovered in the nineteenth century in the Aegean area: the Cycladic, the Minoan and the Mycenaean. For this reason, the school guide also explains in this context the myth of the Minotaur (prominently represented on the cover), even if it is represented within the replica of the Palace of Knossos in 'Grécia'. As the Palace has already been used in the other area, there is no reference to Knossos in 'Las Islas', nor is everything limited to the 'Aegean civilization'; on the contrary, archaic Greek sculpture and art connected to the sanctuary of Delos is also represented here.

The themed area is organized into two parts, both arranged around a square. The first, on the 'mainland' next to Greece and Egypt, hosts the attractions 'Mithos' and 'La cólera da Akiles' and a theatre, the 'Auditorio de Pandora', built around reconstructions of the Megaron of the Palace of Tiryns [Fig. 11]. The entrance is decorated with copies of the Flying fish fresco from Phylakopi, Melos,

Fig. 11 'Auditorio de Pandora', *Terra Mítica*, Benidorm, Spain © imageBROKER / Alamy Stock Photos.

and of the Bull Sacrifice and the Funereal Cult from the Hagia Triada sarcophagus, Crete; both originals were realized rather far from Tiryns and reveal, even in their great attention to detail, the 'equivalence' of Aegean, Minoan and Mycenaean art and culture, mixed together in the creation of the style of this area in an 'abstracted' representation of Greece 'before the Classical time'. This building originally hosted 'La sorpresa de los dioses', an interactive show that was part movie, part live-acted, part animatronic, which told the story of the myth of Pandora's box. It was later transformed into 'Nintendopolis' and then a theatre for the shows 'Tarantela' (in which a silly clown awakens the god of the Circus Maximus) and 'El sueño de Pandora', which returned it to the narrative of the original design of the building; in 2018 the show 'Numen' was dedicated to the Muses. In front of the theatre, facing the bridge which leads to the island, is a reproduction of the Sphinx of Naxos, placed, as with the original, on an Ionic capital (although this is in the park on a relatively short and stout pillar and not, as with the original, on a 12.5m high column, which would hinder its visibility). This famous statue from the archaic period (around 560 BCE) was displayed in Delphi. Still, it was an offering to the Delphic sanctuary by the Cycladic island of Naxos, is made in Naxian marble and was probably sculpted on the island before being shipped; it might thus be perfectly in context within this section of the park, as an expression of the 'pre-Classical' art of the Cyclades.

Once the bridge to the island is crossed, the visitor is confronted with a kouros and a kore, representatives of the most typical and well-known iconography of archaic Greek sculpture, confirming how all of what is 'pre-Classical' has merged together into a pictogram of 'archaic Greece', independent of the specific origin of the artworks. Even if it is not clearly indicated anywhere, the specific models are easily recognizable, and both Athenian: the kore is the Peplos Kore (around 530 BCE), while the kouros mostly resembles the Kouros of Sounion (615–590 BCE), albeit much smaller (the original is a colossal statue) and whole (the original is fragmentary). The pedestals of both statues further confirm this confluence of everything pre-classical: they are decorated with a reproduction of the Phaistos disc, the most famous linear A inscription. The kouros and the kore are flanked on the external sides by bronze tripods on pedestals, a ritual object which is once again mainly connected to the sanctuary of Delphi and the archaic and heroic world: in Homer, they are often the prize for athletic competitions, or a gift. Facing the statues is a refreshment area, hosting a series of vending machines under a roof held up by blue columns with meander decorations; in front of this, the restaurant 'Rodas' again refers to Minoan and Aegean themes. While the name recalls the largest island of the Dodecanese, the signs for the restaurant represent a man holding a sword in the Orientalizing style of the seventh century BCE. Architecturally, the restaurant is dominated by the immediately recognizable Minoan columns, as known from the Palace of Knossos, but in blue, thus evoking a maritime environment. Inside the restaurant, copies of famous Minoan frescoes decorate the room: the Ladies in Blue and the Tauromachy Fresco, from Knossos. Walking further, visitors encounter another Trojan horse. This is again a sign of a rather relevant overlapping between the two Greek areas; however, the fact that 'Las Islas' is dedicated to the Bronze Age and mythology, with special attention dedicated to travel myths, makes the presence of the wooden horse necessary, especially in connection with the attraction 'El Rescate de Ulises', located directly next to it. In front of the horse was the shop 'Isla Golosina' (since moved to 'Grécia', in the former 'Portico del Agora'), a sweets shop located in the reconstruction of a house from Malia, Crete. The interior is again covered in reproductions of Minoan paintings: the sarcophagus of Hagia Triada and the Geese from the Heraklion Museum. Next to this shop, the attraction 'Rápidos de Argos' completes the themed area.

'El Rescate de Ulises'

The main attraction of this themed area is a water dark ride, which opened one year after the rest of the park, in 2001, closed in 2005 and subsequently reopened in 2013 within *Iberia Park*. Built with a huge investment and greeted in the beginning as the biggest ride in Spain (8000 m^2),[78] the dark ride by Hafema Water Rides did not apparently fulfil the park's expectations,[79] and did not meet the taste of the public. The narrative derives from the myth of Odysseus, although attention is shifted from Odysseus to his son Telemachus who, as narrated in the *Odyssey*, leaves Ithaca to look for his father.[80] Approaching the ride, visitors see a huge monumental structure that recalls a fortress with Cyclopean walls (thus again the Late Bronze Age and Mycenaean architecture), which rises from rocks next to the Trojan horse. This is obviously Troy, Odysseus' point of departure after the war and the point from which Telemachus' adventure begins. Here the narrative does not follow Homer, who had Telemachus travel to Pylos and Sparta, not to Troy. The sign at the entrance of the attraction, as well as the drawing on the park's map, evokes the most famous adventure experienced by Odysseus, the meeting with the Cyclops Polyphemus, which is meant to create an expectation of thrill.

The queuing area, characterized by ruins, and the pre-show make clear that Troy has already been conquered. A series of reliefs, illuminated at different moments, evoke moments and feelings which allow visitors to understand the underlying narrative. The myth is so well-known that a complete story is not required, and scenes such as Penelope with the Suitors or Telemachus with Athena can be easily identified, along with the scene which constitutes the main narrative bulk as well as the main deviation from the ancient myth: Odysseus as a prisoner of Poseidon who, after his son Polyphemus has been blinded, does not allow the hero to return home. It is now up to Telemachus to free him. In the pre-show, Telemachus (who wishes to find his father) finds an ally in Golias, and Athena convinces the twenty wisest and strongest men of Ithaca to leave with Telemachus and help him. As in 'Laberinto del Minotauro', the technical aspect of the ride is integrated into the narrative, even if this time with no support from ancient sources: indeed, the original boats had twenty seating places.[81] The boarding station represents an ancient and disrupted harbour, located in a cave; this is not the harbour of Troy as described in the Homeric poems, but the mysterious place where the visitors (who in the narrative accompany Telemachus on his quest) embark. In the original ride, each boat was staffed with an actor representing Telemachus, who provided further narrative details and enhanced the immersion; since the reopening, the boats are smaller and there are no performers.

The dark ride consists of nine scenes: the first, 'El paso del Océano', shows a ghostly shore, with fog and figures which, wrapped in clothes and with luminescent eyes, are barely human, inspired by the Homeric Cimmerians, who live in eternal fog next to the entrance of Hades (*Od.* 11.12–19). Odysseus visits them at the beginning of the *Nekyia*. As with the Homeric location at the entrance of Hades, visitors here also see Charon, the mythical ferryman who brings the souls of the dead across the Styx and the Acheron, even if he is never mentioned in the *Odyssey*. In the next scene, the riders encounter the god Aeolus, accompanied by four winged blue creatures, who cause a huge storm. While the 'companions', two boys and two girls, might be a reference to the six sons and six daughters with whom (according to the Homeric poem) Aeolus lives on the island of Aeolia, his role here is exactly the opposite of that in the *Odyssey*, where he is actually friendly towards Odysseus and his friends, hosting them for a month, then giving them a favourable wind, along with a set of unfavourable winds closed in leather sacks (*Od.* 10.1–76). The ancient traditions surrounding Aeolus are nonetheless many, and while the idea of the god of winds creating a storm is a rather easy narrative device for a dark ride based on sailing, the existence of a tradition by which Aeolus was a son of Poseidon, and therefore a half-brother of Polyphemus, may underlie this narrative twist.[82]

The third scene is the Cyclops. The visitors first see goats, which evoke Polyphemus' flock (hiding among which Odysseus and his friends manage to escape the cave in the *Odyssey*); opposite this is the Cyclops, raising a huge rock that he clearly aims to throw at the boat, and in front of him is a fountain, symbolizing the wall of water created by Athena to protect Telemachus. Next come the Sirens. These are represented as half-woman and half-fish, as is customary in the modern Western tradition, in spite of the fact that this iconography only developed during the Middle Ages, and that the ancient Sirens were half-woman and half-bird.[83] Their chants can be heard, and they sit next to and above the entrance of a cave in which they attract the boat (rather than on an island as in Homer); this proceeds without damage, but it is clear that others were not so lucky: at the entrance of the cave are signs of a previous shipwreck. This cave now becomes Hades, the reign of the dead, in a scene clearly recalling the *Nekyia*. Here visitors see Tantalus pushing his giant rock (as seen by Odysseus in *Od*. 11.582–592) and two souls in cages, then pass between the thrones of Hades and Persephone. The 'afterlife' is represented as a realm of pain and punishment, in a way that seems more akin to Christian hell than the pagan Hades: indeed, the scene is called 'El Infierno' (The Hell) in the ride's script. This allows a stronger level of recognition, by adapting the representation of Hades to the imaginary of hell in modern Western Europe. The next scene abandons the Odyssean tradition even more clearly, in favour of Spanish folklore: in 'Los duendes del olvido', the visitors encounter a population of duendes traditional goblins from the Iberian tradition (and from the Spanish colonies). Nonetheless, their ideation as duendes of oblivion, which allow all worries to disappear, establishes a connection with another Homeric episode, that of the Lotus-eaters.[84]

Returning once again to the sunlight, riders now meet Circe, represented in her most popular role as an evil witch transforming men into animals, as represented here by two figures which are still in the process of transition, showing both human and animal characteristics. Immediately after seeing Circe, the visitors bump into a feast, animated by musicians who spit water onto the boat. At the centre of the feast is a character supposed to be Hermes, here represented as the god of music. After the fun of the feast, danger returns in the form of Scylla and Charybdis. Here they are represented as two dragons: a 'normal' one, and one with six heads, in front of which is a vortex swallowing a ship. As seen in *Belantis*, the vortex is traditionally connected to the danger represented by Charybdis. Yet here the strait is between the monsters and the vortex, while Scylla and Charybdis are sitting next to each other on the same side. While the most usual iconography of Scylla is that of a sea monster with a maiden's head and dog heads sprouting from her body, it has been argued that the Odyssean description (*Od.* 12.73–126; 234–262) more strongly recalls a dragon, and indeed one with six heads;[85] additionally, the dragon allows riders to connect to the iconography of many other scary mythological figures broadly known in popular culture. The fact that Charybdis, as a dragon, only has one head, leads the two monsters to have seven heads in common, which may be the product of a conflation with the myth of the Hydra of Lerna, killed by Heracles in one of his labours. Finally, in the last scene, the visitors encounter Poseidon. In a cave with fountains, which evoke his role as god of the waters, among the ruins of an enormous temple, with huge broken columns, the deity shows only his giant head surmounted by a crown representing a ship, a trident and a hand holding a pearl. According to the script, he offered the gift of 'eternal energy' to Telemachus' companions, trying to push them against each other, though without success. They were able to free Odysseus, held prisoner within a clam: by throwing a pearl, Telemachus was able to break the magic holding his father prisoner. At this point, sailing through broken columns, the visitors are brought to the station where they disembark. When compared to the 'Fahrt des Odysseus' in *Belantis*, 'El Rescate' is certainly a far more ambitious and more expensive ride, but the basic mechanisms are the same. While in *Belantis* the visitors identify with Odysseus' companions, here the narrative device has the visitors become the companions of Telemachus looking for his father and, with the traditional flexibility of ancient myths, they experience the episodes from his father's travels, not those ascribed to him by ancient tradition.

'Los Rápidos de Argos'

This attraction, a water rapids ride realized by Intamin, confirms for 'Las Islas' the same pattern identified in 'Grécia': surrounding a main, heavily themed attraction ('El Rescate') is a series of attractions with much less theming. However, with the park's main attention directed to theming the architecture and decoration of the area, this kind of 'indirect' theming through setting also allows such minor attractions to achieve a good level of immersion. As the name reveals, and the didactic guide confirms, the ride is themed to the myth of the Argonauts, that is, their sea travels to reach Colchis and return with the Golden Fleece, which are symbolized by the rough course of the rapids ride.[86] The Argo, the mythical ship realized by Argos for the Argonauts, had according to the story been built with a piece of magical wood from Dodona on the prow, allowing the ship to speak and prophesize; the Argo is thus often represented (as are most ancient ships) with eyes on the prow, as if it were a sort of face. This imagery is replicated on the ride vehicles which, even while round, are decorated with pairs of eyes. A ship with eyes in a storm is also the logo of the ride. Aside from this and the queuing area (which is themed to Minoan architecture, this time based on the Palace of Phaistos with its characteristic columns, confirming the connection between the age of mythology and the Bronze Age), the ride displays very little theming. Only plants have been employed to decorate the course of the ride, and these are quite noticeable, as they depart from the Mediterranean vegetation which characterizes 'Grécia', replaced with tall reeds and trees, giving a sense of narrowness and shadow. While this may be useful on a hot Spanish summer day, it also evokes the Argonauts' travel away from the Mediterranean to the swampy areas of Colchis, which is traditionally located on the eastern shore of the Black Sea. Some parts of the ride have no plants, and are decorated as a rocky, desert shore, again alluding to the many different places the Argonauts had to cross on their travels.

A few sculptures recall the adventures of the myth, yet they are hardly recognizable to the general public, because the myth of the Argonauts is certainly less known, in its details, than those of Homer. Just as the way in which the *Odyssey* is represented in the park attracted criticism for not being recognizable to visitors with only a very simple idea of the myth,[87] the theming of 'Los Rápidos', based on such isolated hints, is beyond the grasp of most riders. For example, a sculpture representing a hairy, winged figure blowing is a reference to the Harpies, which the Argonauts have to chase in order to get the help of the blind seer Phinaeus; at another point, a cave through which the boats have to pass resembles the mouth of a dragon, alluding to the dragon which protected the Golden Fleece and which had to be put to sleep by Medea's magic arts. At the other end of the cave, the Fleece is small and easy to miss; hanging from a wooden structure is a goat's skin, with the goat's head still very lively, looking into the eyes of the visitors. Funnily enough, it is grey. After this, the second part of the ride (the journey of the Argonauts back to Greece) is not themed: the boats simply move back towards the station, passing beneath a stone bridge. This is no surprise, as this part of the trip includes episodes such as the slaughter of Medea's brother, a journey on foot through the desert, and the generally problematic character of Medea.[88]

Other rides

More popular than the Argonauts' is the myth of Achilles' anger against Agamemnon, which opens the *Iliad*. The theming of the ride inspired by it, however, is given only by its name, 'La colera de Akiles'. The ride is a Super Nova by Mundial,[89] and consists of a replica of an ancient ship (with eyes on the prow) which, thanks to two mechanical arms at the two extremities that move independently, can be made to turn and spin.[90] As the rage of Achilles was certainly not directed at sailors who incurred a storm, it is clear that the name is simply meant to recall both the world of the popular Homeric heroes and a general idea of violence deriving from the hero's anger. This ride belongs, as with 'Synkope', to a moment when the park built new thrill attractions to attract more visitors, while not having the financial capacity to truly invest in their theming, thus simply buying 'ready-made' rides. 'La Cólera' was realized in 2006 and positioned next to 'La Sorpresa de los dioses'. A previous building, the seated restaurant 'Corfú', was destroyed to make space for it, following a strategy to reduce the number of shops and restaurants, which were originally planned in excessive numbers. Only two walls from the previous structure are visible; these were left standing to create an image of ruins befitting both the 'ancient' theming and the idea of the hero's destructive rage.

The last attraction, 'Mithos', is a carousel which occupies a part of the square in front of 'La Sorpresa de los dioses'. While its general style recalls the fairground attractions from the early twentieth century, just as 'Los Icaros' in 'Grécia', its theming is based on the fact that the 'creatures' the children can ride on are mostly mythical creatures from ancient Greek mythology: centaurs, dolphins (the pirates who captured Dionysus were transformed into these), deer (in connection to Acteon), Pegasus, seahorses (which dragged Poseidon's chariot), Sirens and unicorns. The carousel also hosts normal horses and bulls, as well as Cinderella-like chariots. In spite of some mistakes (the unicorn is not an ancient mythological figure; some ancient authors simply mention it as if it really existed), the particular theming of the carousel merely confirms once more how myths represent the best-known and most expected part of ancient Greek culture in a theme park, and especially in a theme park called *Terra Mítica*. Its location in 'Las Islas', while providing an attraction for smaller children that is a staple of every theme park, provides a very convenient theming, which allows it to be consistent with the park and the area with little effort, while maintaining a very strong connection to the ride and its tradition, as well as its recognizability as a fairground attraction.

4

Ancient Greece, the United States of America and the Theme Park

The presence of ancient Greece in US American (popular) culture

This chapter takes us away from the geographical area in which the actual ruins of classical civilization are found, and to the country where theme parks were born, and where they are still considered to be highly typical: the United States. It is well known that geographical distance has done nothing to hinder the influence of classical culture in the United States. Created in the American Revolution, the institutions of the state were inspired by ancient models and the founders of the American republic – most of them college graduates with a background in classical studies[1] – had knowledge of ancient political theories and experiences, and reflected on them thoroughly.[2] It has also been argued that classical culture has played a central role in shaping the society of the United States, as 'the humanists' construction allowed classical culture to serve as a common source of identification and differentiation for the European settlers without sapping the authority of their cultures of origin. Ancient Greece and Rome served as an image-repertoire for the colonists, a source of the values they wished to see in themselves: liberty, uprightness, frugality, courage, patriotism, concern for the common good, hatred of tyranny and corruption'.[3] From this starting point, classical antiquity has consistently been negotiated 'as a precursor – or metaphor – for American society itself'.[4] Even if the revolutionary phase and the constitution were mostly inspired by the Roman Republican model,[5] it has been shown that the antebellum period (c. 1800–1860) witnessed a shift from a focus on Rome to a focus on Greece, with Athens moving to the centre while the concept of democracy was gaining momentum.[6] In the years leading up to the Civil War, democratic Athens was also taken as a point of reference and a historical parallel by the Southern States, due to the climate, the settlement structure, and of course the slavery, which allowed the elite their leisure time and intellectual production.[7]

All this is reflected in the architecture of the revolutionary and post-revolutionary period, with most of the public buildings adopting classical forms. The Second Bank of the United States, for instance, realized by William Strickland in Philadelphia between 1818 and 1824, has the form of a Doric temple with eight columns on the front; compared to the 'stereotypical' Greek temple, it only lacks sculptures on the pediment and reliefs on the metopes. Indeed, the Greek forms dominated over the Roman ones during the period known as the 'Greek Revival', between 1820 and 1845, which 'characterised buildings with Federal and Republican functions throughout the country. The most typical forms were the temple, single-story wings, two-story wings, and the portico.'[8] Unsurprisingly, the dominant architectural model became the Doric temple, meaning the Parthenon (or rather its front), often composed with elements from other ancient Greek and Roman buildings.[9] This was, as everywhere else, the most famous product of Greek architecture, while at the same time being symbolically loaded with political meaning through its construction at the highpoint of Athenian democracy, under the supervision of Pericles.[10] The idea of Greece as political referent, in relation to democracy, is dominant, especially in this early period, thus 'Greece' is essentially just Athens: Sparta, for example, remains more marginal than in Europe, and limited in popular knowledge to the Battle of Thermopylae as a model of heroism and sacrifice for one's own country (more recently also due to Frank Miller's *300* and its filmic version), or to the idea of a 'Spartan education', creating strong, brave and disciplined men/soldiers.[11] During the twentieth century, the strong associations of Sparta with Prussia (and subsequently the Third Reich) contributed to making the 'military State Sparta' even less popular and more suspect.[12]

It is in this context that, to clarify the importance of the symbol, a copy of the Parthenon was realized in the American south-east. The Parthenon in Nashville, Tennessee, was built in the area of the Centennial Park for the Tennessee Centennial and International Exhibition of 1897; after this, it was the only structure that was not removed, as it was highly appreciated by the population, and still represents the centrepiece of the park.[13] The fact that Nashville was known at the end of the nineteenth century as the 'Athens of the South' played a role in choosing a Parthenon replica as the central structure for the exhibition, but as it was a celebration of the one hundred year anniversary of Tennessee's accession to the Union (1796), it was also perfectly in keeping with the ancient inspiration for the ideals of democracy, as well as with the federal architecture. One year before, in 1896, the United States had participated in the first edition of the new Olympic Games in Athens: most of the athletes were connected to universities (with a 'Princeton team' joining the expedition), and viewed Athens through a philhellenistic lens, while newspapers at home accompanied this participation with articles about the glory and heritage of ancient Greece and the ancient Olympic Games. The victories in the competitions (American athletes won the most medals) reinforced the idea of a continuity between classical Athens and the modern United States, and of the body of the American athlete as a resurrection of the ancient body.[14]

Ancient Greece is therefore present in US American popular culture as the cradle of democracy, as a civilization which achieved high cultural and artistic standards. In comparison to Europe, there is a much stronger detachment of ancient Greece from Greece as a tourist destination, and a weaker characterization of Greece as a maritime culture. Somehow, the geographical distance of the United States imposes a more 'romanticised' vision of Greece than in Europe: a fairytale, never changing landscape, as Jenkins has highlighted in reference to Henry Miller's *The Colossus of Maroussi* (1930), in which 'Greece is an integral part in the intellectual, or at least spiritual, formation of every American'.[15] During the first decades of the twentieth century, the development and success of racial theory famously led to James Henry Breadsted arguing that there was a racial kinship between ancient Greeks and Americans.[16]

This scholarly classicism reached a crisis point at the end of the nineteenth century, and its influence on popular culture steadily decreased from this moment on, as Classics lost their pre-eminence within the American educational system.[17] Nonetheless, they left behind a set of concepts, images, names and references which are still anchored within popular culture; in 1989, for instance, in the movie *Bill and Ted's Excellent Adventure*, the two protagonists meet Socrates.[18] In 1999, the President of the United States Bill Clinton could declare, during a visit to Athens, that 'we are all Greeks',[19] and modern forms of reception, such as cinema (for example *Troy* and *300*) still make ancient Greece popular in the States: 'most Americans, regardless of their level of formal education, have a sense that democracy was invented in Athens, Aphrodite was a literal sex goddess, Leonidas and his band of three hundred Spartans bravely fought the Persians at the Battle of Thermopylae, and (Eric Bana's) Hector was no match for (Brad Pitt's) Achilles in the Trojan War'.[20] Athenian democracy was thus used as an explicit term of comparison for 'Disney's Electronic Forum' at *Epcot*, where people could participate in polls of different kinds.[21]

Alongside the traditional academic education and the revolutionary ideals, another element has contributed to the diffusion of images of Greece within the United States, beginning just when the academic side was entering its crisis: the community of Greek immigrants. Greek Americans, estimated to account for between 1.3 and 3 million people, are a deep-rooted and strong community within the United States, with a strong presence in American popular culture: numerous examples exist, from the movies *My Big Fat Greek Wedding* (Joel Zwick, 2002) and its sequel (Kirk Jones, 2016), to the popularity of Telly Savalas and *Kojak*, to the TV series *Full House*, in which a major role was played by the Greek character Jesse Katsopolis, to the successful representation offered by Greek American authors such as David Sedaris and Jeffrey Eugenides. The first significant community developed in New Orleans in the 1850s; numbers then rose little by little during the second half of the nineteenth century before booming in the twentieth.[22] Each community presented themselves in forms that mostly derived from a desire to express their history, tradition, civilization and contribution to the advancement of US society; these forms were then stereotyped and perpetuated in the perception of other communities: 'nearly universally, immigrants and native populations have wanted to maintain their cultures, and those cultures have invariably had an impact both on how they responded to the changes following migration and on how they were perceived by outsiders'.[23] From this ensue 'ethnical traditions' which can be very different from those of the country of origin, as they derive from a very specific and locally American need.[24] The Greeks, as an 'ethnic group' with 'distinct national, socio-historical, socio-cultural, and religious orientations ... and socio-cultural traits'[25] form an important and well-studied community within US American society, with cultural traits that have often remained strong into the third generation in the form of 'symbolic ethnicity'.[26] The Greek community is not a special case, as the development of such strong 'ethnic communities' was typical for migrants from Europe at that time: while 'Americans at mid-century held out to immigrants the possibility of complete assimilation, provided immigrants conformed to the prevailing ideology and culture of the society', the Europeans rather asserted 'their right to equal status within American society without conforming culturally',[27] thus developing their own traditions, feasts, celebrations and so on.[28] Even if the Greek Orthodox Church is the main point of aggregation for this community,[29] within this group, references to Greek antiquity and its role in the birth of Western thinking and of modern democracy represent a further important element of identification. This additionally allows the Greek American community to neatly separate an ancient Greek past, with which they identify and which fosters their pride of belonging to the community, from the 'Greek present': most members of the community are born in the United States, and can generally represent modern Greece as a form of decadence from ancient splendour, in this way 'narrativizing' why their families left to move to America. As explained by Sollors, 'it is always the specificity of power relations at a given historical moment and in a particular place that triggers off a strategy of pseudo-historical explanations that camouflage the inventive act itself'.[30]

Indeed, the process of construction of 'ethnic heritage' exploded during the second half of the twentieth century in forms that were entirely detached from the themes, images and socio-economic milieus of the previous century. In part influenced by the Black Power movement of the 1960s and its revindications,[31] the multi-ethnic movement and the single ethnic connections of the members of each community were practised by people who identified as such by descent, but were born and educated in the United States:

> The celebration of ethnic heritage spread in the 1970s and 1980s from marginal indigenes to regional and immigrant groups. Minority heritage became a fount of old-time virtues ... Americans especially yearn for the intensity of minority roots – the more ethnic, the more desirable.[32]

The logical consequence of this would be, in the 1990s, the multiculturalism movement with its central claim: 'that multiethnicity and multiculturalism were not merely a passing phase of American history', but 'a permanent feature'.[33] Within the Greek community, this meant reconnecting to the motherland through its glorious past, and antiquity became the main pivot around which Greek American identity was constructed, which was also due to its recognizability among non-Greeks. The Greek community is thus known to have paraded in New York on Fifth Avenue on 25 March, the day of the declaration of the Greek War of Independence, showing a model of the Parthenon to the city;[34] in 1998, the Greek community of New York received a statue of Athena as a gift from the mayor of Athens, which was then placed in the Athens Square Park, in the district of Astoria, the 'little Greece' of the American metropolis.[35] Antiquity thus represents, together with Orthodoxy, the core of self-identification for ethnic Greeks, and the bulk of their connection with the motherland: the 'metaphor of the dispersed antiquities as the dispersed Greek national body is one that links the 'Emigrant Hellenism' with its metropolis'.[36] Against this background, Greece (and Greek mythology as the best-known part of ancient Greek culture) can be deployed in different contexts and with different aims, ranging from the creation of the idyllic landscapes of ruins within the previously analysed Greek scenes of 'It's a Small World', to the celebration of the community of Greek immigrants and their contribution to the American dream within the *Mt. Olympus Theme and Water Parks*.

Glimpses of ancient Greece in US parks

Disney parks

'It's a Small World', as shown in the first chapter, provides a first example of the romanticized, 'Millerian' way of visualizing ancient Greece in the United States: a mythological landscape of ruins, solitary people (always only one) dressed in modern Greek traditional costumes, but most of all living in peace with animals (mostly sheep and goats) and nature. Greece becomes, in the minimalistic visualization in Anaheim and the larger, more metaphysical representation in Orlando, the idealized imagination of a pristine, 'more natural' way of life, from which civilization derives, but which is not in itself civilization, or better: which shows the traces of a previous civilization that will be a source of inspiration somewhere else. The idea, deriving from the role of Greece in the traditional education system, is that the ancient Greeks were a race of thinkers, philosophers and inventors, whose wisdom put mankind (meant as the Western world) on the path to civilization. Future discoveries, inventions, and technological advances made life much less 'primitive' as it was in ancient Greece, but could not have happened without their initial intellectual achievements.

This image is confirmed in other visualizations of Greece by Disney: 'Spaceship Earth', in *Epcot*, Orlando, is one of a series of rides which aim to show history as progress, specifically as technological advancement. The dark ride, hosted in the best-known and most iconic building of the park, is a 15-minute summary of the history of communication, from prehistory to modern technology.[37] After the invention of cave paintings, the introduction of papyrus in ancient Egypt and the invention of the alphabet by the Phoenicians, the Greeks appear on stage. Originally, they were represented through theatre, conceived as a major achievement of Greek civilization, and confirming the basic identification of 'ancient Greece' with democratic Athens: a masked actor uttered lines from Sophocles' *Oedipus King*. Since 2008, after a renovation of the ride, the Greeks are portrayed as the inventors of mathematics (depending on the popularity of figures such as Pythagoras or Euclides). Against a minimal background evoking Greek architecture (white columns and walls and cypress trees, creating a touch of Mediterranean flair), an old man teaches a younger man. This follows a common visualization of ancient Greece, leading back to the image of Athenian philosophical schools, which was already present in Raffaello's 'School of Athens' (1509–11): a place where wisdom is transmitted at every corner by experienced philosophers who spend all their time on the agora. The narrator's voice explains how mathematics allowed the development of technology. The Greeks are not the ones who invented communication, but their intellectual achievements did pave the way for 'real' modernity and 'real' science.

The value of ancient Greece as a sort of 'golden age', made of naturality and bounty, goes well beyond the reproduction and adaptation of ancient narratives: between 1986 and 1996, and again between 2010 and 2015, Disney parks showed the 4D sci-fi short movie 'Captain EO', in which the captain (Michael Jackson) battled (musically) with the evil and monstrous Supreme Leader (Anjelica Huston), before finally transforming her into a good, human queen. The leader's iconography is clearly inspired by the iconography of Medusa and in the 'evil world', shapes resembling columns are seen in the background; after the transformation, when the world becomes coloured and joyful, the Supreme Leader's building loses its futuristic, metallic look, assuming the character of classical architecture: gigantic classical columns with plants wrapped around them, a stylobate, and stone walls (with a Roman arch). In this Greek theatre/temple (in the final view from outside, the shape of the Greek temple is unmistakable), peace reigns and butterflies fly around.[38] Classical antiquity is thus again idealized here as the faraway place of utopia.

Even if Disney theme parks have never developed a truly Greek setting, the pictographic representations of this ancient civilization are known and recognizable, especially the elements connected to mythology. The only explicitly ancient Greek element in Disney theme parks have been the Hercules parades, inspired by the eponymous Disney movie (1997).[39] As part of the initiatives to promote the motion picture, *Disneyland* (Anaheim) hosted the 'Hercules Victory Parade' for a year, starting in June 1997; at the same time, *Disney's Hollywood Studios* in Orlando showed a variant called 'Hercules "Zero to Hero" Victory Parade'.[40] From July to October of the same year, the parade was also organized in *Tokyo Disneyland* ('Hercules the Hero'), while a shorter mini-parade was also shown in 1997 in *Disneyland Paris* ('Hercules Happening'). In the same spirit, other events were organized outside the parks, most notably the 'Hercules Electrical Parade', which ran on Broadway, New York, on 14 June 1997 to celebrate the release of the movie and the reopening of the New Amsterdam Theatre.[41] These parades were developed as part of the usual Disney strategy of mutual reinforcement and advertisement of the various branches of the company, and in 1998 they were all replaced by parades inspired by the new Disney movie, *Mulan* (also because *Hercules* was, ultimately, not a particularly successful movie).[42] The movie and the parade reinforced some of the points stressed above: the fact that ancient Greece is mostly known through its mythology, that this is a highly recognizable subject, particularly apt for entertainment (at the beginning of the project, the company was only in doubt as to whether to pick Heracles or Odysseus). At the same time, classical mythology, despite the high recognizability of its characters, is dealt with in a very flexible way: thus for Disney, Hera is Hercules' mother, and Hades is his enemy. Importantly, this was why Disney chose Heracles over Odysseus: Heracles is well known as a character (also because of the very long history of his reception as the model of the muscular hero),[43] but the individual episodes of his myth are less well-known and can therefore be altered with more freedom, while the *Odyssey* is popularly known in much more detail and thus implies greater constraints.[44]

The Disney Hercules also clearly demonstrates an important difference between European and American receptions of classical Greece. While the age of myth in European receptions is generally identified as the Bronze Age and therefore represented through the architecture and the material culture of the Minoan and Mycenaean worlds, this is less the case in the United States. Here, at a far greater distance from the archaeological sites, and influenced by the cultural models discussed above, only the classical period can achieve the level of recognizability sufficient to be deployed in theme parks. Ancient mythology is thus set amidst Doric or Ionic columns: the most recognizable visual symbols of ancient Greece are the 'Greek temple', the marble statue, and the vase with black figures, which is indeed a recurring element in the Hercules products.[45] There are also examples of 'Bronze Age settings' in classical reception in the United States, but these are in the minority, and had only a limited impact on subsequent receptions. Eric Shanower's graphic novel *Age of Bronze*, for example, retells the entire story of the Trojan War and sets it, as the title reveals, in the cultural context of the Mycenaean and Minoan civilizations; however, this is a deliberate choice by the author, who engaged with the 'mission impossible' of allowing all the different variants of the myth to converge into an authoritative, 'objective' version, situated in the context of what has been considered the setting of the (non-existent) 'historical' Trojan War since the nineteenth century.[46] The movie *Clash of the Titans* (1981) sets the adventures of Perseus and Andromeda in Minoan-Mycenaean settings; yet this was a UK–USA co-production, and the British elements are visible in many of the choices (Laurence Olivier and Maggie Smith have leading roles, for instance). The remake of the movie, from 2010, and its sequel, *Wrath of the Titans* (2012) do not follow this choice and 're-classicize' the settings (which appear mostly in ruins) while simultaneously employing a sort of sci-fi aesthetic. This becomes clear when the Medusa scene in the movies from 1981 and 2010 is compared: in the former, Medusa moves among typical Minoan columns in a setting which immediately recalls the Palace of Knossos;

in the latter, the fight takes place among fallen and destroyed examples of monumental classical architecture, with huge Doric columns and architectural sculptures (metopes are visible throughout the scene).

The never-realized 'Fantasia Gardens' would also have been inspired by classical mythology. The idea of a ride based on the movie *Fantasia* (1940) was developed in the 1960s for *Disneyland* in California; it was then planned to replace an older attraction during the 1980s in Florida's *Magic Kingdom*; then subsequently intended for *Animal Kingdom*, opened in 1998 within *Walt Disney World* in Orlando. According to the original concept, this park would have been divided into three areas that corresponded to three categories of animals: existing, extinct, and mythological. The latter would have been represented in 'The Beastlie Kingdomme', a themed area which was never realized due to financial constraints, but within which visitors would also have found representations of mythical animals from Greek mythology.[47] Based on what is known of the original plans, 'Fantasia Gardens', a boat ride, would have brought visitors face to face with centaurs, fauns, and Pegasus, which in the movie animated Beethoven's sixth symphony (*Pastoral*). This section of the movie was entirely inspired by ancient mythology and features gods such as Dionysus, Zeus and Hephaestus. The animals from this section would have been a perfect fit for the 'Beastly Kingdom' and would have represented a further example of the role played by Greek mythology in popular imagination.

The Disney parks thus confirm the forms through which ancient Greece is present in US American popular culture, as well as some of the differences from the European forms of reception: a concentration on the classical period; a focus on certain selected, well-known myths; the role of the ancient Greeks as 'initiators' of a path to civilization, in the political, philosophical, and scientific-technical sense. And yet, the role of Greek migrant communities has also been celebrated by Disney: *Disneyland Resort* in Anaheim hosted the special event 'Opa! A Celebration of Greece' on 25–27 May 2013. This followed previous events that celebrated American multiculturalism and focused on the Chinese (festivities for the Lunar New Year, which still take place every year) and Mexican (Día de los Muertos) communities. Alongside 'It's a Small World' in *Disneyland* and within the 'Paradise Gardens' in *Disney California Adventure*, while Mickey Mouse appeared in fustanella, visitors were offered events such as 'Olympic training with Hercules' (a 'meet and greet' which allowed the brand to reference and advertise the 'Greek product' from Disney, while referring to the popular connection between ancient Greece and sports),[48] as well as live performances offered by the Greek community (for example Greek dancers from Long Beach) and tastings of

Greek food; Greek music was played in the background the whole time. On the evening of 26 May, a special dinner in the 'Golden Vine Winery' was hosted by the Greek chef Argiro Barbarigou and the winemaker Christina Boutari.[49] The stages displayed obviously white columns and blue meanders, accompanied by golden Corinthian capitals, while some employees (called 'The Citizens of Greece' for the occasion) wore white and had a golden laurel crown. Others represented ancient soldiers; the 'meet and greet' with Hercules also displayed a large red vase painted with the image of the demi-god, and visitors could make their own laurel crowns.[50] Antiquity thus played a major role in this special event, as a crucial component of the identity and memory of the Greek communities within the United States,[51] a role which should not be underestimated.

Other parks

Not many other theme parks in the United States refer to ancient Greece. However, two further examples are noteworthy for the forms of reception of classical Greece in America. The 'reduction' in the set of popular and recognizable elements and styles, when compared to Europe (and thus the 'disappearance' of Crete and Mycenae) also exists alongside a tendency to conflate Greece and Rome into a general picture of 'the Classical', which becomes a symbol and a referent for European, and especially southern European, culture: at this point, it is not only the distinction between Greek and Roman culture that becomes fuzzy, but also that between Italy and Greece. A good example of this can be seen at *Busch Gardens Williamsburg* in Virginia. The park, opened in 1975, was earlier called *Busch Gardens: The Old Country* and *Busch Gardens Europe*: its theme is Europe, with all the stereotypes that the European countries have in American eyes.[52] The different areas display England, Scotland, Ireland, Germany, France (as well as French Canada!), and Italy. Greece is not represented – as in *Epcot*'s 'World Showcase', the modern country does not represent a firm reference point for the American public and its tourism. But Italy is represented by two areas: one, 'San Marco', evoking Venice (which also dominates *Epcot*'s depiction of the country), the other, 'Festa Italia', evoking celebrations for Marco Polo's return from China. In both, classical antiquity plays a role, revealing the collapse of temporalities that is typical of how Italy is represented.[53] 'San Marco' thus hosts 'Escape from Pompeii', and 'Festa Italia' features the 'Roman Rapids'. But in the latter area, there is also a steel roller coaster, themed to an ancient Greek god: 'Apollo's Chariot'. This, the first hyper coaster, realized by Bolliger & Mabillard, is very lightly themed: only the cars display on their front the face of a young man, which seems to owe more to classical representations of Dionysus than Apollo; the structure is purple, a colour traditionally associated with antiquity, but more specifically with the Roman Empire. It is true that Apollo was also a god for the Romans, who adopted him from Greece and engaged in his cult; still, Apollo was for the Romans and is still perceived today as the 'Olympian sun god'.[54] What is occurring here is thus the insertion of a popular Greek element – through its association with 'antiquity in general', and thus with Rome and then with Italy – into a different thematic area; the chain of associations described here makes sense for the local public, who do not find this insertion inappropriate.

While there is a lack of thematic areas entirely dedicated to Greece (the only exception is the theme park *Mt. Olympus*), occasional references to Greece do refer to individual well-known aspects, characters or episodes related to ancient Greece, such as classical mythology. At *Dorney Park and Wildwater Kingdom* in Allentown, Pennsylvania, for instance, a wooden coaster, which was inaugurated in 1989 establishing a new record for the highest drop, was called 'Hercules', hinting at the 'heroism' of the riders and at the 'superhuman' challenge it represented. When this coaster was dismantled in 2003, it was replaced by a steel floorless coaster which, with a tongue-in-cheek reference to the predecessor, is called 'Hydra the Revenge' (which opened in 2004). At *Universal Studios Orlando*, the walk-through indoor attraction 'Poseidon's Fury. Escape from the Lost City' (opened in 1999) takes from the myth of Odysseus the tradition of the wrath of the god of the seas and transposes it into a new narrative. The timeframe is modern: visitors accompany an archaeologist, their guide, through the ruins of a temple of Poseidon.[55] The architecture here is not very classical – in spite of some Minoan-looking columns in the first room, it more closely resembles pre-Columbian American ruins, such as Maya or Aztec temples [Fig. 12]: this occurs both in reference to local stereotypical images of archaeology and to images of the 'adventurous archaeologist', such as Indiana Jones, which are often connected to central American settings. Pyrotechnics and water shows accompany the narrative, which deals with the clash between Poseidon and the evil high priest Lord Darkenon. The ride, with its insistence on the dangers and secrets of archaeological research, is therefore fitting for the themed area in which it is inserted, the 'Lost Continent'. Indeed, the movie explaining the narrative, featuring Jeremy Irons as Poseidon, is 'Escape from the Lost City', which stresses that archaeology is dangerous and adventurous, a sort of arcane discipline which can release powerful and dangerous buried, ancient spirits.[56] Decorative elements, such as large skulls sculpted on the walls, skeletons with spiderwebs, domed structures, and large human faces sculpted into the rock (from the mouth of one of these flows a waterfall) have little to no connection with ancient Greece, instead originating from the repertoire of images connected to adventure and horror movies, as well as to Atlantis. The connection of this ride to Atlantis is evident not only from the plot: from the first room, the visitors and their guide move into an undersea world, where the main action takes place, before they are brought back to the 'temple'.

The literary creation by Plato developed into an important and highly popular modern myth and is, as we have already seen, conceptually and visually connected to classical Greece,[57] as is the case at other theme parks. While the story of Atlantis has always been very well known among a very broad public, it reached a special peak between the late 1990s and the early 2000s, when alongside 'Poseidon's Fury', Disney's film *Atlantis: The Lost Empire* (2001) was released, and the three *Sea World* parks opened their 'lifting' rides 'Journey to Atlantis' (Orlando 1998, San Diego 2003, San Antonio 2007).[58] These are water coasters produced by the German Mack Rides, and the connection of Atlantis to water and therefore to *Sea World* is obvious. The main narrative and the iconography of the three rides is rather similar. In Orlando, riders first go through a dark ride: here, an apparently friendly Siren leads them to the lost city of Atlantis. Alas, the Siren then reveals her true evil nature, and visitors go up and down the coaster section before they

Fig. 12 'Poseidon's Fury. Escape from the Lost City', *Universal Studios*, Orlando, USA © Solarysys / Alamy Stock Photos.

return to the station. Not only is the Siren derived from Greek mythology: columns, pediments, fountains, vases and architectural sculptures recall Greek art and architecture. The general aesthetics, with houses with balconies and domes, and delicate yellow and blue colours, are generically 'Mediterranean', and they could equally be used to theme the Italian Renaissance, especially because of the abundant use of curved elements such as arches and domes, which were unusual in ancient Greek architecture.

There is only a trace of 'Minoan taste': certain buildings have the merlons typical of the Palace of Knossos. Interestingly, this element is missing in San Diego, where the ride is much more lightly themed: the 'Mediterranean aesthetic' is built with a stronger reference to Oriental architecture (as is evident from the blue domes), and a steampunk aesthetic, sometimes typical of the Atlantis myth, prevails. As Apollo can be in Italy, Islamic architecture can evoke this same sense of 'Mediterraneanness' which makes it suitable to Greece. Finally, the San Diego style is adopted in the even lighter theming of the San Antonio version, in which only a single blue dome seems to evoke the Greek islands. Even the boats, holding a lamp in front, here seem to be early modern rather than ancient, although the reason for this may be banal: the San Antonio ride is a SuperSplash model by Mack, and the same lamps decorate the vehicles of Mack's 'Atlantica SuperSplash' in *Europa-Park*, which is themed to the Portuguese explorations of the sixteenth century. It seems that after the success of the Orlando ride, *Sea World* decided to go ahead and build the next two, while nonetheless realizing that the strong theming of the first had not been crucial to its success, and in particular that the architecture developed for the occasion was not so recognizable to the American public as to make it an essential element of the ride. On the contrary, the next two rides developed the thrill aspect by dramatically reducing the narrative parts (in San Diego the Siren is simply a voice, and the dark ride section has disappeared), while using the same boats that Mack Rides had themed to a different attraction. The blue domes and the sense of 'southern Europe' are more than enough for American theme park visitors to connect the ride with the idea of Atlantis.

Mt. Olympus, Wisconsin Dells, Wisconsin

History and structure of the park

The only theme park in the United States with an entirely Greek theme is *Mt. Olympus* in Wisconsin Dells, Wisconsin. The small city, with less than 3,000 inhabitants, is located in a very picturesque area, characterized by the Dells of the Wisconsin River, which have been attracting tourists since the mid-nineteenth century. The tourism industry developed in the second half of the twentieth century, becoming by far the most important sector in the area, and attracting visitors in particular from the Midwest.[59] A special focus of the touristic development has been, since the 1970s, the construction of water parks with resorts, and the city registered the slogan 'The Waterpark Capital of the World' as their trademark, as proudly shown by the Wisconsin Dells Visitor and Convention Bureau.[60] It is in this context that *Mt. Olympus* has become one of the biggest amusement parks of the area.

Mt. Olympus is composed of four areas: an indoor theme park, an outdoor theme park, an indoor water park and an outdoor water park. The resort is completed by a hotel and a series of 'villages' scattered around the complex that offer accommodation. The villages, which were not built by the park but progressively acquired from its neighbours, do not show a uniform architecture, although they have all been redecorated to have white and blue, the colours of the Greek flag, as their dominant colours;[61] one of them is decorated with a white windmill with blue vanes, recalling the Greek islands. This village is called 'Mykonos', as this island is also one of the most popular destinations in Greece for American tourists. *Mt. Olympus* also confirms the general 'pan-ancient' approach to classical antiquity which characterizes the United States: the hotel 'Rome' is visible from a distance because of a reproduction of the Colosseum next to it, which hides the actual building; Roman antiquities are reproduced in each room (e.g. paintings of the Colosseum, the Arch of Constantine, Roman aqueducts), again mixed with Greek elements. In the room that we occupied, these 'Roman' frescoes were accompanied by a painting of a Trojan horse. In the corridors are large chests, decorated with reproductions of Italian and Greek postal stamps, not necessarily connected to antiquity. Roman elements can also be found scattered in the park, further confirming the lack of separation between the Greek and Roman cultures: one of the cut-outs placed in the parking lots to remind visitors that they cannot bring their own food and drinks into the park, for instance, is a comic figure of a Roman Emperor, while another represents a family of Cyclopes.

The other landmark visible from a distance is the Trojan horse, which rises near the main entrance of the park [Fig. 13], while the sign on the road that marks the entrance to the park represents the ruins of a Greek temple: three Doric columns supporting a stone wall hold the sign 'Mt. Olympus Water and Theme Park'. The entrance is in monumental classicizing style: the ticket booths

Fig. 13 The Trojan Horse in *Mt. Olympus*, Wisconsin Dells, USA © Dennis MacDonald / Alamy Stock Photos.

are within a structure which resembles a Roman triumphal arch but is entirely built without curved elements; next to it, the small building for group sales has the very basic form of a Greek temple [Fig. 14]. From here, visitors access the outdoor theme park, and through it they can move to the indoor theme park and the two water parks. Hotel guests enter directly from the hotel, which is at the opposite side of the resort: they can directly access the two water parks.

The strong Greek theme, as well as the complicated structure, derive from the park's history; the park is very proud of its origins, and celebrates them both on a commemorative monument in the outdoor theme park, as well as on the park's Facebook page.[62] The founder, Demetrios 'Jim' Laskaris, was born in Greece in 1937; in 1951 he moved to New York, then to Chicago and from there, in 1970, to Wisconsin Dells. While in Chicago, Laskaris and his wife Fotoula had already operated fast food stands; when they arrived in Wisconsin, they opened a fast food diner, which they soon enlarged with a three wheeler dirt track and then with go-kart tracks.[63] This first activity had no Greek theming: it was called *Big Chief* after a statue that Laskaris had bought, and further enlargements of his activities, which did not yet consist of themed environments, would instead show an interest in American and Native American themes (e.g. an Indian

Fig. 14 The Entrance to *Mt. Olympus*, Wisconsin Dells, USA © Ilene MacDonald / Alamy Stock Photos.

Ceremonial and a Western show). Soon, Laskaris was supported by his son Nick, who began as a mechanic and went on to construct the go-karts and go-kart tracks. The Greek theme started to appear in the mid-1990s: between 1995 and 1997 the Laskaris built one roller coaster per year, calling them 'Cyclops', 'Pegasus' and 'Zeus'; the giant Trojan horse then appeared to signal the park to visitors. The Greek theme was strongly desired by Nick Laskaris, who from this moment on (and even more clearly following Demetrios' death in 2003), systematically deployed it as a proud symbol of his family enterprise. Indeed, it was after 2003, as a sort of monument to Jim's memory, that the park was renamed from *Big Chief Amusement Park* to *Big Chief's Mt. Olympus Theme Park*, and Greek theming was added to each part. This happened at record speed, in only six weeks, mostly thanks to the use of a CNC foam cutter.[64] In 2004, *Mt. Olympus* merged with two water parks on adjoining properties: *Family Land Waterpark*, which became the outdoor theme park, and *Treasure Island Resort*, whose 'Bay of Dreams' became the indoor water park; the latter also owned the hotel which, after renovation, would become the Hotel 'Rome' in 2007.[65] This merger was facilitated by the difficulties that Mattei, the owner of both *Family Land* and *Treasure Island*, had experienced since 1999, when a four-year-old boy drowned at the 'Bay of Dreams' and the boy's family sued the park for 4 million dollars.[66] The company now took the name of *Mt. Olympus Water and Theme Park*.[67] Meanwhile, in 2006, the indoor theme park was also added to the complex.[68] The Laskaris family proceeded to buy other motels in the surrounding area, thus enlarging the accommodation on offer at *Mt. Olympus*, which reached 1300 rooms and 70 campsites.[69] The motels and accommodation possibilities were consistently renovated and renamed (to 'Mykonos', 'Santorini', 'Poseidon' and 'Zeus') to better fit the general theming of the park.

Mt. Olympus is thus a 'heritage park'; however, it does not celebrate a national or regional heritage, but an individual one, that of the Laskaris (and their success story), and of the community of migrants to which they belong. Despite how the park developed, the entire narrative told within *Mt. Olympus* revolves around Demetrios 'Jim', not Nick: Demetrios is the poor boy who arrived in the United States and who, as the real self-made man of the 'American dream', achieved honour and wealth as the 'Big Chief'. In this sense, he represents the success of the Greek American community, and his achievements are iconically themed to the culture of his country of origin, or rather to its best-known phases and aspects; this means that even this park, with its strong and individual 'Greek' connotation, adopts generic 'classicizing' motifs, which do not differentiate between Greece and Rome, as is frequently the case in American popular culture.

'Medusa'

In 2004, part of the *Treasure Island Resort* was transformed into the indoor water park; a re-theming was somehow conceived but never realized, and only a very few elements (which are rather easy to miss) hint at a Greek reconceptualization. Previously, this area was called 'Bay of Dreams' and themed to central America and the Maya. While it is officially now called 'Medusa Indoor Water Park' (and thus renamed according to Greek mythology), very few signs actually show this name (and sometimes a head of Medusa), while the old name still prominently appears on at least as many signs. Even if the snack bar has been renamed to 'Mythos Grill', again confirming the association of classical Greece with its mythology (while advertising margaritas, daiquiris and pina coladas that are much more in keeping with the old Caribbean setting), the theming within the indoor water park has not been touched. The indoor water park thus features a series of slides, pools and water attractions set within a reproduction of Mayan ruins, including references to the jungle and the European conquistadores (in the galleon 'Hispaniola'). The names of the attractions have not been changed, either: in May 2016 they were still 'Anaconda', 'Boa', 'Cobra', 'Diamondback', 'Jaguar Hot Tub', 'Sacred Well Hot Tub', 'Mayan Raging River', and 'Hispaniola Bay'. These names do not always correspond to those on the signs next to the single attractions, revealing once again a degree of haste and imprecision in the transformation of 'Bay of Dreams' into 'Medusa', even aside from the theming. Visitors also encounter a 'Mystical Tower Tube Slides' and a 'Warriors Basketball Pool': even if the latter could refer to the Mayan ball games rather than to ancient Greek sporting experience, both these names may also have been intentionally left generic to distance them from both the Mayan and Greek themes. In a context in which the park administration has decided not to invest money and energy in the creation of a strict and precise theme (and since the 'Bay of Dreams' had encountered great success even before its acquisition by the Laskaris, even being shown on the Travel Channel's show 'America's Hottest Places to Cool Off' in 2001), the decision to leave the 'Bay of Dreams' as it was can therefore be understood and explained. The only Greek element in the indoor theme park is thus an automatic machine containing a Zeus robot which, upon receiving a coin, pronounces his oracles. While the Maya, as a past culture, do not contradict the general idea of a park dedicated to antiquity and archaeology (and past cultures are in this sense almost equivalent), the indoor water park more generally reveals the park's general (and 'soft') attitude towards theming.

'Parthenon'

The indoor theme park opened in 2006 with the explicit aim of increasing the park's (and Wisconsin Dells') entertainment on offer in winter. From the beginning, it was called 'Parthenon' and thus had a clear connection to the general theme of the park and the Greek identity of the family, reified in the most famous building from Greek antiquity. The building hosting the indoor theme park is a large white tent, covering a 43,000-square-foot area, and occupies what used to be an empty space between the indoor water park and the outdoor theme park.[70] Only one of the tent's long sides faces the rest of the park, along the path from the hotel and the indoor water park to the main entrance and the outdoor theme park. This was thus decorated with a series of columns, which represent the main theming element of the entire section. The seventeen Doric columns, which pretend to each consist of twelve drums, hold an architrave and a Doric frieze, alternating triglyphs and metopes. On top of these, another architrave hints at a pediment. Indeed, on top of the first column, next to the entrance, one can see what appears to be the beginning of the pediment. The decoration therefore represents the side of a Doric Greek temple, whose façade would have been where the entrance is (and is thus consistent with the identification of the entire building as the Parthenon). This temple is represented not in its pristine, ancient state, but in ruins, exactly as the Parthenon is today, as it can be seen by tourists who visit Greece, and therefore in its most recognizable form. Consistent with this, the metopes are also quite extensively degraded and are barely recognizable. If there is any sort of classical inspiration, it is almost impossible to understand, and surely it is not from the Parthenon. One of these shows a man dragging a bull or a horse, while another depicts a woman dragging another woman. Only one metope seems to more directly evoke an ancient model: the metope from the Temple of Zeus at Olympia with Heracles taming the Cretan Bull, although even this is reproduced in a very approximate fashion.

The main attraction of this area was the wild mouse coaster 'Opa!',[71] which closed in April 2014 after a man fell from the ride and was severely injured.[72] After this incident, the entire indoor theme park was closed, and I could not visit it during my field trip in May 2016; in summer 2018 the indoor park was still closed and 'under construction': only the arcade games, which are substantially independent, were accessible. In the indoor park, theming took the form of columns and walls realized as if they were built with large (white) stone blocks. The 'Tea Cups', for example, which were originally located here and later moved to the outdoor theme park, were not themed, but set within a sort of tholos, built on Doric columns. Overall, the theming of this section is consistent with the overarching theme of the park but is still a sort of patch added to the structure rather than a systematically conceived theming.

'Neptune's Outdoor Water Park'

As with the indoor one, the outdoor water park also has a general name consistent with the theme of *Mt. Olympus*: 'Neptune's Outdoor Water Park'. The name is significant, as the desire to recall the classical god of the seas results in using his Roman name, not the Greek, again revealing a lack of differentiation between Greek and Roman culture. The outdoor water park is divided into two sections: one for resort guests only and one for the general public. The former serves to provide the resort guests with extra facilities in the high season, when the park can be quite crowded. Alongside a series of slides and a very quiet flume ride for children ('Endless River'), neither of which have a meaningful name or theming,[73] it hosts 'The River Troy', a flume ride whose only theming is in the name. This is written in block letters on a wall next to the attraction and accompanied by a depiction of a Corinthian helmet, the most popular form of an ancient Greek helmet, one that is generally recognizable and well-known to many people, particularly as it is a characteristic attribute of the Marvel character Magneto and is, in its plumed variant, represented on the coat of arms of the United States Military Academy.

The section open to the general public also displays a rather low level of theming, mostly focusing on the names, with a more consistent engagement in the last years: the newest attractions are all named after themes from the classical world. So, the children's area 'Huck's Lagoon' evokes Huckleberry Finn, Tom Sawyer and the adventures described by Mark Twain (the decoration shows a big wheel, from a mill or a steamboat, wooden structures and a palm), as it already did when it was a part of *Treasure Island Resort*, while three water slides which show no theming in the decoration have been named after the Greek marine god Triton: 'Triton's Challenge', 'Triton's Fury' and 'Triton's Rage'. 'Poseidon's Rage' (opened 2007) is a wave pool with little theming beyond the name: on the side facing the street, where 'Poseidon's Beach' opened in 2010, Doric columns support a frieze with triglyphs alternating with lilies; in front of it is the bust without arms of a bare-chested ancient warrior, recognizable from the crested helmet (which resembles a Roman one). The sculpture is covered in sand, thus connecting it to the beach on which it is located, and hints that it might be something realized by the children playing on the beach. The park is keen to let its visitors know that this was the old statue of a Native American which gave the name 'Big Chief' to the original enterprise. After the Greek theming was implemented, it was cut at the waist, the feathered cap was replaced with an ancient helmet and it was positioned at the entrance of the park; in 2010, it was sandblasted and brought to 'Poseidon's Beach', but still placed in a way that makes it perfectly visible from the road.[74] The same beach still hosts a bar which, bowing to the stronger evocation in American culture of seaside and holidays through Hawaiian and Polynesian images, is called 'Tiki'. In 2012, the park opened the 'Lost City of Atlantis', a complex of seven different water slides.[75] The reference to Atlantis is consistent with the Greek theming, as we have already seen: in a way which can be considered typical of how the Lost Continent is represented, especially in the United States, the decoration mixes Greek elements (Corinthian columns, Poseidon sitting on a throne, a relief showing Triton with a trident, meanders, ancient Greek warships drawn on the slides), with Mayan elements (such as masks) to represent a generic 'lost civilization', as well as generally maritime decorative props (seahorses), and tall domes in a steampunk style.

Finally, in 2016 the park opened 'The Great Pool of Delphi', a giant swimming pool decorated with a reproduction of the famous three columns of the Delphic Tholos, repurposed as a waterfall.[76] For the first time, the name and the theming were brought together through the use of a replica of a real and well-known archaeological site. As already highlighted for *Terra Mítica*, however, the outdoor water park enjoys a form of indirect theming through the 'Parthenon'. This is clearly visible from most of the slides and attractions, and thus contributes to the construction of what aims to be a Greek immersive environment.

In this section, visitors also encounter a small 'shopping street' ('Shops at *Mt. Olympus*'), which connects the outdoor water park and the outdoor theme park, while simultaneously providing a further form of indirect theming. The shops are hosted in a building which rises next to the columns of the indoor theme park (from which it is separated by the 'Parthenon Arcade', continuing the series of triglyphs and metopes of the 'temple'), in front of 'Poseidon's Rage'. The building is a classicizing architecture, even if not a Greek one, instead inspired by Roman imperial architecture and European neoclassicism. At the centre of the building are three pediments, disposed symmetrically, without sculptures. These are placed above two orders of Doric columns and pillars: the lower one surmounted by an architrave, the upper displaying balconies and arches that correspond to the pediments. Both orders are surmounted by a frieze with triglyphs. The decoration is evocative of a 'classical' style, again intended to be generally Graeco-Roman, in continuity with the decoration of the 'Parthenon' and providing a background to the attractions of the water park. The best view, however, is not from within the park, but from the road: as a visual display meant to attract further visitors, these buildings offer a sort of scenography that is 'inhabited' by the visitors currently in the park performing for those outside, attempting to convince those outside to enter this park, rather than one of the other water parks of Wisconsin Dells. Indeed, the specific economic structure of the town explains why the entire park is essentially oriented towards the road and why the most important factor is the gaze of the external passer-by.

The names of the shops continue the theming through naming: we find 'Aphrodite Gifts and Apparel' and 'Pandora's Candy and Kids Shop'. Here there are also dining opportunities, which again insist on the origin of the park, the history of the family and the cultural references to the Greek American community, thus revealing once again the rationale behind the choice of the theme: visitors can eat at the 'Greek Tycoon' or at the 'Big Fat Greek Pizza Joint'. In general, the outdoor theme park, especially in the section open to the general public, shows a greater attention to theming than the indoor sections, thanks to details consistently developed in the last few years. This is consistent with the general history of the park, which appears to still be in the process of transforming into a more systematically constructed themed environment, but is doing so proceeding step by step, as new attractions are built or old ones are in need of maintenance or replacement.

'Zeus' Playground'

The outdoor theme park, 'Zeus' Playground', is the biggest area and the original nucleus of the park, where the 'Big Chief' Go Kart tracks were located: 'Poseidon Go Karts' and 'Trojan Horse Go Karts' were already present at that stage but were not themed. This is also the most systematically themed section of the park. This applies to both the individual attractions, which have a greater abundance of Greek decorative elements than the other areas, but also to the general decoration politics of the section. The outdoor park consists of a series of go kart tracks (the original focus, preserved as a form of 'family tradition'), some roller coasters and a few additional attractions. The tracks are all named after Greek mythological figures: 'Poseidon' (the name given to a track which causes the visitors to drive underground, or rather 'underwater'),[77] 'Hermes', 'Orion', 'Tiny Heroes', 'Helios', and 'Titans Track'. All of these have themed entrances, which vary from a simple entrance sign raised on two Doric columns ('Tiny Heroes', 'Hermes'), to a larger wooden structure imitating the form of a Greek temple ('Helios', 'Poseidon'). A more complex level of decoration is visible only in the 'Trojan Horse' track: here, the cars drive through the large wooden horse which, located next to the parking lot and the street, serves the additional function of marking the entrance of the park to visitors [Fig. 13].

The roller coasters, built during the 1990s, were the first elements with a Greek theming, at least in their names, even before the complex became *Mt. Olympus*. 'Cyclops', 'Pegasus' and 'Zeus' have two further companions, the children's coaster 'Little Titans', and 'Hades', built in 2005 and renamed 'Hades 360' in 2012, when a 360-degree inverted roll was added. As is the case with the go-kart tracks, aside from the names, the roller coasters have certain props which are consistent with the theming. The entrance to the waiting lines are often in classicizing style, though not necessarily Greek: the entrance to 'Hades' is a sort of Roman triumphal arch, whose posts are nonetheless flanked by Doric columns and decorated with a wave motif; the coaster runs through the 'Greek ruins' of a building, of which only the columns and a pediment are visible [Fig. 15]. All the coasters are wooden, a choice that could also derive from the idea of wooden

Fig. 15 The roller coaster 'Hades 360', Wisconsin Dells, USA © Ilene MacDonald / Alamy Stock Photos.

coasters as being more consistent with an ancient theme; indeed, wooden coasters are well represented in areas themed to antiquity, such as 'Magnus Colossus' in the Roman area of *Terra Mítica* or 'Tonnerre de Zeus' in *Parc Astérix*.

While the four attractions for smaller guests in the children's area, 'Kiddie Train', 'Kiddie Swing', 'Kiddie Biplane' and 'Kiddie Balloon Ride' are completely without theming, the other attractions confirm the pattern described. 'Pan's Animal Farm' is a petting zoo, displaying a statue of a young shepherd representing an American boy from the Midwest. 'Almighty Hermes', which lets the visitors 'fly over' 'Poseidon's Rage', and 'Manticore' (named after a Persian mythical monster known to ancient Greeks, but also after an evil character from DC comics), is a very tall swing ride of the 'sky screamer' type, opened in 2015.[78] Painted in the colours of the rainbow, 'Manticore' has no theming other than the name. The same applies to the pendulum ride 'Apollo's Swing', which closed in 2016; the 'Catapult', a slingshot, evokes in its name the ballistic device invented by the ancient Greeks that describes the principle of the thrill ride rather well, but shows no further theming. The ride was closed and removed in 2015 after an accident.[79]

The outdoor theme park also has a strong component of 'indirect theming', based on further decorative props (such as a couple of Ionic columns that support a pediment) and on the architecture and decoration of the shops and restaurants. Hence, different buildings, including functional buildings and small shops, such as 'Athena Gifts and Apparel', continue the theme, alongside the friezes with triglyphs and lilies already encountered in the shopping street of 'Neptune's Outdoor Water Park'. 'Artemis Apparel' occupies the 'naos' of a Greek temple with Doric columns, in whose pronaos are lockers, children carts to rent, and picnic tables. Restrooms are within a structure that resembles a classical temple with pediment, displaying on the frieze not only the usual triglyphs, but also a meander motif and Greek palmettes. The restaurant 'Hades BBQ Pit' has the same shape, but between the columns are cobra snakes holding the architrave, and the frieze is also decorated with snakes that have no reference in classical art. In this case, the snake is evocative of a sense of challenge and danger, connected to the name of Hades (and to the connection between the ancient Hades and the Christian hell, which evokes images of fire, and therefore of the barbecue; the signs also all feature fire and flames), the name inserted within a general structure which is still recognizably Greek. The bar 'Get Shipwrecked', playing with the popular knowledge of the *Odyssey*, represents a typical Greek ship, with eyes painted on the bow and oars sticking out; finally, the 'Delphi Funnel Cakes' are hosted in a round structure with Doric columns which are meant to evoke a classical tholos.

Overall, *Mount Olympus* thus shows highly varying levels of theming and consistency, which is mostly the result of the history of the park, the moments of acquisition and the construction of the individual parts, and the need to renovate or reconstruct individual parts at various stages. While the heritage of the Laskaris has determined the choice of a Greek theme as part of their self-celebration as members of the 'nation of peoples', the theming is less precise than in the European parks considered previously, and responds to a more general lack of differentiation between Greek and Roman elements within a large section of American popular culture. The park aims to evoke an idea of classicism and antiquity, which is also achieved through images, as with the emperor in purple or the triumphal arch, which belong to ancient Rome. This is taken to extremes in sections of the park that also use central American, or more precisely Mayan, iconography, without considering it contradictory with the Greek theme. A demonstration is provided both by the 'Medusa' water park, for which no renovation and re-theming seem to be planned, and by the forms assumed in Wisconsin Dells by the lost continent of Atlantis, which clearly derive from American forms of visualization which can be quite different from the European ones.

5

The Far East, Ancient Greece and the Theme Park

Ancient Greece in Eastern Asia

The role played by classical antiquity in non-Western societies has until now been a rather neglected topic within classical reception studies. For example, until very recent times little has been written on the reception of the ancient Greek (and Roman) world in Eastern Asia, in spite of a quite remarkable number of pop culture products that reuse and reference ancient European cultures, in particular classical mythology.[1] Beyond studies on the introduction of classical texts in East Asia by Christian, and particularly Jesuit, missionaries, the only (partial) exception to this was a series of studies on classical antiquity in Japanese movies and comics, as seen for example in the *manga* and *anime* genres.[2] For Eastern Asian societies, Western classical civilizations are exotic and do not directly belong to the cultural memory of the country and peoples in the region.[3] In this sense, the level of foreknowledge that can be assumed at a popular level is more limited, and mostly focused around a few key themes and characters, which are already known through other popular media:

> the 'classics' in manga and likewise in Japanese culture are precisely not classical. They are not the foundation of an intellectual/literary history whose reception of Greco-Roman ideas, stories and whatnot informs in various ways how that history has developed and are therefore not afforded a somewhat privileged status by the educational institutions that teach and perpetuate the intellectual history of the West ... Knowledge of their reception in the West and of their proper context may as often be misleading as informative because manga and Japanese literature are marked much more by a lack of engagement with Greco-Roman classical materials than by an obvious and concerted reception thereof.[4]

Yet the visual referents are also similar to the cases already analysed, and the Greek temple is the same kind of pictogram as in Europe or in North America:

the Japanese *Tobu World Square*, hosting miniature reproductions of world's monuments displays, quite obviously, a copy of the Parthenon;[5] the Acropolis represents Greece in the park *Window of the World* in Shenzhen, People's Republic of China, containing miniature replicas of buildings from all over the world. *Spa World* in Osaka, Japan, a themed bathhouse with sections representing different Asian and European cultures, includes not only the quite obvious Roman section (parallels between the ancient Roman and Japanese bathhouse cultures are well established, and lie behind the very popular manga and movies *Thermae Romae*):[6] Greece is there, too, both in the form of 'the Parthenon on the Acropolis ... where goddesses of the Erechtheion linger', and as Atlantis, 'the sunken city of Greek mythology'.[7] Already in 1973, on the Japanese island of Shōdoshima,

> an entrepreneur hotelier decided to promote both tourism and philanthropy by building a replica of a Greek temple at the highest point on the island and planting a park of olive trees around it. The temple, which contains a Shinto shrine, was to be a symbol of peace in the reconstruction of Japan after the devastation of the Second World War, and the olive was chosen for the peace-making associations of 'the olive branch'. A festival with Greek themes is held annually. The island now has a thriving industry of olive production and a museum of Greek history and mythology, and is twinned with the Aegean island of Milos.[8]

In Eastern Asia, Greece is much more popular than Rome, up to the point that scholars speak of a 'Japanese philhellenism' which developed from the nineteenth century;[9] similar to the other contexts we analysed, the presence of Greece is primarily the presence of its mythology, as the adventurous narratives of the mythological hero, their 'universal' value and their easy adaptability, make them suitable for the most diverse cultural products.[10] Their popularity is thus strong, here as in the West, while still preserving their exotic character.[11] Homer is popular in China, and the Homeric poems have had multiple Chinese translations, in verse and in prose, since the beginning of the twentieth century; this is in contrast to Vergil, whose reception is much less widespread. The cultural change in China at the beginning of the twentieth century (the 'New Culture Movement') developed new heroic models which were deeply entangled with (European) philhellenism, and in particular with the Homeric ideal. As demonstrated by Jinyu Liu, the new heroes had to be strong and masculine, to challenge societal and divine rules, to rebel against power, and to fight for their State. The Homeric model thus appealed to a new understanding within China of the exemplary hero, alongside the myth of Prometheus and the historical – yet mythologized – episode of the Spartans at Thermopylae. Such attention for Western Classics was not only developed by intellectual figures who took a critical stance towards China's Confucian past and culture – it could also mean recognizing a superiority of Greek culture, highlighting the parallels between China and Greece as ancient high cultures and bringers of civilization,[12] and 'trying to forge an alliance between Western and Chinese antiquities'.[13]

As formulated by Huang, 'to the Chinese mind, ancient Greece is more fascinating than ancient Rome is. There are at least two reasons for this prejudice. One is that ancient Greece, not Rome, is seen by the Chinese as the cradle of the whole of Western civilization'[14] – and as such, it can be presented in parallel to Chinese culture. According to Ren, for example, in the People's Republic of China a particular 'order of the world' is communicated, structuring all civilizations into three categories: primitive, ancient and modern.[15] Greece can thus be genetically interpreted as 'ancient', on a level with the Chinese society BCE. This background idea, as well as the need to make such 'exotic' content palatable to the local public, generates throughout Eastern Asia a rather typical and widespread strategy of inserting the ancient Greek plots and characters into 'local' forms of visualization; alongside the examples that will be shown in the course of this chapter, one can consider, for example, how the gods of the Olympus eat with chopsticks and sleep on a futon in the anime *Little Pollon* (1982–3).[16]

At the same time, the 'exoticism' of this world, its extraneousness to Eastern Asian cultural memory, also imply the necessity of recurring a variety of elements which do not necessarily belong to the culture of reference in order to guarantee recognizability: the mixture of Greek and Roman antiquity we have already seen in the United States becomes here a more complex mixture of 'European' cultures, including the Middle Ages and modern times, which contribute to the creation of an 'Occidentalism' which is as simplifying as Western Orientalism.[17] The system of abstraction typical to theme park representations here operates at another scale: it is not just the abstraction of all ancient Greek temples into one stereotypical Greek temple, or not only this; it is sometimes the conflation of the entirety of Western history and culture into some pictograms representing them.

Classical receptions are obviously not the same throughout Eastern Asia, and the presence of Greek and Roman civilizations in Japan does not necessarily share many similarities with that of China, South Korea or other countries; still, the Occidentalist simplification is a recurrent feature, together with a strong pre-eminence of Greek culture over the Roman one: Greek mythology constitutes almost the sole aspect of Graeco-Roman antiquity with a significant presence in popular culture in Eastern Asia. Between 2004 and 2015, for instance, Macau hosted the *Casino Greek Mythology*, greeting visitors with a Poseidon fountain in the parking lot; Zeus decorated the top of the entrance stairs, sat upon a throne holding lightning and framed by a structure of columns and roof with a front pediment, mimicking a Greek temple and its cult statue. Meanwhile, the 'Filipino doormen, dressed as Roman Sentries' confirmed the lack of distinction between Greece and Rome.[18]

While, as mentioned above, considerations about the change in 'time regime', the development of postmodern aesthetics and the consequent history boom do not automatically apply outside the cultural context of Western capitalist societies, therefore, it is still worth considering how classical antiquity, and particular classical Greece, are represented in themed environments in Eastern Asia, in order to understand the meaning of this 'exotic representation' and its functionalization in a different cultural context, and to compare this to the 'appropriations of Greece' in Western Europe and North America.

Happy Valley Beijing, People's Republic of China

Happy Valleys

Theme parks have had a growing success in Asia in general and in particular in China; many are now established throughout the country, with cultural themes being the most widespread and most successful.[19] *Happy Valley* is a chain of eight theme parks operated by the state-owned company Overseas Chinese Town Enterprises, worldwide the second biggest theme parks company for revenue after Disney, which also developed many other cultural amusement and theme parks, such as *Splendid China*, *China Folk Culture Village*, or *Window of the World*, sometimes together with China Travel International Investment, another company majority-owned by the state-owned China Travel Services Holdings.[20] The first *Happy Valley* park opened in Shenzhen in 1998, followed by Beijing (2006), Chengdu and Shanghai (2009), Wuhan (2012), Tianjin (2013), Chongqing (2017), and Nanjing (2019). All these parks are made up of multiple themed areas, which very often refer to different historical periods and cultures. These range from local examples, referring to the history of the region where the park is built ('Shanghai Beach' in Shanghai, 'Old Chongqing' in Chongqing, and

'Great Szechwan' in Chengdu), to national Chinese themes, even very delicate ones ('Shangri-La' in Shenzhen, Beijing and Shanghai),[21] to exotic themes such as the Maya ('Lost Mayas' [sic] in Beijing, the water parks 'Playa Maya' in Shenzhen, Shanghai, Wuhan, and Chongqing). While seas and islands are recurring themes, these are not so automatically connected to Greece and the Aegean as in Europe, but rather to the Caribbean (represented not only through the 'Playa Maya', but also further areas in all the parks except Beijing), to a generic image of the Ocean (Shanghai, Wuhan, Tianjin), sometimes to Great Britain in the nineteenth century, represented in the form of a Victorian coastal town ('Sunshine Harbour', Shanghai).

The themed area 'Dream of Mediterranean' in *Happy Valley Chengdu* also has little connection to ancient Greece.[22] The Mediterranean represented here is a touristic one, mostly consisting of southern France (Spain is also present as a Mediterranean utopia in 'Spanish Square' in Shenzhen), and the narrative behind the themed area is the love story between Antoine de Saint-Exupéry, the author of the popular children's book *The Little Prince* (translated into Chinese in 1979), and his wife. Most elements are connected to planes and flights (as in the roller coaster 'Flying over the Mediterranean'), a well-known passion of Saint-Exupéry. The presence of a fountain called 'Poseidon's Trident', evoking the power of the trident to generate enormous (and dangerous) waves, is thus not inserted into a representation of ancient Greece, nor does it feature any recognizable decorative elements connected to classical antiquity. At stake here is a general idea of the Mediterranean as a faraway sea, exotic and (as we will see better later) romantic, but also evoking recognizable mythological figures.

Happy Valley Beijing and the 'Aegean Harbour'

In Beijing, ancient Greece is present in a much stronger and clearer way, as it is the theme of an entire area of the local *Happy Valley* [Fig. 16]. The park was inaugurated in 2006 in the Chaoyang district of Beijing,[23] and stands next to a themed residential and shopping area, the *Vecchio Plazza*, which is themed to European and more specifically (modern) Italian culture,[24] one of the numerous themed environments characterizing the Chinese urban sprawl, which have been defined by Campanella as 'mimetic utopias'.[25] These are architectural forms which characterize the fast development of the Chinese suburbs: closed enclaves with commercial spaces, amenities and residential areas in which 'developers employ a diversity of architectural and geographic themes to distinguish their products in a competitive marketplace. They offer buyers not just shelter but a

Fig. 16 The themed area 'Aegean Harbour' in *Happy Valley Beijing*, People's Republic of China © View Stock / Alamy Stock Photos.

suite of globally legible markers signalling status, prestige, and 'arrival'. Selling a theme is also about fantasy and illusion'. They are in this sense 'sanctuaries for the consumer elite that offer imported scenes of tranquillity and timeless order'.[26] Such mimetic utopias use globalized symbols of status and prosperity, and focus almost exclusively on Western, and particularly European themes.[27] In this sense the *Vecchio Plazza* is comparable to the *Roman Vision* settlement in Nanjing, which is themed to the Italian countryside,[28] or the nine towns built around Shanghai, each evoking a European country, including Italy.[29] The Mediterranean atmosphere has a relevant appeal in these suburban settlements, and Greece is not extraneous to this: in Chengdu, the *Mid-Mountain Acropolis* was built to provide its inhabitants with a Mediterranean-style life.[30] And yet, Europe is also perceived in a monolithic, 'Occidentalizing' way, mixing cultural elements from different areas and countries, as in the *Acropdis Park*, an estate in Nanjing which mixes London and Athens: 'the Chinese name of the development is itself a study in borrowed geography: Hai De Wei Cheng refers both to London's Hyde Park (Hai De) and the Acropolis in Athens (Wei Cheng, literally 'defensive castle'), which is then fused rather clumsily in English as Acropdis Park'.[31]

Through this positioning, *Happy Valley Beijing* mostly targets 'domestic leisure class consumers'.[32] From the start, the park hosted a themed area dedicated to Greece, 'Aegean Harbour'. This presence, which as noted is not automatic and does not recur in any of the chain's other parks, is motivated by one of ancient Greece's most popular 'themes' throughout the world: sports, and more specifically the Olympic Games. The attention given to classical Greece in the People's Republic of China and its capital increased sharply at the beginning of the twenty-first century, as in 2001 Beijing was assigned the organization of the Games of the XXIX Olympiad, which took place in 2008. This was a long-awaited occasion, and an opportunity for national redemption: in 1993, Beijing had very unexpectedly lost the assignation of the XXVII Olympiad to Sydney at the last moment.[33] The Australian city won by two votes after Beijing had dominated in all the previous rounds. 2008, however, was a year of great glory, not only for the city but also the entire country, and implied a long period of preparation that also consisted of major architectural projects.[34] All this had major repercussions on *Happy Valley Beijing*, planned and built during the years between the Games being assigned and their organization, and explains the existence of the themed area, as well as its structure and many of its characteristics. Yet the motives represented in the themed area are not only connected to sports, but also to classical mythology that, as has already been made clear, is the most popular set of notions and stories from Greek antiquity in China.

Next to this, there are seven further areas: six are arranged in a loop around a central lake, at whose centre is an island hosting the seventh themed area, 'Atlantis'. Distinct from the European examples, as well as taking to extremes the process seen in US representations of the Lost Continent, Atlantis is here completely devoid of any reference to classical antiquity, and is instead a hyper-technological, yet steampunk, lost civilization, with a special focus on the topic of (clean) energy (for example the attractions 'Energy Collector', 'Crystal Wing', 'Energy Storm', 'Holy Crystal Castle'). While at the time of our visit (the area is now called 'Dessert Kingdom'), 'Ant Kingdom' was dedicated to a comic image of the life and world of insects (funny ants in different colours are the mascots of the park), most other areas are inspired by ancient or legendary civilizations: 'Atlantis' and 'Aegean Harbour' are accompanied by 'Happy Time' which, as with the other parks of the chain, represents a European fair with its attractions,[35] 'Shangri-La' (another staple of many parks of the chain, which should be read in connection to the Chinese appropriation of Tibet and its myths);[36] 'Lost Maya', which represents a colonial Central America at the time of the first (adventurous!) exploration of the Maya ruins; and 'Wild Fjord', the smallest area, which represents the Vikings. *Happy Valley* thus detaches itself from the Chinese tradition of theme parks that, as highlighted by Stanley, is far from 'the easy visual cultural stereotypes of *Epcot*, as well as from 'the internationalist universalism to be found throughout Disney creations and copied assiduously in other Western parks'.[37] The topography of the park is a little more complicated than that of Western parks, but it is impossible to deny the presence of a Western visual language and structure, as well as of an 'internationalist universalism'.

The eighth themed area, the indoor 'FantaSea' which opened in 2014, is located next to the 'Aegean Harbour' and only accessible from it. The area is broadly themed to the marine world and predominantly hosts attractions for small children themed to fish, sea horses and creatures of the sea, with a 'procession of marine life' featuring dancers in fish costumes. But although most of the area is in this sense not themed to a specific sea, two attractions clearly connect this sector with the 'Aegean Harbour' and reveal that the sea should be understood as the Mediterranean: 'Sparta's Arena' and 'Flying over the Aegean Sea'. The central space of 'FantaSea', where the parade takes place, is also decorated with the signs of the European zodiac: the twelve zodiac signs are derived from Babylonian astrology, but through a very strong reception of Hellenistic culture; in China and Eastern Asia, they are perceived as a symbol of Westernness and Europeanness, specifically referring to ancient Greece and its mythology. In this sense, as we will see below, they also appear in *E-Da*, but also for example in Japanese popular culture, most famously in the anime *Saint Seiya* (1986–90). Importantly, 'FantaSea' is indicated on the park's plan as being part of 'Aegean Harbor', with reference to the more detailed map just above. In China, Greece's connotation as a maritime culture and the reference to the sea (the Aegean, represented in the very name of the themed area) is thus also strong. The logo of 'Aegean Harbour', as visible on the merchandising, is two square structures with domes surmounted by crosses (evoking, as in many other examples already discussed, the church architecture of Aegean islands such as Santorini or Mykonos) and an olive branch. Interestingly, the colour is not blue but green, even if blue is the colour of the themed area (and of 'FantaSea') on the park maps. Somehow, the connection of Greece to the sea still brings blue to the fore as the colour-coding for this region and culture, although not with the same automatism and exclusivity we have seen until now (it must also be considered that the Chinese public may be far less familiar with the Greek flag than European and American audiences).

Greece as a touristic destination is host to a growing number of Chinese tourists;[38] since theme parks in China have become popular for offering comfortable, sanitized areas, gated communities which represent landscapes of privilege for the middle and upper classes,[39] the target public of park visitors may coincide with those who can afford to travel abroad to Europe on holiday (and in this sense, the themed area resonates with the themed shopping mall just outside the park). At the same time, the concentration on ancient mythology still places a strong focus on navigation, on islands and on the sea, especially in connection with the myths of Odysseus and the Argonauts. The fact that 'Sparta's Arena' is in the 'FantaSea' area also reveals a less differentiated picture of Greece than in Europe or in the United States: Sparta, differently from Athens, is in Europe not connected with the idea of a particular development of theatre. That Sparta was not by the sea and not primarily a maritime power is a view that is strongly established in Europe (albeit oversimplified and partially wrong), but seems to be less present in *Happy Valley Beijing*. The connection between ancient Greece and the modern touristic destination is also visible in the outdoor area, where the attraction 'Ocean Star', a Condor ride, is themed to Ocean liners: the symbol is a white life buoy with orange ropes, which is clearly recalled in the shape and colour of the ride vehicles. More generally, all the water attractions of the park are in this area: 'Happy Bubble', featuring large plastic balloons within which children can move on the water's surface; the 'Aegean Harbor Ferry'; and the water coaster 'Journey of Odyssey' (sic), on which more will be said below. All in all, the 'Aegean Harbour' in Beijing is a blend of classical mythology, the classical Greece of Olympia and of the Olympic Games, and a stereotypical imagination of a modern touristic Greece; as such, it is not (at least in terms of approach and spirit) very different from the other representations of Greece analysed until now.

If the visitors follow a counter-clockwise path after the entrance, which is the same as the path taken by the train travelling around the park, the entrance to the Greek area comes from 'Wild Fjord'. The border is marked by a sort of disrupted aqueduct which belongs, stylistically, to the Scandinavian area, and the visitor must walk through one of its arcades. On the other side, visitors are immediately confronted with the building hosting 'FantaSea' to the right, which opens onto the road with the entrance to 'Sparta's Arena', 'King's Treasure', a store marked by candy sticks that appear from out of the white and blue building, and the restaurant 'Kitchen Klosos', named after the Cretan city of Knossos and marking the transition from the outdoor to the indoor area. On the left side, the first attraction of the Greek area is dedicated to the Trojan horse and shows the same association between mythology, Bronze Age and Minoan architecture that we have already encountered. This style is confirmed by the small restaurant 'Troians' (sic) located next to the attraction, within a smaller structure with the same characters as the 'Minoan fortress' on the other side of the horse. While the blue and white tables and chairs and the reproduction of the Dolphin Fresco from Knossos confirm this pattern, the sign for the name of the restaurant – the O including a cross and the I as the spear of a knight – to Western observers is more indicative of medieval times, consistent with a generally 'monolithic' vision of Western history that resurfaces at certain points, even within such a well-thought-out and carefully themed park as *Happy Valley*.

The Minoan style is abandoned immediately afterwards (although this cannot be understood as a movement 'through time', as Bronze Age architecture will return, as we will see), where visitors come to a bifurcation. Both paths are connected as part of a loop: if visitors move left and choose a clockwise path, they pass over water on a bridge surmounted by four gigantic statues of Greek warriors holding shields and spears [Fig. 17]. While these statues do not have ancient models, they immediately evoke the Spartans at Thermopylae, as they are depicted in the act of 'blocking the passage'; the Battle of Thermopylae is very popular in China, especially after the success, even here, of the 2006 movie *300*. This is attested by references to Sparta and the Spartans in a variety of contexts, such as a famous and unfortunate advertising stunt for a salad which involved dozens of Western young men in 'Spartan dress' storming Beijing in 2015 – only to be arrested by police.[40]

Fig. 17 *Happy Valley Beijing*: Greek warriors © Jeremy Thompson (Creative Commons license).

After the bridge is the part of the themed area most explicitly dedicated to sports and the Olympic Games. One building shows on its front four identical figures of Atlas holding a roof (while curiously also holding in one hand a loincloth to cover his nudity – a necessity in China), as well as the symbols for the famous sport brands Nike and Adidas. Directly in front, the ride 'Happy World' is hosted in a Greek temple which reproduces the temple of Zeus at Olympia [Fig. 2]. This is explicitly stated on the front of the building, where 'Olympia' is written in big letters, and unmistakably in the font that is associated with the Japanese optic manufacturer Olympus all over the world. On this square there is also a small cart for food and refreshments, strangely named 'Plato's Bookcase', the 'Aegean Harbor Ferry', which in an 'Occidentalistic' way appears rather like a modern galleon on the signs, and 'Happy Bubble'. Between the temple and the Nike/Adidas building is the path leading back to the bifurcation; this passes through two passages beneath the lift and the drop of the 'Journey of Odyssey', whose temples can therefore be constantly seen. In between is the 'Olympic Culture Square' (in which the reference to the games is again very explicit): a large amphitheatre with a monumental scenography, made up of many small houses rising on a steep, rocky coast (evoking the Aegean), framed by the temples and walls of the water coaster. Many of the small houses are white with blue domes, and thus resemble the well-known churches of the Aegean islands; others are yellow and pink, a character that in the Western world is more connected to the Italian Mediterranean, as in Portofino [Fig. 16]. Indeed, some of the houses have signs qualifying them as shops or 'tourist information' centres, and many signs are in Italian ('veranda', 'Piccolo', 'Pizzeria-Spaghetteria'), once again revealing the somewhat monolithic perception of the Western world, in particular of Mediterranean Europe. The general conflation of classical cultures (Greece and Rome) and Mediterranean cultures (Italy and Greece, and eventually France and Spain) is part of a sometimes much broader conflation which can expand to the entire Western world: a frisbee ride in 'Lost Maya', for instance, is called 'Apollo's Wheel' – here, the centrality of the Sun in Mayan culture is conflated with the solar role of the Greek god Apollo.

The square thus evokes the image of Greece as a touristic destination and attraction, confirmed when crossing to the other side of the water coaster, to the 'Greek Small Town Business Street', which is actually a sequence of small stores, mostly in classicizing architectures and with names evoking Greece ('Mycenae Store', 'Aigaia Thalassa', 'Greek Bar', 'Athena's Mirror' etc., although churros are also sold here, as part of 'tourism to the West') on two streets that join in the shape of an L, displaying the unavoidable white windmill and white building with blue dome, alongside fisherman's nets, buoys and small fishing boats brought ashore. At the bifurcation, a platform allows visitors to see the drop of the water coaster while protected behind a glass wall, as the boats raise huge waves. This platform, which creates a crossing of the gaze between the people on the ride and other visitors,[41] also allows visitors to see part of the Culture Square and, on the front, a few more façades of the same kind. These are decorated with black figures of men and women and a centaur, recalling the paintings on Greek vases (and their aesthetics, which are also known from comics and animation movies), but also the lives of tourists in Greece: the most prominent thing to see from the platform is a sign that reads 'Exchange'.

'Trojan Horse'

As mentioned, the 'Trojan Horse' adopts the same decorative language previously encountered in other countries, associating mythology with the Bronze Age. The first building the visitors encounter is inspired by Minoan and Aegean architecture, even if this is represented in a much more original way than in Europe, less constrained by the model of Evans' reconstruction of the Palace of Knossos. While the usual red columns consistently contribute to the theming, the buildings more closely resemble towers and fortresses, with round windows and a prominently yellow-beige colour. While the shape of the merlons somehow still evokes the Cretan style, the general appearance would, in the Western world, be rather evocative of a medieval setting. Next to the ride's entrance is the classicizing statue of a goddess: this is not only consistent with a lack of differentiation between Minoan and classical Greek culture, but also with a general lack of differentiation between classical and neoclassical. Indeed, the statue is unmistakably inspired not by ancient art, but by European neoclassical sculptures of the eighteenth and nineteenth centuries, in particular those of Canova [Fig. 18]: distinguishing between ancient and neoclassical is not a part of local popular culture, and both styles look 'Greek' enough. As we draw closer to the attraction, the building gives way to a series of Minoan columns – with no ceiling – allowing a view of the large wooden horse, which is situated directly next to the lake in the centre of the park. The connection between the two parts is shaped by two columns holding what are clearly the ruins of a collapsed building, evoking the destruction of Troy. Across the waiting area are weapons, shields, wheels, abandoned helmets and general signs of destruction and war.

This setting is in keeping with the ride: 'Trojan Horse' is a top spin ride,[42] whose spinning part is the central section of the horse's body; the bottom part of

Fig. 18 Statue next to 'Trojan Horse', *Happy Valley Beijing* © Jeremy Thompson (Creative Commons license).

the spinning device is decorated as if it were wood, and features small circular windows that evoke ancient war ships, like those on which the Achaeans came to Troy [Fig. 19]. The ride was developed by the German company Huss, but the theming and the decoration were chosen by the park, which hired a Chinese company;[43] we must therefore assume intensive research, one that goes well beyond the basic knowledge of classical antiquity present in Chinese popular culture. This shows the high level of investment in the park and its consequent theming, as great attention has been dedicated, in the political and cultural context explained above, to increasing knowledge of and fascination for ancient Greece within the Chinese capital. As with *Terra Mítica*, in *Happy Valley Beijing* the attractions are accompanied by explanatory signs which contain not only safety instructions (who can use the ride and such), but also some technical data and information about the background story, helping visitors to contextualize the ride within (for 'Aegean Harbour', at least) Greek mythology.

'Journey of Odyssey'

The explanatory sign for the 'Trojan Horse' establishes a direct connection with the largest attraction of the area (and its most important eye catcher, through its integration into the scenography of the 'Olympic Culture Square'), by inviting

Fig. 19 'Trojan Horse', *Happy Valley Beijing* © Jeremy Thompson (Creative Commons license).

the visitors to join Odysseus (who is consistently called Odyssey in the English translations throughout the park) in conquering Troy. A few steps farther along, visitors can then experience the journey of the hero back to Ithaca after the conquest of the city. The entrance to the ride is now located next to the platform from where visitors can see the riders plunge into the sea, at the beginning of the 'Business Street', and is marked by a reproduction of an ancient ship emerging from the wall of the small building. The entrance looks rather out of place for such a central attraction of the park and is indeed not the original one, which is much more monumental, and located a few steps further, in front of 'Ocean Star' (the decision to move the entrance was taken to dramatically increase the size of the queuing area). The building, in the shape of a fortress and with architectural elements that recall the Bronze Age (with the usual red columns and merlons) also features maritime elements, such as drawings of a shark or masts above the main entrance. As with the architecture surrounding 'Trojan Horse', the impression of a fortress, with small windows and a light whitish colour, would in other parts of the world evoke the idea of the Middle Ages, once again revealing a conflation of the various ages of Western history, even in such a well-themed park. In front of this are two Sphinxes, inspired by the Naxian Sphinx of Delphi which, as in *Terra Mítica*, represents archaic Greek culture and therefore the mythic age, in spite of the temporal distance which separates it from the Minoan and Mycenaean eras. The decoration of the waiting area is not so different from that of the 'Trojan Horse': on the walls are paintings freely inspired by the Minoan frescoes, in much brighter colours and with graphics that recall comics. For instance, elements and motifs from the Griffin Fresco of Knossos are enriched by a shield and two crossed swords; the shield has at its centre a sparkling star, which evokes Captain America more than classical antiquity. These motifs connect the old and the new waiting areas, as the old one also has wall decorations that are predominantly inspired by the Griffin Fresco and the Blue Monkeys Fresco of Akrotiri.

The older part of the waiting area is decorated with pictures of the ride itself and the themed area in the outdoor part; the indoor section then features the usual Minoan columns and Hellenizing statues. These are interestingly not white, but rather green, thus evoking bronze, the material in which indeed Greek statues (and not their Roman copies that are known to us) were mostly realized. The decoration again shows a lack of distinction between different Western (ancient) cultures, thus displaying a Roman soldier, for example. The most prominent figure is that of Poseideon, which is consistent with the story being narrated. The many labrys that stand around are once again the product of some very well-informed theming, as these were a symbol of power in Minoan society. A shield and bows on the wall are also compatible with the usual Bronze Age setting of classical mythology and with the story of Odysseus, who is ultimately recognized, within the *Odyssey*, through the test of the bow (*Od.* 21.1–423). Once at the loading station, under the cover of a wine pergola (which is central to any evocation of a Mediterranean environment, and is here decorated with the Tauromachy Fresco), riders encounter an explanatory sign that again establishes a connection with the 'Trojan Horse', explaining that Odysseus was its inventor, who was then punished for his arrogance by Poseidon. The arrogance motif, unconnected to Poseidon's rage in Homer, is a recurrent scheme within simplified versions of the contrast between gods and heroes in classical mythology, which also underlies the narrative of *Europa-Park*'s 'Poseidon' and the *Terra Mítica* show on the Trojan War.[44] The sign also explicitly mentions the sculptural decoration – both the Sphinxes at the old entrance, which 'represent his journey', and the gods Athena, Poseidon and Helios (the Roman soldier) in the waiting area, all important deities in the *Odyssey*.

The ride, realized by the Chinese company Golden Horse from Zhongshan, is a shoot-the-chute. In the first section, boats move through architectural structures, which host more figures from the epics. Of particular interest is the representation of the Cyclops, who is recognizable because of his one eye, but is represented in a clearly East-Asian style, thus achieving recognition for the mostly Chinese public, instigating a conciliation between Chinese and ancient Greek mythology. After this, the boats go up, floating behind the scenography of the Olympic Square, across many ruins of ancient temples characterized by broken columns, until they come to the final 'danger', a small, slightly less disrupted temple, from which hangs a multi-headed sea serpent (the Hydra?); this is represented in a very unconventional way, with extremely long teeth sprouting from both the upper and lower jaws, again reconciling the Western iconographies with the local imagination of dragons. After this comes the extremely high plunge, causing a giant wave which can be seen from the platform mentioned above, protected by a glass wall. A further possibility for interaction between riders and visitors is provided, as in *Europa-Park*, by a series of water-shooting cannons that can be directed at the already-soaked riders. In fact, riders become so soaked that they are compelled to wear ponchos (provided by the British company Haystack Dryers, which prominently advertises these exact ponchos on their homepage).[45]

'Flying over the Aegean Sea'

The last two rides to be analysed symptomatically cover the three perspectives from which *Happy Valley Beijing* views ancient Greece and thus constructs its image: on the one hand, the cultural and historical aspects of classical mythology, which are also deeply entrenched in the ever-present image of Greece as a touristic destination; and on the other the Olympic Games, which establish a connection between Olympia and Beijing. 'Flying over the Aegean Sea' is a flight motion simulator located within the indoor area of 'FantaSea' which shows a seven-minute movie that takes the riders through space and time to ancient and modern Greece. The trip begins in outer space, where riders move among planets and asteroids before plunging into a vortex. This first section evokes the creation of the Universe, and the time before life. When riders emerge out of this sort of black hole, however, no dinosaurs are in sight, but rather classicizing architecture: two columns frame a picture of a woman floating above the waves and playing a lyre. The iconography is well known, in antiquity as in modernity, and represents a Muse, thus immediately evoking the beginning of the epic poems, most famously the *Iliad*. This is demonstrated by the next scene: as the riders fly into the picture, the Muse becomes animated and flies above the waters and huge waves. Spectators follow her, until they arrive to a huge ancient city, as the Muse disappears just before the city comes in view. It is not explicitly stated what city the riders fly into, but this is made clear by the intertextual and intermedial cross-referencing with the rides outside: the architecture of the gigantic walls – the first thing the riders see in the video – is the same as the small buildings next to the 'Trojan Horse' as well as the original entrance to the 'Journey of Odyssey'. Their 'medieval' appearance here carries a further meaning: the presence of two rectangular towers that frame the city gates, and then of a huge linear wall on the outer sides (whose corners cannot be seen) also evokes the Great Wall of China, which is not far from Beijing. So, while the Muse and the external references allow visitors to immediately identify the city as Troy, there is a further pattern of identification for local visitors, along the lines of a comparison between the Chinese and the Greek cultures as the two seminal high cultures from which civilization originated.

Passing over the gate in the company of an eagle, riders fly through the streets of a city at peace, seeing the inhabitants of Troy going about their daily lives. The architectural style is definitely classicizing: the 'Minoan' elements are left at the city gate, and what appears here are columns, classical statues of goddesses, and round temples. Some red columns are the only elements that still evoke Knossos, although their shape is not that of typical Minoan columns. Eventually the flight continues to a large palace: this uses the decorative language seen outside the attraction. The palace does not look like a fortress, but rather reuses the merlons and other architectural elements to represent a huge building, with a rather chaotic structure and no recognizable plan, characterized by the presence of many different floors and many columns – something not so far from the reconstructions of the Palace of Knossos. Flying into the palace, riders travel through time to the next scene, as they now witness the destruction of the city they just visited. Flying through the same streets, they now see fires, fear, and knights slaughtering people (as always, according to the principle that mythological deaths are de-semantized and therefore also representable within a theme park), riders are then eventually raised up to see the Trojan horse, which is also burning, demonstrating that the city has fallen. Once again, the visual reference to the Trojan horse, which is spinning a few metres from the riders, creates narrative consistency and consolidates the sense of immersion into Greek antiquity. The fire of the burning horse connects to the next scene: from these flames, the movie switches to other flames, which burn in the torch held by the Colossus of Rhodes. The golden Colossus is represented in a rather Olympic form, which reconnects to the rest of the themed area: he holds the torch in his right hand and keeps it high, while looking at it, more closely recalling the gesture of the lighting of the Olympic flame than a representation of the Sun god. Flying down along the statue and over some ships, riders then turn back to see the whole Colossus, the city behind him and impossibly high mountains covered in snow in the background, thus establishing a connection with traditional Chinese watercolour landscape painting, while at the same time relating Rhodes to another very famous image of Europe, the Alps.

The flight over part of the city soon dissolves to show the next historical stage: classical architecture is again present, in the form of a tholos and some columns, but as ruins. On a road that used to lead to the round temple, a group of people are walking in a very ordered way, evoking a ritual, with a figure leading them holding a torch, and following these, a second group of people cheer on the action. The ceremony is the lighting of the Olympic torch in Olympia, which has taken place every four years since Berlin 1936. The representation allows the riders, in connection with the Colossus, to establish a continuity between ancient Greece and China as constructed in the Olympic Games of 2008, to contextualize the ride within the broader theme of the entire region, as well as ultimately to develop a further inter-ride cross-reference with 'Happy World'. The ruined sanctuary is in an idyllic green landscape; this scene marks the connection between antiquity and modernity, and the last part of the video brings the riders to modern-day Greece as a touristic destination. In doing so, it demonstrates why one would wish to visit: the intact nature and the beautiful landscape, shown through rafting activities on small rivers and within canyons, before moving to a high waterfall leading down back to the sea, into which the riders plunge to see beautiful maritime fauna and some fellow tourists scuba diving. Even the sharks do not disturb – accompanied by dolphins, the riders can emerge once more in front of a beautiful island at sunset (the chronological structure of the video is reinforced through the symbolism of the times of the day). Alongside sailboats, motor boats and jet skis, the riders approach the island in the warm light of late afternoon, flying over the city made of small white houses, blue domes, a swimming pool, and windmills, before arriving to the Church of Panagia Platsani, Santorini, which they enter to the sound of bells chiming to see a wedding. The strong Eastern Asian fascination for Western wedding ceremonies has a particularly strong connection to Greece, and to Santorini. Here, an important 'wedding industry' has developed on the island (900 weddings in 2015),[46] which strongly appeals to the Chinese market. Chinese agencies organize wedding packages to Santorini, and trips to Santorini are often the prize for Chinese wedding competitions.[47] With a reference to this most famous reason for the Chinese public to travel to the Aegean, the trip is over. Riders fly out of the church to see that the sun has set, and that over Santorini there hangs a beautiful starry sky full of falling stars (so many that it actually seems more like a sci-fi battle scene).

The ride, even if it only opened with the rest of 'FantaSea' in 2014, is of central importance to the organization of the entire Greek theme, and to reinforce its significance. With a movie lasting seven minutes (and thus the possibility of a show every 15–20 minutes) and a huge capacity, as well as being appropriate for most visitors, it is a much-visited attraction. The movie connects the various meanings and aspects of ancient Greece which are known to the local public (the Olympic Games, mythology, tourism and the wedding industry), tying them to each other in a continuous intermedial dialogue with the other rides of the themed area, authoritatively establishing the meaning of Greece in the city of Beijing's popular culture: an ancient high culture, seminal to the development of the Western civilization, thus comparable to Chinese culture, a connection that is sealed and reinforced through the long-desired Olympic Games of 2008, which lie at the heart of the final ride we will analyse.

'Happy World'

'Happy World', opened in 2014, is the main attraction of the Greek area, together with 'Journey of Odyssey'. As previously explained, the Olympic Games of 2008 were the main reason for the level of interest and enthusiasm for the ancient Greek culture in Beijing during the years leading up to this important event. After the games, it was a prominent interest to memorialize the games and transform them into a central part of the city's cultural memory. But more importantly, the next Olympic challenge was in sight: in 2013, Beijing entered their bid to host the Winter Olympic Games of 2022, and in 2014 were revealed to be one of the three finalists. The bid was eventually successful in 2015, thus transforming Beijing into the first city in the world to host both the summer and winter Olympics and reinforcing the importance of the 'Olympic' identity to the self-representation of the Chinese capital.

The Olympic references are already clear when visitors stand before the attraction and see signs that refer to Olympia and to sports. The entrance to the ride is, as we have seen, a 'pictographic' Greek temple with four Ionic columns on the façade; the pediment is decorated with a cartoon-like wooden boat, with the image of an ant (the mascot of the park) on the bow and people from the different continents on board [Fig. 2]. This temple hosts a reconstruction of Phidias' statue from the Temple of Zeus at Olympia. It is already clear at the entrance how the Olympic Games are celebrated within the ride: they are represented as the most important sporting event in the world, a celebration of the international community and the peaceful interaction of all nations, which fits with the special Chinese focus on 'the world' as the most popular (cultural) theme in Chinese theme parks.[48] Coherent with this spirit, the water-based dark ride is strongly inspired (also in its name) by Disney's 'It's a Small World';[49] the music consists of sounds that evoke the various styles and traditions, with recurring variations on Beethoven's 'Ode to Joy', which is used to symbolize the peaceful cohabitation of nations.[50]

The large waiting area is decorated with wall paintings that evoke Greece and its history, from various periods: there are drawings inspired by Byzantine mosaics, alongside others reproducing Minoan frescoes and figures wearing the fustanella. The main focus, nonetheless, is on sports and activities that are physical and could be considered 'sporty': boxing, represented in forms that evoke Greek vase painting; female figures in the waves which invent ancient models for synchronized swimming; discus throwers and runners, but also the figures of judges; even St. George killing the dragon seems to be connected to riding sports. Interspersed among these figures are further images of ancient Greek inspiration, which consistently confirm the theming: Agamemnon's Mask, Athena, the Hagia Triada sarcophagus with the sacrifice scene. The sports–Olympics–Greece connection is clear: and so, after boarding the boats, visitors first encounter ancient Greece, and indeed ancient Greece during the Olympic Games. The representation is a mixture of ancient and modern themes: two priestesses stand next to a brazen tripod where the Olympic flame burns, while three columns of different heights form a podium, whose second place is occupied by a dog. Behind these we see classicizing architecture with columns and pediments and many people cheering, and in the background is a high mountain, Olympus, with a temple on its top. Ionic columns are everywhere, and in front of them stand soldiers (who actually evoke Roman legionaries, although this is a distinction that would be difficult to make even in the West). A centaur plays a horn to celebrate the winners, and the Olympic logo is clearly displayed with its five circles, making absolutely clear why Greece is celebrated and important. This Greek section abruptly turns into a celebration of the modern Olympics, with pictograms for the different sports and the flags of many modern countries.

The theme of the dark ride, and its journey around the world, is twofold. On the one side, the journey evokes the movements of the Olympic flame, from Greece (and symbolically from ancient Greece, as it is lit in Olympia), throughout the world – to China, which is represented in the last section of the ride (the Olympic torch relay of 2008 was the only one that set foot on all the inhabited continents). On the other side, the various continents and countries are represented through their most famous festivities and celebrations (such as the Oktoberfest, Christmas, and Valentine's Day, which is also a very important celebration and commercial occasion in China, Thanksgiving, the Brazilian Carnival, etc.). The Olympic Games, which open and close the ride, are thus represented as a worldwide occasion for celebration. The representation of the world in this form also allows us to repeatedly jump back and forth in time: while the United States, with their typical festivities, are clearly set in the 'Wild West'; there is also a representation of ancient Egypt, with pyramids, hieroglyphs, Anubis, and Caesar and Cleopatra (the representation of Cleopatra as Egyptian, in ways similar to those of the pharaonic times, is very present in popular culture worldwide),[51] evoking the annual Nile river flooding festival. For China, at the end of the journey, local festivities are represented, such as the Lantern Festival and the Chinese New Year, ending with a representation of monuments and famous buildings from the entire country, summarizing in one picture the idea of unity through diversity of the People's Republic. It ends with a scene of fireworks, which recalls the opening ceremonies of the Olympic Games, when the torch reaches its destination.

'Happy World' is a summary of *Happy Valley*'s approach to ancient Greece: sport constitutes the most important reason for ancient Greece to be perceived as relevant to the Chinese public of the twenty-first century, via the connection established through the Olympic Games in Beijing. From this, a parallel between China and Greece is established, one that creates an implicit equivalence between the two 'high cultures' of antiquity, both perceived as seminal cradles for the modern cultures of the West and the East. In *Happy Valley*, Greece is not represented as 'the ancestor' of the culture of reference, of its mentality and political forms, as in Europe, but as a double alterity, historically and geographically, which is nonetheless perceived as being relevant to the entire world history and as being 'connected' to China and its history. If classical mythology still represents the most important repertoire of stories and narratives, due also to their adventurous nature, and the idea of Greece as a tourist destination is present, it is undoubtedly the Olympic side which is prominent here, and which makes a representation of ancient Greece meaningful.

E-Da, Kaohsiung, Republic of China

E-Da World

E-Da is a resort built just outside the city of Kaohsiung in the Republic of China (Taiwan). This resort is significant for a number of reasons: first, it is a perfect demonstration of the trend, as highlighted in scholarship on Asia, 'of integrating theme parks, casinos, retail spaces and museums into single developments', deriving from 'a strategy for unifying a particular space and creating it as a 'destination', where it was not intended'.[52] *E-Da World*, even if it has not (yet) been completely realized, was planned to be (and is) a huge mixed-use complex, including a theme park with museum, hotels, an exhibition centre, an outlet mall, residential areas, a space for an open market, an international school and a University, a golf range, a hospital and residences for elderly people. As the brochure of the resort proudly states, 'E-DA World is currently Taiwan's largest and most comprehensive landmark complex of recreational, tourism, shopping and entertainment facilities'.

In this sense, *E-Da* is a hyperbolic amplification of the 'mimetic utopias' identified by Campanella: it follows the principle of the *Vecchio Plazza* in Beijing but expands it to the creation of a parallel city. *E-Da* also shares the general theme with *Vecchio Plazza*: Europe. At the beginning of the twenty-first century, it was already noted that the Taiwanese middle classes (one of the target publics of the resort, those who are more reasonably expected to buy flats and villas within the residential area) have an ever-growing interest in European historical culture, partially as a consequence of the growing levels of tourism to Europe.[53] This explains not only the presence of Greece, again in both the forms of antiquity and of the tourist destination, but also the theming of the other parts of the resort. It is impossible to provide here, for reasons of space, a complete overview of all the sections of *E-Da World* and their theming; it will be sufficient to highlight that the 'Fashion Street' is inspired by Paris, and that the 'Outlet Mall' has a different theming for each section, including a replica of the Moor Fountain of Piazza Navona in Rome, set among huge columns of pink marble that support a ceiling painted as a blue, slightly cloudy sky. The first floor is decorated with balconies which also allude to Italian architecture.

This interest in historical Europe also expanded to the culturally immersive environments dedicated to local history and culture: the *Formosan Aboriginal Culture Village*,[54] for example, includes a 'European Palace Garden'. Such local cultural theme parks are the other main feature of the Taiwanese themed environment landscapes. This is no surprise, as Taiwanese national identity and cultural identity are highly contested, a consequence of the birth of today's Republic in 1949 when Chiang Kai-shek moved to the island while fleeing the Maoist revolution. Following the democratization processes that began in the 1980s, Kai-shek's Kuomintang is still one of the most important political parties in the Republic of China.[55] The KMT stands for a 'natural' belonging of Taiwan to China, and the existence of a strong relationship between the island and mainland China since prehistory ('one-China policy');⁵⁶ the sticking point is that according to this ideology, thanks to Kai-shek and the foundation of the Republic of China, only Taiwan preserved the true, authentic Chinese identity, while in the People's Republic it has been destroyed by the Cultural Revolution. This position is broadly held, even if 'it was, ironically, only after Taiwan was ceded to Japan after the Sino-Japanese war of 1894–95 that the island was considered an essential part of China'.⁵⁷ Taiwan remained under Japanese control until the Second World War, becoming part of the Republic of China for five years before Chang Kai-shek's flight, during which the nationalistic argument for a 'restitution' of Taiwan to China by the defeated Japanese and the 'joy' of the Taiwanese to rejoin their countrymen became fully developed.⁵⁸

The other side of the local political spectrum, the Democratic Progressive Party, also pursues a nationalistic agenda, but one based on a specifically Taiwanese identity, independent of China, thus re-evaluating the local indigenous cultures and their languages against a domination by Chinese language, culture and ethnicity. This side generally favours the theory that Taiwan was the place from which all Austronesian peoples originated, thus meaning that the aboriginal people were of Taiwanese origin, contrary to theories of their migration from China (and that of their migration from the South, from Indonesia).⁵⁹ This political contestation has often manifested itself in the creation of immersive and themed environments which, through strategies of living history, sometimes aim to foster these competing visions of national identities, as can be seen in the *Taiwan Folk Village*, which strongly supports Kuomintang's politics of identity, or in the *Aboriginal Village*.⁶⁰

Before investigating the specific political aspects of *E-Da*, which become particularly visible in the 'Taiwan Story House', it is necessary to linger a little more on the general structure of the resort. Construction started in March 2006, with festive ceremonies and the presence of local authorities.⁶¹ The E-Da Development Co. was created for construction, founded and chaired by Lin I-Shou, an important magnate of the Taiwanese steel industry who was also chairman of E United Group, an industrial giant created from the Yieh United Group in 2003.⁶² Different sections opened at various different times, with the theme park becoming operative in 2010. A press statement released on the occasion insisted on the European character of the enterprise, making clear that visitors to *E-Da* 'are welcome to feel European holiday emotions without going abroad'.⁶³ These were years when the discussion over Taiwan's identity and ethnicity was still very much ongoing: Ma Ying-jeou (KMT), president of the republic between 2008 and 2016, is a firm supporter of the idea that Taiwan belongs to China.[64]

The mascot of the resort is a rhino – also the mascot of E United Group – which in 2012 also became the mascot of the baseball team *E-Da Rhinos*, the new name given to the Sinon Bulls after they were purchased by E United (the group sold the team at the end of 2016, and since 2017 it has been called the Fubon Guardians).[65] The rhino, called Dae, wears different clothes in different parts of the park, highlighting the specific theming. In the outlet, for instance, it appears in various European costumes: as Napoleon, in the uniform of the Queen's Guard, or in an elegant suit representing Italy. In the Greek version, it is sometimes represented as Poseidon. The rhino is accompanied by four friends, who are not as 'versatile': these are present everywhere in the resort and make it clear that Greece is one of the dominant and overarching themes within the general European theming of the entire resort. They are a pelican (Dian Dian), traditionally connected to the Greek islands and particularly to Mykonos (although this pelican, as the park flyer explains, was born on Santorini); a rather crazed-looking donkey named Donkey (another animal that is traditionally connected to Greece – the flyer highlights that the Greeks traditionally use donkeys for transportation; Donkey is represented with a sword among flames, and a carrot belt which resembles the explosive belts of terrorists, either as Ares or Hades); and lastly two ancient gods, Apollo (as the Sun god) and Diana. The use of the Latin name rather than the Greek should not surprise: the goddess, here represented mostly as goddess of the moon, is probably better known under this shorter and easier name, and the general lack of differentiation between Greek and Roman antiquity makes this naming entirely unproblematic.[66] Greece is the main *Leitmotif* recognizable in most sections of *E-Da World*: the 'Flea Market' square is enclosed by a neoclassical structure hosting golden reproductions of ancient Greek sculptures in its niches: the *Apoxyomenos*, the Capitoline Venus, Aristogeiton from the sculptural pairing with Harmodios, the Aphrodite of Knidos, the Doryphoros (with a different head), and a Venus de Milo with arms. While the *E-Da Royal Hotel* is not themed to Greece, its pool is, with Doric columns, rotundas and (neo)classicizing architecture. Next to it, a maxi screen is framed by four columns (two on each side) and a pediment, and it broadcasts cartoons of the five *E-Da* mascots, all set in ancient Greece. Generally the plot is always the same: Da-E and friends find funny ways to ruin the plans of the Trojans (portrayed as evil) – in fact, they are the heroes within the Trojan horse![67] Greece has a rather varied set of reasons for playing this role: it is a popular touristic destination, especially among the younger generation and middle to upper classes and is connected to ideas of history, nature and romance. Greek mythology (more than history) provides a set of narratives which are rather well-known in Taiwan, partially through the popularity of American movies such as *Clash of the Titans* or *300*; last but not least, ancient Greek culture is not only a part of the European history celebrated in general in *E-Da World*, but – in a widespread and very simplified fashion – can also be seen as the seminal origin of European culture and, as in Beijing, can run in parallel to Chinese culture for Eastern Asia.

'Taiwan Story House'

Visitors who arrive at the theme park from the resort can access it directly from the 'Outlet Mall' – through an internal passage, visitors get to the ticket booths and the ticket control, located indoor at one extremity of the mall. But visitors who arrive from outside, from the parking lots and the bus stops, must enter a small building surmounted by a huge rhino. From its upper floor they can then walk over a pedestrian bridge to the other side of the road, where another entrance to the park is located (for those who already have a ticket and groups), or from where they can join the other visitors at the main entrance. The building that most visitors thus have to pass through is a small museum, the 'Taiwan Story House'. This is exemplary of the presence of museums within theme parks, which aim to combine educational initiatives with entertainment, a particularly popular combination in Asia.[68] It is here that the political agenda behind *E-Da* becomes visible, and that the choice of classical Greece gets an explanation. Entering the building, visitors are (surprisingly, given the name of the museum) confronted with rooms explaining the geography of today's Republic of Greece – its statistics, pictures of its most famous monuments and a collection of souvenirs, hinting at the role of Greece as a tourist destination. The souvenirs gathered here show once again that there is no clear differentiation of Greece from other European countries: the 'Mediterranean' atmosphere is what counts, and thus it is not problematic to include souvenirs from Sardinia or other Italian destinations in the collection. Children can test themselves on what they have learned about the European nation with a Q&A game before also learning, accompanied by the five mascots, about ancient Greek culture, its gods and goddesses and mythological figures; the Western zodiac with its 12 signs is also present in this explanation of classical Greek culture. The following steps bring visitors closer to ancient Greece through another recurring topic: sports. While the explanatory signs concentrate on the Olympic Games while presenting a series of Olympic sports, the rooms also celebrate (or at least they did until March 2017) the baseball team formerly owned by the same company operating the park. The *E-Da Rhinos* thus appear as the true heirs of the Greek sporting spirit, and a first connection between ancient Greece and Taiwan is established.

At this point, visitors move from the ground floor to the first floor, which is entirely dedicated to the history of Taiwan. The presence of the mascots (especially Apollo and Diana) in Chinese traditional costume hints at the underlying idea: Greece and China as the two seminal high cultures from which Western and Eastern civilizations developed. The 'Taiwan Story' represented here has no space for indigenous Taiwanese cultures and is instead a celebration of the Chinese culture on the island, sticking to the Kuomintang's idea that the true Chinese culture, destroyed by the People's Republic on the continent, has only been preserved on Taiwan. A strong insistence on 'vintage Taiwan', for example through pictures of old Taipei and records of Taiwanese singers, nostalgically evokes the time of the one-party rule before the democratization of the 1980s. The other explicitly national/nationalistic element of the theme park, the ride 'Taiwan Formosa' located in the 'Trojan Castle' (see below), is – not by chance – a flight motion simulator that showcases the beauty of the country and insists on natural elements and modern aspects, such as Taipei 101, while carefully avoiding aboriginal heritage. On the contrary, there is a clear display of the Grand Hotel Taipei, a Chinese palace-style hotel that was planned by Chiang Kai-Shek in 1952 and which replaced a Shinto temple from the time of the Japanese rule.[69] The insistence on topics which were portrayed in relation to Greece on the ground floor, for instance religion and religious architecture, as well as the changing of the mascots' clothes, serve to visualize the parallelization of Chinese and Greek cultural achievements until the end of the visit. This end is marked by a festoon holding a series of meaningful flags: the flag of the Republic of China, the flag of the Kuomintang, and a blue flag with a representation of Greater China as conceived by the Kuomintang (including Mongolia, whose independence, proclaimed in 1911, had never been recognized by Chiang Kai-Shek). After this extremely clear political statement, the visitors (in particular groups, and thus also school classes) can cross the pedestrian bridge and arrive at the entrance of the theme park.

E-Da Theme Park

As is proudly stated by *E-Da* in their brochure, the theme park in the resort is 'the only Greek-themed park in Taiwan'.[70] The interest of the Taiwanese and Chinese middle and upper classes for Europe, the growing touristic offerings connected with Greece, as well as the ideological underpinnings of a similarity between Chinese and Greek cultures, all serve to explain this choice. The main entrance area, reached from the 'Outlet Mall', is a good summary of all the elements present in the park: populated by park workers dressed in ancient costumes, this indoor entrance area is decorated with wooden elements and Mediterranean plants. The dominant colours are blue and white; on the walls are pictures of the Aegean islands, particularly Santorini, and everywhere are souvenirs from Greece (dishes painted with Greek landscapes, or flip-flops displaying Santorini and the Aegean). Antiquity is not absent, as two large vases containing plants are decorated with reproductions of ancient paintings; curiously, one does not reproduce vase paintings, but frescoes, similar to the Ladies in Blue from Knossos. The second is a variation of the Athena from the Panathenaic amphora by the Marsyas Painter, housed in the Harvard Art Museum; the vase (and therefore the background of the picture) is white, and the crest on the goddess' helmet has been tinted blue, to better fit into the colour scheme of the area.

After the ticket control, visitors move to the first indoor area of the park. Given the climate of Taiwan and its heavy seasonal rains, combined with a wish to keep the park open all year round, *E-Da Theme Park* is divided into three themed areas, each of which is subdivided into an indoor and an outdoor section. During the typhoon season, for example, or when it is very hot, it is possible to spend the entire day at the theme park only in the indoor sections, which are connected by a monorail train. This structure has strong implications for the theming politics: the outdoor areas are the most consistently themed, as larger architectural endeavours can be better displayed and larger rides can be constructed with a stronger focus on the Greek theme. Meanwhile, the indoor areas are characterized by smaller flat rides and fairground attractions, often for children, generally with a low level of theming beyond the constant presence of the five park mascots. The three areas correspond to the three main 'topics' connected with classical Greece, which we have identified all over the world: the first and smallest area, 'Acropolis', evokes the culture of the classical polis; the second, 'Santorini', relates to the touristic Aegean Greece; the final one, 'Trojan Castle', reconnects to the world of mythology, and its visualization through Bronze Age forms.

The three areas are built in a sequence: the entrance (and exit) is from 'Acropolis', from which the path guides visitors through 'Santorini' and then up to 'Trojan Castle'. This easy map, which corresponds to the relatively small dimensions of the park (albeit greatly increased by the many-storeyed buildings of the indoor areas) generates one main street, the 'Greek Avenue', connecting the three outdoor sections. In each section, the street broadens to form a square – the 'Acropolis Plaza', the 'Volcano Plaza' in 'Santorini', and finally at the very end of the street, the largest, 'Trojan Plaza', unmistakably decorated with a huge Trojan horse [Fig. 20]. The wooden horse, one of the main symbols of the park, wears a mask and other parts of a horse's armour; the hooves also appear to be metallic, and are decorated by round motifs that recall wheels. This is both an allusion to the wheels on which the Trojan horse was moved and an evocation of steampunk aesthetics. The practice of barding, and particularly the use of metal chanfrons, are attested in classical antiquity (as in the case of the cataphracts), although these are mostly associated with the European Middle Ages. Western history appears, here too, at times conflated into a homogenous block. More interestingly, barding in metal, and especially the use of lamellar in horse armour, was also widely practised in medieval China. *E-Da*'s horse can therefore be reasonably argued to represent the Trojan horse as a war horse that is highly recognizable to a Chinese public, thus once again stressing the connection between China and Greece as the two 'oldest' and 'seminal' cultures.

The main street and the Trojan square host the park's parade each day at 2.00 pm, which during our visit was called 'Return of Hades' and began with a dance show on the 'Trojan Plaza'. There is essentially no connection between

Fig. 20 Trojan Horse on the 'Trojan Plaza', *E-Da Theme Park*, Kaohsiung, Taiwan © Ralf Lüchau.

what happens in the show and the classical Hades: the name is here synonymous with 'Evil', or the 'Devil', in a way that mixes pagan and Christian conceptions of the afterlife, but which also references the most famous Hades-as-a-wrongdoer, that of Disney's *Hercules*. Hades has a chest from which the forces of evil appear in a recollection of Pandora's box (the Mandarin title of the show is 'Pluto's Treasure Chest'). This chest is placed on a stage that has the form of a Greek temple, to which stairs lead flanked by Corinthian columns, while inside the temple are flames forming a diabolical mask. In the show, an 'army of good', led by the rhino Da-E (the group look like sci-fi cosmic warriors) fights alongside Eros against an 'army of evil', which is led by a black samurai-like devil and composed of a number of snake-girls and dragon-boys, as well as two black figures in small wooden boats, evoking Charon. After the final victory of the good guys (and some pictures with the public), the performers parade from the 'Trojan Plaza' along the 'Greek Avenue' down to the 'Acropolis'.

'Acropolis'

Most shows, however, take place in the 'Acropolis' area, a large part of which is taken up by the 'E-Da Royal Theater', which is accessible from both within and outside the park (as it also hosts shows unconnected with the park's activity). With a capacity of 1810 seats, the theatre is built entirely in a neoclassical style, which does not clash, in terms of local sensibilities, with the ancient theming of the park – neoclassicism is additionally a widespread architectural style in Taiwan, that has experienced an intense revival since the 1990s, especially in the construction of luxurious apartments and hotels.[71] In this way, the theatre can adopt a double purpose – on the one hand, ancient Greece and its role in the development of theatre in general, and on the other the European theatres of the nineteenth and early twentieth centuries and the society that used to gather there, playing thus with the widespread fascination among Taiwanese middle and upper classes for European culture.[72] The ceiling is decorated with the twelve signs of the Western zodiac, and the connection to ancient Greece is made explicit in the resort's brochure: 'the 20-meter-high, horoscope-inspired ceiling of the auditorium is accentuated by ingenious lighting to evoke the illusion of gazing up at the starry sky depicted in Greek mythology'.[73] Greek mythology is at the centre of the shows staged here; this was certainly the case during our visit, particularly in the show 'Journey of Hero'. Beginning with a scenography inspired by the Athenian Acropolis, but with the Parthenon displaced to be more visible at the front (and curiously represented in bright colours), a group of dancers in 'ancient Greek' costumes move while holding spears; three of them kill the main performer, the hero, who thus begins his (or rather his soul's) 'journey' of acrobatic performances through green valleys and waterfalls. With a change of scenery, the hero finds himself once again in a 'Greek' or rather 'ancient' city, surrounded by an army of warriors; on the screen in the background are scenes of battle and blood, until a huge fire makes us understand that we are now moving within Hades/Hell (following the typical mixing we have already encountered), dominated by a monster with long teeth and very long horns, which appears to be a Minotaur paying homage to Chinese demons. Through further acrobatic movements, the hero frees a friend, who is chained within a sort of cube. At this point, and against images of the sky, a group of four girls enter and perform acrobatic movements, the most notable of which are made while suspended from the ceiling. During these scenes, the background shows a series of mythological monsters: Cerberus, Medusa (as represented in the movie *Clash of the Titans*), the Minotaur, a kouros with huge wings, a centaur and a gryphon. The final scene shows the hero, his friend and the principal female character return to a Greek city, recognizable from its hexastyle temple and two white statues of men wearing a sort of chiton. In the city, dancing breaks out to celebrate their arrival and, rather anachronistically, so do fireworks. While the fireworks can again insist on the parallel between China and Greece, as they are a celebrated Chinese invention and have been used in China since the seventh century to scare evil spirits, the show is generally an occasion for acrobatic performances that are loosely tied together by referencing a series of different and disconnected Greek myths. The concept of a journey could refer Odysseus, although this is a journey into the afterlife, which would apply more to Heracles and yet, the only reference to his twelve labours is the brief appearance of Cerberus. It is therefore useless to search for a specific referent, beyond the general idea that Greek mythology contains stories of heroism and deliverance and the appeal provided by mythological references, even if they are mixed up in such way (and contaminated with representations of Christian Hell).

The general mixture of different 'Western' elements is visible in other parts of the Acropolis area, particularly on the second floor of the indoor area, which is a sequence of shops leading to the monorail station. Next to the station is a golden statue of the rhino Da-E as the Sun god. Wearing a crown of rays and holding a lyre in his left hand and a torch in the right, the rhino stands on top of a column in the centre of a fountain. While the inspiration may have been the Colossus of Rhodes, the lyre could evoke both Apollo (present in the park in the form of another mascot) and even more strongly the emperor Nero, whose colossal statue as the Sun god was built in Rome and gave the name to the Colosseum. Again, there is probably a plurality of models and inspirations: the combination of Greek and Roman should not surprise, nor should the presence of Nero, who is not as well known in local (and more generally Eastern Asian) cultural memory as a tyrant and autocrat as he is in the Western world. The rest of the floor has decorations that look more neoclassical than ancient (such as columns decorated with gold), but also contains references to the Western Middle Ages. A shop directly next to the monorail, the 'Mystical Corner', clearly evokes European medieval castle architecture, and the association with magic and mysticism also connects much more with the imaginary of the Middle Ages than with that of classical antiquity (because of this connection, the shop has Halloween motifs all year round). Just next to the shop is a small café where visitors can sit at tables within a space arranged with trompe l'oeil to look like France, as if they were sitting in front of the Café de Paris in Place du Tertre, in Montmartre. Europe is Europe, and this holds true in spite of the name of the café, 'Greek Wedding Cafés' (European weddings, and particularly Greek ones, are a big theme within *E-Da*).

The rest of this themed area, the smallest, essentially serves to control the flux of visitors between the entrance, the indoor and outdoor areas, and the monorails; it is thus loosely themed. The outdoor section consists of only one ride, the 'Booster', a pendulum ride from Fabbri. The model itself is called booster,[74] and the lack of any effort to rename the ride corresponds to the lack of any kind of theming applied to it. It is nonetheless important to highlight that this a common rule in *E-Da*: rides are called by the English name of their mechanical device. The first floor of the indoor area contains two further attractions which are not directly themed to ancient Greece: a 4D movie theatre, which during our visit showed a sort of *Jurassic Park*-like movie in which riders drove with a jeep among dinosaurs; and a smaller performance area, where the 'Water Tamer' show takes place, a dance show with one dancer and water jets that move rhythmically. The only theming is on the ceiling of the entire floor of the building: another representation of the zodiac.

'Santorini'

There is little space for antiquity in the second themed area of the park, which focuses on the touristic aspects of Aegean Greece. The area, as its name suggests, seeks to replicate one of the most famous tourist destinations in the Eastern Mediterranean and provide visitors with the atmosphere of the island, or rather its towns. One potential reference to antiquity could be the insistence on the volcanic nature of Santorini: not only is the square here the 'Volcano Plaza', but a huge volcano also rises behind the buildings. This is not an imitation of Santorini's actual volcano, which consists of a huge caldera mostly under water, but is instead what appears to be a reference to the history of the island and its most famous eruption, that of the sixteenth century BCE, which has at various times been connected to the end of the Minoan culture and/or the Platonic myth of Atlantis. Apart from three rides located at the edge of the area, directly at the border with the 'Trojan Castle' (which are analysed below), the presence of antiquity is otherwise limited here to only the representation of ruins, that is, antiquity as perceived today when touring Greece. In the indoor area in particular, there are broken columns and ancient ruined elements; the many pictures on the wall represent Santorini and its touristic attractions (including beaches), but also archaeological areas, even those with no connection to the island (the Acropolis of Athens appears quite prominently on the second floor). Even the Donkey character is represented in this area wearing what appears to be the uniform of the Evzones, the most recognizable modern Greek army uniform.

The larger part of the themed area is made up of a group of buildings, hosting a three-storeyed indoor area, but also characterized by streets and passages that allow visitors to move between the different levels outdoor. As is to be expected, the buildings are replicas of famous constructions on Santorini, such as the windmill of Oia, next to which there is a bell tower that appears to be a simplified version (with brighter colours) of that of the Catholic Cathedral in Fira, the typical white and blue houses, but also the yellow and orange houses that belong to the landscape of Santorini's main centre. Finally, at the top of the 'village' which subsumes all the towns of the Greek islands, there is the obvious white chapel with a blue dome, imitating just the central upper part of the Ekklisia Panagia Platsani of Oia (whose iconic bell tower is also present, but disconnected from the church). Considering what we have already noted concerning the Santorini wedding industry (and the pre-eminence of mainland Chinese visitors in the park), it will come as no surprise to learn that this chapel is used for weddings – the organization of 'Greek weddings' within the park is indeed an important factor at *E-Da*, as advertised through posters and flyers throughout the resort.

This section of the park in general appears to have the aim of creating a perfect hyperreality, blurring the boundaries between 'Santorini' and Santorini to the extreme. This is particularly evident in the shops located in the indoor area, which sell *E-Da* merchandising, but which is not directly and immediately identifiable as such (for example, a postcard representing the wooden horse of *E-Da* is marked with the name 'Santorini') and, more significantly, souvenirs identical to those that could be bought on Santorini: fridge magnets, purses, tee-shirts and further merchandising marked with the words Greece or Santorini, produced in Taiwan for shipment to and sale in Greece. These items are identical to those that actual tourists to Greece would bring back from there, which also serves to enhance the immersion and hyperreal authenticity of the experience after leaving the park when the magnet displayed on the fridge at home means your friends won't know whether you travelled to Greece, or to *E-Da*.

This is likely why this section of the park is much more carefully themed, avoiding the 'generic Western' theming that we encountered in 'Acropolis'. Only a painted egg with a hat and ears, perhaps connected to Easter, which is placed on the street in front of a Santorini building appears to be the exception, and while the food served in the local restaurants is definitely not Greek, the decoration is carefully Mediterranean: outside terraces, pergolas, blue and white colours, as in the 'Oia Café', which has a ceiling covered with flags from all over the world – perhaps a further reference to the Olympic Games. Even the store 'Candy Kingdom', decorated with huge candies and bright colours, tries to follow the theming, with candy windmills; more generally, sections such as this one which do not really fit with the Santorini theme are identifiable, set apart, and obviously 'unreal'. This also applies to the only attraction in the indoor area, '5D Ship of Souls', a walkthrough haunted house with a pirate theme, which is therefore completely separated from the main theme. Indeed, the hyperreal Santorini is most effective outdoors, in spite of the important role of the shops. Great care has been taken in creating the village, and for this reason it hosts no rides, which would disturb this immersive environment. The four main rides of the area (and probably the entire park) are located behind the village and the volcano, at the border with the 'Trojan Castle'. One of them, 'Pirate Ship', has little to do with pirates (even if the ride's sign does adopt a skeleton and swords motif); the reason for the name is, as already noted, the ride's genre, which in English is called a pirate ship. The level of theming is otherwise low, although the ship itself hints at the representation of an ancient warship; the typical eyes on the prow are missing, but its shape, and the decoration of the sides with holes for oars, appears to be inspired by ancient galleys.[75]

Rather unsurprisingly, 'Flume Ride' – which stands alongside the 'Pirate Ship' and allows riders to sail just next to it – is a flume ride, again with a low level of theming.[76] The very few elements that do appear still attempt to establish a connection between Greek mythology and the Chinese visual language. In this sense, the sign for the ride is an angry, bearded Poseidon holding a trident; his menace is what awaits the riders – a plunge. Yet the main visual element, beyond certain marine themes, is a huge three-headed dragon. It is hard to know if this represents a sea monster or is in some way evocative of Scylla and Charybdis, or of the Hydra (or even of Cerberus, given the three heads?); its iconography is derived purely from Chinese dragon iconography. However, Chinese dragons have only one head and are a positive symbol, not menacing creatures; indeed, it is hard to tell whether this dragon is menacing us or simply there to decorate the ride. The ambiguity is likely intentional, as it is functional to this mixture of languages, which is even more explicit in the ride opposite.

This is a big air coaster ('Big Air'), realized as a custom design for *E-Da* by Vekoma, which opened around half a year later than the park itself, in 2010.[77] The theming here is provided by two sculptures that stand next to the coaster track, representing Odysseus and the Cyclops [Fig. 21]. The statue of Odysseus, a little cracked to represent its age, shows a rather traditional Greek hero, holding his round shield and his sword, with an Illyrian helmet and sandals; however, Polyphemus again represents a fusion of the West and the East, through an iconography that is incompatible with his Western representations: the helmet with four spikes at the base, the sword behind the back and the hilt with four spikes all evoke a ninja iconography, and thus Japanese. Considering the Japanese domination of Taiwan and the political orientation of the park, it is not so surprising to see Japanese iconography in the representation of the evil Cyclops, who menaces the hero. Odysseus is also the main protagonist of the last ride of this area. As its entrance is just in front of 'Big Air', the statue of the Greek hero actually functions as a marker and a theming element for both of them. Another ride with a self-evident name, 'Splash Battle', has a built entrance representing the forms of a Minoan palace in grey, thus anticipating and smoothing the passage to the 'Trojan Castle', which is visible just behind it. The building is also accessible from one side, where it hosts a shop and bar ('Apollo Palace'), whose entrance is marked by a snake that surmounts the door, two golden soldiers with Corinthian helmets, as well as drawings of the mascots Apollo and Diana. Apollo is here meant as the Sun god, as the theming is entirely solar, including sunflowers and representations of the sun chariot.

The queuing area makes it clear what the ride is about, as the walls are decorated with comic-like representations of the adventures of Odysseus: the Olympus as a temple atop the clouds; the Sirens; the Cyclops throwing rocks at Odysseus' boat; Scylla and Charybdis; sailing within a deep and scary cavern, likely representing the *Nekyia*. The ride vehicles are shaped like small ancient galleys and travel

Fig. 21 The Cyclops from 'Big Air', *E-Da Theme Park*, Kaohsiung, Taiwan © Ralf Lüchau.

through columns and ruined classical architecture, past shipwrecks and a series of monsters evoking Odysseus' adventures, or adventures from Greek mythology that are generally connected to the seas. Indeed, the large octopus stretching its tentacles towards the boats has little to do with Odysseus, nor the Medusa, which is represented by the same iconography as in the movie *Clash of the Titans* (1981). A volcano with an evil face also seems out of place in the *Odyssey*, while the army of zombies is rather evocative of Jason's battle with the army raised from the earth. A huge dragon head hanging from the wall of the entrance building, which is visible at all times from the ride, is again strongly tied to the Chinese iconographical tradition. Only the huge Poseidon, accompanied by dolphins and his quadriga of water-blue horses, reconnects riders with the Odyssean tradition.

'Trojan Castle'

'Trojan Castle' is the biggest area of the park and, in keeping with the tradition of calling things clearly by their names, it is exactly that: a building in the shape of a fortress, characterized by all the architectonical elements that can be identified as Minoan, connected here – as everywhere else in the world – with the age of myth and heroes. Only the metopes decorating the spaces between the big red columns, which alternate between displaying Athenas and owls, fail to fit it, instead belonging to the archaic period in Athens. Beyond the 'Trojan Plaza' (whose floor decoration features, unsurprisingly, the zodiac), this area is only developed indoors (on five floors) and on the roof of the castle, which hosts a restaurant, a wild mouse coaster, a chain swing ride and a samba tower by Zamperla. Within the castle, as in the other indoor areas, the theming is very light: the red columns can be found on every single floor; there are further metopes representing side portraits, at times derived from ancient coins (as with the owls and the Athenas), and the walls are sometimes decorated with classical columns, reproductions of ancient ruins, statues recalling ancient figures, small details (a bronze relief replicating the Ladies in Blue) and ornamental motifs such as palmettes. Again, these are intermingled with iconographies and symbols from Chinese traditions, such as dragons, which appear frequently. This theming is not consistently applied to the rides (mostly flat rides), which show an amazing plethora of styles and themes, each specific to an individual ride, from a barn to the fire brigade. The main ride of the area, 'Dark Ride', is a junior coaster themed to hidden resources and wealth (mines, precious stones) and reaching the centre of the earth (Jules Verne may have been the source of inspiration here) travelling through the internal court of the Trojan Castle, where riders can cross gazes with other visitors. The ceiling of this internal court, made of steel and glass, appears to be tied in to the steampunk atmosphere of this main ride, which is prominently represented by the form of a giant drilling machine, alongside which are the coaster tracks. Only a few individual rides show an ancient theme, as in the case of the chain swing ride decorated with painted reproductions from Greece: ancient and modern, touristic and historical, from the Ladies in Blue, the Parthenon and the Prince of the Lilies to the church of Panagia Paraportiani on Mykonos, through to representations of a sunset on the (Mediterranean) sea.

Restaurants and shops, for which the application of ancient or neoclassical motifs is easier and cheaper, at times have stronger references to the theme of the park. The 'Troy Restaurant' is decorated with bronze lamps, paintings evoking the conquest of Troy and reproductions of ancient frescoes – yet, curiously, Egyptian and Etruscan ones (even if their addition here would be understandable, as what is reproduced is the famous fresco from Tarquinia representing Achilles ambushing Troilus). The 'Ice World' bar on the ground floor is hosted by an ancient warship with eyes on the prow; an ancient warship in comic style is also the centrepiece of the shop 'Da-E's Home', right next to a Trojan horse. The merlons, however, present in connection with the idea of the 'Trojan Castle', mean the walls of the shop are decorated with forms connected to medieval castles, for instance a walkway on the walls, behind the merlons. A medieval castle also decorates the wall of the local monorail station. Other restaurants and shops, as in 'Acropolis', aim instead to produce and offer a more generic European atmosphere, as is the case with the 'Love Pea Café', which offers pastries and cake within a central European environment. Particularly interesting is a wall decoration on the second floor: what is represented is a stereotypical ancient temple, with six Doric columns on the front. But the central two columns are surmounted by a *quadriga* which is unmistakably the one from Berlin's Brandenburg Gate: classical and neoclassical are again conflated. The gaze towards Athens and Santorini, in Kaohsiung as in Beijing, is very different from the gaze from Europe or from the United States, representing ancient Greek culture, its achievements and its mythology as an experience of pure exoticism and alterity. Even the possibility of underlining parallels and similarities between ancient Greece and ancient China does not reduce this component of otherness: it is always two traditions, expressed in the most symbolic way by the various 'horoscopes' (which explains the success of the zodiac as a symbol of ancient Greece). And yet the two cultures do find points in common that can interact and form a dialogue with the intention of universal understanding: these occur mostly through sports, whether the Olympic Games in Beijing or the *E-Da Rhinos* in Taiwan.

6

Ancient Greece in France: The World of a Gallic Warrior

Re-mediatization and the theme park

This last chapter takes us back to Europe, more precisely to France, a country in whose cultural memory ancient Greece is strongly present, in ways not entirely dissimilar to Germany and Spain. Yet this chapter appears last because the park to be investigated is very different in nature to those analysed thus far. No representation of history is 'direct' (as has been stressed many times) and every visualization of ancient Greece derives from previous forms of reception and representation in a 'reception chain', which continuously develops and influences future forms of representation of the past; however, we have until now explored parks that are themed to 'Ancient Greece'. They therefore worked with the best-known, most widespread and most stereotypical images for their target audience. The park presented in this chapter works in an entirely different way: its theme is not ancient Greece, nor historical cultures, but the world of the Gallic warrior Astérix, as (re)presented and made famous by the comics first drawn by Goscinny and Uderzo, which since their creation in 1959 have enjoyed incredible popularity throughout the world. What happens here is a form of re-mediatization, which translates a world created first in comics, then into animated movies, and into a theme park (this same world has subsequently been re-mediatized in motion pictures, too). The references are therefore somewhat narrowed down: ancient Greece in *Parc Astérix* is ancient Greece as it has been represented in the Astérix comics and animated movies. As Astérix itself has been defined as a contemporary myth, especially because of its qualities as a foundational, atemporal and collective narrative,[1] the representations in *Parc Astérix* are all of a mythological nature; where Greek mythology is represented, it is not as Greek mythology, but as a component of the Astérix mythology.[2] What is not directly provided in the comic albums can still be subsumed in this mythical universe and thus be represented, grasping for the widespread knowledge and presence of Greece in

French cultural memory (most park visitors are French); however, this must also be mediated by and translated into the specific visual language of the Astérix world, as well as its specific forms of humorous and anachronistic representations of antiquity. The recognizability is therefore above all the recognizability of the Astérix style, and through it that of symbols and themes from classical antiquity. The presence of Greece in French culture and cultural memory is therefore important here, just as it has been in the other nations and parks, and will be discussed in the first paragraph; yet it is even more important (in a second stage) to understand what images of Greece are available in the Astérix comics and movies to serve as a model, and what can/must be integrated into the theme park – which will be the subject of the rest of the chapter.

Ancient Greece in France

The origins of France's relationship (almost a love story) with Greece are not so different from those of Germany: France, Germany and Great Britain are the political contexts in which the combination of neoclassicism and nationalism produced the most visible results. Starting with the seventeenth century, the French élite started to become interested in collecting Greek antiquities, and from that moment on their travels, paintings, and purchases of archaeological materials grew steadily. 'What European artists and their clients really wanted, however, were images that revealed the scenery of the imagined classical Greek world, a world that was mythologized according to their expectations. Once again, it was the formalized, literary past, not the present, that was the attraction of Greece'.[3] The idea of Greece as the cradle of the Western civilization has been highly present in French intellectual circles since the Enlightenment; the political convulsions of the early nineteenth century and Greek War of Independence against the Ottoman Empire attracted huge sympathy in philhellenic circles, which compared and contrasted the value of Greece, seen from a strongly neoclassical perspective, with the Orientalist stereotypes deployed in describing the Ottomans. In the *Voyage pittoresque de la Grèce* (1782–1812), de Choiseul-Gouffier appealed for help to return Greece to its independence and ancient glory;[4] he was followed by many other visitors, in a trend which famously culminated in Chateaubriand's *Note sur la Grèce* (1825).[5] In 1826, Delacroix' painting 'Greece on the Ruins of Missolonghi', which was the culmination of a series of 'Greek paintings' that also included 'A Greek Warrior' (1821) and 'The Massacre of Scio' (1824), provided a visual manifesto for the ideal of a 'resurrection' of Greece and its values (meant as Christian and ancient), and its detachment from the 'Orient', and France was generally greatly moved in support of the Greek independence.

The Second Empire had a strong connection with classical antiquity, preferred to the 'Medieval' Franks, but was more focused on highlighting the Gallic and Roman heritage of France,[6] within which Greece played a minor role;[7] but the Third Republic, which originated from the defeat of Sedan (1870) and lasted until the Nazi invasion (1940), established an even stronger ideal connection with ancient Greece. As a Republic, France rejected the imperial model of Rome, instead focusing on their genetic derivation from the Gauls, while also reconnecting to the ideal image of Athenian democracy already deployed during the Revolution and the first two Republics. Ancient Greece was thus perceived as the spiritual ancestor of modern France: Paris was often presented as the New Athens, idealizing both the ancient Greek polis and the modern French capital as a centre of intellectual, literary and artistic life, a beacon of civilization. Additionally, the presence in Paris of masterpieces of ancient Greek art (most notably the Venus de Milo since the 1820s and the Nike of Samothrace since 1884, perceived as being equivalent to the British appropriation of the Parthenon sculptures) provided an additional 'nationalistic' touch to many references to ancient Greece.[8] In this context, it is no surprise that neoclassical architecture was systematically developed for the buildings hosting political institutions.[9]

Beginning with the defeat of Sedan in 1870, a rhetorical argument was developed in France that asked the French people to recover a 'Greek body' (meant as a perfectly trained one) as the only means of gaining revenge over the German Empire and redeeming national pride.[10] In a similar way to the previously mentioned German idealization of the Greek body, 'at the center of the new, militaristic, ethnic, and indeed ethno-racial, visions of France was the Greek physical ideal'.[11] This was true not only for men but also women, who were expected to follow the model of the Venus de Milo.[12] 'Greek identification had far-reaching and specifically practical consequences in post-war France. In order to regain their lost Greek body, the French had to change their way of life: they had to care for their body as their Greek ancestors had done. They should do gymnastics, and make trips to the Mediterranean south of France, and especially Provence, where the roots of France were supposed to lie. Contact with the Mediterranean Sea, sunshine, open air and the way of life of Provence were expected to revive the nation'.[13] This also implied highlighting and celebrating the Greek origin of French people in the genealogical sense,[14] through the history of certain southern cities, mostly Marseille (founded as Massalia by Phocaean colonists - the foundation had been the subject of the artistic competition of the *concours de Rome* in 1865)[15] and Nikaia/Nice (founded around 350 BCE by the Massalians). Ancient Greece thus became the apple of discord between philhellenist nationalists within Germany and France, the latter claiming a stronger connection to the noble, ancient ancestors through their 'Mediterranean' nature.[16] In contrast to contemporary ideas of the ancient Greeks as blond, French intellectuals thus started thinking of them as dark-haired, emphasizing the common belonging to a 'Mediterranean complexion'.[17] The fact that the modern Olympic Games (which began in 1896) had been invented and realized by Pierre de Coubertin, a Frenchman, was also perceived as a special reason of national pride and a further connection to ancient Greece.[18] Coubertin himself, a few years after realizing this project (which in spite of its internationalism derived from French anxiety about German dynamism)[19] commented that the revival of the Olympic Games was a French achievement.[20] The direct competition with Germany had a further component, as the archaeologists who began to excavate at the site of the ancient sanctuary of Olympia in 1875 were German; this represented a point of national pride and resentment, especially after the war of 1870, which was only partially compensated in 1882 by the beginning of the French excavations at Delphi.[21]

In Germany, the insistence on Greek sports, the Olympic Games, and the Greek body were greatly reduced after the Second World War, due to their importance to the Third Reich, especially in connection with the Olympic Games held in Berlin in 1936 – a focus that impacted on the perception of an event that was generally intended to be international and peaceful.[22] France did not go through the same experience, however, and the memory and celebration of Pierre de Coubertin is still alive and well. In general, the French approach to ancient Greece has not changed much since the Second World War, nor have the references to ancient Greece as precursor and model for the Republiques (i.e. the Fourth and the Fifth) diminished. As has been demonstrated by Miriam Leonard, Greece was everywhere in the French intellectual production from the 1950s onwards, and 'post-war France's encounter with the Greeks gave rise to a new interrogation of the political',[23] based once again on Athens and its political and philosophical tradition.[24] Antiquity has been a source of inspiration in all areas and a point of reference in French literature throughout the post-war period.[25]

In French secondary school, Greek history is taught rather briefly and not in a very detailed way;[26] the main focus is on art and literature, much less on social and political history, even if the history programmes for schools do include citizenship in antiquity (and therefore the dynamics of inclusion and exclusion in the Athenian democracy) as a topic relevant to the modern age.[27] The general concentration of French reception on Athens – due to its connection with French Republicanism, the idea of democracy, and the exaltation of Paris as the capital of art, literature, and culture in general – has a further consequence in French historical culture: Sparta, presented here as the prototypical totalitarian State, the anti-Athens, is very negatively characterized, and absent from the school programmes.[28]

Ancient Greece in the Astérix world

All the Astérix stories are set between around 50 and 44 BCE: the former year is prominently mentioned at the beginning of each comic album, and Caesar is always present, and thus still alive.[29] In the fiction of the comics, the Roman Empire is already entirely 'built up', stretching from the Iberian peninsula to the eastern provinces, from Britannia (in reality only conquered by the Romans around a century later) to North Africa, and is marked by clearly defined boundaries, which the Roman Empire never had.[30] While such anachronisms have a mostly narrative function, or refer to recognizable stereotypes about ancient societies (and can be revealed as such only by experts of ancient history),[31] humorous anachronisms are one of the staple features of the Astérix comics:[32] they bring this particular world closer to our own experience, thus creating fun effects entirely based on the possibility of recognizing referents used to associate the ancient and the modern.[33] This is very different from the anachronisms of other cartoons and comics, such as *B.C.* or *The Flintstones*; Astérix does not have a proto-car or a proto-TV, yet in Britain he meets the ancient parallel to The Beatles, his Belgi fry potatoes, and his Goths wear the Prussian Pickelhaube.[34] As highlighted by Rouvière, humour in Astérix is deployed to make fun of three different levels of stereotypes: knowledge about the ancient Gauls; stereotypes about the French (at a national and regional level); and common images of foreign nations.[35] At all three levels, the main set of foreknowledge required from the reader can be located in the content of history teaching in French schools immediately before and after the Second World War.[36] Indeed, the comics were and still are written first and foremost for a French public (and it is important to stress that the theme park is also primarily directed towards a French public). In this sense, most stereotypes about history, nations, traditions and so on are those that are valid in France and often directed towards (or against) France's neighbours and traditional enemies.[37]

The particular kind of humour within the comic – its continuous reference to motifs of French nationalism (both in the construction of the Gauls and the Romans, as well as in representations of the Germans) and its strong use and parody of historical clichés and stereotypes built up during the Third and Fourth Republic[38] – leads to a sort of neglect for Greek antiquity. Subdued by the Romans, Greece is here not the classical world of the polis, nor the world of mythology located in the Bronze Age that we have seen in other theme parks: it is the world of a previously great civilization, now resentful of Roman control, engaged in preserving its culture and cultural heritage. It is not Sparta, and it can be Athens only in the sense of the artistic and intellectual achievements of the Athenian democracy, which are admired and respected. And yet for Astérix and his friends, who visit Greece in the first century BCE, the Athenian Acropolis is a touristic, musealized destination, not the religious centre of the city. It is less ruined, but is otherwise today's Acropolis (very obviously white):[39] it is full of offers for tourists, including the painter who makes instant souvenir-portraits on a vase, with red figures.[40] Throughout all the chapters, we saw that modern Greece mostly appears as a holiday destination, and the touristic visit to the Acropolis, together with huge groups of international visitors, clearly also plays upon this perception of the modern nation. Such anachronisms are more frequent in the theme park than in the comics, however, which stems from the architectural nature of the park: the houses and buildings, inspired by the available images of Greece (and therefore small white and blue houses from the Aegean islands) can be used for humorous jokes.

The humorous anachronisms deployed in relation to Greece clearly show a lack of recognizable references to modern Greece, which could be comparable to those available for the Brits (drinking tea, having bad traditional cuisine, wearing tweed, etc.) or other modern nations. The stereotypical references to the Greeks derive from the classical world, perceived and reproduced as the most important, basic form of 'Greekness' to which one can refer. A 'contamination' between ancient Greece and the modern nation is most visible in the frequent definition of Greek characters in the comics as being 'Greek' (i.e. not Athenians or Spartans).[41] Greeks are recognizable in the comic mostly from their aspect and their language. The speech bubbles of the Greeks are written in a different font, an angular writing that imitates the Greek alphabet (but in its ancient, epigraphic form, not its printed form today!),[42] thus making them immediately recognizable, along with their names, which all end in -as or -os.[43] The most important repository of potential references (also in an anachronistic sense) to ancient Greece derives from sports, thus not from modern Greece but from a modern international institution – the Olympic Games – which has an ideal connection to ancient Greece. These references always involve Greek men having extremely muscular bodies, reminiscent of ancient sport and ancient sculptures, and generally being characterized by a particular nose that today we would generally call a 'Greek profile', which derives from ancient sculpture, or rather its interpretation in the nationalistic and racist literature of the nineteenth century.[44] Elderly men always have beards, derived from the ancient representation of philosophers. Greek women, with long black hair, are irresistibly beautiful and Minoan in character, their breasts and hairstyles recalling the Snake Goddess and the Ladies in Blue. Agecanonix (English: Geriatrix), in the comic album bringing him and the Gallic heroes to Olympia, on which more will be said just below, defines them all as 'statues', not missing the chance for another joke based on the stereotypical idea of the perfect bodies of classical Greek sculptures.

This stereotyping becomes highly visible in a scene from *Les Lauriers de César* (1972). Astérix and Obélix are in Rome and offer themselves to a slave trader, in the hope of becoming Caesar's slaves. They are displayed at the slave market on a tribune together with the other slaves on sale at a luxury trader's, Tifus. The slave market recalls the images proposed by the French artists of historical paintings with an Orientalist style, such as Boulanger's 'Le marché aux esclaves' (1882), thus ironically referencing known images within French national culture. There are also other slaves on the tribune: a Breton dressed in tweed for instance, and a Greek slave who ends up being hit by Obélix. The Greek (p. 16) has an impressively muscular body, is only very partially covered by a small white cloth, evoking (and correcting) the nudity of most Greek statues, and his movements reproduce the position and postures of famous classical statues (the Apollo from the pediment of the Temple of Zeus at Olympia, the Laocoön Group, Praxiteles' Hermes, and the Discobolus). The only modern, anachronistic reference that does not connect him to Greece (but rather to France) is the first statue he poses as, when the Gallic heroes arrive, Rodin's neoclassical *The Thinker* (1902), perhaps mixed with the Hellenistic Boxer from the Museo Nazionale Romano.[45]

Sport is essentially only the Olympic Games, which resonates with the national tradition of celebrating Pierre de Coubertin and the role of France as the 'new Greece' in their revival: the only comic album which brings the Gallic heroes to Greece is *Astérix aux jeux Olympiques* (1968), that became a film in 2008 (directors Forestier and Langmann). After learning that a Roman from a nearby legionary camp has been chosen for the Olympic Games, the Gallic village decides to participate too; even if the games are only open to Greeks and Romans, they insist that Caesar claims to have conquered all of Gaul, thus making them

Romans. Astérix and Obélix are chosen to represent the village, but everybody accompanies them to Greece. Arriving in Athens, the Gauls perform the previously mentioned guided tour of the city. Here we also see the only references to modern Greece: Greek food (and quite obviously what readers recognize and eat today),[46] Greek dances (Zorba's dance), and a joke, when the tourist guide hired by the Gauls suggests one of his cousins for every kind of service or need, thus playing on the stereotype of the huge, strongly interconnected Greek family. This also forcefully emerges, for instance, in the movie *My Big, Fat Greek Wedding*,[47] and is here connected to general stereotypes about Mediterranean societies and the greediness of a society living off international tourism.[48]

The representation of Olympia, clearly inspired by didactic material and history books,[49] is symptomatic of the reception of classical Greece in popular culture. In antiquity, the sanctuary consisted mostly of earthwork buildings, but this would not be acceptable to the stereotypical representation of ancient Greek architecture; the panoramic view of the sanctuary in the comic thus reproduces a recognizable Temple of Zeus, containing a representation and explanation of the Hellanodikeon, Bouleuterion and Prytaneon, but also shows a huge number of buildings in marble with Doric columns and a stadium built entirely in stone and surrounded by tribunes on all four sides, shown a second time from within (p. 28).[50] At the entrance of the precinct is a gate with an arch, unusual in Greek architecture, with a caricature of Goscinny and Uderzo accompanied by real ancient Greek 'insults' between the two. Ancient sport is also shown in a way recognizable to the public, identical to modern sport. The opening ceremony of the games is created along the lines of the modern ones, with the different cities and regions of Greece and the Roman Empire entering the stadium in procession after a sign indicating their provenance; here again the humoristic effect is created with puns on the ancient world, as with the statement that the inhabitants of Samothrace are sure of their Victory, or that the inhabitants of Rhodes have sent only one champion, but a colossal one (p. 38).[51] There is no trace of the religious context of the ancient games, and even the ceremonies after the sporting events are modelled on the modern Olympics: while in antiquity only the winner got a prize, in the Astérix world there is also a prize for second and third, and the three of them stand on a podium, decorated with Roman numbers. As we have already seen in *Terra Mítica* (which may have been inspired by Astérix), this is a rather understandable and easy form of representing ancient sport to a broad modern public.[52] Some elements are historically accurate for antiquity, but they are deployed to humouristic aims. For example, the comic correctly references that women were forbidden to enter the stadium, and an angry Greek woman leaves shouting that one day women would be able to not only watch the games, but also participate in them; a laughing man answers that for sure, they will also be allowed to drive carts. The historical element is therefore built into a humorous construction which, from the perspective of the modern Olympic Games (and modern roads), functionalizes it for the sake of fun. This becomes even more apparent when one considers that such a historical element is used here somewhat incorrectly: only married women were not allowed to assist the games; young unmarried girls could.[53]

To further confirm that the world of Astérix relies on the same stereotypes and motifs that we have encountered all over the world, classical mythology also plays an important role, as a repertoire of known, adaptable narratives. While this is extraneous to the world of the Gallic heroes (who do not follow the Olympic religion), and religion is generally alien to the comics (which represent a very rational and lay world, modelled on France – and this applies to the theme park, too),[54] very well-known classical myths can still provide a background, inspiration or reference point to be used in different stories and various moments. So, for example, the long journey of Astérix and Obélix to the Middle East to get petroil for the magic potion is called *L'Odyssée d'Astérix* (1981). The most notable inspiration from classical mythology in the Astérix world, however, is the animated movie *Les douze travaux d'Astérix* (1976), later also released as an illustrated story. As the title already makes clear, the plot is inspired by the myth of Heracles. While this is famous everywhere, it is particularly successful in France, and was already the topic of an enormous number of paintings in the second half of the nineteenth century; the reception of this myth thus has a particularly fertile background in the French context, as 'since the French Revolution Heracles has been seen as a prototype of the mass of the French people laboring with his hands for the benefit of the community, cleaning stables and using his physical strength to eliminate its enemies'.[55]

The Gauls from the unconquered village are challenged by Caesar to deal with twelve labours that he creates – if they are able to successfully complete all of them, he will admit that they are gods and give them the control over Rome. The twelve labours of Heracles are briefly summarized at the beginning of the movie in a series of humorous drawings imitating ancient Greek vase paintings and characterized by the usual anachronisms (the cleaning of the Augean stables is, for instance, represented by Heracles using a vacuum cleaner). It is no surprise that these same drawings are represented on a giant amphora located in *Parc Astérix*, thus making the connection to Greek black figures painted on vases even clearer [Fig. 22]. Some of the labours are inspired by classical mythology, even if not directly by the Heracles myth: for instance, the Isle of Pleasure

Fig. 22 The 'Vase of Heracles', *Parc Astérix*, Plailly, France © Carmen García Bueno.

(Astérix' fourth labour) is directly inspired by the Odyssean myth of the Sirens, mixed in with the ancient idea of the Islands of the Blessed. Labour number 10 sees Astérix and Obélix meet the Old Man of the Mountain, who challenges them with a riddle, which is a parody of detergent advertisements on TV.[56] The Olympic gods are shown for the first and only time in Astérix (they are otherwise only present in exclamations by Greek characters, just as the Gauls often reference the names of their gods, as do the Romans): not only does Astérix have to identify Olympus, the detergent they use for their laundry, but the Olympic gods are shown in council (as the Homeric tradition teaches), discussing whether they should really let Astérix and Obélix join them; Venus proposes this, but Jupiter clearly refuses it. However, in this movie, Greece is mostly present through references to sports and the Olympic Games: the first three labours the Gauls have to face are all connected to defeating the champions in three disciplines: running (where they beat a Greek at the marathon – the only character explicitly defined as an Olympic champion), javelin throwing (the champion is a Persian), and fighting (the champion is a German who, in an anachronistic way, uses karate techniques).

In sum, Greece is present in the Astérix world as a reference, as a part of the ancient Mediterranean world in which the adventures of the Gallic warrior take place; yet it is not a main component. The reasons for this must be sought in the stereotypes that exist concerning Greece in French popular culture, which permit only a limited development of the specific form of anachronistic humour that is typical of Astérix. Yet it is precisely this background which explains why the representation of Greece in the world of Astérix is easier within the theme park, where the use of architecture and multimedia forms (such as the possibility of referencing well-known element of narratives from classical Greece, like mythology, without having to embed them into a consistent plot) make their display and activation less complicated than in a comic.

Parc Astérix

History of the park

The first park dedicated to Astérix was opened in 1967 in Nice but turned into a financial disaster and was soon forced to close. The project of a theme park dedicated to the famous comics was revived when, in 1981, Uderzo visited Disneyland in Anaheim and decided that France should host a similar park for the Gallic hero. In 1985, the company Parc Astérix SA was founded,[57] and the park opened its doors in 1989 at Plailly, on the outskirts of Paris, near an important highway and the main airport of the capital.[58] In the first phase, the park had five themed areas: 'Via Romana'; the village of the Gauls; the Roman city; a street from Paris; and the big lake ('Grand Lac'), which already had a partially Greek theming, stressing the connection between Greece and water, as we have observed in many other parks. In 1990 a new themed area was added, 'Square in Gergovia'. In 1992, *Parc Astérix* suffered a major blow from the opening of *Disneyland Paris* but was able to recover thanks to a very strict operational campaign and the opening of a new themed area,[59] which was developed in 1994 from a section of what was previously the 'Grand Lac' and dedicated to Greece. From then on, the park continued to change: the 'Place de Gergovie' in 1995 became the 'domain lacustre', which was then joined to the 'village d'Astérix' to form an area called 'La Gaule' and later 'Bienvenue chez les Gaulois'. In 2006, another sector of the 'Grand Lac' was transformed into a Viking area, and in 2012 the newest sector of the park was opened, representing Ancient Egypt, in honour of the famous album and movie *Astérix and Cleopatra*. The park today thus consists of six themed areas, five of which represent ancient cultures, as experienced by Astérix and his friends in their adventures (Gaul, Rome, Greece, Egypt and the main street), while the other (earlier 'Rue de Paris', today 'À travers le temps') illustrates the history of Paris and France from the Middle Ages through to the twentieth century.

With 2,000,000 visitors in 2017, *Parc Astérix* is the fifth most-visited theme park in France and is an established reality in the landscape of European theme parks.[60] The map of the park resembles, from many perspectives, that of the *Magic Kingdoms*: from the entrance, visitors are led through the 'Via Romana', a main street that hosts buildings in various styles and inspirations. This does not recall any specific Roman street, but rather all the different cultures, styles and regions visited by Astérix during his adventures. As with 'Main Street U.S.A.' in the Disney parks, this area is very poor in attractions and consists of shops and restaurants. At the end of the street, a huge menhir, on which Astérix is sitting, is the 'weenie' to which visitors are attracted. It marks the entrance to the central area of the park, representing Gaul. At the end of the 'main street', visitors can either enter this Gallic area by walking straight ahead, or turn left and enter the Roman sector, at the end of which they reach the large lake that represents the biggest water mass in the park. If they decide to walk around the lake counter-clockwise, visitors pass through Greece then the Viking area, before finally reaching the 'Parisian' sector. The shores of the lake thus belong to Greece, to the Vikings and, on the eastern side, reachable directly from Rome, to Gaul; here is the 'Lutèce Plage', which ironically hints at the Paris-Plage. The Gallic area is the largest, occupies the entire central area of the park and is reachable from almost every other area (only Greece does not have a direct border with it). The Egyptian sector, located in the north-eastern corner, is a later addition that can only be reached from the Gallic area. In sum, the park is structured around a loop, in which the central part is represented not by a square, as in the *Magic Kingdoms*, but by an entire area.

Next to the big lake there are other water elements, such as the river flowing around the Gallic village, although the structure of the park essentially highlights a clear differentiation between cultures that revolve around water (the Vikings and the Greeks), the Gauls, who have both the shoreline (the village, in the comics, is on the coast) and the forests, and civilizations which are not connected to water (Egypt and Rome). The latter is understandable when we consider the role of Rome in the comics, whereby Romans are mostly represented as infantry soldiers. The themed area in general represents the Roman Empire, not the city of Rome, and thus imagines it as a land extension. The Roman sector has only one water ride, 'Romus et Rapidus', a river rapids ride built by Intamin in 1989, which was originally part of 'Grand Lac' (and later 'Grèce'); it had a Greek theme and was called 'La descente du Styx', evoking the adventurous aspect of descending along the river which, in Greek mythology, marked the boundary between the Underworld and the Earth. In 2006 a six-year-old Belgian visitor drowned on the ride, so it was closed until 2008, then reopened and reassigned to the Roman area, with a name that distances it from any associations with death and the Underworld. The ride now evokes the foundation of Rome and the fact that the twins Romulus and Remus were abandoned on the Tiber, which overflowed but then deposited them safely on the spot where the she-wolf would find them.

'Grèce'

The Greek area 'Grèce' was created in 1994, further developing the Greek aspects already inserted in 'Grand Lac', which hosted structures and attractions relating to Greek mythology, such as the previously mentioned 'Descent du Styx', the ride 'Le Cheval de Troie' (a magic carpet ride built by Zierer with a quite low level of theming)[61] and the large Theatre of Poseidon ('Théâtre de Poseidon'), which can host up to 2,000 visitors and is used for shows with dolphins and seals.[62] The theatre, which still represents one of the main attractions of the Greek area, once again confirms the stereotypes at stake: Greece as a maritime land, and therefore the perfect location for the much-loved shows with sea animals (the show is called 'Réverence' and takes place three times a day).[63] The name of the structure evokes both the god of the seas (in direct relation to the dolphins and seals involved in the performances) and the great importance of the theatre for ancient Greeks, another piece of information that is well known across many different groups and cultural backgrounds. Considering the position of the Greek area in the western part of the park, bordering on land which can be used to expand, its narrow and long shape along the shores of the lake, and its previous marginality, it is easy to understand why in recent years the largest investments have been concentrated on this area, which is thus now bound to attract more visitors than before thanks to a radically increased density of attractions. The two newest (and most heavily advertised) attractions, built in 2016 and 2017, are both here: 'Discobélix' and 'Pégase Express'.[64]

The scarcity of references to Greece in the comics makes the representation of Greece in *Parc Astérix* much 'freer' than that of the other regions and cultures. The theme park therefore assembles different allusions, references and styles in a paratactic way so that the theme, once defined, does not necessarily require a consistent narrative. The lack of strong motifs and recurrent themes to re-mediatize from the other Astérix products (the only element in this sense is the vase with drawings appearing in *Les douze travaux d'Astérix*) means that what is chosen are the stereotypical images and ideas about Greece, which are the same as we have met across Europe and throughout the world. While we expect references to the Olympic Games in connection to the only adventure which brought the Gallic heroes to Greece, these would in any case be present because of their significance to the reception of ancient Greece. Alongside these, references to classical mythology are positioned among a landscape of white houses and blue roofs, evoking the well-known image of touristic Greece, with a focus once again on the Aegean islands (windmills are not absent, either).

Yet even in the absence of direct references to the adventures of Astérix, the style of the comic is consistently deployed: in the graphical elements (such as the font used for signs, which copies the 'Greek' as represented in the comic albums), or in the typical forms of 'anachronistic humour'. These are very widespread throughout the area and once again reveal the stereotypical knowledge that is expected from visitors. Next to the theatre of Poseidon, for example, there is a small 'shop window': it is a mode boutique, called 'Au vrai chic Athénien' which displays six different forms of fig leaves. The joke is clear, referring to the fig leaves (entirely unknown to antiquity) that were added to ancient statues in the Vatican during the sixteenth century (and therefore to the Roman copies of ancient Greek statues) to cover their genitals, which by the early nineteenth century had become synonymous with antiquity, in spite of their modern origin.[65] Next to the entrance of the ride 'Le Cheval de Troie', a small door with chains hints at a doghouse – the name written above it is Cerberus, as it would be written on Snoopy's doghouse as drawn by C. Schulz. Ajax has a laundry, with a joke that alludes to the name of a modern soap, while elsewhere a door has the sign 'Penelope. Couture – tapisserie', alluding to the never finished tapestry; a few metres away, Odysseus has a travel agents' office. As in the comics, these details are scattered everywhere and sometimes very easy to miss, as they are positioned in blind spots, or on walls which mark the areas not accessible to the public. And yet their function is crucial, as they activate all the stereotypical knowledge of ancient Greece and transpose it onto the typical style of the Astérix world. Mythology and holidays also appear as the theme of shops and restaurants: next to a small parlour for French fries called 'Fritapopoulos', playing with modern Greek surnames, the area has only one restaurant, called 'Taverne Dionysos'. The god of wine is an apt figure to evoke a pleasant and refreshing stop dedicated to eating and drinking.[66] Next to it is the souvenir shop 'Au comptoir des mers', which refers only to the maritime and touristic side of Greece's popularity and sells products connected to life on the beach. The connection with water was also highlighted earlier through a small area with water games, where it was possible to take a walk or go for a run, and to get soaked on hot summer days. This area, 'Les jeux d'Odous', playing with the French expression 'jeux d'eau' and with the

Greek suffixes, displayed a very simple decoration, based mostly on white columns, as is to be expected in a popular ancient Greece.[67]

Entering the Greek area from Rome, visitors see Poseidon's theatre on their right, while on the left there is the 'Cheval de Troie', and immediately behind it the newest attraction of the sector, the launched roller coaster 'Pégase Express', realized in 2017 by Gerstlauer. Located at one extremity of the park, the long coaster track is weakly themed: the dominant colour is blue, which is coherent with the entire themed area, and there are only a very few decorative elements with motifs from classical mythology, such as a small Greek temple in ruins dominated by the head of Medusa on the façade; it also appears in the inner part, which functions as a sort of station on the track, from which the trains then roll backwards after having been cursed by the Gorgon. Still, most of what the riders see during the more than three-minute-long ride are backstage structures and the parking lots.[68] The waiting area and the station imitate Aegean churches, through their recognizable white structure with a blue dome. With typical Astérix humour, it is a station: the Gare Montparnassos, which both evokes the Parnassus, the mountain of Delphi, and the Gare Montparnasse in Paris (from which, incidentally, all trains to Armorica leave). The narrative underlying the coaster is clear, needing only a very broad knowledge of classical mythology: that Pegasus was a winged horse, with which one is therefore supposed to fly (the park's homepage also insists on his transformation into a constellation of stars).[69]

'Le Vol d'Icare', 'L'Hydre de Lerne', 'La Rivière d'Elis'

'Le Vol d'Icare' is probably one of the most paradigmatic rides to show the reception of classical Greece in the theme park in general, and in *Parc Astérix* in particular. This family coaster by Zierer, built in 1994 for the the opening of 'Grèce',[70] is a further example of the reception of mythology in a Minoan visualization.[71] The waiting area and loading station are situated within a replica of the Palace of Knossos, which is represented as a ruin, consistent with the general setting of the park's theme in the first century BCE. We have already seen that the Bronze Age is the most common setting for mythology, and the connection is even stronger in the case of the myth chosen here, that of Daedalus and Icarus, who tried to escape from the Cretan Labyrinth that Daedalus had built, in which he had been imprisoned together with his son by Minos (at least according to a popular version of the myth). In this sense, the architectural choice is entirely disconnected from the Astérix comics, where Minoan architecture is only deployed to represent Atlantis in the adventure *La galère d'Obélix* (1996). The waiting area builds up a narrative of Daedalus' studying to escape the Labyrinth. Beginning from a sign representing the Labyrinth with the indication 'you are here', which perfectly fits with the humorous style of Astérix, these rooms show various ideas and experiments for Daedalus' flight. The visitors essentially move through an archaeological excavation, seeing traces of something which happened there 'a long time ago'; something like being in ancient Greece, but in Roman times. The experiments and inventions represent Daedalus as a sort of mad scientist, who has already designed Leonardo's flying machines. The roller coaster is thus the adventurous flight of Icarus:[72] after the initial lift hill, the cars move along a sculpture representing the sun, whereupon riders suddenly remember what happened to Daedalus' son (and his wings held together by wax) when he got too close to the sun. It is highly likely they do, as the myth is very well-known, as demonstrated by its frequent use for rides in theme parks (we have already come across this myth in *Europa-Park*, in *Belantis* and in *Terra Mítica*). Luckily, the riders don't fall in the water, but return to the station after a few bumps.

Alongside this coaster was installed, a year later, the octopus ride 'L'Hydre de Lerne', by Gerstlauer. The reference is again to classical mythology, more precisely to one of Heracles' labours, the killing of the Lernaean Hydra. This has been represented since archaic times as a multi-headed snake or dragon, the number of heads often changing (also because, according to the myth, every time one was cut off, two more would grow from the wound). Heracles thus had to use fire to burn the stumps after each decapitation, killing the Hydra.[73] Nothing so brutal happens here. The idea of a multi-headed monster is simply a very good, easy way to theme a ride of this kind, which is characterized by multiple arms, and thematically reconnects with Heracles, as the huge vase representing his labours is positioned just a few metres away. The ride's arms do not represent the necks of the monster, though – the seven heads are instead all in the centre of the ride. The arms hold the vehicles, which are shaped in the form of small boats. While the iconography of the boat with its oars is once again recognizable as belonging to Mediterranean antiquity, one cannot avoid noticing that the myth of the Hydra has little to do with navigation, in spite of the name of the monster, and it being connected to water (at times it is defined as a 'sea monster'). The reason for the boats must be sought elsewhere: while the shape is technically very convenient for such a ride, as it allows the riders to sit inside them and comply with all safety regulations, the idea of Greece as a maritime country also influences the representation of the Hydra, which here is fought by Greeks arriving by boat, possibly with an 'interference' of the other multi-headed dragon, Scylla, which we have already seen in other theme parks.

Up to this point, Greece has thus been visualized through classical mythology and the postcard images of Aegean Greece, seen as its seaside tourist destinations. The element which was missing until now, Olympia, becomes prominent in the second section of the themed area. 'La Rivière d'Elis' is in this sense somehow a connecting element. A tow boat ride realized by Mack and opened in 1997, it is a family attraction, allowing riders to sail slowly across a fantastic landscape populated by mythological figures,[74] with sculptures scattered across the landscape, all realized in a 'cartoon' style. Yet here one can find no traces of the humour or anachronisms of the Astérix world; the image this ride wishes to convey is that of a slow and relaxing trip within a fantastic world, more closely resembling the classical mythology as represented in Disney's *Fantasia* than the world of the Gallic heroes. The ride starts from a rock dominated by a small round temple, which might also evoke the (Roman) *tropaeum Alpium* in La Turbie to a French public, and is accompanied by relaxing, smooth music. The boats, surmounted by gilded bars holding a roof, have the shape of an egg and recall, with their decoration, the neoclassical and French imperial style. They move through Mediterranean vegetation animated by scattered amphoras, an Eros with his arch and glasses (with very thick lenses), winged horses (some hatching from colourful eggs), Sirens, centaurs and satyrs.[75] Classical mythology is again dominant, this time represented by a magical landscape, full of sweet and amusing creatures, none of which have any evil feelings, and without any hint of possible adventure.

The connection with the next section derives merely from the name: instead of being named after Arcadia (which we generally tend to connect to this sort of landscape, along with a tranquil pastoral life), the ride is named after another Peloponnesian region, Elis, home of the sanctuary of Olympia. This is not a reference that can be grasped by all visitors, and will likely be missed by the average one; yet the park management seems to have decided to insert here their first Olympic reference, one that hints, tongue-in-cheek, both to one of the main components of the reception of ancient Greece in popular culture and to the only story of the Astérix saga that plays out in Greece.

'Discobélix'

Parc Astérix had no explicit and direct reference to the Olympic Games until 2016. This clearly marks the difference of the Greek area from the others within the theme park. While the other areas are entirely dominated by the comic adventures which took place in the corresponding regions, this does not apply to 'Grèce'. Built with a heavy use of the widespread stereotypes about (ancient) Greece, and recurring to the same visual language and repertoire of motifs as many other parks already analysed, for a very long time the area simply had no clear reference to the only adventure of the Gallic heroes set in Greece. This can be explained in various ways: from the visualization of Greece as a 'sea nation', which distances it from the topic and content of the comic adventure to the lack, in *Astérix aux jeux olympiques*, of any 'strong' and memorable Greek character that could be redeployed here as the titular name of a ride. Yet it is nonetheless relevant that, while the vase with Heracles' labours still represents a direct reference to an Astérix movie, there is not even a decorative podium (such as that we encountered in *Terra Mítica*) to refer to the Gallic adventure in Olympia.

This changed in 2016 with the opening of 'Discobélix', located between 'La Rivière d'Elis' and 'La Tonnerre de Zeus', directly on the lake's shore. The ride is a Disk'ò Coaster built by Zamperla: a spinning ride that moves along a track with a camelback hump, mixing the thrill of a coaster with that of a spinning ride.[76] While there is no need to look for a special reason for the construction of this ride, it is nonetheless worth highlighting that a stronger sensitivity for the topic at that stage may also have been motivated by the candidature of Paris to host the 33rd Olympic Games in 2024, a possibility that was still active in 2016 and would indeed lead to the Games being assigned to the French capital in 2017. The large vehicle on which the riders sit has the shape of a disk, which gives the model its name. But in connection with ancient Greece, a disk immediately evokes Myron's Discobolus and the launch of the disk as a sport, practised in antiquity and still present at the Olympic Games. In true Astérix style, the word Discobolus is Gallicized with an -ix and, thanks to the presence of the letters ob, transformed into the name of one of the most important characters – Obélix, who is represented at the ride's entrance by an obviously white 'marble' statue that 'launches' the disk, more or less in the posture of the Discobolus [Fig. 23]. The entrance is a round structure with Ionic columns that provides a rather faithful reconstruction of a historical building in the sanctuary of Olympia, the Philippeion (a small representation of this is also present in the overview of Olympia found in the comic). Built by Alexander the Great in honour of his father Philip II, it is chronologically in keeping with the 'Roman Greece' represented in Astérix. The track runs over a construction which, along with its hump, forms a bridge framed by Ionic columns that looks like monumental ancient architecture (yet considering the bridge and its arch, is much more Roman than Greek). The riders, spinning on the huge disk thrown by Obélix

Fig. 23 'Discobélix', *Parc Astérix*, Plailly, France © Frédéric Vielcanet / Alamy Stock Photos.

with his incredible strength, fly along this up and down, finishing on the water before then rising once more to a brazier, inside of which burns the Olympic flame.

'La Tonnerre de Zeus'

The most iconic ride of 'Grèce', the one that is also reproduced on the postcards that represent this themed area, is the wooden roller coaster 'La Tonnerre de Zeus' (Zeus' thunderbolts).[77] Realized in 1997 by Custom Coasters International, the ride has received many awards, which have contributed to its popularity and success: it was recognized as the best wooden coaster in the world in *Mitch Hawker's Wooden Coaster Poll* for three years in a row, from 1999 to 2001.[78] The name of the coaster evokes both the typical rumble of wooden coasters (a big part of the thrill they generate in riders) and the role of Zeus as god of the atmosphere, in particular of thunder and lightning.[79] Again, a reference to modern French culture is crucial to understanding the humour hidden behind the name: *La Tonnerre de Jupiter* (Jupiter's Thunderbolts) is a famous early French mythological movie, realized in 1903 by Georges Méliès, the 'national hero' of early cinema. The movie displays 'a dwarfish Olympian throwing cardboard lightning bolts onto the stage. They explode, he does a few amusing flips, and the Muses appear behind him'[80] – with this reference in mind, the roller coaster acquires again a humorous undertone, typical of Astérix and his park.

The coaster is also signposted from a great distance away by a huge statue of Zeus, who stands holding thunderbolts with a very menacing character (see book cover). This iconography was already well attested in antiquity and is very popular, as not only is it very common in ancient sculpture and vase paintings but is also frequently found within modern reception products (comics, the cover of the famous video game *Age of Mythology*, etc.). And yet, this dangerous-looking Zeus also falls prey to the humour that pervades all corners of the Astérix world: when visitors walk between his legs to enter the queuing area, they realize that he is wearing underwear decorated with flowers. While the connection between the wooden coaster, the thunder and Zeus is sufficient to explain the choice of name and the theming of the ride, there is also the fact that the only one of Astérix's adventures to be located in Greece also takes place in Olympia, in the sanctuary of Zeus, and indeed the comic features an image of a statue of Zeus looking rather menacing and holding thunderbolts. Yet the statue in the comic is entirely different from that in the park, and neither have anything to do with Phidias' statue that we encountered in *Terra Mítica* and *Happy Valley Beijing*. The olive tree of the entrance area, which is around 1000 years old,[81] also hints at ancient Greek religion.

The waiting area and station of the coaster, as well as the small building where riders can buy the pictures taken during the ride, are both structured as Greek temples: Doric columns, a pediment with a decoration representing thunderbolts, and a coffered ceiling. Yet rather curiously, they are not white. The lower parts and the capitals of the columns are red, the abacuses are blue with a meander motif, the pediment has a yellow decoration against a blue background; blue and yellow also dominate in the frieze, where the triglyphs are blue, with yellow (empty) metopes [Fig. 24]. These colours are also applied to the two trains: originally blue, they were later (2004–15) one red and one blue, and since 2015 are again both blue. As previously noted, ancient Greek temples were indeed polychrome, and red, yellow and blue were surely dominant colours; but this is not how they are represented and imagined in popular culture.[82] This also applies to *Parc Astérix*: a photo opportunity dedicated to Heracles, for example, is formed by an altar with the name of the hero, surmounted by a dead lion (clearly the Nemean one), on which visitors can climb and have their pictures taken against a background representing an ancient Greek city (or rather the ancient Greek city of popular knowledge, Athens). Once again, in spite of the chronological conundrum, Heracles is supposed to stand in front of the Periclean

Fig. 24 Loading station of 'Tonnerre de Zeus', *Parc Astérix*, Plailly, France © Carmen García Bueno.

Acropolis, which is entirely white, showing from a distance the purity of its marble. It is therefore hard to argue that these structures are coloured following any sort of faithfulness to more precise reconstructions of ancient architecture, which would be very far from the spirit and general inspiration of the park. The colours of the buildings, which are also in contrast to the representations of Greek architecture in the comics, seem to have been chosen to give them a 'lighter' image, to 'desacralize' the image of serious antiquity in marble, almost as if from far away a white marble temple and the brazen statue of a menacing Zeus would have appeared too distant from the ironic touch that characterizes the entire park. The colours are, in this sense, somehow the equivalent of Zeus' underwear.

This is one of the ways in which, in *Parc Astérix*, the mechanisms of re-mediatization (i.e. the dependence on the model featured in the comics, which lie behind the theme park and justify its very existence) influence and 'change' the reception of classical Greece. Yet as we have seen, this rather seldomly happens. Not only is Greece represented too scarcely in the comics to generate a truly complete, specifically Astérix-ian vision of Greece, but the comics also play with the same stereotypes and visualizations of Greece that are available in broader society and all over the world. Of the two great strings of reception of Greece that we have identified – antiquity and tourism – the comics mostly deploy the first, while the theme park, due to its nature of place and its need to create an architectural context, rediscovers the white-and-blue of the Aegean islands that represents the ciphre of Greece all over the world. Once freed from the creation of a consistent plot (and therefore the functionalization of characters, structures, narratives and decoration for the development of that plot), even the world of Astérix adds little to what is perceived, received and retransmitted concerning ancient Greece in all the other parks we considered: classical mythology, columns and templar architectures, and the dream of a summer holiday on an Aegean island.

7

Greece – In the Form of a Conclusion

The study of representations of classical Greece in theme parks throughout the world is a study in glocalization. Glocalization is also connected to postmodern aesthetics: as has been argued by Svetlana Boym, nostalgia is the 'result of a new understanding of time and space that made the division into "local" and "universal" possible'.[1] The 'nostalgic creature' internalizes this division, and thus somehow both aspires for the universal and yearns for the particular. Glocalization thus emerges as the 'bridge' that covers this aesthetic and cognitive gap. Scholars have highlighted how glocalization works in theme park chains, adapting the staples of parks that have diffused worldwide into the different regions where they have been built; special attention is paid to the local cultures involved, as well as the local visitors, who must find in the theme park images and stimuli to which they can respond: in this way, 'locality continues to reassert itself'.[2] Chang and Pang have very effectively shown how these mechanisms work in *Universal Studios* parks;[3] the forms of adaptation to the different localities in Disney theme parks have also been the object of intensive study:[4] *Tokyo Disneyland* has thus been interpreted as 'the recontextualization of the American signs so that the Japanese are able to make them their own'.[5] The adaptations of how Greece is represented in 'It's a Small World' provide another good example.[6]

Ancient Greece is, of course, not an international theme park chain, but rather an ancient culture that is recognized worldwide as being a part of cultural heritage; it is a highly valued past, even in countries which do not recognize it as a part of their own history.[7] It is therefore a trope, one with universal value, but at the same time particularized and localized in different places.[8] In this sense, ancient Greece is a global culture, characterized by symbols and signs that are recognized globally, and present everywhere, a lowest common denominator of Greekness which, through the tourism industry, self-promotion, school books, and so on has defined the 'brand Greece' everywhere in the world. Lash and Urry have noted that from the perspective of the real economy, the 'reproduction' (for instance of a work of art) is actually the production;[9] branding thus assumes a crucial role, which not only applies to the stardom system, music, or Hollywood movies.¹⁰ Indeed, what we have seen throughout this book is no less than the product of the 'branding' of classical Greece, and its 'production' in different areas of the world.

The Greek pavilion within the *Global Village* in Dubai is a good example of all the elements that are stereotypically recognizable as 'Greek': characterized by an extreme whiteness and decorative elements in blue, the pavilion has an entrance formed by two pillars (not columns) holding a pediment, on which the name 'Greece' is shaped in very angular golden letters and framed by two golden circular decorations (evoking a sun motif). In front of the pillars, a copy of the Venus de Milo and an antiquizing statue of a soldier holding spear and shield (not derived from any ancient model) strengthen the connection to the classical as the most recognizable phase of the entirety of Greek history. At the same time, the other popular dimension of Greece, that of the Aegean islands and modern tourism, is evoked not only by the colour coding, but also by the 'silhouette' of the bell tower of the Paraportiani church on Mykonos. Through philhellenism, ancient Greece has been imagined and idealized to become a realm of fantasy, compared by George Zarkadakis, in this sense, to *Disneyland*.¹¹

In a more proper way, ancient Greece can be defined as a 'supersystem'. Marsha Kinder defines it as

> a network of intertextuality constructed around a figure or a group of figures from pop culture who are either fictional...or 'real'...In order to be a supersystem, the network must cut across several modes of image production; must appeal to diverse generations, classes, and ethnic subcultures, who in turn are targeted with diverse strategies; must foster 'collectability' through a proliferation of related products; and must undergo a sudden increase in commodification, the success of which reflexively becomes a 'media event' that dramatically accelerates the growth curve of the system's commercial success.¹²

Of course, there are many differences between the Teenage Mutant Ninja Turtles (the object of Kinder's analysis) or Disney,¹³ and classical Greece. Yet if we broaden the definition provided above to include a culture next to figures, we realize that ancient Greece cuts across many modes of image production, appeals to different sectors of the population all over the world, assumes a different meaning in different 'historical cultures', and is correspondingly 'functionalized' (Kinder's 'targeting'), is 'collectable' in the form of travel experience, travel souvenirs, memorabilia (including the 'authentic Greek' souvenirs made in Taiwan and sold in *E-Da*), and can experience sudden increases in commodification in connection with special events that activate this special field of historical memory. Examples of this range from a successful movie such as *300* to the Olympic Games, whose impact on the image of ancient Greece throughout the world was mentioned repeatedly.

Following Baudrillard, the sign-value of an object, like the simulacrum of a simulacrum, entirely disembeds the object from its relation to exchange-value and use-value – it 'cuts away the last remaining foundations of an already almost foundationless object'.[14] The 'economy of sign and space' would thus produce signs which are emptied both of material and symbolic content.[15] It is hard to accept this perspective, however, and not only because it increases the reflexivity of the subject.[16] Starting from a post-structuralist and Latourian perspective which challenges the subject/object divide and recognizes the agency of the object, one must also admit that the sign, the 'object', is not emptied in the dramatic way that Baudrillard (or Lash and Urry) described. Indeed, the deterritorialization just identified in the transformation of ancient Greece within a system of symbols is not a purely globalized emptiness: the Acropolis, or the Trojan horse may be deterritorialized – a Trojan horse is not always the same, and can indicate the cunning behaviour of the Greeks, as in the show in *Terra Mítica*, or the beginning of Odysseus' travels, as in *Belantis*, or the destruction of Troy and the sense of disruption, as in *Happy Valley Beijing* ... However, this does not mean it is 'empty'; 'on the contrary, deterritorialization makes objects more elastic and absorptive, and it allows them to be filled up with more than one meaning'.[17] As we have seen, the global images of Greece – in each cultural, political, economic, social, historical context – can assume a different nuance, or a different value, depending on the specific connection with modern Greece, as well as the specific value of ancient Greece in the local 'historical culture'. It also depends on the extent to which the ancient Greek culture is known at a popular level in the various countries – the global symbols must therefore be adapted to each individual location and context, thus becoming 'glocal'.

Returning to the concept of authenticity discussed at the beginning,[18] Greece in the theme park can ultimately be 'more authentic' than the modern Republic of Greece, exactly as *Disneyland*'s New Orleans in Eco's stupefied statement. Famously, Heidegger was very disappointed when travelling to Greece, as upon crossing the border he could not feel the 'Greekness' that the German philhellenic tradition had trained him to expect from his encounter with the 'cradle of culture'; in Olympia, he felt thoroughly underwhelmed by the village and the touristic structures.[19] This does not happen (or rather, should not happen) to the average visitor for whom the park is created, in the Greece of the theme park, which represents a sublimation of those parts of Greece which compose the expected and recognizable Greekness. Quite obviously, disappointment, or plain outrage, can be generated by theme park representations among those who have different (and minority) expectations: a philhellenic philosopher, a classicist, or perhaps a Greek national.

The process of ancient Greek culture (which is perceived as a global heritage) becoming glocal in the individual areas and contexts in which it is received, generates a third and crucial aspect, alongside the difficult polarity between the perception of classical Greek heritage as being both national (in the modern nation of Greece) and global, as investigated, for instance, by Lowenthal and Yalouri.[20] It will not have escaped the attention of the reader that one country is missing from this book: Greece. Of course, it would have been extremely interesting to study the representation of ancient Greece in theme parks within modern Greece, where the heritage presented is local, and offered both to a national public and to foreign tourists.[21] And yet, there is no theme park that represents ancient Greece in Greece.[22] Surely, a partial reason for this can be found in the relatively low level of success of theme parks in south-eastern Europe in general, although this cannot be an exhaustive answer in a country that depends so heavily on international tourism. The answer must rather be sought in the complicated dynamics between local, glocal and global in the appropriation of Greek heritage, and specifically in the tensions experienced in this sense within Greece, where classical antiquity represents an extremely important source of symbolic capital, serving as a crucial authoritative resource (following Giddens' terminology).[23]

As Yalouri has shown, there is in Greece a strong resistance against any kind of commercial activity, monetary transaction, or even just 'open exchange' in connection with antiquities and classical heritage, as these are perceived to be a dangerous commodification which undermines the values of national identity:[24] as so often happens, transactions that transform 'symbolic capital' into economic capital must be masked and hidden.[25] This ties in to the particular history and content of Greek nationalism, as well as to the highly difficult and consistent confrontation with an antiquity that is perceived as glorious and of universal significance, while at the same time belonging to the modern Greeks. This antiquity raises, nationally and internationally, fears and complexes of forever being unable to maintain the same stakes as their ancient precursors (what Nikos Dimou has called the 'National Inferiority Complex').[26] In substance, it ties in with the construction of ancient Greece as a heterotopia.[27] 'Earning money' with antiquities is unacceptable, but it is also unacceptable to 'play with them', or 'parody' them; it is unacceptable to undermine the 'objective authenticity' of the classical ruins for the 'sensorial authenticity' of the immersive environment, as this would give rise to a reduction in the importance and uniqueness of the Greek cultural heritage.[28] The theme park, in its connection to postmodern aesthetics, is substantially anti-auratic and anti-hierarchical, one of the forms which 'do not proclaim their uniqueness, but are mechanically, electronically and digitally reproduced and distributed'.[29] The first and principal examples of this are the Disney parks, as we have seen, and even individual rides within them, such as 'It's a Small World'. The adaptation to local cultures and circumstances does not, and cannot, change this 'loss of aura'; it is thus clear that, from a Greek perspective, it is unacceptable to dismantle the separation between the 'real ruins' – the archaeological heritage of the nation – and their 'copies'. These ruins must therefore be considered, in a modernist way, as being somehow still defined by the divide between high and low culture and thoroughly inserted, in the words of Bourdieu, within the 'cultural economy', with a non-convertible cultural capital.

The construction of a sort of classicizing fake gate at the stadium of Athens for the opening ceremony of the Athletics World Championships of 1998 caused great resentment and discussion within Greek society;[30] the Olympic Games of 2004 were strongly criticized for the excessive commodification of the Olympic spirit they gave rise to and propagated, as 'the prospect of Greece hosting the modern, commodified version of the Games presented for some the dreaded likelihood that "the Olympic spirit will die in the very land where it was born"'.[31] All this explains well enough why no *Acropolis Park* has been realized at the most popular touristic destinations. Not that similar initiatives have never been proposed – more meaningfully, plans to create ancient Greek theme parks in Greece have thus far failed. At the beginning of the 1990s, the project *Mythos Park*, a theme park based around classical mythology that was to be built in the outskirt of Athens, was made public.[32] On the eve of the Olympic Games of 2004, when considering how to further improve Greek tourism, Tassos Chomenidis, the managing director of the Hellenic Tourist Properties S.A., was still insisting on the project. Noting that there were no theme parks in south-eastern Europe, and demonstrating little knowledge of the European market (through the claim that *Disneyland Paris* was the only major park on the continent), the manager proposed a park with water attractions and mythological themes, which could attract tourists from Europe and Russia and bring them to Athens, which is often avoided while visiting the Aegean and the islands.[33] Yet nothing more was ever heard of this project. The plans for a theme park dedicated to Alexander the Great, to be realized in Thessaloniki, were more concrete. The reasons for this plan were mostly political, connected to the dispute with North Macedonia (then officially called Former Yugoslav Republic of Macedonia) around the use of the name 'Macedonia', as well as the cultural heritage connected to it, above all Philip II and Alexander the Great. The idea came from the Greek diaspora in the United States:

> The Chicago-based Alexander the Great Foundation, Inc. had kicked off a minor media circus in 2002–3 with plans for an Alexander-sanctuary of its own: an educational theme park centred on a 260-foot Mount Rushmore-style portrait carved into the face of Mount Kerdyllion. Abandoned in the face of protests by local archaeologists and environmentalists, this mega-Alexander would have gazed out towards Mount Athos, famously the never-used canvas on which the ancient Greek sculptor Dinocrates had hoped to carve an even larger Alexander of his own.[34]

What ultimately does exist in Greece are amusement parks which reference classical mythology, often in direct connection to the area where they are, such as the *Olympia Aqua Park*, in Kyllini, around 60 km from the ruins of the sanctuary, a water park that does not show any reference to classical antiquity beyond the mascots Hercules and Olympia.[35] Similar is the case of the park *Labyrinth* on Crete, near Hersonissos.[36] This is 'inspired by the Minoan culture', but does not contain any reproduction of the Palace of Knossos or its north portico; the contents of mythology and antiquity can be used, as long as the material sites of heritage – the archaeological sites and the ruins – are not (as they would thus be 'desacralized').[37] Despite sometimes being defined as a theme park, the *Aristoteles Park* in Stagira, where the ancient philosopher was born, is nothing of the kind, but rather a park celebrating the intellectual achievements of the famous ancient citizen of Stagira, in particular his research into what we would today call the natural sciences.[38] The rest is an aulic celebration of the ancient cultural heritage.

Yet this cannot be considered a revenge of 'museological authenticity', nor a bastion of the differentiation between high and low forms of culture. The nationalistic appropriation of ancient Greek heritage and culture is rather one of the 'strategies of targeting', to again use Kinder's vocabulary and model. Within the Republic of Greece, the global supersystem of symbols identified as 'Classical Greece' is catered to a specific function and a specific public, thus implying that only certain specific forms of its presentification are useful and acceptable. Outside of this (rather paradoxical) form of nationally and nationalistically laying claim to what is simultaneously presented and exalted as a universal heritage, other targets, strategies, and events 'decline' the vocabulary of symbols, images, and stereotypes connected to ancient Greece; this is also the case within the theme parks. But even if the meanings, uses and the functionalizations are at times very different, and encroach upon locally specific cultural issues, dominating discourses, even contingencies and occasions, the 'words' which can in various ways be declined are, in general, always the same. In the United States just as in Taiwan, in France as in Spain, blue and white, a windmill, a white Doric temple, some columns and a wooden horse are the grammatical elements that compose the phrase 'Greece'. It's a small world, after all.

Notes

Chapter 1: Representing History in the Theme Park: The Case of Ancient Greece

1. 'It's a Small World' is therefore an example of 'lifting', 'attractions or other elements which are largely or entirely duplicated in multiple parks' (Younger 2016: 392).
2. http://time.com/82493/its-a-small-world-50th-anniversary/ [23/04/2018].
3. See Fjellman 1992: 274–6; van Maanen 1992: 13.
4. On the colonialist underpinnings of 'It's a Small World', see Hom 2013.
5. Carlà-Uhink, Freitag, Mittermeier and Schwarz 2017: 9–10.
6. Carlà, Freitag, Mittermeier and Schwarz 2016: 326–8.
7. On-ride video: https://www.youtube.com/watch?v=bIOPXLEMCQo [23/04/2018].
8. Hom 2013: 34.
9. On the Greek communities in the United States, see pp. 107–10.
10. https://www.youtube.com/watch?v=yveW8Q-dLCU [23/04/2018]. On *Tokyo Disneyland* and the choice of certain elements within it from Orlando rather than from Anaheim, see van Maanen 1992: 15–16.
11. Hendry 2000: 34–6.
12. On-ride video: https://www.youtube.com/watch?v=7bNWkXvNDTE [23/04/2018].
13. Lukas 2016. See also Gottdiener 2001: in particular 73–144; Kolb 2008: 109–14.
14. Bryman 1999: 33: 'Disneyland's originality lies in the combination of the transformation of themed *attractions* into one of themed environments with the transformation of the world's fair/exposition concept into a *permanent* site' (italics in the original). See also Clavé 2007: 23–7.
15. Kagelmann 1993: 407–8. See also Fichtner and Michna 1987: 7–9; King 2002: 3–4; Clavé 2007: 28–9; King and O'Boyle 2011: 5–7; Carlà and Freitag 2015c: 135–6; Carlà-Uhink, Freitag, Mittermeier and Schwarz 2017: 10; Lukas 2013: 16.
16. King 2007: 838.
17. See Harris 1997; Clavé 2007: 3–18; King 2007; Lukas 2008: 21–80; King and O'Boyle 2011: 7–9. On antecedents of theme parks, see, among many others, Young and Riley 2002. On the theme park as an expression of postmodern architecture, see Hannigan 1995; see also Fjellman 1992: 398–9.
18. Steinkrüger 2013: 180–1. See also Davis 1997: 31–4.
19. See Roseberry and O'Brien 1991: 8, on the representation of non-Western civilizations as 'an array of neatly bounded units', mostly intended to highlight

their difference from European and more generally Western culture. See also Hendry 2000: 50–60.
20 Steinkrüger 2013: 123–4.
21 Roseberry and O'Brien 1991: 1.
22 Anderson 1984: 17–21; Hitchcock 1998: 127–8; Hendry 2000: 134–6; Conan 2002. See also Kirshenblatt-Gimblett 1998: 39–41.
23 See Muzaini 2016: 245–7. See also Wallace 1996: 10–12.
24 King 1981: 121.
25 In some parks the ritual crossing of the boundary is made even more evident through further actions: in the former *Glücks-Königreich* in Japan, for instance, a theme park representing Germany, tickets looked like a German passport, which was stamped at the entrance of the park: Hendry 2000: 21.
26 See King 1981: 127–8; Fichtner and Micha 1987: 13–15.
27 Francaviglia 1981: 141.
28 Lukas 2013: 69. See also Urry and Larsen 2011: 125–6.
29 King and O'Boyle 2011: 11; see also King 2002: 10.
30 Fichtner and Michna 1987: 26–7.
31 See, among others, Hendy 2000: 104 (on *Taman Mini Indonesia*); Bruner 2001: 886–90 (on *Bomas of Kenya*); Schlehe 2004: 303–9; Hitchcock 2005; Hitchcock and Stanley 2010: 73–5; 79–81; Salazar 2010: 95–7; Schlehe and Uike-Bormann 2010: 73–85 (on *Taman Mini Indonesia*); Hom 2015: 195–204 (on *Italia in Miniatura*); Carlà 2016: 21–2; Feige 2017 (on *Mini Israel*); Paine 2019: 65–8.
32 Feige 2017: 165–6.
33 See e.g. Mittermeier 2017.
34 Hochbruck and Schlehe 2010: 8.
35 Bryman 2004: 18.
36 Folch 2017: 161.
37 Schlehe and Uike-Bormann 2010: 57. See also Dicks 2004: 103–7, adopting the definition of 'ethnographic theme park'; Paine 2019: 15; 75–81 ('culture park').
38 Ong and Jin 2016.
39 My definition of 'historical theme park' therefore places a clear accent on 'theme park' and is completely different from other definitions which consider 'historical theme park' as being more or less a synonym of 'living history museum', stressing the educational purposes of such structures, and their generally governmental or non-profit making nature (e.g. Moscardo and Pearce 1986: 471). King (2007: 838) in this sense calls *Colonial Williamsburg* a 'historic theme park', and *Archeon*, Alphen an der Rijn, Netherlands, is defined as 'archaeological theme park' (Ijzereef 1999). Hjemdahl (2002) uses the concept of 'historical theme park' to describe private initiatives offering immersive experiences of the past to visitors and schools along the principles of living history museums, and therefore without attractions.

Although she never explicitly defines the concept, it is clear that it is quite different from that adopted here, as the label of 'ethnic theme parks', used for attractions representing the ethnic diversity or the traditional ethnicities of a region or a state, generally with shows and reconstructions, but without rides (see e.g. Yang 2011: 321–2). Nor can I accept the definition of 'theme park' or the idea of 'themeparkization' deployed in reference to archaeological sites, despite the possible usefulness of such an approach for the study of tourism, cultural heritage, and of preservation. Mortensen (2009), for instance, uses this approach for Copán, underlining that the archaeological site, organized as an 'archaeological industry', resembles a theme park, with loads of tourists arriving in the morning, staff 'keeping open' and cleaning while the tourists are there, and highly staged appearances of the archaeologists. If we take the classification provided by Blockley (1999: 15), who argues that the 'five main forces behind the creation of reconstructions' are 'interpretation; education; tourism development; experiment/research; local or cultural identity', I consider theme parks to be only those moved by the third force, and eventually by the fifth, as in the case of the political miniparks such as *Taman Mini Indonesia Indah* mentioned above. I therefore consider historical what, from a different perspective, Paine (2019: 3) calls 'mythology', 'history' and 'foreign culture' parks.

40   Carlà 2016: 19–20.
41   Schlehe and Hochbruck 2010: 11.
42   Chapman 2018: 36–7.
43   See also King and O'Boyle 2011: 12–14 on the connection between representation and the memory of the visitors.
44   See Füßmann 1994: 35: historical information only becomes relevant when it connects to the horizons of expectation and experience of the public addressed. On recognizability see also Boym 2001: 35; Kolb 2008: 111, 116–17; McCall 2018: 406–7.
45   See e.g. van Maanen 1992: 21, on how the ride 'Pirates of the Caribbean' is received in Tokyo by some visitors, who are unfamiliar with Western pirate stories. See also Davis 1997: 164.
46   Lowenthal 1998: 163.
47   See Salazar 2010: 94. See also Fjellman 1992: 29–30.
48   Howe 2011: 196. See also Hendry 2000: 158.
49   See for example Horne 1984: 16–17.
50   Friedman 1992: 845–6; Holtorf 2005: 135–6; Lukas 2010: 136–9; 2013, 111–13. Jameson (1991: 12) argues that the existential model of authenticity and inauthenticity has been repudiated by postmodernism.
51   Yang 2011: 321. See also Horne 1984: 27; Dicks 2004: 58.
52   MacCannell 1973.

53 Knudsen and Waade 2010: in particular 12–16.
54 Orvell 1989: xxiii.
55 Eco 1987: 6–7. See also Hom 2015: 17–19.
56 Lash and Urry 1994: 4.
57 As already highlighted by Moscardo and Pearce (1986), who claimed that 'the existing definitions of authenticity have failed to consider the time dimension, they were intended for classifying present day settings' (473).
58 Steinkrüger 2013: 222.
59 Lowenthal 1998: 165. See also Winnerling 2014: 159.
60 Wallace 1996: 23. See also Anderson 1984: 60–1; Hendry 2000: 127–9.
61 Lowenthal 1998: 154–5.
62 Gable and Handler 2004.
63 Baudrillard 1976: 61–73; 1981: 121.
64 Hom (2013: 27), for themed environments, explicitly refers to simulacra of the second order; also Hom (2015: 10) seems to feel the sense of the conundrum when using the concept of simulacra and defining them 'copies that are visited more than is the original'.
65 Baudrillard 1981: 10.
66 Baudrillard 1981. 9.
67 See Fjellman 1992: 61: 'this is not the space-time continuum of modernism, which, however folded, remains connected. Rather, we have here the disconnected, discrete space-time packages of postmodernism'; Knight 2003: 325–6.
68 Baudrillard 1981: 108.
69 On this, from the perspective of media studies, see Großklaus 1995: 98–9. Even if Großklaus works within Baudrillard's categories, he highlights (108) that the images of images, reaching a medial autonomy, reinforce the 'veridicity' of a 'remaining starting point-reality' (*Rest-Ausgangs-Realität*); see also 127–42: here Großklaus seems to imply that the 'third level' of simulacrum is intrinsic to computer simulation.
70 Hendry 2000: 70.
71 Baudrillard 1981: 6.
72 Adey 2007: 153.
73 Ren 1998: 18–20: 'a landscape of cultural representation assembling knowledge of culture into a form realigned entirely through consumption'.
74 Holtorf 2017: 6.
75 See n. 31.
76 Rowan 2004: 262. On religion in theme parks, see Paine 2019.
77 See e.g. Bryman 2004: 15. See also Kolb 2008: 111–12.
78 Kirshenblatt-Gimbett 1998: 146–7.
79 Lowenthal 2002: 11. Italics in the original. It has been argued that theme parks generally let visitors pay an entrance fee, while all the attractions within the park

are afterwards free, also because having to pay at every moment would imply an overly strong and continuous contact with 'reality': see Fichtner and Michna 1987: 39–40. See also Paine 2019: 92.
80   See Fjellman 1992: 61: 'there is little about the present at WDW'.
81   Teo, Chang and Ho 2001: 6.
82   Balme 1998: 55–6. See also Hendry 2000: 141–2.
83   Dicks 2004: 103–4.
84   Carlà 2016: 19–21. See also Salazar 2010: 93; Paine 2019: 65–71.
85   Francaviglia 1995.
86   See Carlà 2016: 19.
87   Jonker 2009: 38; Gorbahn 2011: 11.
88   Holtorf 2007b; 2009; 2017. See also Hochbruch and Schlehe 2010: 8–9, and Winnerling 2014: 152; 161–2, on video games.
89   Urry and Larsen 2011: 3.
90   Steinkrüger 2013: 58–62.
91   See Kolb 2008: 116.
92   Kolb 2008: 123. This is particularly evident when the 'theme' is one involving danger; in this case, the themed environment represents it as 'riskless risk' (see Hannigan 1998: 67–70).
93   Urry and Larsen 2011: 3–4.
94   Hahn 2012: 28; Pinzer 2012: 109.
95   Graburn 1977: 2. Großklaus 1995: 240–3 calls it a 'tactile time travel'.
96   Samuel 2012: 177–8. See also Holtorf 2017: 13.
97   See Carlà 2016: 20–1.
98   See Wallace 1996: 134; Edgerton 2001.
99   Chapman 2018: 14.
100 Bryman 2004: 1.
101 Bryman 1999; 2004. See also Clavé 2007: 177–87.
102 Zukin 1991: 20.
103 Bryman 1999: 26–7; 2004: 5–10.
104 Stone and Planel (1999: 8), for example, used the concept of 'Disneyfication' to describe archaeological sites built up for tourism that offer it in a 'final' form, and not continuously updated according to new research theories, opposing it to 'correct' experimental archaeology. The concept of 'Disneyfication' is also used for Knossos by Hitchcock and Koudounaris (2002: 52).
105 Gable and Handler 2004: 168
106 Olalquiaga 2002: 291.
107 See, in general, the contributions to the symposium 'Disney and the Historians: Where do we go from here?', in *Public Historian* 17.4 (1995); Wallace 1996: 163–73; Carlà 2016: 25–6; Mittermeier 2016.

108 Mittermeier 2016: 133–5. See also Lukas 2007b: 275–6.
109 Fjellman 1992: 59–63.
110 Lowenthal 1998: 170. On the historians' approach and the wish that 'distory' might aid a reconsideration of historical methods and assumptions, see Hollinshead 1998: 94–5. See Mittermeier 2016: 139–140, on professional historians siding with Disney in the dispute.
111 See pp. 84–5. An analysis of the didactic offer of *Sea World San Diego* is provided by Davis 1997: 117–51.
112 Huyssen 2001: 66. On the end of the high/low culture dichotomy in postmodernism, see below, n. 154.
113 Winnerling 2014: 160, referring to video games.
114 Grever and Adriaansen 2017. See also Rüsen 1994: 3–4.
115 Rüsen 2014.
116 Rüsen 1994: 18; 1995: 514–18.
117 See Howe 2011: 197–8.
118 Rüsen 1994: 7–8.
119 Rüsen 1994: 9.
120 Rüsen 2004.
121 Carlà and Freitag 2015c: 140–1. See also Francaviglia 1981; King 1981: 129–130; Zukin 1991: 221–2; Fjellman 1992: 169–76; Wallace 1996: 135–7; Knight 2003: 329–32.
122 See Lukas 2007b: 276–80.
123 Hardtwig 2010: 44–5.
124 Boym 2001: 78.
125 Blockley 1999: 18.
126 Lowenthal 2015: 502–5. See also Hjemdahl 2002: 106–7.
127 Lowenthal 1998: 148–62.
128 Carlà and Freitag 2015c: 136–9.
129 Fichtner and Michna 1987: 19–20; Wallace 1996: 137–8; Hochbruck and Schlehe 2010, 13.
130 Duke 2007: 89.
131 Lowenthal 2002: 15.
132 King and O'Boyle 2011: 15: 'Theming communicates by use of "carrier" symbols as a shorthand system'.
133 Nisbet 2008: 97.
134 Winnerling 2014: 158.
135 See also Holtorf 2010: 30.
136 For a history of the reconstruction of polychromy, with particular reference to the Parthenon, see van Zanten 1994.
137 Yalouri 2001: 176–9. See also Horne 1984: 29.

138 Salmon 2018: 81–2; Hanink 2017: 111–12, highlighting that Winckelmann already knew that the ancient statues were polychromic, but played it down in his reconstruction of ancient art.
139 Lowenthal 1988: 730.
140 Hanink 2017: 191. See also Plantzos 2008: 11–14.
141 King and O'Boyle 2011: 11.
142 Winnerling 2014: 158.
143 See Dicks 2004: 122–5.
144 Lukas 2007a: 76. See also Schlehe 2004: 298–9.
145 Lukas 2013: 136–8.
146 See in general Lukas 2007a. See also Pinzer 2012: 108–10.
147 See Dicks 2004: 19–21.
148 On this, see Eldridge 2006. See also Grütter 1994: 48.
149 Eldridge 2006: 195.
150 See Carlà 2016: 22–5.
151 Lowenthal 2002: 11–12.
152 Walsh 1992: 53–69.
153 See, among many others, Grütter 1994; Hardtwig 2010, 11.
154 Jameson 1991: 2; Huyssen 2001: 66; Hardtwig 2010: 30.
155 Samuel 2012.
156 Rowan and Baram 2004: x.
157 See e.g. Rowan and Baram 2004, in particular the introduction to the volume by Uzi Baram. Most literature in this sense adopts the concept of the 'theme park' as the scaremonger of a complete commodification of cultural heritage (Rowan and Baram 2004: 10: 'the next stage of archaeological sites, when they are transformed into theme parks for even greater ease of visitation').
158 Baudrillard 1981: 43.
159 Huyssen 2001; Gumbrecht 2010; Assmann 2013.
160 Koselleck 2000. See also Walsh 1992: 11–38.
161 Huyssen 2001; Gumbrecht (2010: 104) specifies that this temporality is 'postmodern' because postmodern thought, particularly Lyotard, has provided the conditions for the conceptualization of this shift. See also Jameson 1991: 16: 'we now inhabit the synchronic rather than the diachronic'; 27.
162 Grütter 1994.
163 Assmann 2013: 225–8.
164 Gumbrecht 2010: in particular 132–4.
165 Huyssen 2001: 70–1.
166 Braidotti 2013: 160.
167 Paradis 2007: 60. See also Jameson 1991: 284–7; Project on Disney 1995: 65–6.
168 Boym 2001: xiv. See also King 1981: 130–1.

169 Gumbrecht 2010: 67. See also Großklaus 1995: in particular 11–71.
170 Jameson 1991: 18–19; Boym 2001: 30.
171 On this, see, among many others, Walsh 1992: 94–115; 160–75; Wallace 1996: 135; Hannigan 1998: 925; Stone and Planel 1999 (and the entire volume into which this chapter is inserted); Chappell 2002; Hjemdahl 2002; Oesterle 2010; Urry and Larsen 2011: 151–4.
172 Boym 2001: xv.
173 See Agnew 2007.
174 Winnerling 2014: 152.
175 Anderson 1984: 10; Holtorf 2007b; 2009; 2017.
176 Gumbrecht 2010: 53.
177 Boym 2001: xviii; 41.
178 Olalquiaga 2002: 298.
179 Olalquiaga 2002: 293.
180 Wolf 1999; Schulze 2005; Pine and Gilmore 2011: especially 1–39. Gumbrecht (2010: 46) connects this with the change in the regime of temporality and with globalization. See also Bryman 2004: 26–7; Urry and Larsen 2011: 53–4.
181 Stone and Planel 1999: 6. See also Urry and Larsen 2011: 120–2, on themed architecture and its connection with the experience economy.
182 Schlehe and Hochbruck 2010: 8–9.
183 See e.g. Hendry 2000: 179–99; Bosker 2013: 22–9.
184 Holtorf 2005: 127–9; 2010, highlighting three requisites of pastness: materiality, an appearance that confirms preconceptions, and the existence of plausible and meaningful narratives.
185 Jameson 1991: 118.
186 Carlà, Freitag, Mittermeier and Schwarz 2016: 329–30.
187 Olalquiaga 2002: 145–6.
188 Van Eeden 2007: 121.
189 See e.g. Beard 2002: 22.
190 Carlà 2015; Carlà and Freitag 2015a; 2015b; 2015c. The problems highlighted by Clavé (2007: xiv), in particular the 'intellectual aversion' to theme parks, can surely in part explain this lack of scholarship.
191 Gottdiener 2001: 178.
192 Wyke 1997: 147; Melotti 2008: 53–76; Hom 2015: 4–5.
193 On the global character of ancient Greek heritage, see Yalouri 2001: 5–17.
194 Nisbet 2008: viii.
195 See on this Winnerling 2014: 159–60.
196 Nisbet 2008: 38–9.
197 Nisbet 2008: 16.
198 See Großklaus 1995: 113–16.

199 Winterer 2002: 66–7.
200 Nisbet 2008: viii.
201 Lowenthal 2002: 16–17.
202 Gohrbahn 2011: 13–14.
203 Lowenthal 2002: 17.
204 Holtorf 2007a: 8.
205 Herzfeld 1987: 54–5; Leoussi 1998: 21–4; Lowenthal 1988: 731–2; 1998: 199–200; 243–5; Hanink 2017.
206 Tsigakou 1981: 11. See also Hamilakis and Yalouri 1996: 122.
207 Tsigakou 1981: 42–9; Herzfeld 1987: 28–9; Morris 1994: 22–3; Hanink 2017: in particular 70–147.
208 Kaplanis 2014: 95–7.
209 On 'historical culture' in Greece, especially in relationship to classical antiquity, see, among others, Herzfeld 1987; Hamilakis and Yalouri 1996; Lowenthal 1998; Yalouri 2001; Hamilakis 2007; Damaskos and Plantzos 2008; Tziovas 2014; Yalouri 2014.
210 Herzfeld 1987: 1–5; quote p. 2.
211 Tsigakou 1981: 71–7; quote p. 76.
212 Yalouri 2001: 128.
213 Duke 2007: 23; on GNTO and its ways of advertising tourism in Greece, see González-Vaquerizo 2017.
214 Lowenthal 1988: 730–1.
215 Rhodes 1995: 18.
216 Yalouri 2014: 166–7.
217 See, among others, Kondaratos 1994: 37–49.
218 Tsigakou 1981: 29. On its value even today, see the episode narrated by Yalouri 2001: 5; 2014: 171, speaking of the Parthenon as a Panopticon. On the importance of the Parthenon within Greek culture, see also Philippides 1994.
219 Lambrinou 2018: 130–3. See also Connelly 2014: ix–xvii.
220 Nisbet 2008: 39. See also Horne 1984: 13.
221 Not by chance is the Parthenon also the symbol of UNESCO: see Hanink 2017: 21.
222 Rhodes 1995: 1–6.
223 Tsigakou 1981: 63; Yalouri 2001: 35–6; 55; Beard 2002: 99–102; Plantzos 2008: 15; Hanink 2017: 151–70.
224 Gorbahn 2007: 180.
225 Nisbet 2008: 76–7 highlights the strong 'militarisation' of modern images of Sparta.
226 Gorbahn 2007: 181–2.
227 Nisbet 2008: 87.
228 Nisbet 2008: 7.

229 Toner 2017: 178–9.
230 Carlà and Freitag 2015b: 148–50.
231 See Hanink 2017: 235–8.
232 Gorbahn 2007: 182.
233 Gorbahn 2007: 182. Classical mythology, and ancient religion in general, is presented mostly in an anecdotal way, not as what moderns would understand as a religious experience. See Paine 2019: 81–3.
234 See e.g. Leoussi 1998: 173–4 with a quantitative study on the presence of Greek myths in British painting.
235 Boym 2001: 7–8.
236 Sparkes 1971.
237 Solomon 2001: 124–5.
238 Nisbet 2008: 65.
239 Gorbahn 2011: 161.
240 Hamilakis and Momigliano 2006: 25–8.
241 Duke 2006: 82–3. See also Hamilakis 2002: 5–13.
242 Momigliano 2017: 2 for the association with myth. On Evans' reconstruction of the Palace of Knossos, see Hitchcock and Koudounaris 2002.
243 Solomon 2006: 172–3.
244 Nisbet 2008: 34.
245 Solomon 2006: 165–8.
246 See Gohrbahn 2007: 177–8.
247 Gohrbahn 2007: 177–8.
248 Gohrbahn 2007: 187–8.
249 Nisbet 2008: 2.
250 Gohrbahn 2011: 265–6.
251 Yalouri 2011: 152–3.
252 On the 'historiography of Greek sport', see Koulouri 2011.
253 Yalouri 2001: 39–40; 2014: 173–4. See also Hanink 2017: 170–6.
254 Leoussi 1998: 15. This conviction was also widespread in Greece: see Koulouri 2004: 25.
255 Leoussi 1998: 46.
256 See Leoussi 1998: 91–2; 101–3; 2016; 2018: 106–18.
257 See Koulouri 2004: 41; Yalouri 2004: 295. See also p. 170.
258 Gorbahn 2007: 182–3. See for example Rhodes 1995: 78–80, for an enthusiastic description of the realism of the *Doryphoros*.
259 Leoussi 2001: 481–3.
260 https://www.themetraders.com/greek-props-theme [27/03/2018].
261 https://www.eventprophire.com/themes/greek?currentPage=0&totalPages=6 [27/03/2018].

262 http://torino.repubblica.it/cronaca/2016/06/04/foto/in_aeroporto_vestiti_da_divinita_greche_volano_gratis_ad_atene-141277769/1/#1; http://www.lastampa.it/2016/06/04/multimedia/cronaca/volo-gratis-per-atene-solo-se-vestiti-da-antichi-greci-DziP6DbfNL5VTRFvD9OPSK/pagina.html [13/06/2016]
263 Carlà, Freitag, Grice and Lukas 2016.

Chapter 2: German Philhellenism in the Theme Park

1 Lambrinou 2018: 136–7.
2 Before that moment, philhellenism was often connected to a liberal and at times republican and radical political agenda, and thus viewed with some suspicion by institutions: see Marchand 1996: 32–5. See also Tsigakou 1981: 46–9.
3 Marchand 1996: 152.
4 Marchand 1996: xiii–xix; Leoussi 2016: 52–3.
5 Marchand 1996: xix–xxi. This does not contradict the fact that, within the academic structure, it was the discipline of classical philology which assumed a dominant position: see, among others, Werner 2011.
6 Morris 1994: 16–19; Sünderhauf 2004: 1–46.
7 See Meid 2012: 1–8.
8 Marchand 1996: 302–40.
9 Sünderhauf 2004: 139–53.
10 Leoussi 1999: 80–1; 2016: 48–51.
11 Leoussi 2016: 52–3; 84–6.
12 See Biddiss 1999, and p. 169.
13 Telesko 2004: 118–20. See also Squire 2011: 18–23.
14 See Wildmann 2018.
15 Sünderhauf 2004: 344–52.
16 Marchand 1996: 341.
17 However, it would be wrong to assume an easy and direct connection between philhellenism and nationalism, as shown by Most 2003.
18 That the Greeks were Aryans was a staple belief of racist literature since the nineteenth century; see Leoussi 2001: 473–6.
19 Marchand 1996: 343–54; Wildmann 1998: 23–6; Sünderhauf 2004: 295–334; Wiedemann 2018; Wildmann 2018.
20 Telesko 2004: 120–1.
21 The 'Greeks' are also often presented as a homogeneous group in school books, and in this case modelled on Athens (Gorbahn 2011: 137).
22 Gorbahn 2011: 14.

23 Gorbahn 2011: 209–10. See Gorbahn 2011: 227–42, for an analysis of the representation of Sparta in German school books.
24 Gorbahn 2011: 106–7.
25 Marchand 1996: xxiv; 354–75.
26 https://de.wikipedia.org/wiki/Griechen_in_Deutschland [26/05/2016]. See also Pantazis 2002: 71–6.
27 http://www.zeit.de/2010/20/Deutschlandkarte-Griechen [26/05/2016].
28 www.ifd-allensbach.de/uploads/tx_reportsndocs/prd_0313.pdf [26/05/2016].
29 http://www.dekochef.de/Griechenland_1 [31/05/2016].
30 http://www.partydeko.de/mottoparty/land/griechenland.html [31/05/2016].
31 http://www.ebay.de/gds/Tipps-zur-Dekoration-im-griechischen-Stil-/10000000178691809/g.html [31/05/2016].
32 Pantazis 2002: 71.
33 http://www.handelsblatt.com/unternehmen/dienstleister/tourismus-in-griechenland-warum-die-deutschen-hellas-trotzdem-lieben/11488824.html [26/05/2016].
34 Images of archaeological sites, and in particular of the Athenian Acropolis, are also widespread throughout illustrations in school books: see Gorbahn 2011: 259.
35 http://www.alltours.de/urlaub/griechenland/ [31.05.2016].
36 Gorbahn 2011: 213–14.
37 Gorbahn 2011: 168–91.
38 See pp. 35–6.
39 See Leoussi 2001: 481.
40 Schulz 2002: 389–91. On the presentation of Greek history in German school books, see Gorbahn 2011 – in general (102) Greece takes up more space in German school programmes than Egypt or the Ancient Near East, but much less than Rome.
41 Gorbahn 2011: 106. Myth represents, under the heading of 'religion' a central element in the chapters on ancient Greece from German school books (Gorbahn 2011: 158–61).
42 http://www.berliner-zeitung.de/immer-mehr-griechen-kehren-ihrer-heimat-den-ruecken-und-kommen-voller-hoffnung-nach-berlin--als-erstes-lernen-sie-deutsch-schoene-straende-sind-nicht-genug-15153242 [30/05/2016].
43 http://www.focus.de/magazin/archiv/jahrgang_2010/ausgabe_8/ [30/05/2016].
44 On this cover and the articles of these issues, their colonialist content, and the outrage they sparked in Greece, see Hanink 2017: 199–201.
45 http://www.focus.de/magazin/archiv/jahrgang_2010/ausgabe_18/ [30/05/2016].
46 Tsiovas 2014: 14–16.
47 TEA 2017: 11.
48 Clavé 2007: 149–51; Europa-Park 2015: 10. On the early history of the park, and for certain interesting insights on the plans for its development at the end of the 1990s, see Kreft 2000.

49 Europa-Park 2015: 24–5.
50 Heck 1997: 45.
51 See Klein 2000: 70; Europa-Park 2015: 12.
52 Klein 2000: 157; Europa-Park 2015: 16–17.
53 Schlehe and Uiko-Bormann 2010: 59.
54 Heck 1997: 46–7; Dawid 2004: 27.
55 Europa-Park 2015: 69.
56 Heck 1997: 52–3.
57 Schlehe and Uiko-Bormann 2010: 59.
58 Heck 1997: 48–9.
59 Schlehe 2004: 301–2.
60 Dawid 2004: 27.
61 http://www.europapark.de/de/park/themed-areas/griechenland [31/05/2016]
62 This is explicitly acknowledged by Europa-Park 2015: 60–1.
63 http://www.beazley.ox.ac.uk/XDB/ASP/recordDetails.asp?id=4C877B3C-6F6B-4A61-A757-04CF54736278&noResults=&recordCount=&databaseID=&search= [23/01/2017].
64 Carlà-Uhink and Freitag 2018: 284.
65 Gorbahn 2011: 131–5.
66 Rieche 2012: 193.
67 Europa-Park 2015: 69.
68 As stressed in Europa-Park 2015: 60–1.
69 A complete list can be found at http://www.epfans.info/?id=1637,12,& [21/09/2016].
70 Europa-Park 2015: 70.
71 A definition for a water coaster is provided by Younger 2016: 428.
72 Carlà-Uhink and Freitag 2018: 295–7.
73 Carlà and Freitag 2015a: 244–6.
74 Europa-Park 2015: 63.
75 On this, see Schwarz 2017.
76 Dawid 2004: 27–8.
77 See pp. 33–4.
78 Europa-Park 2015: 63.
79 On-ride video: https://www.youtube.com/watch?v=Hs53RHzWsxs [20/07/2016]
80 Carlà-Uhink and Freitag 2018: 297.
81 On VR coasters, see Younger 2016: 428.
82 However, the visitors opting for Coastiality had to queue in a different line, missing the entire theming of the waiting area. The virtual reality show was a promotional movie for the film *Happy Family* (2017).
83 Holtorf 2007a: 63–75.
84 Rieche 2012: 194–5.

85 Holtorf 2007a for a comprehensive study.
86 Holtorf 2007a: 36.
87 Boym 2001: 33.
88 Offride video: https://www.youtube.com/watch?v=EGPRgcIZI68 [22/07/2016]
89 See Mittermeier 2017.
90 Blanshard and Shahabudin 2011: 212; Carlà and Freitag 2015b: 156.
91 https://www.youtube.com/watch?v=B_kudFKPJxU [10/10/2016, a video from 2006]; https://www.youtube.com/watch?v=DRd_nFqcNxk [10/10/2016, a video from 2009].
92 Younger 2016: 70.
93 Europa-Park 2015: 68, tells the myth of Icarus only to state that today people can fly in safety, for instance in the ride's balloons.
94 See p. 32.
95 On shooters, see Younger 2016: 421.
96 See pp. 116–17.
97 The name of Atlantis, in the case of low levels of theming, can also be simply connected with images of the oceanic depths: one example is the condor ride 'Atlantis' (2016) in *Kernies Familienpark / Kalkar Wunderland* (Kalkar, Germany), on which pictures of various kinds of fish and coral decorate a ride on which, if one excludes the female figures that adorn the prows of the ships/gondolas, there are no traces of human presence.
98 In the Astérix comic *La galère d'Obélix* (1996), for instance, Atlantis is represented entirely through the forms of Minoan architecture; on this Astérix album, see also Müller 2017: 276–80. See Hamilakis 2006: 146–9, stressing that the Minoans were presented – and still are, in popular perception – as a utopia, as free people, traders, peace-loving and so on; this makes them very apt for a setting as myth, and particularly a utopian myth such as Atlantis.
99 Plato is mentioned and thus used as an explanation for the location of the ride in the Greek area in Europa-Park 2015: 67.
100 Ciardi 2011: 139–43.
101 Plat., *Tim.* 20d–25d; *Crit.* 108e–121c.
102 See, among others, Vidal-Naquet 2005; Ciardi 2011.
103 E.g. Strab. 2.3.6
104 Olalquiaga 2002: 104–16.
105 Olalquiaga 2002: 118.
106 Jules Verne, *Twenty Thousand Leagues Under The Sea*, Part 2; Chapter 9 ('A Vanished Continent'); transl. W. Butcher.
107 Ciardi 2011: 131–2.
108 On the movie, see Müller 2017: 280–2.
109 On-ride video: https://www.youtube.com/watch?v=cOTLrDy2SQ4 [15/09/2016].

Notes to pp. 58–67

110 On madhouses, see Younger 2016: 453.
111 Europa-Park 2015: 66 explicitly suggests reading the tables in the queuing area, as otherwise the narrative of the ride is hard to grasp. On this ride, see Paine 2019: 102.
112 Galanova 2009: 256–8.
113 On-ride video: https://www.youtube.com/watch?v=A10usWc2IWo [15/09{2016].
114 The text is available at http://madhouse-guide.com/?lang=de&id=2&sid=4&ssid=7 [15/09/2016].
115 Kessler 2012: 147.
116 https://www.parkerlebnis.de/belantis-besucherzahlen-2016_34240.html [06/09/2018].
117 A new themed area had been announced as a project for 2018 (http://www.freizeitpark-welt.de/freizeitparks/belantis/belantis_start.php?id=2&nid=2461 [06/09/2018]), but the project seems to have been abandoned.
118 Schröder 2012: 206–7.
119 On this as a character of many theme parks, see Fichtner and Michna 1987: 60.
120 Kessler 2012: 147–9; Schröder 2012: 205.
121 Interestingly, an episode (546, 2003) of the popular German crime TV show *Tatort* was shot in the theme park which, in the fiction, was named *Atlantis*.
122 Mitrašinović 2006: 139.
123 Francaviglia 2011: 60.
124 Freizeitparks 2017: 16–17.
125 Kessler 2012: 153.
126 In 2011, the topic was Pinocchio; in 2012 the show, dedicated to the park's mascot, was called 'Buddelshow'; after this, 'Immer Ärger mit Schneewittchen' ('Always Trouble with Snow White') followed in 2014, and in 2015–16 a version of *The Magic Flute* for children.
127 The name is a pun related to the 'Pythagorean cup', which is also called, in German, 'Schale des Pythagoras'.
128 Carlà-Uhink and Freitag 2018: 287–8. On tow-boat rides, see Younger 2016: 426.
129 Full on-ride video: https://www.youtube.com/watch?v=_a8g0r0LpaI [23/09/2016].
130 Personal communication.
131 Cuisinier 2003: 277–85.
132 Ulf 2003.
133 See e.g. Cuisinier 2003: 153–5. For a critical perspective, see Cobet 2003; 2006; Zimmermann 2006.
134 Cuisinier 2003: 316–21. On the Strait of Messina as the place of the myth of Scylla and Charybdis, see Carbone 2018.
135 For the on-ride video of 'Fluch des Pharao': https://www.youtube.com/watch?v=ko_1B6_mUvE [25/09/2016].

136 Carlà-Uhink and Freitag 2018: 288.
137 See Berti 2015 for a detailed explanation of this evolution in Circe's reception.
138 Carlà-Uhink and Freitag 2018: 288. The Homeric Circe seems to have a lot in common with Athena, as stressed by Berti (2015: 115–16), although this surely played no role in the genesis of this iconography.
139 Cuisinier 2003: 221–3.
140 Cuisinier 2003: 295–7.
141 The Sirens are otherwise generally located off the Campanian coast (Cuisinier 2003: 304–6).
142 See Berti and Carlà-Uhink 2018: 207–8.
143 Personal communication. For the standard skydive by Sunkid, see http://www.sunkidworld.com/sunkid-produkte0/sunkid-summer-world0/skydive-freizeittechnik.html [10/10/2016].
144 http://www.gerstlauer-rides.de/assets/downloads/brochures/SkyRoller.pdf [07/10/2016].
145 On-ride video: https://www.youtube.com/watch?v=EG8u36aaW84 [07/10/2016].
146 http://www.zierer.com/mainmenu/produkte/rundfahrgeschaefte/jet-skis/; http://www.inno-heege.de/index.php/grossanlagen/wasserrondell.html [11/10/2016].
147 Offride video: https://www.youtube.com/watch?v=66dJcFzAmv0 [11/10/2016].
148 See pp. 18–19.
149 Offride video: https://www.youtube.com/watch?v=Hi-OBTT-Cwc [11/10/2016].
150 Personal communication.

Chapter 3: Spain, Ancient Greece and the Land of Myths

1 Also opponents of Franco's regime, such as Ortega y Gasset, considered the Visigoths to be the decisive factor in the birth of the Spanish nation (see Cortadella Morral 1988: 18).
2 Corbí 2009: 2. The autochthonist idea, and the strong continuity with prehistorical times, is particularly developed in the work of Almagro Basch (see Cortadella Morral 1988: 20–1).
3 Corbí 2009: 3.
4 Corbí 2009: 34–6.
5 Duplà Ansuategui 1992: 205–6. This ambiguity is less present in etic representations of Spain: in the Japanese *Parque España*, for example, Roman antiquity is presented as an integral part of Spanish history and identity (see Hendry 2000: 26).
6 Duplà Ansuategui 1992: 204–5.
7 On 'Numantinismo' and its origins, see Gracia Alonso 2017: 67–73. See also Ruiz Zapatero and Alvarez-Sanchís 1995: 216–17.

8   See Aguilera Durán 2014.
9   Díaz-Andreu 1993: 75.
10 http://thurrakos.blogspot.de/ [05/12/2016].
11 Corbí 2009: 4–10; 15–19 on the example of Pericot.
12 Ruiz Zapatero and Alvarez-Sanchís 1995: 216.
13 Díaz Andreu 1993: 78. See also Cortadella Morral 1988: 22.
14 Gracia Alonso 2017: 73–94.
15 Díaz-Andreu 1997: 160.
16 See Díaz-Andreu 1997: 159–60.
17 See Olmos 1991.
18 Kirshenblatt-Gimblett 1998: 136.
19 For the Greek presence in Spain from a scholarly perspective, see Domínguez 2006. As an example of the popularization of these contents, see for example the page 'The Greeks in Spain' on the website 'Spain then and now', edited by two retired professors: http://www.spainthenandnow.com/spanish-history/the-greeks-in-spain/default_39.aspx [05/12/2016].
20 A complete collection of all ancient sources referring to Tartessos is offered by Freeman 2010.
21 On the reception of Tartessos in popular culture, in particular the homonymous comic, see Iguácel 2008. On Tartessos in Francoist historiography, see Martí-Aguilar 2003; Corbí 2009: 32–3.
22 Gorbahn 2007: 184–5.
23 Díaz-Andreu 1997: 158.
24 Corbí 2009: 22.
25 Corbí 2009: 14.
26 Díaz-Andreu 1997: 160–2.
27 Ruiz Zapatero 1996: 185; Corbí 2009: 36–48.
28 Ruiz Zapatero and Alvarez-Sanchís 1995: 218–19; Ruiz Zapatero 1996: 180–7; Ruiz Zapatero 2003. See also Ruiz, Sánchez and Bellón 2003. In general, on the historiography of the Iberians, see Díaz-Andreu 1997.
29 Ruiz Zapatero 1996: 189–90. See also Ruiz Zapatero and Alvarez-Sanchís 1995: 223–4.
30 García Santa María and Pagès Blanch 2008: 698–9. See also 710–13.
31 García Santa María and Pagès Blanch 2008: 703.
32 García Santa María and Pagès Blanch 2008: 707.
33 García Santa María and Pagès Blanch 2008: 713–14.
34 Gorbahn 2011: 345.
35 http://www.rtve.es/alacarta/audios/mediterraneo/ [14/12/2016].
36 Dietler 1994: 595–6; Díaz-Andreu 1997: 163.
37 Clavé 2007: 367.

38 Plat., *Phaid.* 109b.
39 https://web.archive.org/web/20070517170958/http://www.rcdb.com/document48.htm [14/12/2016].
40 http://elpais.com/diario/2006/07/28/cvalenciana/1154114290_850215.html [14/12/2016].
41 http://economia.elpais.com/economia/2010/07/27/actualidad/1280215984_850215.html [14/12/2016].
42 http://www.levante-emv.com/comunitat-valenciana/2012/06/28/venden-terra-mitica-67-millones/916465.html [14/12/2016].
43 http://www.pa-community.com/articulos/iberia-park-la-nueva-ocionia-de-terra-mitica [14/12/2016].
44 http://www.terramiticapark.com/en/social-celebrations.html [15/12/2016].
45 http://www.dailymail.co.uk/news/article-2684277/teenager-dies-falling-rollercoaster-called-Hell-Benidorm-theme-park-harness-failed.html [14/12/2016].
46 http://www.abc.es/espana/comunidad-valenciana/abci-terra-mitica-amplia-mercado-hotel-vender-paquetes-entrada-y-alojamiento-201607131256_noticia.html [15/12/2016].
47 Lowenthal 1998: 188.
48 Video of the show: https://www.youtube.com/watch?v=vRFcHt7y1dY [15/12/2016]. See Carlà and Freitag 2015a: 247; Carlà-Uhink and Fiore 2016: 202.
49 Video of the show: https://www.youtube.com/watch?v=0Kbn-EXzbS4 [16/12/2016].
50 Video of the show: https://www.youtube.com/watch?v=R-ieu2jug8g [16/12/2016].
51 The scenography and costumes were realized by the architect Curt Allen Wilmer Goodman, who then worked for GPD s.a.: http://estudiodedos.com/trabajos/barbaroja-terra-mitica; http://estudiodedos.com/trabajos/barbaroja-terra-mitica∞icio [16/12/2016].
52 See the special flyer, available at http://www.terramiticapark.com/ProgEscolarWeb-TM.pdf [16/12/2016].
53 As the guide to 'Las Islas' does not include the ride 'El Rescate de Ulíses', which closed in 2005, it must have been created after this year.
54 http://www.terramiticapark.com/es/escolares.html#center_guias [16/12/2016]
55 *IG* I³, 127. See Lawton 1995: 88–9; with a photographic reproduction on Plate 7.
56 Carlà, Freitag, Mittermeier and Schwarz 2016: 328–9.
57 https://www.youtube.com/watch?v=OKVpXAC84N8 [09/02{2017].
58 It may be interesting to highlight that, as the Hellenistic period as such is not particularly present in popular history, it has been 'split' in *Terra Mítica* according to the geographic areas: in 'Egipto' there is a reproduction of the Pharos of Alexandria, placed directly next to the structures evoking Pharaonic Egypt.
59 Carlà-Uhink and Freitag 2018: 284.

60 The booklet for schools, while explaining the statue of the Athena Lemnia, also recalls the myth of the contest between Athena and Poseidon for the control of Attica.
61 Nisbet 2008: 32–3.
62 Video of the show: https://www.youtube.com/watch?v=Lckx2rb5DNI [03/02/2017].
63 In the ancient myth, women were used by the lion to attract men who wanted to rescue them into the cave.
64 On this ride, see Carlà and Freitag 2015a: 252–6; 2015b: 152–4. What is presented here is a shorter version of the analysis conducted there.
65 On-ride video: https://www.youtube.com/watch?v=FrUaNYa0wNU [03/02/2017].
66 http://www.animala.es/en/portfolio/terra-mitica/ [11/05/2018].
67 See pp. 30–1.
68 On this sort of ride, see Freitag 2016: 128.
69 http://www.themeparkinsider.com/columns/kevin/238.cfm [17/01/2018].
70 http://www.achus.net/noticias/2006/terra-mitica-estrena-nueva-pelicula-en-el-simulador-de-grecia.php [20/02/2017].
71 On Intamin spillwater rides: https://intaminworldwide.com/wp-content/uploads/2016/12/spillwater_12_15_20_web.pdf [09/02/2017].
72 On-ride video: https://www.youtube.com/watch?v=Tbaqci6ZABM [07/02/2017].
73 Carlà-Uhink and Freitag 2018: 292–4.
74 http://mondialrides.com/rides/parkrides/revolution [09/02/2017].
75 Personal communication with Menno Draaisma, Mondial Rides, on 10/02/2017.
76 http://www.terramiticapark.com/es/el-parque/grecia/atracciones/los-icaros.html [09/02/2017].
77 See p. 32.
78 https://www.hosteltur.com/02668_terra-mitica-presenta-hoy-rescate-ulises-nueva-atraccion-ha-supuesto-inversion-3000-millones-pesetas.html [10/02/2017].
79 A personal communication from Paul Sommer (Hafema Water Rides) has highlighted that the ride was built by the company which later gave life to Hafema; they did not play any role in the theming, though, as this had been completely realized, with storybook, by the Spanish company Patali.
80 Carlà-Uhink and Freitag 2018: 288–91. On–ride video: https://www.youtube.com/watch?v=SoR89cJXc3U [10/02/2017]. For a thorough description of the attraction and its script: http://themeparkzone.es/2014/07/08/terra-mitica-el-guion-descriptivo-de-el-rescate-de-ulises/ [10/02/2017].
81 Carlà-Uhink and Freitag 2018: 289.
82 Carlà-Uhink and Freitag 2018: 290.
83 See Berti and Carlà-Uhink 2018: 205–13.
84 Carlà-Uhink and Freitag 2018: 290–1.
85 Ogden 2013: 129–35.

86 On-ride video: https://www.youtube.com/watch?v=Yl3QlsvP730 [20/02/2017].
87 http://www.themeparkinsider.com/columns/kevin/238.cfm [20/02/2017].
88 Carlà-Uhink and Freitag 2018: 294–5.
89 http://mondialrides.com/rides/transportable/super-nova [20/02/2017].
90 Offride video: https://www.youtube.com/watch?v=Cb7Aj9hrUGQ [20/02/2017].

Chapter 4: Ancient Greece, the United States of America and the Theme Park

1 Winterer 2002: 16–17.
2 See, among others, Wyke 1997: 14–17; Bederman 2009; Frank 2011: 480–5; Heun 2011.
3 Connolly 2010: 79, who also highlights how these references to classical culture were instrumental in differentiating the European colonists from other groups, and therefore enforcing different forms of domination over African Americans, Native Americans and women.
4 Jenkins 2015: 8.
5 Winterer 2002: 18–20.
6 Winterer 2002: 61–76; Yalouri 2004: 299–300.
7 Winterer 2002: 74–5.
8 Frank 2011: 491–2. See also Mattern 2011.
9 Lambrinou 2018: 141–4.
10 The Parthenon played a central role as model in the nineteenth century and was also perceived to be the highest point of art in Great Britain, where many projects for a reconstruction of the temple were realized: see Fehlmann 2007.
11 Loseman 2011.
12 On Sparta in the historical culture of the Third Reich, see pp. 40–1.
13 Beard 2002: 5–7; Lambrinou 2018: 149.
14 Yalouri 2004.
15 Jenkins 2015: 30–2.
16 Vinson 2004: 57–8.
17 Winterer 2002: 178.
18 Hanink 2017: 32–3.
19 Yalouri 2001: 6. George Bush also spoke of the ties between the United States and Greece (McEnroe 2002: 67).
20 Hanink 2017: 22.
21 Fjellman 1992: 381–2.
22 Kourvetaris 1997: 17–31; Kourvetaris 1999: 249–51.
23 Barkan 1999: 13.

24 Conzen 1989: 48. In this sense, ethnicity should be understood from a constructivist perspective (Sollors 1989: xiv–xv).
25 Kourvetaris 1997: 1.
26 Kourvetaris 1997: 6–7.
27 Conzen 1989: 55. See also Kourvetaris 1999: 248–9.
28 See Conzen 1989 for examples taken from the German community in the United States during the nineteenth century.
29 Kourvetaris 1999: 251–2.
30 Sollors 1989: xvi.
31 Barkan 1999: 4–5.
32 Lowenthal 1998: 81–2.
33 Barkan 1999: 3.
34 Yalouri 2001: 71.
35 Yalouri 2001: 73.
36 Yalouri 2001: 71.
37 See Fjellman 1992: 87–91; Wallace 1996: 144–6. On-ride video: https://www.youtube.com/watch?v=UaVHkwmwWiA [07/03/2017].
38 See Project on Disney 1995: 73. The movie is available at: https://www.youtube.com/watch?v=ONRTzWy26Ko [27/09/2018].
39 The movie *Hercules* has been already thoroughly analysed from the perspective of classical reception: see Blanshard and Shahabudin 2011: 194–215.
40 https://www.youtube.com/watch?v=HeoJktA1sEI [07/03/2017].
41 Blanshard and Shahabudin 2011: 200–1.
42 Blanshard and Shahabudin 2011: 201.
43 Scholarship on the reception of Heracles is abundant: see, among others, Stafford 2012: 201–44, more particularly 237–9 for Disney's movie.
44 Blanshard and Shahabudin 2011: 197.
45 Blanshard and Shahabudin 2011: 209; Stafford 2012: 239.
46 Shanower 2011; 2013.
47 http://www.disneyparkhistory.com/animal-kingdom.html; http://www.wdwforgrownups.com/articles/rides-never-were-walt-disney-world-%E2%80%93-beastlie-kingdomme-animal-kingdom; http://progresscityusa.com/2009/06/19/neverworlds-the-magic-kingdoms-fantasia-gardens/ [24/03/2017].
48 https://www.youtube.com/watch?v=zHHL7OLyEsI [23/04/2018].
49 https://disneyparks.disney.go.com/blog/2013/03/opa-a-celebration-of-greece-coming-to-disneyland-resort-may-25-27/ [23/04/2018]; http://www.neomagazine.com/2013/10/argiro-barbarigou-showcases-greek-cuisine-in-the-us/ [23/04/2018].
50 https://www.youtube.com/watch?v=lE1SH1A0Pvo [23/04/2018]; http://www.mouseinfo.com/forums/content/2252-look-opa-greek-celebration-disneyland-park.

html [23/04/2018]; http://www.mouseinfo.com/forums/content/2249-opa-disney-california-adventure-celebrates-greek-culture-food-entertainment-more.html [23/04/2018]. The logo of the event had only one reference to classical antiquity, a crown made of olive leaves, which surrounded a central space with the word OPA! written in angular letters. Beneath this was a banner with the writing 'A celebration of Greece'. Apart from the green leaves and a small golden Disney logo on the bottom, the entire logo was blue and white, the colours of the Greek national flag.

51 See, for instance, the comments by a visitor at https://ocmomblog.com/opa-a-celebration-of-greece-at-disneyland-resort/ [23/04/2018]: 'Having some Greek in my blood, it is important to share my heritage with my children, and Disneyland created a magical celebration of my heritage this weekend.'
52 See Lukas 2008: 138–9.
53 See p. 1.
54 https://seaworldparks.com/en/buschgardens-williamsburg/Attractions/Rides/Apollos-Chariot/ [07/03/2017].
55 https://www.youtube.com/watch?v=X__VWgtSkvE [27/09/2018].
56 See Holtorf 2007a: 88–90.
57 See pp. 56–7.
58 Orlando: https://www.youtube.com/watch?v=cMMslhVyF9w; San Diego: https://www.youtube.com/watch?v=9lzppeAtCs0; San Antonio: https://www.youtube.com/watch?v=YbkupOfjwjY [08/03/2017]. On lifting, see Younger 2016: 392.
59 The Dells 1999: 39–55.
60 http://www.wisdells.com/wisconsin-dells.htm [30/06/2017].
61 http://www.wiscnews.com/wisconsindellsevents/news/local/article_426b10ab-f174-5168-a348-17b5a030e035.html [08/03/2017].
62 https://www.facebook.com/notes/mt-olympus-resorts-parks/history-of-mt-olympus-resorts/324431177602933/ [08/03/2017].
63 http://www.legacy.com/obituaries/sunsentinel/obituary.aspx?page=lifestory&pid=1646801 [08/03/2017]. The food service industry is the business area in which most Greek immigrant entrepreneurs worked (Kourvetaris 1997: 140–1).
64 http://www.hotwiredirect.com/customers/mt-olympus-theme-park/ [08/03/2017].
65 http://www.wiscnews.com/wisconsindellsevents/news/local/article_5f7f305a-ba2f-5467-9786-197def25e9c9.html [30/06/2017].
66 http://www.angelfire.com/wi3/wisconsindells/ [08/03/2017].
67 http://archive.jsonline.com/business/123694669.html [08/03/2007].
68 http://www.wiscnews.com/wisconsindellsevents/news/local/article_862f33bb-f6ec-5286-b93d-96b87aea3df4.html [23/06/2017]
69 http://host.madison.com/wsj/news/local/wisconsin-dells-theme-park-owners-plan-major-expansions-along-the/article_bec0309a-1f5f-11e0-8d94-001cc4c03286.html [08/03/2017]; http://archive.jsonline.com/business/123694669.html [08/03/2017];

Notes to pp. 121–130

http://www.wiscnews.com/wisconsindellsevents/news/local/article_89a85d0a-e39c-11df-9030-001cc4c03286.html [08/03/2017].
70 http://www.wiscnews.com/wisconsindellsevents/news/local/article_862f33bb-f6ec-5286-b93d-96b87aea3df4.html [23/06/2017].
71 https://www.youtube.com/watch?v=MCJ-pLz4R4w; https://www.youtube.com/watch?v=PSDHeJR12pw [23/06/2017].
72 http://www.wiscnews.com/baraboonewsrepublic/news/local/article_90299ce8-e2d1-51b6-924a-a1e527183124.html [23/06/2017].
73 With the sole partial exception of 'Thunder and Lightning', which might refer to Zeus' arts, the names of the other water attractions in this area are very generic, such as 'speed slides', 'tube slides', 'mat or no mat slides' etc.
74 https://www.facebook.com/notes/mt-olympus-resorts-parks/history-of-mt-olympus-resorts/324431177602933/ [30/06/2017].
75 http://www.wiscnews.com/wisconsindellsevents/news/local/article_9b340f9a-543b-11e1-990c-0019bb2963f4.html [30/06/2017].
76 http://www.wiscnews.com/wisconsindellsevents/news/local/article_85301309-ce06-5a58-afa5-9362a9a7d7c8.html [30/06/2017].
77 https://www.mtolympuspark.com/parks/outdoor/theme-park/poseidon-underwater-go-kart-track/ [30/06/2017].
78 http://www.wiscnews.com/wisconsindellsevents/news/local/article_76fdba2f-a86e-5a48-a5cc-dd03e7269eee.html [30/06/2017].
79 http://www.channel3000.com/news/local-news/family-thankful-son-is-alive-after-cable-breaks-on-dells-ride_20161116051905116/163047778 [30/06/2017].

Chapter 5: The Far East, Ancient Greece and the Theme Park

1 Renger and Fan 2019 is now a seminal work on the topic.
2 Takada 2010; Theisen 2011; Castello and Scilabra 2015; Pigeat 2015; Scilabra 2015; Wieber 2017: 335–48; Scilabra 2018; Kawana 2019; Scilabra 2019.
3 The 'Western Alterity' can even be used to represent complete otherness, or even the 'evil side' (Scilabra 2015: 101–2; 2019: 300–2).
4 Theisen 2011: 59. See also Kawana 2019: 262–3.
5 Hendry 2000: 3.
6 On *Thermae Romae*, see Kawana 2019.
7 http://spaworld.co.jp/english/european.html [22/04/2019]. It might be noted that ancient Rome is here represented by the Trevi fountain, confirming the monolithic 'Occidentalism' discussed in the chapter. See Hendry 2000: 149.
8 Hendry 2000: 46.
9 Nara 2019.

10 See e.g. Cardi 2019 on translations of Greek literature and reelaborations of classical myth in Japanese literature.
11 Scilabra 2015: in particular 93–5.
12 Liu 2015; 2019. Similar ideas of a parallelism with Greece as 'seminal Western culture' were developed in Japan, too (Nara 2019: 184–5). See also Saussy 2010; Wieber 2017: 336; Huang 2019: 363–5.
13 Liu 2019, 107.
14 Huang 2019: 372.
15 Ren 1998: 95.
16 Castello and Scilabra 2015: 183–4; Scilabra 2015: 99–100; 2018: 36–9; 2019: 294.
17 Castello and Scilabra (2015: 180) speak of a 'monolithic reception of the Western world: an ideal perception of the Western world as a whole'. See also Teo, Chang and Hp (2001: 6), who show that 'cultural connections' are 'multiscalar', even if they use the reversed example of the European perspective on South-East Asia, perceived as a macro-region in spite of the big differences between its components.
18 Simpson 2010: 62–4.
19 Hannigan 1998: 166–71; 174–7; Ren 1998: 20–1; Teo and Yeoh 2001: 143–4; Ap 2002, highlighting that after a first moment of development there was a moment of 'crisis' in the Chinese theme park industry in the 1990s. As Ap explains, this crisis was due to a lack of good management and too much confidence on a purely replicated model; it is quite easy to explain that the successive further development of Chinese theme park industry was now based far more on a search for an individual character and more careful planning, also following the development, in 1999, of the Standard Rating System for Quality Tourist Attractions; Clavé 2007: 72–85; Ren 2007: 100–1; Campanella 2008: 248–69; Ong 2016: 192–3; Erb and Ong 2017: 152–4. The discussion of whether Eastern Asian and more specifically Chinese theme parks should be considered a form imported from the West, or a different form of space, strongly influenced by local traditions and local approaches to culture and heritage, is not central to the topics dealt with in this chapter. On this, see Ren 2007: 99–100; Erb and Ong 2017: 156–9.
20 Ap 2002: 197–8; Clavé 2007: 142–4. On CTS and OCT, see Ren 1998: 61–78. See also Campanella 2008: 254–8; Lukas 2008: 84–5.
21 See Clavé 2007: 180, on the importance of local themes in Asian theme parks.
22 http://cd.happyvalley.cn/Park/dizhonghai.shtml [19/10/2017].
23 The only information I could find on visitor numbers dates to 2008 and refers to 2 million visitors/year: http://www.parkworld-online.com/oct-group/ [20/10/2017].
24 On Italian 'brandscapes', see Hom 2015: 19–20.
25 Campanella 2009. See also Campanella 2008: 205–14; 262–5; Bosker 2013, locating this phenomenon within the Chinese 'culture of the copy'; Erb and Ong 2017: 158–9.

26 Campanella 2009: 81.
27 Ren 2007: 100–1; Bosker 2013: 39–40.
28 Campanella 2009: 82.
29 Campanella 2008: 88–90.
30 Campanella 2009: 83.
31 Campanella 2009: 82. See also Campanella 2008: 207.
32 Ren 1998: 97.
33 The park *Chinese Ethnic Culture Park* was part of the campaign for the Olympic Games of 2000, intended to present China to guests from all over the world (Ren 1998: 83).
34 Campanella 2008: 121–4.
35 http://sz.happyvalley.cn/park/hlsg.shtml [20/10/2017].
36 On representations of Tibet in Chinese theme parks, see Paine 2019: 67–78; 102–3.
37 Stanley 2002: 272.
38 In 2016, 150,000 Chinese tourists are reported having visited Greece, but this number, which has been growing over the past years, is expected to have boomed from 2017: see e.g. https://www.bloomberg.com/news/articles/2017-05-09/fosun-targets-bringing-10-times-more-chinese-tourists-to-greece [05/12/2017];
39 Ong 2016: 189, speaking of an 'aestheticized landscape of privilege'.
40 http://edition.cnn.com/2015/07/23/asia/china-spartans-marketing-police/index.html [24/11/2017].
41 As in *Europa-Park*: see p. 41.
42 An on-ride video from 2013 can be found here: https://www.youtube.com/watch?v=1-hFPWXoAMs [24/11/2017].
43 Personal communication from Kathrin Siegert, Huss Park Attractions GmbH.
44 See above, [GERMANY + SPAIN]
45 https://www.haystack-dryers.com/post.php?s=2016-08-06-happy-valley-beijing-add-a-cyclone [05/12/2017]
46 See for example http://www.santoriniweddings.net/Greek-Weddings.html [03.01.2018].
47 http://www.greece-is.com/santorini-weddings-arent-seem/ [06/12/2017]; http://www.orchardtimes.com/why-chinese-are-in-love-with-santorini [06/12/2017].
48 Ren 2007: 100–1; Ong and Jin 2016: 228–9.
49 On-ride video: https://www.youtube.com/watch?v=kqeokMl8Dp4 [13/12/2017].
50 For a more detailed analysis of this attraction and its relationship to 'It's a Small World', see Carlà-Uhink and Freitag forthcoming.
51 Carlà-Uhink and Wieber 2020: 9–14.
52 Erb and Ong 2017: 145. See also Teo and Yeoh 2001: 147–9. For examples from the People's Republic, see Ren 2007: 101–2. Indeed, it is important to highlight that the target public of tourists to *E-Da* is mostly composed not of Taiwanese tourists, but

those from the People's Republic of China and Hong Kong; in this sense, a similarity in the development of such successful structures is to be expected.

53 Stanley 2002: 277–8.
54 See Stanley 2002: 275–8; Hitchcock and Stanley 2010: 75–9.
55 See Rubinstein 2007; Metzler 2017: 69–76.
56 Metzler 2017: 79; 85–6 on the later development of this view. On KMT's presentation of aboriginal peoples, see e.g. Ren 1998: 144–63.
57 Andrade 2009: 261; the same author writes on p. xvi: 'In many ways Taiwan is more Chinese than its assertive neighbor. Three decades of Maoism stripped away parts of mainland China's traditional culture, but Taiwan preserves customs, festivals, and schools of thought that were extinguished across the strait'; for Taiwan, Metzler 2017: v–vi speaks of '5000 years of Chinese history'. On the history of such theories of Taiwan's 'Chinese identity', also in connection with theories on the origin of Taiwan's Aborigines, see Zorzin forthcoming.
58 Metzler 2017: 21–38.
59 Metzler 2017: 79–80; 94–6. On the 'politics of Taiwan aboriginal origins', see Stainton 2007 and Zorzin forthcoming.
60 Stanley 2002: 272–8.
61 http://www.edaworld.com.tw/en/hl_detail.aspx?h_id=120 [30/12/2017].
62 http://www.e-united.com.tw/Index/eng [30/12/2017].
63 http://www.edaworld.com.tw/en/hl_detail.aspx?h_id=140 [30/12/2017].
64 Metzler 2017: 119.
65 http://www.edaworld.com.tw/en/hl_detail.aspx?h_id=146 [30/12/2017].
66 It is difficult to know if the choice of Apollo and Diana, brother and sister in classical mythology, is also somehow influenced by Phebos (also Apollo) and Athena, who were the mascots for the Olympic Games of Athens in 2004.
67 For example: https://www.youtube.com/watch?time_continue=1&v=vUiqc3TxjQs (including a representation of a park's ride, 'Big Air', see below); https://www.youtube.com/watch?v=64OChwEW-2I; https://www.youtube.com/watch?v=mDm1ErZ3tXU [03/01/2018]. Many of these cartoons can be found on the YouTube channel of the *E-Da* theme park: https://www.youtube.com/channel/UCtYht0uOztpYHWrwGpRok7g [03/01/2018].
68 Hochbruck and Schlehe 2010: 11.
69 On-ride video of 'Taiwan Formosa' (unfortunately low quality): https://www.youtube.com/watch?time_continue=4&v=rfz2M0FoWGg [08/01/2018].
70 E-Da World: 3.
71 Hsu 2019: in particular 351–4.
72 Hsu 2019: 353.
73 E-Da World: 14.
74 http://www.fabbrigroup.com/portfolio-item/booster-75-24/ [02/01/2018].

75 Offride video: https://www.youtube.com/watch?v=kTiU0OC7gGc [03/01/2018].
76 On-ride video: https://www.youtube.com/watch?v=S_PR8eCfKGI [03/01/2018].
77 Personal communication by Charlotte van Etten, Sales and Marketing at Vekoma. For this kind of ride: https://www.vekoma.com/index.php/experience-thrill-coasters/big-air-coaster [03/01/2018]. Offride video: https://www.youtube.com/watch?v=jjT_StiIDWY [03/01/2018].

Chapter 6: Ancient Greece in France: The World of a Gallic Warrior

1 Maguet 1998.
2 See Lukas 2008: 67–8.
3 Tsigakou 1981: 28–9.
4 Tsigakou 1981: 43.
5 Tsigakou 1981: 46–7.
6 On the role played by the ancient Gauls in shaping French national identity in the nineteenth and twentieth centuries, see also, among others, Dietler 1994; Agulhon 1998.
7 Leoussi 1998: 181–2.
8 The Venus de Milo did represent the French nation, for instance, in the now lost sculpture by Emmanuel Frémiet 'Gorille emportant la Vénus de Milo' (*c.* 1871), in which the gorilla represented Prussia.
9 Leoussi 2016: 48.
10 Leoussi 2016: 58–66.
11 Leoussi 2016: 59. See also Leoussi 1999: 89–94.
12 Leoussi 1999: 91–3.
13 Leoussi 2016: 65. See also Leoussi 1998: 183–99.
14 Leoussi 1998: 180–1.
15 Leoussi 1998: 182–3; 1999: 90–1.
16 And sometimes, as with Armand de Quatrefages, denying that the Germans were Aryans, and thus Greeks, defining them as Finnish: see Leoussi 1999: 93–4.
17 Leoussi 1998: 115.
18 See Loussi 2016: 61–2.
19 Biddiss 1999: 126–7.
20 Coubertin had also planned to host the first Olympic Games in Paris, in 1900, which became the second Olympic Games of modern times (Biddiss 1999: 129–30).
21 See Himmelmann 1976: 175–9; Biddiss 1999: 131–2; Wittenburg 2010.
22 See p. 43.
23 Leonard 2005: 3.

24 Leonard 2005: 13–14.
25 Leonard 2005: 216–20.
26 Schulz 2002: 392.
27 Schmitt-Pantel 2002: 57–9; on p. 60 the author highlights that cultural differences, such as the 'invention' of the barbarians in Greek antiquity, are completely neglected in the school programmes that teach ancient history.
28 Schulz 2002: 396–7.
29 Cadotte 2000.
30 Brodersen 2008: 12–13.
31 Rouvière 2015: 22–3.
32 Stoll 1974: 95–6; Rouvière 2008: 200.
33 See, in particular, Kauffmann 1998.
34 Brenne 1999: 111–13.
35 Rouvière 2008: 19.
36 Rouvière 2008: e.g. 321–3.
37 Will 2008: 33. See also Stoll 1974: 97–104.
38 Rouvière 2008; Rouvière 2015.
39 The Gallic heroes also fly over the Acropolis in *Astérix chez Rahâzade*, 23 (1987). Brenne (1999: 115) argues that this view is probably derived from a model reconstruction, that found in *Astérix aux jeux Olympiques,* from a postcard or a photograph.
40 This is indeed an anachronism of the first kind, as this kind of vase painting was no longer practised in the first century BCE (Brenner 1999: 113).
41 E.g. *Astérix legionnaire*: 18: 'Plazadetoros, je suis Grec, par Zeus'.
42 Rouvière 2008: 301. See also Stoll 1974: 145–6.
43 Rouvière 2008: 203–4.
44 This is also comically highlighted by Obélix in *Astérix aux jeux olympiques*: 22. See Rouvière 2008: 205. On the origins of the Grecian profile and its importance in nineteenth-century racist literature, see Leoussi 1999: 83–4.
45 Stoll 1974: 116; Brenne 1999: 117; Ax 2008: 129.
46 Rouvière 2008: 214.
47 This stereotype is again partially evoked two stories later, in *Astérix in Hispanie* (1969): the young Iberian hostage, Pépé, is actually called Pericles, because the family has Greek ancestors, in a storyline that clearly has ramifications throughout the Mediterranean.
48 Rouvière 2008: 265–8. The stereotype of the greedy Greek is confirmed by the Olympic judges, who are very interested in using the games as an occasion for increasing tourism and earning money, and by the Greek soldier in *Astérix legionnaire* (1967) who, with his typical nose and Corinthian helmet, wildly over-negotiates his payment (19).

49 Rouvière 2008: 323.
50 Rouvière 2008: 215; Sinn 2008: 159–60.
51 Brenne 1999: 117; Rouvière 2008: 223–4.
52 See p. 87.
53 Sinn 2008: 174–6.
54 Stoll 1974: 159–60; Rouvière 2008: 231–5; Spickermann 2008: 105–14; Paine 2019: 85.
55 Leoussi 1998: 192–5. Quote on p. 192.
56 Spickermann 2008: 112–13.
57 Since 2001, the company has been called Grévin et Cie, and has started acquiring other theme and amusement parks in France and in Europe (Clavé 2007: 133–5).
58 See Kuisel 2012: 160.
59 On *Parc Astérix*' success after the opening of *Disneyland Paris* and its possible reasons, see Renaut 2011: 135; Kuisel 2012: 160–1; 170–1.
60 TEA 2017: 55.
61 The waiting area is placed in a white building with blue domes, evoking the stereotypical Greek architecture from the Aegean islands; the ride itself, painted in blue, is decorated with meander motifs. See https://www.parcasterix.fr/attractions/sensations-fortes/cheval-troie [14/02/2018].
62 On the dolphinarium, see http://dauphins.parcasterix.fr/ [15/02/2018].
63 https://www.parcasterix.fr/spectacles-du-parc/reverence [14/02/2018].
64 As both rides were inaugurated after my last field trip to *Parc Astérix*, they have not been the subject of an autoptic analysis.
65 Squire 2011: 4–5.
66 https://www.parcasterix.fr/offres/restauration/restaurants/la-taverne-de-dionysos [14/02/2018].
67 https://www.youtube.com/watch?v=XZewiySxM2M [14/02/2018].
68 On-ride video: https://www.youtube.com/watch?v=thnmdrD18rI [14/02/2018].
69 https://www.parcasterix.fr/attractions/famille/pegase-express [14/02/2018].
70 https://www.parcasterix.fr/attractions/famille/vol-dicare [14/02/2018].
71 Carlà and Freitag 2015b: 154–6.
72 On-ride video: https://www.youtube.com/watch?v=Zg24Jewttoc [14/02/2018].
73 On the Hydra of Lerna and its modern reception, see Bièvre-Perrin 2018.
74 https://www.parcasterix.fr/attractions/famille/riviere-delis [14/02/2018].
75 On-ride video: https://www.youtube.com/watch?v=9x6ugb1qo-s [14/02/2018].
76 http://www.zamperla.com/products/disko-coaster/ [14/02/2018].
77 https://www.parcasterix.fr/attractions/sensations-fortes/tonnerre-zeus [15/02/2018].
78 http://www.ushsho.com/woodpoll14yeartable2007.htm [15/02/2018]. This did not help CCI, the construction company, which failed in 2002. See Latotzki 2015: 238–41.

79 On-ride video: https://www.youtube.com/watch?v=kVsD2Hb9LSg&t=7s [15/02/2018].
80 Solomon 2001: 103.
81 Latotzki 2015: 238.
82 See pp. 18–19.

Chapter 7: Greece – In the Form of a Conclusion

1   Boym 2001: 11.
2   Teo and Yeoh 2001: 144–5.
3   Chang and Pang 2016.
4   E.g. Hendry 2000: 90–4; Bryman 2004: 161–4; Groves 2011; Renaut 2011; Kuisel 2012: 165–7; Freitag 2015. Francaviglia (1981: 149–55) has already noted the differences between *Disneyland* in California and the *Magic Kingdom* in Orlando.
5   Van Maanen 1992: 16.
6   See pp. 1–3.
7   Hanink 2017: 21.
8   See Huyssen 2001: 24, attributing this definition of 'trope' to the Holocaust.
9   Lash and Urry 1994: 122–3.
10 Lash and Urry 1994: 137–8.
11 Hanink 2017: 203.
12 Kinder 1991: 122–3.
13 Kinder's definition must be broadened to apply to Disney, too, as Disney also offers much more than a systematic 'group of figures'. Yet Zukin (1991: 223–4) had developed a model similar to Kinder's 'supersystem' (though of course not using this word) and applied it to Disney (230).
14 Lash and Urry 1994: 14.
15 Lash and Urry 1994: 13–17.
16 Lash and Urry 1994: 31–59.
17 Yalouri 2001: 113.
18 See p. 8.
19 See Urry and Larsen 2011: 16–17.
20 Lowenthal 1988; Yalouri 2001.
21 See pp. 11–12 on the limits of the concept of externality.
22 It is interesting to highlight by way of contrast that the situation in Italy is very different, with theme parks and immersive environments that celebrate the country's history and its antiquities: see Hom 2015: 184–212; Melotti 2017.
23 Hamilakis and Yalouri 1996.
24 Yalouri 2001: 101–35.

25 Hamilakis and Yalouri 1996, 119–21.
26 See Hanink 2017: 205–6.
27 Hamilakis 2007: 17; Plantzos 2008: 14.
28 See in particular Yalouri 2001: 112.
29 Urry and Larsen 2011: 98–9.
30 Yalouri 2001: 119–20.
31 Yalouri 2011: 158–62; 2014: 175–82.
32 https://www.independent.co.uk/news/by-zeus-meet-the-gods-in-a-theme-park-1360370.html [28/12/2018]. See Paine 2019: 81–2.
33 http://www.washingtonpost.com/wp-adv/specialsales/spotlight/greece/art3.html??noredirect=on [02/09/2018]
34 Nisbet 2008: 137–8.
35 https://www.rivieraolympia.com/water-park-hotel.html [12/08/2019].
36 http://www.labyrinthpark.gr/en/home [02/09/2018].
37 I do not consider here the 'biggest themed waterpark in Europe', as it proudly claims, *WaterWorld* at Ayia Napa, Cyprus: the political situation on Cyprus after the Turkish invasion of 1974, and particularly Ayia Napa's position in the southern, and Greek-controlled, part of the Famagosta district, cause here a different saliency and 'use' of ancient Greek in shaping identity and historical culture than in the Republic of Greece.
38 http://www.dimosaristoteli.gr/en/sights/aristotle-park [04/01/2019].

Bibliography

Adey, P. (2007), '"Above Us Only Sky": Themes, Simulations, and Liverpool John Lennon Airport', in S. A. Lukas (ed.), *The Themed Space: Locating Nature, Nation, and Self*, 153–66, Lanham and Plymouth: Lexington Books.

Agnew, V. (2007), 'History's Affective Turn: Historical Reenactment and Its Work in the Present', *Rethinking History*, 11 (3): 299–312.

Aguilera Durán, T. (2014), 'L'eroe indomito. Viriato nella mitologia nazionalista spagnola', in J. Bassi and G. Canè (eds), *Sulle spalle degli antichi: Eredità classica e costruzione delle identità nazionali nel Novecento*, 165–79, Milano: Unicopli.

Agulhon, M. (1998), 'Le mythe gaulois', *Ethnologie Française*, 28 (3): 296–302.

Anderson, J. (1984), *Time Machines: The World of Living History*, Nashville: American Association for State and Local History.

Andrade, T. (2009), *How Taiwan Became Chinese. Dutch, Spanish, and Han Colonization in the Seventeenth Century*, New York: Columbia University Press.

Ap, J. (2002), 'An Assessment of Theme Park Development in China', in A. A. Lew, L. Yu, J. Ap and Z. Guangrui (eds), *Tourism in China*, 195–214, Binghamton: Haworth Hospitality Press.

Assmann, A. (2013), *Ist die Zeit aus den Fugen? Aufstieg und Fall des Zeitregimes der Moderne*, München: Carl Hanser.

Ax, W. (2008), 'Die Loorbeeren Caesars – oder: Vom Sieg der gallischen über die römische Rhetorik', in K. Brodersen (ed.), *Asterix und seine Zeit. Die große Welt des kleinen Galliers*, 3rd edn, 128–142, München: Beck.

Balme, C. B. (1998), 'Staging the Pacific: Framing Authenticity in Performances for Tourists at the Polynesian Cultural Center', *Theatre Journal*, 50 (1): 53–70.

Barkan, E. R. (1999), 'Introduction: America – A Nation of Peoples', in E. R. Barkan (ed.), *A Nation of Peoples. A Sourcebook on America's Multicultural Heritage*, 1–18, Westport and London: Greenwood Press.

Bartsch, S. (2019). 'The Ancient Greeks in Modern China: History and Metamorphosis', in Renger and Fan (2019): 237–56.

Baudrillard, J. ([1976] 1990), *L'échange symbolique et la mort*, Paris: Gallimard; Italian transl. *Lo scambio simbolico e la morte*, Milano: Feltrinelli.

Baudrillard, J. ([1981] 1994), *Simulacres et simulation*, Paris: Galilée; English transl. *Simulacra and Simulation*, Ann Arbor: University of Michigan Press.

Beard, M. (2002), *The Parthenon*, London: Profile Books.

Bederman, D. J. (2009), *The Classical Foundations of the American Constitution*, Cambridge, UK: Cambridge University Press.

Berti, I. (2015), 'Le metamorfosi di Circe: dea, maga e femme fatale', *Status Quaestionis*, 8: 110–40. Available online: http://ojs.uniroma1.it/index.php/statusquaestionis/article/view/13143 [27/06/2016].

Berti, I. and Carlà-Uhink, F. (2018), 'Mixanthropoi: Die mittelalterliche Rezeption antiker hybrider Kreaturen', in U. Rehm (ed.), *Mittelalterliche Mythenrezeption. Paradigmen und Paradigmenwechsel*, 193–221, Köln: Böhlau.

Biddiss, M. (1999), 'The Invention of the Modern Olympic Tradition', in M. Wyke and M. Biddiss (eds), *The Uses and Abuses of Antiquity*, 125–43, Bern et al.: Peter Lang.

Bièvre-Perrin, F. (2018), 'The Different Faces of the Lernean Hydra in Contemporary Pop Culture: From Cinema to Videogames', *thersites*, 8: 67–84 Available online: https://thersites-journal.de/index.php/thr/article/view/108/167 [10/11/2019].

Blanshard, A. and Shahabudin, K. (2011), *Classics on Screen: Ancient Greece and Rome on Film*, Bristol: Bristol Classical Press.

Blockley, M (1999), 'Archaeological Reconstructions and the Community in the UK', in P. G. Stone and P. G. Planel (eds), *The Constructed Past: Experimental Archaeology, Education and the Public*, 15–34, London and New York: Routledge.

Bosker, B. (2013), *Original Copies: Architectural Mimicry in Contemporary China*, Honolulu and Hong Kong: University of Hawai'i Press and Hong Kong University Press.

Boym, S. (2001), *The Future of Nostalgia*, New York: Basic Books.

Braidotti, R. (2013), *The Posthuman*, Cambridge, UK and Malden: Polity Press.

Brenne, S. (1999), 'Asterix und die Antike', in T. Lochman (ed.), *Antico-mix: Antike in Comics*, 106–19, Basel: Skulpturhalle Basel.

Brodersen, K. (2008), 'Die kleine Welt des großen Galliers', in K. Brodersen (ed.), *Asterix und seine Zeit: Die große Welt des kleinen Galliers*, 3rd edn, 12–18, München: Beck.

Bruner, E. M. (2001), 'The Maasai and the Lion King: Authenticity, Nationalism, and Globalization in African Tourism', *American Ethnologist*, 28: 881–908.

Bryman, A. (1999), 'The Disneyization of Society', *The Sociological Review*, 47 (1): 25–47.

Bryman, A. (2004), *The Disneyization of Society*, London: Sage.

Cadotte, A. (2000), 'Astérix et l'Histoire', *Chronozones*, 6: 46–55.

Campanella, T. J. (2008), *The Concrete Dragon: China's Urban Revolution and What It Means for the World*, New York: Princeton Architectural Press.

Campanella, T. J. (2009) 'Mimetic Utopias: Theming and Consumerism on China's Suburban Frontier', in S. Ramos and N. Turan (eds), *New Geographies: After Zero*, 78–85, Cambridge, MA: Harvard University Press.

Carbone, M. B. (2018), 'Chronotopes of Hellenic Antiquity: The Strait of Reggio and Messina in Documents from the Grand Tour Era', in R. Rovira Guardiola (ed.), *The Ancient Mediterranean Sea in Modern Visual and Performing Arts. Sailing in Troubled Waters*, 33–54, London and New York: Bloomsbury.

Cardi, L. (2019), 'Retelling Medea in Postwar Japan: The Function of Ancient Greece in Two Literary Adaptations by Mishima Yukio and Kurahashi Yumiko', in Renger and Fan (2019): 154–71.

Carlà, F. (2015), 'Atena e l'ottovolante: 'affective turn', estetica postmoderna e ricezione dell'antico', *Status Quaestionis*, 8: 7–36. Available online: https://statusquaestionis.uniroma1.it/index.php/statusquaestionis/article/view/13138 [04/10/2018].

Carlà, F. (2016), 'The Uses of History in Themed Spaces', in S. Lukas (ed.), *A Reader in Themed and Immersive Spaces*, 19–29, Pittsburgh: ETC Press.

Carlà, F. and Freitag, F. (2015a), 'Ancient Greek Culture and Myth in the Terra Mítica Theme Park', *Classical Receptions Journal*, 7 (2): 242–59.

Carlà, F. and Freitag, F. (2015b), 'The Labyrinthine Ways of Myth Reception: Cretan Myths in Theme Park Rides', *Journal of European Popular Culture*, 6 (2): 145–59.

Carlà, F. and Freitag, F. (2015c), 'Strategien der Geschichtstransformationen in Themenparks', in S. Georgi et al. (eds), *Geschichtstransformationen. Medien, Verfahren und Funktionalisierungen historischer Rezeption*, 131–49, Bielefeld: transcript.

Carlà, F., Freitag, F., Grice, G. and Lukas, S. A. (2016), 'Research Dialogue: The Ways of Design, Architecture, Technology, and Material Form', in S. A. Lukas (ed.), *A Reader in Themed and Immersive Spaces*, 107–12, Pittsburgh: ETC Press.

Carlà, F., Freitag, F., Mittermaier, S. and Schwarz, A. (2016), 'Zur Formierung der komplexen Zeitlichkeit von Themenparks', in M. Gamper et al. (eds), *Zeiten der Form – Formen der Zeit*, 317–41, Hannover: Wehrhahn.

Carlà-Uhink, F. and Fiore, D. (2016), 'Performing Empresses and Matronae: Ancient Roman Women in Re-enactment', *Archäologische Informationen*, 39: 195–204.

Carlà-Uhink, F. and Freitag, F. (2018), '(Not so) Dangerous Journeys: The Ancient Mediterranean and Ancient Mythological Sea Travelers in European Theme Park Attractions', in H. Kopp and C. Wendt (eds), *Thalassokratographie. Rezeption und Transformation antiker Seeherrschaft*, 283–300, Berlin and Boston: de Gruyter.

Carlà-Uhink, F. and Freitag, F. (forthcoming), 'Theme Park Imitations: The Case of "Happy World" (Happy Valley, Beijing)', *Huaxia Wenhua Luntan / Chinese Culture Forum*.

Carlà-Uhink, F., Freitag, F., Mittermeier, S. and Schwarz, A. (2017), 'Introduction: The Complex Temporalities of Theme Parks', in F. Carlà-Uhink, F. Freitag, S. Mittermeier and A. Schwarz (eds), *Time and Temporality in Theme Parks*, 9–16, Hannover: Wehrhahn.

Carlà-Uhink, F. and Wieber, A. (2020), 'Introduction', in F. Carlà-Uhink and A. Wieber (eds), *Orientalism and the Reception of Powerful Women from the Ancient World*, 1–15, London and New York: Bloomsbury.

Castello, M. G. and Scilabra, C. (2015), 'Theoi Becoming Kami: Classical Mythology in the Anime World', in F. Carlà and I. Berti (eds), *Ancient Magic and the Supernatural in the Modern Visual and Performing Arts*, 177–96, London and New York: Bloomsbury.

Chang, T. C. and Pang, J. (2016), 'Between Universal Spaces and Unique Places: Heritage in Universal Studios Singapore', *Tourism Geographies*, 19 (2): 208–26.

Chapman, A. (2018), *Digital Games as History: How Videogames Represent the Past and Offer Access to Historical Practice*, New York and Abingdon: Routledge.

Chappell, E. A. (2002), 'The Museum and the Joy Ride: Williamsburg Landscapes and the Specter of Theme Parks', in Young and Riley (2002): 119–56.

Ciardi, M. (2011), *Le metamorfosi di Atlantide: storie scientifiche e immaginarie da Platone a Walt Disney*, Roma: Carocci.

Clavé, S. A. (2007), *The Global Theme Park Industry*, Wallingford and Cambridge, MA: CABI.

Cobet, J. (2003), 'Vom Text zur Ruine: Die Geschichte der Troia-Diskussion', in C. Ulf (ed.), *Der neue Streit um Troia*, 19–38, München: Beck.

Cobet, J. (2006), 'Schliemanns Troia', in M. Zimmermann (ed.), *Der Traum von Troia: Geschichte und Mythos einer ewigen Stadt*, 149–64, München: Beck.

Conan, M. (2002), 'The Fiddler's Indecorous Nostalgia', in Young and Riley (2002): 91–117.

Connelly, J. B. (2014), *The Parthenon Enigma*, New York: Alfred A. Knopf.

Connolly, J. (2010), 'Classical Education and the Early American Democratic Style', in S. A. Stephens and P. Vasunia (eds), *Classics and National Cultures*, 78–99, Oxford: Oxford University Press.

Conzen, K. N. (1989), 'Ethnicity as Festive Culture: Nineteenth-Century German America on Parade', in W. Sollors (ed.), *The Invention of Ethnicity*, 44–76, New York and Oxford: Oxford University Press.

Corbí, J. F. M. (2009), 'El franquismo en la arqueología: El pasado prehistórico y antiguo para la España "Una, Grande y Libre"', *Arqueoweb: Revista sobre Arqueología en Internet*, 11: 1–6. Available online: https://webs.ucm.es/info/arqueoweb/pdf/11/corbi.pdf [22/12/2018].

Cortadella Morral, J. (1988), 'M. Almagro Basch y la idea de la unidad de España', *Studia Historica. Historia Antigua*, 6: 17–25.

Cuisinier, J. (2003), *Le périple d'Ulysse*, Paris: Fayard.

Damaskos, D. and Plantzos, D. (eds) (2008), *A Singular Antiquity: Archaeology and Hellenic Identity in Twentieth-Century Greece*, Athens: Benaki Museum.

Davis, S. G. (1997), *Spectacular Nature: Corporate Culture and the Sea World Experience*, Oakland: University of California Press.

Dawid, A. (2004), 'Poseidon, Pommes und Piraten – zum Unterhaltungswert der Archäologie im Europa-Park Rust', *Museumsblatt*, 38: 26–30.

Díaz-Andreu, M. (1993), 'Theory and Ideology in Archaeology: Spanish Archaeology under the Franco Régime', *Archaeology*, 67: 74–82.

Díaz-Andreu, M. (1997), 'Nationalism, Ethnicity and Archaeology – The Archaeological Study of the Iberians Through the Looking Glass', *Journal of Mediterranean Studies*, 7 (2): 155–68.

Dicks, B. (2004), *Culture on Display. The Production of Contemporary Visitability*, Maidenhead: Open University Press.

Dietler, M. (1994), '"Our Ancestors the Gauls": Archaeology, Ethnic Nationalism, and the Manipulation of Celtic Identity in Modern Europe', *American Anthropologist*, 96 (3): 584–605.

Domínguez, A. J. (2006), 'Greeks in the Iberian Peninsula', in G. R. Tsetskhladze (ed.), *Greek Colonisation: An Account of Greek Colonies and Other Settlements Overseas*, Vol. I, 429–505, Leiden and Boston: Brill.

Duke, P. (2006), 'Knossos as Memorial, Ritual, and Metaphor', *Creta Antica*, 7: 79–88.

Duke, P. (2007), *The Tourists Gaze, the Cretans Glance: Archaeology and Tourism on a Greek Island*, Walnut Creek: Left Coast Press.

Duplà Ansuategui, A. (1992), 'Notas sobre fascismo y mundo antiguo en España', *Rivista di Storia della Storiografia Moderna*, 13 (3): 199–213.

E-Da World (2014). *E-Da World: Cultural Creative Ind / Shopping / Amusement / Business / Holiday / Theater / Exhibitions / Medical / Education*, Kaohsiung: E United Group.

Eco, U. (1987), *Travels in Hyperreality: Essays*, San Diego, New York and London: Harcourt Brace Jovanovich.

Edgerton, G. R. (2001), 'Introduction. Television as Historian: A Different Kind of History Altogether', in G. R. Edgerton and P. C. Rollins (eds), *Television Histories: Shaping Collective Memories in the Digital Age*, 1–16, Lexington: University Press of Kentucky.

Eldridge, D. (2006), *Hollywood's History Films*, London and New York: I.B. Tauris.

Erb, M. and Ong, C. E. (2017), 'Theming Asia: Culture, Nature and Heritage in a Transforming Environment', *Tourism Geographies*, 19 (2): 143–67.

Europa-Park (2015). *Europa-Park: Deutschlands größter Freizeitpark*, Köln: Vista Point.

Fehlmann, M. (2007), 'As Greek as it Gets: British Attempts to Recreate the Parthenon', *Rethinking History*, 11: 353–77.

Feige, M. (2017), 'Mini Israel and the Subversive Present', in F. Carlà-Uhink, F. Freitag, S. Mittermeier and A. Schwarz (eds), *Time and Temporality in Theme Parks*, 155–68, Hannover: Wehrhahn.

Fichtner, U. and Michna, R. (1987), *Freizeitparks: Allgemeine Züge eines modernen Freizeitangebotes, vertieft am Beispiel des Europa-Park in Rust/Baden*, Freiburg: Selbstverlag.

Fjellman, S. M. (1992), *Vinyl Leaves: Walt Disney World and America*, Boulder: Westview Press.

Folch, M. (2017), 'A Time for Fantasy: Retelling Apuleius in C. S. Lewis's *Till We Have Faces*', in B. M. Rogers and B. E. Stevens (eds), *Classical Traditions in Modern Fantasy*, 160–86, Oxford: Oxford University Press.

Francaviglia, R. (1981), 'Main Street U.S.A.: A Comparison/Contrast of Streetscapes in Disneyland and Walt Disney World', *Journal of Popular Culture*, 15 (1): 141–56.

Francaviglia, R. (1995), 'Texan History in Texas Theme Parks', *Legacies: A History Journal for Dallas and North Central Texas*, 7: 34–42.

Francaviglia, R. (2011), 'Frontierland as an Allegorical Map of the American West', in K. M. Jackson and M. I. West (eds), *Disneyland and Culture: Essays on the Parks and Their Influence*, 59–86, Jefferson: McFarland & Co.

Frank, T. (2011), 'From Republican to Imperial: The Survival and Perception of Antiquity in American Thought', in G. Klaniczay, M. Werner and O. Gecser (eds), *Multiple Antiquities – Multiple Modernities: Ancient History in Nineteenth Century European Cultures*, 479–97, Frankfurt and New York: Campus.

Freeman, P. M. (2010), 'Ancient References to Tartessos', in B. Cunliffe and J. T. Koch (eds), *Celtic from the West: Alternative Perspectives from Archaeology, Genetics, Language and Literature*, 303–34, Oxford and Oakville, CT: Oxbow.

Freitag, F. (2015), 'Amerikanisierung, Glokalisierung, Branding: EuroDisney, 1992', in J. Ernst and F. Freitag (eds), *Transkulturelle Dynamiken. Aktanten – Prozesse – Theorien*, 165–97, Bielefeld: transcript.

Freitag, F. (2016), 'Movies, Rides, Immersion', in S. A. Lukas (ed.), *A Reader in Themed and Immersive Spaces*, 125–30, Pittsburgh: ETC Press.

Freizeitparks (2017), *Freizeitparks in Deutschland und Europa*, Potsdam: Vista Point.

Friedman, J. (1992), 'The Past in the Future: History and the Politics of Identity', *American Anthropologist*, 94 (4): 837–59.

Füßmann, K. (1994), 'Historische Formungen. Dimensionen der Geschichtsdarstellung', in K. Füßmann, H. T. Grütter and J. Rüsen (eds), *Historische Faszination: Geschichtskultur heute*, 27–44, Köln et al.: Böhlau.

Gable, E. and Handler, R. (2004), 'Deep Dirt: Messing Up the Past at Colonial Williamsburg', in Y. Rowan and U. Baram (eds), *Marketing Heritage: Archaeology and the Consumption of the Past*, 167–81, Walnut Creek: AltaMira Press.

Galanova, O. (2009), 'Das Überlebensgeheimnis einer mythischen Gestalt. Die Alltagsrezeption der Kassandra als Quelle eines vielschichtigen Erinnerns', in G. Kamecke, B. Klein and J. Müller (eds), *Antike als Konzept: Lesarten in Kunst, Literatur und Politik*, 254–60, Berlin: Lukas.

García Santa María, T. and Pagès Blanch, J. (2008), 'La imagen de la antigüedad en la enseñanza de la historia', in P. Castillo, S. Knippschild, M. García Morcillo and C. Herreros (eds), *Congreso Internacional Imagines: La antigüedad en las artes escénicas y visuales*, 691–720, Logroño: Universidad de la Rioja.

González-Vaquerizo, H. (2017), '"Visit Greece and Live Your Myth": The Use of Classical Antiquity by the Greek National Tourism Organization', *thersites*, 6: 241–303; available online at https://thersites-journal.de/index.php/thr/article/view/67/98 [10/11/2019].

Gorbahn, K. (2007), 'Konvergenz oder Divergenz? Überlegungen zur Darstellung antiker griechischer Geschichte in aktuellen europäischen Schulbüchern', in B. Schönemann and H. Voit (eds), *Europa in historisch-didaktischen Perspektiven*, 176–93, Idstein: Schulz-Kirchner.

Gorbahn, K. (2011), *Die Geschichte des antiken Griechenland als Identifikationsangebot. Untersuchungen zur Konstruktion sozialer Identität in neueren Schulgeschichtsbüchern*, Göttingen: V&R.

Gottdiener, M. (2001), *The Theming of America: Dreams, Media Fantasies and Themed Environments*, 2nd edn, Boulder: Westview Press.

Graburn, N. (1977), 'The Museum and the Visitor Experience', *Roundtable Reports,* Fall 1977: 1–5.
Gracia Alonso, F. (2017), 'The Invention of Numantia and Emporion: Archaeology and the Regeneration of Spanish and Catalan Nationalisms after the Crisis of 1898', in A. De Francesco (ed.), *In Search of Pre-Classical Antiquity: Rediscovering Ancient Peoples in Mediterranean Europe (19th and 20th c.),* 64–95, Leiden and Boston: Brill.
Grever, M. and Adriaansen, R. J. (2017), 'Historical Culture: A Concept Revisited', in M. Carretero, S. Berger and M. Grever (eds), *Palgrave Handbook of Research in Historical Culture and Education,* 73–89, London: Palgrave Macmillan.
Großklaus, G. (1995), *Medien-Zeit, Medien-Raum: Zum Wandel der raumzeitlichen Wahrnehmung in der Moderne,* Frankfurt a.M.: Suhrkamp.
Groves, D. (2011), 'Hong Kong Disneyland: Feng-Shui Inside the Magic Kingdom', in K. M. Jackson and M. I. West (eds), *Disneyland and Culture: Essays on the Parks and Their Influence,* 138–49, Jefferson: McFarland.
Grütter, H. T. (1994), 'Warum fasziniert die Vergangenheit? Perspektiven einer neuen Geschichtskultur', in K. Füßmann, H. T. Grütter and J. Rüsen (eds), *Historische Faszination: Geschichtskultur heute,* 45–57, Köln et al.: Böhlau.
Gumbrecht, H. U. (2010), *Unsere breite Gegenwart,* Frankfurt a.M.: Suhrkamp.
Hahn, A. (2012), 'Erlebnislandschaft – Erlebnis Landschaft? Einführung in ein Forschungsprojekt', in A. Hahn (ed.), *Erlebnislandschaft – Erlebnis Landschaft? Atmosphären im architektonischen Entwurf,* 11–37, Bielefeld: transcript.
Hamilakis, Y. (2002), 'What Future for the "Minoan" Past? Re-Thinking Minoan Archaeology', in Y. Hamilakis (ed.), *Labyrinth Revisited: Rethinking 'Minoan' Archaeology,* 2–28, Oxford: Oxbow.
Hamilakis, Y. (2006), 'The Colonial, the National, and the Local: Legacies of the "Minoan" Past', *Creta Antica,* 7: 145–62.
Hamilakis, Y. (2007), *The Nation and Its Ruins: Antiquity, Archaeology, and National Imagination in Greece,* Oxford: Oxford University Press.
Hamilakis, Y. and Momigliano, N. (2006), 'Archaeology and European Modernity: Stories from the Borders', *Creta Antica,* 7: 25–35.
Hamilakis, Y. and Yalouri, E. (1996), 'Antiquity as Symbolic Capital in Modern Greek Society', *Antiquity,* 70: 117–29.
Hanink, J. (2017), *The Classical Debt: Greek Antiquity in an Era of Austerity,* Cambridge, MA and London: Harvard University Press.
Hannigan, J. A. (1995), 'Theme Parks and Urban Fantasy-Scapes', *Current Sociology,* 43 (1): 183–91.
Hannigan, J. A. (1998), *Fantasy City: Pleasure and Profit in the Postmodern Metropolis,* London and New York: Routledge.
Hardtwig, W. (2010), *Verlust der Geschichte – oder wie unterhaltsam ist die Vergangenheit?,* Berlin: Vergangenheitsverlag.

Harris, N. (1997), 'Expository Expositions. Preparing for the Theme Park', in K. A. Marling (ed.), *Designing Disney's Theme Parks: The Architecture of Reassurance*, 19-27, Paris and New York: Flammarion.

Heck, B. (1997), 'Freizeitpark und Museum – Der Europa-Park Rust als Fallbeispiel', *Beiträge zur Volkskunde in Baden-Württemberg*, 7: 39-57.

Hendry, J. (2000), *The Orient Strikes Back: A Global View of Cultural Display*, Oxford: Berg.

Herzfeld, M. (1987), *Anthropology through the Looking-Glass: Critical Ethnography in the Margins of Europe*, Cambridge, UK: Cambridge University Press.

Heun, W. (2011), 'Die Antike in den amerikanischen politischen Debatten in der zweiten Hälfte des 18. Jahrhunderts', in U. Niggemann and K. Ruffing (eds), *Antike als Modell in Nordamerika?*, 65-83, München: Oldenbourg.

Himmelmann, N. (1976), *Utopische Vergangenheit: Archäologie und moderne Kultur*, Berlin: Gebr. Mann.

Hitchcock, L. A. and Koudounaris, P. (2002), 'Virtual Discourse: Arthur Evans and the Reconstructions of the Minoan Palace at Knossos', in Y. Hamilakis (ed.), *Labyrinth Revisited: Rethinking 'Minoan' Archaeology*, 40-58, Oxford: Oxbow.

Hitchcock, M. and Koudounaris, P. (2002), 'Virtual Discourse: Arthur Evans and the Reconstructions of the Minoan Palace at Knossos', in Y. Hamilakis (ed.), *Labyrinth Revisited: Rethinking 'Minoan' Archaeology*, 40-58, Oxford: Oxbow.

Hitchcock, M. (1998), 'Tourism, Taman Mini, and National Identity', *Indonesia and the Malay World*, 26: 124-35.

Hitchcock, M. (2005), '"We Will Know Our Nation Better": Taman Mini and Nation Building in Indonesia', *Civilisations*, 52 (2): 45-56.

Hitchcock, M. and Stanley, N. (2010), 'Outdoor Ethnographic Museums, Tourism and Nation Building in Southeast Asia', in M. Hitchcock, V. T. King and M. Parnwell (eds), *Heritage Tourism in Southeast Asia*, 72-82, Copenhagen: Nias Press.

Hjemdahl, K. M (2002), 'History as a Cultural Playground', *Ethnologia Europea*, 32 (2): 105-24.

Hochbruck, W. and Schlehe, J. (2010), 'Introduction: Staging the Past', in J. Schlehe et al. (eds), *Staging the Past: Themed Environments in Transcultural Perspectives*, 7-20, Bielefeld: transcript.

Hollinshead, K. (1998), 'Disney and Commodity Aesthetics: A Critique of Fjellman's Analysis of "Distory" and the "Historicide" of the Past', *Current Issues in Tourism*, 1: 58-119.

Holtorf, C. (2005), *From Stonehenge to Las Vegas: Archaeology as Popular Culture*, Walnut Creek: AltaMira Press.

Holtorf, C. (2007a), *Archaeology is a Brand! The Meaning of Archaeology in Contemporary Popular Culture*, Walnut Creek: Left Coast Press.

Holtorf, C. (2007b), 'Time Travel: A New Perspective on the Distant Past', in B. Hårdh, K. Jennbert and D. Olausson (eds), *On the Road: Studies in Honour of Lars Larsson*, 127-32, Stockholm: Almqvist & Wiksell.

Holtorf, C. (2009), 'On the Possibility of Time Travel', *Lund Archaeological Review*, 15: 31–41.

Holtorf, C. (2010), 'The Presence of Pastness: Themed Environments and Beyond', in J. Schlehe et al. (eds), *Staging the Past: Themed Environments in Transcultural Perspectives*, 23–40, Bielefeld: transcript.

Holtorf, C. (2017), 'The Meaning of Time Travel', in B. Petersson and C. Holtorf (eds), *The Archaeology of Time Travel: Experiencing the Past in the 21st Century*, 1–22, Oxford: Archaeopress.

Hom, S. M. (2013), 'Simulated Imperialism', *Traditional Dwellings and Settlement Review*, 25: 25–44.

Hom, S. M. (2015), *The Beautiful Country: Tourism and the Impossible State of Destination Italy*, Toronto: University of Toronto Press.

Horne, D. (1984), *The Great Museum: The Re-Presentation of History*, London and Sydney: Pluto Press.

Howe, K. (2011), 'Vacation in Historyland', in K. M. Jackson and M. I. West (eds), *Disneyland and Culture: Essays on the Parks and Their Influence*, 195–206, Jefferson: McFarland.

Hsu, C. L. (2019), 'Politics, Culture, and Classical Architectural Elements in Taiwan', in Renger and Fan (2019): 342–59.

Huang, Y. (2019), 'Classical Studies in China', in Renger and Fan (2019): 363–75.

Huyssen, A. (2001), 'Present Pasts: Media, Politics, Amnesia', in A. Appadurai (ed.), *Globalization*, 57–77, Durham, NC and London: Duke University Press.

Iguácel, P. (2008) 'Tartessos: El mito en lenguaje de cómic', in P. Castillo, S. Knippschild, M. García Morcillo and C. Herreros (eds), *Congreso Internacional Imagines: La antigüedad en las artes escénicas y visuales*, 645–58, Logroño: Universidad de la Rioja.

Ijzereef, G. F. (1999), 'The Reconstruction of Sites in the Archaeological Themepark ARCHEON in the Netherlands', in P. Planel and P. G. Stone (eds), *The Constructed Past: Experimental Archaeology, Education and the Public*, 171–80, London: Routledge.

Jameson, F. (1991), *Postmodernism or, the Cultural Logic of Late Capitalism*, Durham, NC: Duke University Press.

Jenkins, T. E. (2015), *Antiquity Now: The Classical World in the Contemporary American Imagination*, Cambridge, UK: Cambridge University Press.

Jonker, G. (2009), 'Naming the West: Productions of Europe In and Beyond Textbooks', *Journal of Educational Media, Memory and Society*, 1 (2): 34–59.

Kagelmann, H. J. (1993), 'Themenparks', in H. Hahn and H. J. Kagelmann (eds), *Tourismuspsychologie und Tourismussoziologie: Ein Handbuch zur Tourismuswissenschaft*, 407–15, München: Quintessenz.

Kaplanis, T. A. (2014), 'Antique Names and Self-Identification: Hellenes, Graikoi, and Romaioi from Late Byzantium to the Greek Nation-State', in D. Tziovas (ed.), *Re-Imagining the Past: Antiquity and Modern Greek Culture*, 81–97, Oxford: Oxford University Press.

Kauffmann, J. (1998), 'Astérix: le jeu de l'humour et du temps', *Ethnologie Française*, 28 (3): 327–36.

Kawana, S. (2019), 'Cool Rome and Warm Japan: *Thermae Romae* and the Promotion of Japanese Everyday Culture', in Renger and Fan (2019): 259–86.

Kessler, U. (2012), 'Landschaftskritik des Vergnügungsparks Belantis', in A. Hahn (ed.), *Erlebnislandschaft – Erlebnis Landschaft? Atmosphären im architektonischen Entwurf*, 147–69, Bielefeld: transcript.

Kinder, M. (1991), *Playing with Power in Movies, Television, and Video Games: From Muppet Babies to Teenage Mutant Ninja Turtles*, Berkeley at al.: University of California Press.

King, M. J. (1981), 'Disneyland and Walt Disney World: Traditional Values in Futuristic Form', *Journal of Popular Culture*, 15 (1): 116–40.

King, M. J. (2002), 'The Theme Park: Aspects of Experience in a Four-Dimensional Landscape', *Material Culture*, 34 (2): 1–15.

King, M. J. (2007), 'Theme Park', in R. B. Browne and P. Browne (eds), *The Guide to United States Popular Culture*, 837–9, Bowling Green: Bowling Green State University Popular Press.

King, M. J. and O'Boyle, J. G. (2011), 'The Theme Park: The Art of Time and Space', in K. M. Jackson and M. I. West (eds), *Disneyland and Culture: Essays on the Parks and Their Influence*, 5–18, Jefferson: McFarland.

Kirshenblatt-Gimblett, B. (1998), *Destination Culture: Tourism, Museums, and Heritage*, Berkeley and Los Angeles: University of California Press.

Klein, H. (2000), *Von der Illusion und ihrer Wirklichkeit: 25 Jahre Europa-Park*, Rust: Europa-Park Mack & Co.

Knight, C. K. (2003), 'What Time Is It? Subverting and Suppressing, Conflating and Compressing Time in Commodified Space and Architecture', in A. T. Tymieniecka (ed.), *Gardens and the Passion for the Infinite*, 325–36, Dordrecht: Kluwer Academic.

Knudsen, B. T. and Waade, A. M. (2010), 'Performative Authenticity in Tourism and Spatial Experience: Rethinking the Relations Between Travel, Place and Emotion', in B. T. Knudsen and A. M. Waade (eds), *Re-Investing Authenticity: Tourism, Place and Emotions*, 1–19, Bristol: Channel View.

Kolb, D. (2008), *Sprawling Places*, Athens and London: University of Georgia Press.

Kondaratos, S. (1994), 'The Parthenon as a Cultural Ideal: The Chronicle of Its Emergence as a Supreme Monument of Eternal Glory', in P. Tournikiotis (ed.), *The Parthenon and Its Impact in Modern Times*, 19–53, Athens: Melissa.

Koselleck, R. (2000), *Zeitschichten: Studien zur Historik*, Frankfurt a.M.: Suhrkamp.

Koulouri, C. (2004), 'Introduction: Rewriting the History of the Olympic Games', in C. Koulouri (ed.), *Athens, Olympic City: 1896–1906*, 13–53, Athens: International Olympic Academy.

Koulouri, C. (2011), 'From Antiquity to Olympic Revival: Sports and Greek National Historiography (Nineteenth–Twentieth Century)', in E. Fournaraki and Z.

Papakonstantinou (eds), *Sports, Bodily Culture and Classical Antiquity in Modern Greece*, 10–48, London and New York: Routledge.

Kourvetaris, G. A. (1997), *Studies on Greek Americans*, Boulder: East European Monographs.

Kourvetaris, G. A. (1999), 'Greeks', in E. R. Barkan (ed.), *A Nation of Peoples: A Sourcebook on America's Multicultural Heritage*, 248–65, Westport and London: Greenwood Press.

Kreft, M. (2000), 'Europa-Park – von der Unternehmervision zum Marktführer', in A. Steinecke (ed.), *Erlebnis- und Konsumwelten*, 133–44, München and Wien: Oldenbourg.

Kuisel, R. (2012), *The French Way: How France Embraced and Rejected American Values and Power*, Princeton: Princeton University Press.

Lambrinou, L. (2018), 'The Parthenon from the Greek Revival to the Modern Movement', in K. Harloe, N. Momigliano and A. Farnoux (eds), *Hellenomania*, 126–60, London and New York: Routledge.

Lash, S. and Urry, J. (1994), *Economies of Signs and Space*, London: Sage Publications.

Latotzki, R. (2015), *Up&Down: Wooden Rollercoasters in Europe*, Rheinbreitbach: Vista Point.

Lawton, C. L. (1995), *Attic Document Reliefs: Art and Politics in Ancient Athens*, Oxford: Clarendon Press.

Leonard, M. (2005), *Athens in Paris: Ancient Greece and the Political in Post-War French Thought*, Oxford: Oxford University Press.

Leoussi, A. S. (1998), *Nationalism and Classicism: The Classical Body as National Symbol in Nineteenth-Century England and France*, Basingstoke: Palgrave Macmillan.

Leoussi, A. S. (1999), 'Nationalism and the Antique in Nineteenth-Century English and French Art', in M. Wyke and M. Biddiss (eds), *The Uses and Abuses of Antiquity*, 79–105, Bern et al.: Peter Lang Publishing.

Leoussi, A. S. (2001), 'Myths of Ancestry', *Nations and Nationalisms*, 7 (4): 467–86.

Leoussi, A. S. (2016), 'Making Nations in the Image of Greece: Classical Greek Conceptions of the Body in the Construction of National Identity in Nineteenth-Century England, France and Germany', in T. Fögen and R. Warren (eds), *Graeco-Roman Antiquity and the Idea of Nationalism in the 19th Century: Case Studies*, 45–70, Berlin and Boston: de Gruyter.

Leoussi, A. (2018), 'Making Everyone Greek: Citizens, Athletes, and Ideals of Nationhood in Nineteenth-Century Britain, France, and Germany', in K. Harloe, N. Momigliano and A. Farnoux (eds), *Hellenomania*, 100–25, London and New York: Routledge.

Liu, J. (2015), 'Vergil in China in the Twentieth Century', *Sino-American Journal of Comparative Literature*, 1: 67–105.

Liu, J. (2019), 'Translating and Rewriting Western Classics in China (1920s–1930s): The Case of the *Xueheng* Journal', in Renger and Fan (2019): 91–111.

Losemann, V. (2011), 'Sparta-Diskurse in den frühen USA', in U. Niggemann and K. Ruffing (eds), *Antike als Modell in Nordamerika?*, 137–47, München: Oldenbourg.

Lowenthal, D. (1988), 'Classical Antiquities as National and Global Heritage', *Antiquity*, 62: 726–35.

Lowenthal, D. (1998), *The Heritage Crusade and the Spoils of History*, Cambridge, UK: Cambridge University Press.

Lowenthal, D. (2002), 'The Past as a Theme Park', in Young and Riley (2002): 11–23.

Lowenthal, D. (2015), *The Past as a Foreign Country – Revisited*, Cambridge, UK: Cambridge University Press.

Lukas, S. A. (2007a), 'Theming as a Sensory Phenomenon: Discovering the Senses on the Las Vegas Strip', in S. A. Lukas (ed.), *The Themed Space: Locating Nature, Nation, and Self*, 75–95, Lanham and Plymouth: Lexington Books.

Lukas, S. A. (2007b), 'A Politics of Reverence and Irreverence: Social Discourse on Theming Controversies', in S. A. Lukas (ed.), *The Themed Space: Locating Nature, Nation, and Self*, 271–93, Lanham and Plymouth: Lexington Books.

Lukas, S. A. (2008), *Theme Park*, London: Reaktion Books.

Lukas, S. A. (2010), 'From Themed Space to Lifespace', in J. Schlehe et al. (eds), *Staging the Past: Themed Environments in Transcultural Perspectives*, 135–53, Bielefeld: transcript.

Lukas, S. A. (2013), *The Immersive Worlds Handbook: Designing Theme Parks and Consumer Spaces*, New York and London: Focal Press.

Lukas, S. A. (2016), 'Introduction: The Meanings of Themed and Immersive Spaces', in S. A. Lukas (ed.), *A Reader in Themed and Immersive Spaces*, 3–15, Pittsburgh: ETC Press.

MacCannell, D. (1973) 'Staged Authenticity: Arrangements of Social Space in Tourist Settings', *American Journal of Sociology*, 79 (3): 589–603.

Maguet, F. (1998), 'Astérix, un mythe? Mythogénèse et amplification d'un stéréotype culturel', *Ethnologie Française*, 28 (3): 317–26.

Marchand, S. L. (1996), *Down from Olympus: Archaeology and Philhellenism in Germany, 1750–1970*, Princeton: Princeton University Press.

Martí-Aguilar, M. Á (2003), 'Tartesos: Precedentes, Auge y Pervivencias de un Paradigma Autoctonista', in F. Wulff Alonso and M. Á. Martí-Aguilar (eds), *Antigüedad y franquismo (1936–1975)*, 189–215, Málaga: CEDMA.

Mattern, T. (2011), '"Noble Beyond Expression": Die Antike als Vorbild der US-Architektur', in U. Niggemann and K. Ruffing (eds), *Antike als Modell in Nordamerika?*, 277–304, München: Oldenbourg

McCall, J. (2018), 'Videogames as Participatory Public History', in D. Dean (ed.), *A Companion to Public History*, 405–16, Malden: Wiley-Blackwell.

McEnroe, J. C. (2002), 'Cretan Questions: Politics and Archaeology 1898–1913', in Y. Hamilakis (ed.), *Labyrinth Revisited: Rethinking 'Minoan' Archaeology*, 59–72, Oxford: Oxbow Books.

Meid, C. (2012), *Griechenland-Imaginationen: Reiseberichte im 20. Jahrhundert von Gerhart Hauptmann bis Wolfgang Koeppen*, Berlin: de Gruyter.

Melotti, M. (2008), *Turismo archeologico: Dalle piramidi alle veneri di plastica*, Milano: Bruno Mondadori.

Melotti, M. (2017), 'Gladiator for a Day: Tourism, Archaeology, and Theme Parks in Rome', in F. Carlà-Uhink, F. Freitag, S. Mittermeier and A. Schwarz (eds), *Time and Temporality in Theme Parks*, 131–53, Hannover: Wehrhahn.

Metzler, J. J. (2017), *Taiwan's Transformation: 1895 to the Present*, New York: Palgrave Macmillan.

Mitrašinović, M. (2006), *Total Landscapes, Theme Parks, Public Space*, Aldershot: Ashgate.

Mittermeier, S. (2016), '"Windows to the Past": Disney's America, the Culture Wars, and the Question of Edutainment', *Polish Journal for American Studies*, 10: 127–46.

Mittermeier, S. (2017), 'Utopia, Nostalgia, and Our Struggle with the Present: Time Travelling through Discovery Bay', in F. Carlà-Uhink, F. Freitag, S. Mittermeier and A. Schwarz (eds), *Time and Temporality in Theme Parks*, 171–87, Hannover: Wehrhahn.

Momigliano, N. (2017), 'Introduction: Cretomania – Desiring the Minoan Past in the Present', in N. Momigliano and A. Farnoux (eds), *Cretomania: Modern Desires for the Minoan Past*, 1–13, London and New York: Routledge.

Morris, I. (1994), 'Archaeologies of Greece', in I. Morris (ed.), *Classical Greece: Ancient Histories and Modern Archaeologies*, 8–47, Cambridge, UK: Cambridge University Press.

Mortensen, L. (2009), 'Producing Copán in the Archaeology Industry', in L. Mortensen and J. Hollowell (eds), *Ethnographies and Archaeologies: Iterations of the Past*, 178–98, Gainesville: University Press of Florida.

Moscardo, G. M. and Pearce, P. L. (1986), 'Historic Theme Parks: An Australian Experience in Authenticity', *Annals of Tourism Research*, 13: 467–79.

Most, G. W. (2003), 'Philhellenism, Cosmopolitanism, Nationalism', in M. Haagsma, P. den Boer and E. M. Moorman (eds), *The Impact of Classical Greece on European and National Identities*, 71–91, Amsterdam: J. C. Gieben.

Müller, V. (2017), 'Verjüngtes Atlantis: die Rezeption des platonischen Atlantis-Mythos in Kinder- und Jungendmedien der letzten 40 Jahre', in M. Janka and M. Stierstorfer (eds), *Verjüngte Antike: Griechisch-römische Mythologie und Historie in zeitgenössischen Kinder- und Jugendmedien*, 265–86, Heidelberg: Winter.

Muzaini, H. (2016), 'Informal Heritage-Making at the Sarawak Cultural Village, East Malaysia', *Tourism Geographies*, 19 (2): 244–64.

Nara, H. (2019), 'An Adoring Gaze: The Idea of Greece in Modern Japan', in Renger and Fan (2019): 175–201.

Nisbet, G. (2008), *Ancient Greece in Film and Popular Culture*, 2nd edn, Exeter: Bristol Phoenix Press.

Oesterle, C. (2010), 'Themed Environments – Performative Spaces: Performing Visitors in North American Living History Museums', in J. Schlehe et al. (eds), *Staging the Past: Themed Environments in Transcultural Perspectives*, 157–75, Bielefeld: transcript.

Ogden, D. (2013), *Drakōn: Dragon Myth and Serpent Cult in the Greek and Roman Worlds*, Oxford: Oxford University Press

Olalquiaga, C. (2002), *The Artificial Kingdom: On the Kitsch Experience*, Minneapolis: University of Minnesota Press.

Olmos, R. (1991), 'Historiografia de la presencia y del comercio griego en España', *Boletin de la Asociacion Española de Amigos de la Arqueologia*, 30–1: 123–33.

Ong, C. E. (2016), '"Cuteifying" Spaces and Staging Marine Animals for Chinese Middle-Class Consumption', *Tourism Geographies*, 19 (2): 188–207.

Ong, C. E. and Jin, J. (2016), 'Simulacra and Simulation: Double Simulation at a North Song Dynasty Theme Park', *Tourism Geographies*, 19 (2): 227–43.

Orvell, M. (1989), *The Real Thing: Imitation and Authenticity in American Culture, 1880–1940*, Chapel Hill and London: The University of North Carolina Press.

Paine, C. (2019), *Gods and Rollercoasters: Religion in Theme Parks Worldwide*, London and New York: Bloomsbury.

Pantazis, V. (2002), *Der Geschichtsunterricht in der multikulturellen Gesellschaft: Das Beispiel der griechischen Migrantenkinder*, Frankfurt a.M.: Peter Lang.

Paradis, T. W. (2007), 'From Downtown to Theme Town: Reinventing America's Smaller Historic Retail Districts', in S. A. Lukas (ed.), *The Themed Space: Locating Culture, Nation, and Self*, 57–74, Lanham and Plymouth: Lexington Books.

Philippides, D. (1994), 'The Parthenon as Appreciated by Greek Society', in P. Tournikiotis (ed.), *The Parthenon and Its Impact in Modern Times*, 279–309, Athens: Melissa.

Pigeat, A. (2015), 'Imaginaires de l'Antiquité dans le manga, entre mythes et mythologies: Représentations, fonctions et modalités d'apparition', in J. Gallego (ed.), *La bande dessinée historique: Premier cycle: l'Antiquité*, 135–42, Pau: Presses Universitaires de Pau.

Pine, B. J. and Gilmore, J. H. (2011), *The Experience Economy*, 2nd edn, Boston: Harvard Business School Press.

Pinzer, D (2012), 'Erlebniswelten und Technikphilosophie', in A. Hahn (ed.), *Erlebnislandschaft – Erlebnis Landschaft? Atmosphären im architektonischen Entwurf*, 97–120, Bielefeld: transcript.

Plantzos, D. (2008), 'Archaeology and Hellenic Identity, 1896–2004: The Frustrated Vision', in D. Damaskos and D. Plantzos (eds), *A Singular Antiquity: Archaelogy and Hellenic Identity in Twentieth-Century Greece*, 11–30, Athens: Benaki Museum.

Project on Disney (1995), *Inside the Mouse: Work and Play at Disney World*, Durham and London: Duke University Press.

Ren, H. (1998), *Economies of Culture: Theme Parks, Museums, and Capital Accumulation in China, Hong Kong and Taiwan*, PhD thesis, University of Washington, Washington.

Ren, H. (2007), 'The Landscape of Power: Imagineering Consumer Behavior at China's Theme Parks', in S. A. Lucas (ed.), *The Themed Space: Locating Culture, Nation, and Self*, 97–112, Lanham: Lexington Books.

Renaut, C. (2011), 'Disneyland Paris', in K. M. Jackson and M. I. West (eds), *Disneyland and Culture: Essays on the Parks and Their Influence*, 125–37, Jefferson: McFarland.
Renger, A. B. and Fan, X. (eds) (2019), *Receptions of Greek and Roman Antiquity in East Asia*, Leiden and Boston: Brill.
Rhodes, R. F. (1995), *Architecture and Meaning on the Athenian Acropolis*, Cambridge, UK: Cambridge University Press.
Rieche, A. (2012), *Von Rom nach Las Vegas: Rekonstruktionen antiker römischer Architektur*, Berlin: Dietrich Reimer.
Roseberry, W. and O'Brien, J. (1991), 'Introduction', in J. O'Brien and W. Roseberry (eds), *Golden Ages, Dark Ages: Imagining the Past in Anthropology and History*, 1–18, Berkeley et al.: University of California Press.
Rouvière, N. (2008), *Astérix ou la parodie des identités*, Paris: Champs-Flammarion.
Rouvière, N. (2015), 'De l'histoire de l'Antiquité à l'histoire culturelle contemporaine: Quelle est la valeur documentaire d'Astérix?', in J. Gallego (ed.), *La bande dessinée historique: Premier cycle: l'Antiquité*, 21–8, Pau: Presses Universitaires de Pau.
Rowan, Y. (2004), 'Repackaging the Pilgrimage: Visiting the Holy Land in Orlando', in Y. Rowan and U. Baram (eds), *Marketing Heritage: Archaeology and the Consumption of the Past*, 249–66, Walnut Creek: AltaMira Press.
Rowan, Y. and Baram, U. (eds) (2004), *Marketing Heritage: Archaeology and the Consumption of the Past*, Walnut Creek: AltaMira Press.
Rubinstein, M. A. (2007), 'Political Taiwanization and Pragmatic Diplomacy: The Eras of Chang Ching-kuo and Lee Teng-him, 1971–1194', in M. A. Rubinstein (ed.), *Taiwan: A New History*, exp. edn, 436–95, Armonk and London: Routledge.
Rüsen, J. (1994), 'Was ist Geschichtskultur? Überlegungen zu einer neuen Art, über Geschichte nachzudenken', in K. Füßmann, H. T. Grütter and J. Rüsen (eds), *Historische Faszination: Geschichtskultur heute*, 3–26, Köln et al.: Böhlau.
Rüsen, J. (1995), 'Geschichtskultur', *Geschichte in Wissenschaft und Unterricht*, 46: 513–21.
Rüsen, J. (2004), 'Historical Consciousness: Narrative Structure, Moral Function, and Ontogenetic Development', in P. Seixas (ed.), *Theorizing Historical Consciousness*, 63–85, Toronto et al.: University of Toronto Press.
Rüsen, J. (2014), 'Die fünf Dimensionen der Geschichtskultur', in J. Nießer and J. Tomann (eds), *Angewandte Geschichte: Neue Perspektiven auf Geschichte in der Öffentlichkeit*, 46–57, Paderborn et al.: Ferdinand Schöningh.
Ruiz, A., Sánchez, A. and Bellón, J. P. (2003), 'Aventuras y desventuras de los Iberos durante el Franquismo', in F. Wulff Alonso and M. Á. Martí-Aguilar (eds), *Antigüedad y franquismo (1936–1975)*, 161–88, Málaga: CEDMA.
Ruiz Zapatero, G. (1996), 'Celts and Iberians: Ideological Manipulations in Spanish Archaeology', in P. Graves-Brown, S. Jones and C. Gamble (eds), *Cultural Identity and Archaeology: The Construction of European Communities*, 179–95, London and New York: Routledge.

Ruiz Zapatero, G. (2003), 'Historiografía y "uso público" de los Celtas en la España franquista', in F. Wulff Alonso and M. Á. Martí-Aguilar (eds), *Antigüedad y franquismo (1936–1975)*, 217–40, Málaga: CEDMA.

Ruiz Zapatero, G. and Alvarez-Sanchís, J. R. (1995), 'Prehistory, Story-Telling, and Illustrations: The Spanish Past in School Textbooks (1880–1994)', *Journal of European Archaeology*, 3 (1): 213–32.

Salazar, N. B. (2010), 'Imagineering Tailor-Made Pasts for Nation-Building and Tourism: A Comparative Perspective', in J. Schlehe et al. (eds), *Staging the Past: Themed Environments in Transcultural Perspectives*, 93–109, Bielefeld: transcript.

Salmon, F. (2018), 'The Ideal and the Real in British Hellenomania, 1751–1851', in K. Harloe, N. Momigliano and A. Farnoux (eds), *Hellenomania*, 73–99, London and New York: Routledge.

Samuel, R. (2012), *Theatres of Memory: Past and Present in Contemporary Culture*, London: Verso.

Saussy, H. (2010), 'Contestatory Classics in 1920s China', in S. A. Stephens and P. Vasunia (eds), *Classics and National Cultures*, 258–66, Oxford: Oxford University Press.

Schlehe, J. (2004), 'Themenparks: Globale Kulturrepräsentation, nation building oder Freizeitvergnügen?', in K. Beck, T. Förster and H. P. Hahn (eds), *Blick nach vorn: Festgabe für Gerd Spittler zum 65. Geburtstag*, 298–310, Köln: Rüdiger Köppe.

Schlehe, J. and Uike-Bormann, M. (2010), 'Staging the Past in Cultural Theme Parks: Representations of Self and Other in Asia and Europe', in J. Schlehe et al. (eds), *Staging the Past: Themed Environments in Transcultural Perspectives*, 57–91, Bielefeld: transcript.

Schmitt-Pantel, P. (2002), 'Que dire du monde antique à l'école?', in M. Hagnerelle (ed.), *Apprendre l'histoire et la géographie à l'École, Direction de l'enseignement scolaire*, 57–62, Paris: Canopé – CRDP de Versailles.

Schröder, J. (2012), 'Belantis: Erlebnisgestaltung zwischen Funktion und Emotion: Interpretation des Interviews mit dem Architekten Herrn Rudolf', in A. Hahn (ed.), *Erlebnislandschaft – Erlebnis Landschaft? Atmosphären im architektonischen Entwurf*, 201–24, Bielefeld: transcript.

Schulz, R. (2002), 'Alte Geschichte im europäischen Kulturkontext? Die klassische Antike in französischen und deutschen Schulbüchern der Sekundarstufe I und des Collège', *Internationale Schulbuchforschung*, 24: 387–404.

Schulze, G. (2005), *Die Erlebnisgesellschaft: Kultursoziologie der Gegenwart*, 2nd edn, Frankfurt a.M.: Campus.

Schwarz, A. (2017), 'Staging the Gaze: The Water Coaster "Poseidon" as an Example of Staging Strategies in Theme Parks', in F. Carlà-Uhink, F. Freitag, S. Mittermeier and A. Schwarz (eds), *Time and Temporality in Theme Parks*, 97–112, Hannover: Wehrhahn.

Scilabra, C. (2015), 'Vivono fra noi: L'uso del classico come espressione d'alterità nella produzione fumettistica giapponese', *Status Quaestionis*, 8, 2015: 92–109. Available online: https://ojs.uniroma1.it/index.php/statusquaestionis/article/view/13142 [22/12/2018].

Scilabra, C. (2018), 'When Apollo Tasted Sushi for the First Time: Early Examples of the Reception of Classics in Japanese Comics', in F. Bièvre-Perrin and É. Pampanay (eds), *Antiquipop: La reference à l'Antiquité dans la culture populaire contemporaine*, Lyon 2018. Available online: https://books.openedition.org/momeditions/3371 [12/03/2019].

Scilabra, C. (2019), 'Back to the Future: Reviving Classical Figures in Japanese Comics', in Renger and Fan (2019): 287–309.

Shanower, E. (2011), 'Twenty-First Century Troy', in G. Kovacs and C. W. Marshall (eds), *Classics and Comics*, 195–206, Oxford: Oxford University Press.

Shanower, E. (2013), 'Trojan Lovers and Warriors: The Power of Seduction in *Age of Bronze*', in S. Knippschild and M. García Morcillo (eds), *Seduction and Power: Antiquity in the Visual and Performing Arts*, 57–70, London and New York: Bloomsbury.

Simpson, T. (2010), 'Materialist Pedagogy: The Function of Themed Environments in Post-Socialist Consumption in Macao', *Tourist Studies*, 9 (1): 60–80.

Sinn, U. (2008), 'Asterix und Olympia', in K. Brodersen (ed.), *Asterix und seine Zeit: Die große Welt des kleinen Galliers*, 3rd edn, 159–76, München: Beck.

Sollors, W. (1989), 'Introduction: The Invention of Ethnicity', in W. Sollors (ed.), *The Invention of Ethnicity*, ix–xx, New York and Oxford: Oxford University Press.

Solomon, E. (2006), 'Knossos: Social Uses of a Monumental Landscape', *Creta Antica*, 7: 163–82.

Solomon, J. (2001), *The Ancient World in the Cinema*, 2nd edn, New Haven and London: Yale University Press.

Sparkes, B. A. (1971), 'The Trojan Horse in Classical Art', *Greece and Rome*, 18: 54–70.

Spickermann, W. (2008), 'Asterix und die Religion', in K. Brodersen (ed.), *Asterix und seine Zeit: Die große Welt des kleinen Galliers*, 3rd edn, 105–26, München: Beck.

Squire, M. (2011), *The Art of the Body: Antiquity and Its Legacy*, London and New York: I.B. Tauris.

Stafford, E. (2012), *Herakles*, London and New York: Routledge.

Stainton, M. (2007), 'The Politic of Taiwan Aboriginal Origins', in M. A. Rubinstein (ed.), *Taiwan: A New History*, exp. edn, 27–44, Armonk and London: Routledge.

Stanley, N. (2002), 'Chinese Theme Parks and National Identity', in Young and Riley (2002): 269–289.

Steinkrüger, J. E. (2013), *Thematisierte Welten: Über Darstellungspraxen in zoologischen Gärten und Vergnügungsparks*, Bielefeld: transcript.

Stoll, A. (1974), *Asterix: Das Trivialepos Frankreichs: Bild- und Sprachartistik eines Bestseller-Comics*, Köln: DuMont.

Stone, P. G. and Planel, P. G. (1999), 'Introduction', in P. G. Stone and P. G. Planel (eds), *The Constructed Past: Experimental Archaeology, Education and the Public*, 1–14, London and New York: Routledge.

Sünderhauf, E. S. (2004), *Griechensehnsucht und Kulturkritik: Die deutsche Rezeption von Winckelmanns Antikenideal 1840–1945*, Berlin: Akademie Verlag.

Takada, Y. (2010), 'Translation and Difference: Western Classics in Modern Japan', in S. A. Stephens and P. Vasunia (eds), *Classics and National Cultures*, 285–301, Oxford: Oxford University Press.

TEA (2017), Themed Entertainment Association, *Theme Index and Museum Index 2017. Global Attractions Attendance Report*, Burbank: TEA. Available online: http://www.teaconnect.org/images/files/TEA_268_653730_180517.pdf [22/12/2018].

Telesko, W. (2004), *Erlösermythen in Kunst und Politik: Zwischen christlicher Tradition und Moderne*, Wien: Böhlau.

Teo, P., Chang, T. C. and Ho, K. C. (2001), 'Introduction: Globalization and Interconnectedness in Southeast Asian Tourism', in P. Teo, T. C. Chang and K. C. Ho (eds), *Interconnected Worlds: Tourism in Southeast Asia*, 1–10, Amsterdam et al.: Pergamon.

Teo, P. and Yeoh, B. S. A. (2001), 'Negotiating Global Tourism: Localism as Difference in Southeast Asian Theme Parks', in P. Teo, T. C. Chang and K. C. Ho (eds), *Interconnected Worlds: Tourism in Southeast Asia*, 137–54, Amsterdam et al.: Pergamon.

The Dells (1999), *'The Dells': An Illustrated History of Wisconsin Dells*, Friendship: New Past Press.

Theisen, N. A. (2011), 'Declassicizing the Classical in Japanese Comics: Osamu Tezuka's Apollo's Song', in G. Kovacs and C. W. Marshall (eds), *Classics and Comics*, 59–71, Oxford: Oxford University Press.

Toner, J. (2017), 'The Intellectual Life of the Roman Non-Elite', in L. Grig (ed.), *Popular Culture in the Ancient World*, 167–88, Cambridge, UK: Cambridge University Press

Tsigakou, F. M. (1981), *The Rediscovery of Greece: Travellers and Painters of the Romantic Era*, London: Thames and Hudson.

Tziovas, D. (2014), 'Introduction: Decolonizing Antiquity, Heritage Politics, and Performing the Past', in D. Tziovas (ed.), *Re-Imagining the Past: Antiquity and Modern Greek Culture*, 1–26, Oxford: Oxford University Press.

Ulf, C. (2003) (ed.), *Der neue Streit um Troia: Eine Bilanz*, München: Beck.

Urry, J. and Larsen, J. (2011), *The Tourist Gaze 3.0*, Los Angeles et al.: SAGE.

van Eeden, J. (2007), 'Theming Mythical Africa at the Lost City', in S. A. Lukas (ed.), *The Themed Space: Locating Nature, Nation, and Self*, 113–35, Lanham and Plymouth: Lexington Books.

van Maanen, J. (1992), 'Displacing Disney: Some Notes on the Flow of Culture', *Qualitative Sociology*, 15 (1): 5–35.

van Zanten, D. (1994), 'The Parthenon Imagined Painted', in P. Tournikiotis (ed.), *The Parthenon and Its Impact in Modern Times*, 259–77, Athens: Melissa.

Vidal-Naquet, P. (2005), *L'Atlantide: Petite histoire d'un mythe platonicien*, Paris: Les Belles Lettres.

Vinson, S. (2004), 'From Lord Elgin to James Henry Breasted: The Politics of the Past in the First Era of Globalization', in Y. Rowan and U. Baram (eds), *Marketing Heritage: Archaeology and the Consumption of the Past*, 57–65, Walnut Creek: AltaMira Press.

Wallace, M. (1996), *Mickey Mouse History and Other Essays on American Memory*, Philadelphia: Temple University Press.

Walsh, K. (1992), *The Representation of the Past: Museums and Heritage in the Post-Modern World*, London and New York: Routledge.

Werner, M. (2011), 'Philology in Germany: Textual or Cultural Scholarship?', in G. Klaniczay, M. Werner and O. Gecser (eds), *Multiple Antiquities – Multiple Modernities: Ancient History in Nineteenth-Century European Cultures*, 89–110, Frankfurt and New York: Campus.

Wieber, A. (2017), 'Non-Western Approaches to the Ancient World: India and Japan – Classical Heritage or Exotic Occidentalism?', in A. Pomeroy (ed.), *A Companion to Ancient Greece and Rome on Screen*, 329–48, Malden and Oxford: Wiley Blackwell.

Wiedemann, F. (2018), 'The Aryans: Ideology and Historiographical Narrative Types in the Nineteenth and Early Twentieth Century', in H. Roche and K. N. Demetriou (eds), *Brill's Companion to the Classics, Fascist Italy and Nazi Germany*, 31–59, Leiden and Boston: Brill.

Wildmann, D. (1998), *Begehrte Körper: Konstruktion und Inszenierung des 'arischen Männerkörpers' im 'Dritten Reich'*, Zürich: Königshausen & Neumann.

Wildmann, D. (2018), 'Desired Bodies: Leni Riefenstahl's Olympia, Aryan Masculinity and the Classical Body', in H. Roche and K.N. Demetriou (eds), *Brill's Companion to the Classics, Fascist Italy and Nazi Germany*, 60–81, Leiden and Boston: Brill.

Will, W. (2008), 'Die Gallier und ihre Nachbarn – oder: Die Schweiz ist flach', in K. Brodersen (ed.), *Asterix und seine Zeit. Die große Welt des kleinen Galliers*, 3rd edn, 19–33, München: Beck.

Winnerling, T. (2014), 'The Eternal Recurrence of All Bits: How Historicizing Video Game Series Transform Factual History into Affective Historicity', *Eludamos: Journal for Computer Game Culture*, 8: 151–70. Available online at: https://www.eludamos.org/index.php/eludamos/article/view/vol8no1-10/8-1-10-html [10/11/2019]

Winterer, C. (2002), *The Culture of Classicism: Ancient Greece and Rome in American Intellectual Life, 1780–1910*, Baltimore and London: Johns Hopkins University Press.

Wittenburg, A. (2010), 'Olympia und Delphi – deutsche und französische Archäologen im neuen Griechenland', in E. Kocziszky (ed.), *Ruinen in der Moderne: Archäologie und die Künste*, 221–43, Bonn: Reimer.

Wolf, M. J. (1999), *The Entertainment Economy: How Mega-Media Forces Are Transforming Our Lives*, New York: Three Rivers.

Wyke, M. (1997), *Projecting the Past: Ancient Rome, Cinema and History*, London and New York: Routledge.

Yalouri, E. (2001), *The Acropolis: Global Fame, Local Claim*, Oxford and New York: Berg.

Yalouri, E. (2004), 'When the New World Meets the Ancient: American and Greek Experiences of the 1896 "Revival" of the Olympic Games', in C. Koulouri (ed.), *Athens, Olympic City: 1896–1906*, 295–331, Athens: International Olympic Academy.

Yalouri, E. (2011), 'Fanning the Flame: Transformations of the 2004 Olympic Flame', in E. Fournaraki and Z. Papakonstantinou (eds), *Sports, Bodily Culture and Classical Antiquity in Modern Greece*, 151–79, London and New York: Routledge.

Yalouri, E. (2014), 'Possessing Antiquity: Reconnecting to the Past in the Greek Present', in D. Tziovas (ed.), *Re-Imagining the Past: Antiquity and Modern Greek Culture*, 165–85, Oxford: Oxford University Press.

Yang, L. (2011), 'Cultural Tourism in an Ethnic Theme Park: Tourists' View', *Journal of Tourism and Cultural Change*, 9 (4): 320–40.

Young, T. and Riley, R. (2002) (eds), *Theme Park Landscapes: Antecedents and Variations*, Washington, DC: Dumbarton Oaks Research Library and Collection.

Younger, D. (2016), *Theme Park Design and the Art of Themed Entertainment*, Milton Keynes: Inklingwood.

Zimmermann, M. (2006), 'Troia – eine unendliche Geschichte?', in M. Zimmermann (ed.), *Der Traum von Troia: Geschichte und Mythos einer ewigen Stadt*, 11–25, München: Beck.

Zorzin, N. (forthcoming), 'Alternating Cycles of the Politics of Forgetting and Remembering the Past in Taiwan', in V. Apaydin (ed.), *Critical Perspectives on Cultural Memory and Heritage: Construction, Transformation and Destruction*, London: UCL Press.

Zukin, S. (1991), *Landscapes of Power: From Detroit to Disney World*, Berkeley, Los Angeles and Oxford: University of California Press.

Index

Note: Numbers in **bold** refer to figures.

20,000 Leagues Under the Sea (movie, 1954) 57
300 (comic, 1998) 31, 106
300 (movie, 2006) 31, 40, 106–7, 138, 153, 191

Achaeans 34, 141
Acheron 100
Achilles 33, 89–90, 103–4, 107, 165
Acropdis Park, Nanjing, PRC 134
Acropolis of Athens, *see* Athens
Acteon 104
Adriatic Sea 68–9, 71
Aeaea 67
Aegean Sea and islands 29, 36, 42, 44, 49, 59, 61, 78, 83, 96–8, 130, 133–7, 139–41, 144, 146, 155, 159, 172, 180–1, 183, 188, 190, 193, 225
Aelian (Claudius Aelianus) 57
Aeolia 100
Aeolus 95, 100
Affective turn 20, 22
Africa 25, 45, 48, 62, 78, 80, 171, 216
Agamemnon 34, 53, 58, 86, 103, 148
Age of Mythology (video game, 2002) 186
Ajax 180
Akrotiri 52
    Blue Monkeys Fresco 143
    Boxer Fresco 91
Alcmene 69, 90
Alexander III of Macedon (Alexander the Great) 31, 41, 184, 193–4
Alexandria 64, 214
    Pharos of Alexandria 214
Alicante 80
Almagro Basch, Martin 212
Alphen an der Rijn 198

Alps 146
America 9, 14–16, 37, 62, 115, 119, 121, 154, 128–9, 132, 135–6, 216
    see also United States of America
American Civil War (1861–1865) 14, 105
American Revolution (1765–1783) 105
Ampurias (ancient Emporion) 77, 79, 85
anachronisms 1, 158, 168, 171–3, 175–7, 180, 183, 224
Anaheim, *see* Disney, theme parks
Anatolia 65
Andromeda 90–1, 112
anime 129, 131, 136
Anubis 149
Aphrodite 42, 107, 125
    Aphrodite of Knidos 152
    see also Venus
Apollo 93, 114–15, 117, 127, 139, 152, 154, 158, 162, 173, 222
Apoxyomenos, *see* Lysippus
Aqualandia, Benidorm, Spain 80–1
Aquileia 69
Arcadia 3, 30, 183
Archaeology 17–18, 23–4, 26, 28, 30–1, 33–4, 42, 48–9, 52–4, 75, 77–9, 85, 89, 91, 93, 112, 115, 122, 125, 160, 168, 170, 182, 193–4, 198–9, 201, 203, 208
Archeon, Alphen an der Rijn, Netherlands 198
archetype 6, 32, 35, 41, 56
Archimedes 64
Ares 152
Arganthonios 78
Argo (mythical ship) 99, 102
Argonauts 33, 97, 102–3, 137
Argos (mythical character) 102
Aristogeiton 152
Aristoteles Park, Stagira, Greece 194

Aristotle 28, 194
Armorica 181
art nouveau 95
Artemis 93, 128
   see also Diana
Artemision Bronze, see Poseidon
Aryans 40, 43, 78, 207, 223
Asia 2, 37, 129–32, 150, 136, 144, 146, 153,
        159, 220
Astérix 7, 18, 37–8, 43, 76, 127, 167–8,
        171–88, 210, 224–5
Athena 3, 52–3, 58, 60, 63, 68, 73, 87, 92,
        100–1, 109, 128, 139, 143,
        148, 155, 164, 212, 215, 222
   Athena Lemnia 86, 215
   Athena Promachos 73
Athens 19, 28–31, 33–6, 39–43, 47, 53,
        56–7, 63, 78–9, 85–8, 92, 98,
        105–7, 109–10, 134, 137, 157,
        160, 164–5, 169–72, 174, 180,
        186, 193, 207, 208, 222
   Acropolis 25, 30–1, 37, 39, 42–4, 47, 57,
        63, 73, 79, 86–8, 92, 94–5,
        130, 134, 155–8, 160–1, 165,
        172, 187, 191, 193, 208, 224
   Agora 87–8, 110
   Erechtheion (and Porch of the
       Caryatids) 86, 92, 130
   Parthenon 1–2, 25, 28, 30–1, 33, 42–43,
        51–2, 57, 73, 79, 88, 92–3,
        106, 109, 122–3, 125, 130,
        157, 164, 169, 202, 205, 216
   Plaka 88
   Stoa of Attalus 88
   Stoa of Zeus 87
   Temple of Theseus (Temple of
       Hephaestus) 28
Athos, Mount 194
Atlantic Ocean 62, 117
Atlantis 49–50, 56–58, 62, 116–17, 124,
        128, 130, 135, 160, 182,
        210–11
Atlantis, The Lost Continent (movie, 1961)
        57
Atlantis: The Lost Empire (movie, 2001) 58,
        116
Atlas 53, 139
Attica 52, 215
Augustus of Prima Porta 82

Austria 45
Authenticity 6, 9, 24, 46, 52, 91, 151, 161,
        190–1, 193–4, 199–200
Ayia Napa 227
Aztecs 24, 115

B.C. (comic strip, 1958–present) 171
Baba Aruj (Barbarossa, Oruç Reis) 84
Babylon 136
Barcelona 77, 79
Basques 78
Beatles, The 171
Beethoven, Ludwig van 113, 148
Beijing 25, 33, 37–8, 132–5, 137–8, 141–2,
        144–5, 147, 149–50, 153, 165,
        186, 191
   Chaoyang district 133
Belantis, Leipzig, Germany 32, 37–8,
        61–73, 101–2, 182, 191
   'Insel der Ritter' 62
   'Küste der Entdecker' 62
   'Land der Grafen' 62
   'Prairie der Indianer' 62
   'Reich der Sonnentempel' 62
   'Strand der Götter' **62–73**
      'Arena des Zeus' 63
      'Fahrt des Odysseus' **64–70**, 71–3,
         102
      'Flug des Ikarus' 63, 68, **70–1**, 72
      'Götterflug' 63, **71–2**
      'Poseidons Flotte' 68, **72–3**
      'Säule der Athene' 63, **73**
      'Schalen des Pythagoras' 63
   'Tal der Pharaonen' 62
      'Cobra des Amun-Ra' 63
      'Fluch des Pharaos' 63, 66
Belgium 171
Bella Coola 9
Benidorm 15, 19, 25, 80, 86, 96–7
Berlin 40, 46, 54–5, 146, 165, 170
   Berlin Wall 46
   Brandenburg Gate 165
Bes 72
Bill and Ted's Excellent Adventures (movie,
        1989) 107
Bomas of Kenya, Nairobi, Kenya 198
Boulanger, Gustave 173
Boxer at Rest 173
Boy with Thorn 87

Brabant 65
Brazil 149
Breadsted, James Henry 107
bronze age 33–4, 52–3, 56, 66, 86, 91, 97, 99, 103, 112, 138, 140, 142–3, 155, 172, 181
Buenos Aires 27
Buffalo Bill 9
Busch Gardens Williamsburg, Williamsburg, USA 26, **114–15**
   'Festa Italia' 114
     'Apollo's Chariot' **114–15**
     'Roman Rapids' 114
   'San Marco' 114
     'Escape from Pompeii' 26, 114
Byzantine empire 29, 35, 60, 148

Caesar 149, 171, 173, 175
Campania 68–9, 212
Canada 114
Canova, Antonio 140
Capitoline Venus, *see* Venus
Captain America 143
Caribbean 121, 133, 199
carnival 149
Carter, Howard 54
Caryatids 86
Carthage 77–8
Casino Greek Mythology, Macau, PRC 132
Cassandra 49, 58–61, 69
Catalonia 75, 77–80
Catholicism 75, 90, 160
Celtiberians 76, 78
Celts 75, 78–9
   see also Gauls
centaurs 91, 104, 113, 140, 148, 158, 183
Cerberus 91, 158, 162, 180
chaos 93
Charon 100, 157
Charybdis 66–7, 70, 101–2, 162, 211
Chateaubriand, François-René de 168
Chengdu 132–4
Cheops 85
Chiang Kai-shek 150–1, 154
Chicago 119, 194
China (People's Republic) 12, 24–5, 33, 37, 113–14, 130–131, **132–49**, 151–6, 158, 160–5, 220–2

China Folk Culture Village, Shenzhen, PRC 132
China Travel International Investment 132
China Travel Services Holdings 132, 220
Chinese Ethnic Culture Park, Beijing, PRC 221
Chinese New Year 113, 149
Choiseul-Gouffier, Marie-Gabriel-Florent-Auguste de 168
Chongqing 132–3
Christmas 148
Cid, *see* El Cid
Cimmerians 100
Cinerama Holiday (movie, 1955) 31
Circe 65, 67–9, 101, 212
Circeo, Cape 65
Clash of the Titans (movie, 1981) 34, 112, 153, 158, 163
Clash of the Titans (movie, 2010) 112
Cleopatra VII 85, 149, 177
Cleopatra's Needles 85
Clinton, Bill 107
Colchis 102–3
Colonial Williamsburg, Williamsburg, USA 9, 14, 198
colonialism 4, 45, 47, 54, 135, 197, 208, 216
Colonization (Greek), *see* Greek Colonization
colosseum 45, 96, 118, 159
Colossus of Rhodes 145–6, 158, 174
Confucius 131
Copán 199
corinthian helmet 124, 162, 224
corinthian order 87–8, 96, 114, 124, 157
Costa Blanca 94
Coubertin, Pierre de 170, 173, 223
Crete 18, 33–4, 67, 77, 91, 98–9, 114, 123, 137, 140, 181, 194
Cultural memory 29, 75, 84, 129, 131, 147, 159, 167–8
Cultural Revolution 151
Culture Wars 15
Cumae 68
Cyclades 97–8
Cyclopes 50, 65, 68–9, 99–101, 118, 120, 126, 144, 162–3
   see also Polyphemus
Cynic Philosopher 72
Cyprus 227

Daedalus 34, 55, 71–2, 181–2
Dama de Elche 77
Dama Oferente del Cerro de los Santos 82, 84
dark theming 17–18
Darwinism 35
Delacroix, Eugène 168
Delos 97
Delphi 3, 90, 98, 125, 128, 142, 170, 181
    Sanctuary of Athena Pronaia (Tholos) 3, 125
democracy 16, 19, 28, 30, 37, 41, 53, 75, 78–9, 83, 85, 105–8, 110, 150, 154, 169, 171–2
Diadumenos, see Polykleitos
Diana 152, 154, 162, 222
    see also Artemis
Dinocrates of Rhodes 194
dinosaurs 144, 159
Dionysus 42, 104, 113, 115, 180
Discobolus, see Myron
Disney, Walt 5, 11, 17
Disney, company (WDC) 14–15, 18, 57, 91, 110–13, 116, 132, 136, 148, 157, 183, 190, 201–2, 217–18, 226
Disney, theme parks 3, 13–15, 18, 58, **110–14**, 132, 136, 148, 178, 189, 193
    'Captain EO' **111**
    Disney's America **14–15**
    Disneyland Resort, Anaheim, USA 113
        Disney California Adventure 113
            Golden Vine Winery' 114
            'Paradise Gardens' 113
        Disneyland 1, 3, 5, 9, 11, 16, 57, 80, 110–11, 113, 177, 190–1, 197, 218, 226
            'Fantasyland' 1
            'Hercules Victory Parade' 111
            'Main Street U.S.A.' 5, 16, 46, 80, 83, 178
            'Opa! A Celebration of Greece' **113–14**
    Disneyland Paris, Paris, France 1–2, 44, 57, 111, 177, 193, 225
        'Hercules Happening' 111
        'Les mystères du Nautilus' 57
        'Fantasia Gardens' 113
    Hong Kong Disneyland, Hong Kong, PRC 1, 3
    'It's A Small World' **1–3**, 36, 109–10, 113, 148, 189, 193, 197, 221
    Magic Kingdoms 1, 178
    Shanghai Disneyland, Shanghai, PRC 1
    Tokyo Disneyland, Tokyo, Japan 1–2, 111, 189, 197
        'Hercules the Hero' 111
        'Pirates of the Caribbean' 199
    Tokyo DisneySea, Tokyo, Japan 57
    Walt Disney World, Orlando, USA 113, 201
        Animal Kingdom 113
        Disney's Hollywood Studios 111
            'Hercules "Zero to Hero" Victory Parade' 111
        Epcot, Orlando, USA 107, 110, 136
            'Disney's Electronic Forum' 107
            'Spaceship Earth' 110
            'World Showcase' 46, 114
        Magic Kingdom 1–3, 57, 110, 113, 197, 226
Disneyfication 11, 13–15, 201
Disneyization 11, 13–14
Distory 15, 202
Dodecanese 98
Dodona 102
Dolphins 47, 50, 52, 65, 104, 138, 146, 163, 179, 225
Doric order 18, 28, 51, 88, 106, 112–13, 118, 122–6, 128, 152, 165, 174, 186, 195
Dorney Park and Wildwater Kingdom, Allentown, USA 115
    'Hercules' 115
    'Hydra the Revenge' 115
Doryphoros, see Polykleitos
Dresden 61
Dubai 190

E-Da World, Kaohsiung, Taiwan 37–8, 136, **149–65**, 190, 221
    E-Da Theme Park **154–65**, 222
        'Acropolis' 155, **157–9**, 161, 165
            'Acropolis Plaza' 156
            'Booster' 159
            'E-Da Royal Theatre' **157**
            'Greek Wedding Cafés' 159

'Journey of Hero' **157–8**
'Mystical Corner' 159
'Water Tamer' 159
'Greek Avenue' 155, 157
'Return of Hades' **156–7**
'Santorini' 155–6, **159–63**
'5D Ship of Souls' 161
'Apollo Palace' 162
'Big Air' **162**
'Candy Kingdom' 161
'Flume Ride' **161–2**
'Oia Café' 161
'Pirate Ship' 161
'Splash Battle' **162–3**
'Volcano Plaza' 156, 160
'Trojan Castle' 154–5, 160, 162, **164–5**
'Da-E's Home' 165
'Dark Ride' 164
'Ice World' 165
'Love Pea Café' 165
'Taiwan Formosa' 154, 222
'Trojan Plaza' 156–7, 164
'Troy Restaurant' 164
'Fashion Street' 150
'Flea Market' 152
'Outlet Mall' 150, 152–3, 155
'Royal Hotel' 152
'Taiwan Story House' 151
Easter 161
Egypt 55, 62–4, 66, 72, 80–5, 94–7, 110, 149, 164, 177–8, 208, 214
El Cid 91
El Jabato (comic, 1958–present) 76, 83
Elche 77, 80
Elis 181, 183–4
Emporion, *see* Ampurias
England 30, 49, 64, 114
enlightenment 21, 39, 168
Epcot, *see* Disney, theme parks
Eratosthenes 34
Eros 88, 157, 183
Etruscans 80, 165
Euclides 64, 110
Eugenides, Jeffrey 108
Europa (mythological character) 34
Europa-Park, Rust, Germany 18, 24, 32, 37–8, **44–61**, 63–4, 68, 69, 70, 94, 117, 143–4, 182

'Griechenland' **47–61**
'Abenteuer Atlantis' 49, **56–8**
'Fluch der Kassandra' 49, **58–61**
'Flug des Ikarus' 49, **55–6**
'Helena Souvenirs' 50
'Helenas Traum' 49
'Olymp' 49
'Olympia Basketball' 50
'Pegasus' 49, 52, **53–4**
'Penelope Glykos' 50
'Poseidon' 47, 49, **50–3**, 54, 56, 59, 94, 143
'Taverna Mykonos' 50
'Troja Kiosk' 50
'Portugal' 117
'Atlantica SuperSplash' 117
Europe 2–3, 7, 12, 19, 21, 28–31, 34–5, 37, 41, 44–6, 48–9, 54–5, 61–2, 75, 77–80, 101, 105–8, 112–14, 117, 121, 125, 128–37, 139–40, 146, 149–54, 156–7, 159, 165, 167–8, 178–9, 192–3, 198, 216, 220, 225, 227
European Economic Community 2, 79
European Union 61, 75, 79
Eurystheus 90
Evans, Arthur 34, 140, 206
Evzones 160
experience society and experience economy 21, 23
externality 11–13, 226

fairy tales 5–7, 107
Famagosta 227
Family Land Waterpark, Wisconsin Dells, USA 120
Fantasia (movie, 1940) 113, 183
Farnese Heracles, *see* Heracles
Finland 223
Flintstones (1960–1966) 171
Formosan Aboriginal Culture Village, Yuchi, RoC 150–1
'European Palace Garden' 150
France 2, 30, 45–7, 76, 80, 133, 139, 159, **167–88**, 195, 223, 225
Franco, Francisco 75–8, 212–13
Frémiet, Emmanuel 223
Freud, Sigmund 32
Full House (TV series, 1987–1995) 108

Fustanella 2, 113, 148
FYROM, *see* North Macedonia

Gardaland, Castelnuovo del Garda, Italy 55
   'Ikarus' 55
Gauls 167, 169, 171–8, 180, 183–4, 223–4
   see also Celts
German Democratic Republic (DDR) 41
Germans (ancient peoples) 40, 75, 172, 176
Germany (Federal Republic) 15, 23–4, 32, 37, **39–73**, 75, 114, 116, 141, 167–70, 191, 198, 208, 210–11, 217, 223
Geryon 78
Gibraltar 69, 156
Global Village, Dubai, UAE 190
globalization 134, 191, 204
glocalization 189, 191–2
Glücks-Königreich, Obihiro, Japan 198
Göring, Hermann 41
Golden Fleece 102–3
Goths 171
   see also Visigoths
Graces 93
Great Britain 45, 62, 112, 144, 133, 168–9, 171–2, 206, 216
Great Wall of China 145
Greece, Kingdom of 31
Greece, Republic of 47, 153, 191, 194, 227
Greek body 35–6, 40, 43, 71, 87, 107, 169–70, 173
Greek Civil War 41
Greek Colonization 77–9, 170
Greek military junta 41
Greek National Tourist Organisation (GTNO) 29, 205
Greek statues 19, 25, 29, 35–6, 39, 43–4, 71–3, 82, 86–7, 92–3, 98, 112, 132, 143, 145, 147, 173, 180, 184, 186, 203, 215
Greek temple 18, 25–7, 31, 33, 37, 39, 50–2, 54, 73, 86, 93, 106, 111–12, 118–19, 126, 128–32, 138, 147, 157, 165, 181, 186, 188, 195
Greek War of Independence 30, 39, 77, 109, 168
Gryphon 52, 158

Hades 93, 100–1, 112, 126–8, 152, 156–8
Hadrian 76
Hagenbeck, Carl 9
Hagia Triada sarcophagus 91, 98–9, 148
Halloween 81–2, 159
Hansa-Park, Sierskdorf, Germany 61
Happy Family (movie, 2017) 209
Happy Valley parks 132
   Happy Valley Beijing, PRC 25, 33, 37–8, **132–49**, 186, 191
      'Aegean Harbour' **134–49**
         'Aegean Harbour Ferry' 137, 139
         'Greek Small Town Business Street' 139, 142
         'Happy Bubble' 137, 139
         'Happy World' 139, 146, **147–9**
         'Journey of Odyssey' 137, 139, **141–4**, 145, 147
         'Ocean Star' 137, 142
         'Olympic Culture Square' 139–41, 144
         'Plato's Bookcase' 139
         'Troians' 137
         'Trojan Horse' **140–1**, 142–3, 145
      'Ant Kingdom' 135
      'Atlantis' 135
         'Crystal Wing' 135
         'Energy Collector' 135
         'Energy Storm' 135
         'Holy Crystal Castle' 135
      'Dessert Kingdom' 135
      'FantaSea' 136–7, 144, 147
         'Flying over the Aegean Sea' 136, **144–7**
         'King's Treasure' 137
         'Kitchen Klosos' 137
         'Sparta's Arena' 136–7
      'Happy Time' 135
      'Lost Maya' 135, 139
         'Apollo's Wheel' 139
      'Shangri-La' 133, 135
      'Wild Fjord' 135, 137
   Happy Valley Chengdu, PRC 132
      'Dream of Mediterranean' 133
      'Flying over the Mediterranean' 133
      'Poseidon's Trident' 133
      'Great Szechwan' 133

Happy Valley Chongqing, PRC 132
    'Old Chongqing' 132
    'Playa Maya' 133
Happy Valley Nanjing, PRC 132
Happy Valley Shanghai, PRC 132
    'Playa Maya' 133
    'Shanghai Beach' 132
    'Shangri-La' 133
    'Sunshine Harbour' 133
Happy Valley Shenzhen, PRC 132
    'Playa Maya' 133
    'Shangri-La' 133
    'Spanish Square' 133
Happy Valley Tianjin, PRC 132
Happy Valley Wuhan, PRC 132
    'Playa Maya' 133
Harpies 103
Harry Potter 6–7
Harvard University 28, 155
Haymarket 14
Hawaii 12, 124
Hector 89, 107
Heidi 81
Helen 34, 49–50, 89
Helen of Troy (movie, 1956) 34
Helen of Troy (movie, 2003) 89
Helios 52, 110, 126, 143, 146, 152, 158–9, 162
Hell 22, 60, 82, 101, 128, 157–8
Hellenism 32, 79, 85, 87, 136, 173, 214
Hephaestus 113
Hera 69, 86–7, 89–90, 95, 112
    Hera Barberini 86
Heracles 33, 42, 56, 69–70, 78, 89–90, 93, 102, 111–15, 123, 158, 175–6, 182, 184, 186, 194, 217
    Farnese Heracles 93
Heraklion, Greece 99
    Heraklion Archaeological Museum 99
Herculaneum 71
Hercules (movie, 1997) 25, 111–14, 157, 217
Herder, Johann Gottfried 75
Hermes 101, 126–7, 173
Heron 64
Hersonissos 194
Heterotopia 44, 192

Hissarlik 66
historical culture 3–4, 11–12, 15–16, 26, 36, 77, 150, 167, 171, 190–1, 205, 216, 227
history boom 20–2, 132
Hitler, Adolf 40, 43
Hölderlin, Friedrich 39
    Hyperion 39
Holiday Park, Haßloch, Germany 61
Hollywood 111, 190
Holocaust 15, 226
Holy Land Experience, Orlando, USA 11
Homer 28, 33, 50, 52–3, 65–6, 69–70, 86, 89, 98–101, 103–4, 130, 143, 176, 212
    Iliad 103, 144
    Odyssey 57, 64–5, 67, 69–70, 99–103, 112, 128, 143, 163, 175–6
    Nekyia 69, 100–1, 162
Hong Kong, People's Republic of China 1, 3, 222
Huston, Anjelica 111
human zoo 4, 9
Hydra of Lerna 91, 102, 115, 144, 162, 181–2, 225
hyperreality 8, 10, 21, 160–1

Iberia Park, Benidorm, Spain 82, 99
    'Iberia Village' 82
Iberians 76–8, 81, 83, 213, 224
Icarus 34, 49, 55–6, 70–2, 95–6, 104, 181–2, 210
Iceland 45, 82
immersion 4–5, 7, 9–10, 12–15, 19–21, 24–5, 27–8, 33, 37, 52, 60, 63, 85, 87, 94, 100, 102, 125, 145, 150–1, 161, 193, 198, 226
Indiana Jones 54, 91, 115
Indonesia 5, 10, 151, 198–9
ionic order 2, 18, 44, 63, 86–8, 98, 112, 127, 147–8, 184
Ireland 45, 114
Irons, Jeremy 115
Islands of the Blessed 176
Israel 5, 198
'It's a Small World', *see* Disney, theme parks
Italia in Miniatura, Rimini, Italy 198

Italy 1, 3, 5, 26, 45, 47–8, 54, 65, 68, 70–1, 80, 83, 88, 114–15, 117–18, 133–4, 139, 150, 152–3, 220, 226
Ithaca 50, 99–100, 142

Jabato, see El Jabato
Jackson, Michael 111
Japan 2, 129–31, 136, 139, 151, 154, 162, 189, 198, 212, 220
Jerusalem 11
Jesuits 129
Judaea 11
Julius Caesar, *see* Caesar
Jung, Carl Gustav 32
Jurassic Park 54, 159

Kalkar 210
Kaohsiung, *see* E-Da World
Kassel 30
Kazantzakis, Nikos 41
Kenya 198
Kerdyllion, Mount 194
Kernies Familienpark, Kalkar, Germany 210
Kitsch 14, 23
Knossos, Greece 34, 42, 91, 97, 99, 137–8, 143, 145, 155, 199, 201
    Charging Bull Fresco 91
    Dolphin Fresco 138
    Griffin Fresco 143
    Ladies in Blue Fresco 99, 155, 164, 173
    Palace of Knossos 34, 37, 42, 52–3, 79, 86, 90–1, 95, 97, 99, 112, 117, 140, 145, 181, 194, 206
    Prince of Lilies Fresco 91, 164
    Tauromachy Fresco 34, 91, 99, 143
Kojak (TV series, 1973–1978) 108
Kore / korai 98
Korea, *see* South Korea
Kouros / kouroi 98, 158
Kouros of Sounion 98
Kuomintang 150–1, 154, 222
Kyllini 194

La Tonnerre de Jupiter (movie, 1903) 185
La Turbie 183
labyrinth 34, 56, 90, 181–2, 194

Labyrinth Theme Park, Hersonissos, Greece 194
Lantern Festival 149
Laocoön Group 173
Lascaux 10
Leipzig, *see* Belantis
Leonardo da Vinci 182
Leonidas 107
limes 96
Little Pollon (1982–1983) 131
living history 9, 19–20, 22, 46, 151, 198
London 36, 134
    Big Ben 2
    Hyde Park 134
Long Beach 113
Lost City, Moses Kotane, South Africa 25
Ludwig I of Bavaria 39
Lusitanians 76
Lyotard, Jean-François 203
Lysippos 87–8
    Apoxyomenos 87, 152
    Eros Stringing His Bow 88

Macau 132
Macedonia (historical region) 42, 194
Macedonia (Republic), *see* North Macedonia
Magic Kingdoms, see Disney, theme parks
Magneto 124
'Main Street U.S.A.', *see* Disney, theme parks
Malia 99
Manga 129–30
Manticore 127
Maoism 150, 222
Marco Polo 114
Marseille 169–70
Marsyas Painter 155
Maya (ancient people) 24, 115, 121–2, 124, 128, 133, 135, 139
Maya the Bee (character) 81
Medea 103
medievalism 6
Mediterranean Sea 45, 47–9, 53–4, 62, 65, 75, 79–85, 87–8, 92, 94, 96, 103, 110, 117, 133–4, 136, 139, 143, 153, 155, 159, 161, 164, 169–70, 174, 176, 182–3, 224

Medusa 49, 53, 111–12, 121–2, 128, 158, 163, 181
Méliès, Georges 185
Melos 97, 130
Merkouri, Melina 41
Messina, Strait of 65–6, 211
Mexico 24
Mid-Mountain Acropolis, Chengdu, PRC 134
Middle Ages 6–7, 11, 45, 55, 60, 62, 64–5, 70, 78, 83, 92, 101, 131, 138, 140, 142, 145, 156, 159, 165, 169, 177
Middle East 2, 175
Miller, Frank 31, 106
Miller, Henry 107, 110
mimetic utopia 133–4, 150
Ming dynasty 24
Mini Israel, Latrun, Israel 198
miniature parks, miniatures 5, 10, 130
Minoan civilization 18, 33–5, 52–3, 56, 91, 97–9, 103, 112, 115, 117, 137–8, 140, 143, 145, 148, 160, 162, 164, 173, 181, 194, 210
Minos 34, 90, 181
Minotaur 34, 56, 86, 90–1, 97, 100, 158
Minujín, Marta 30
Mississippi river 13
Missolonghi 168
modernism 15, 193, 200
Mongolia 154
Mouskouri, Nana 41
Mt. Olympus Water and Theme Park, Wisconsin Dells, USA 37–8, 109, 115, **117–28**
  'Medusa' **121–2**, 128
    'Anaconda' 122
    'Boa' 122
    'Cobra' 122
    'Diamondback' 122
    'Hispaniola Bay' 121–2
    'Jaguar Hot Tub' 122
    'Mayan Raging River' 122
    'Mystical Tower Tube Slides' 122
    'Mythos Grill' 122
    'Sacred Well Hot Tub' 122
    'Warriors Basketball Pool' 122
  'Mykonos' 118, 121
  'Neptune's Outdoor Water Park' **123–6**, 128
    'Aphrodite Gifts and Apparel' 125
    'Big Fat Greek Pizza Joint' 125
    'Endless River' 123
    'Greek Tycoon' 125
    'Huck's Lagoon' 124
    'Lost City of Atlantis' 124
    'Pandora's Candy and Kids Shop' 125
    'Poseidon's Rage' 124–5, 127
    'Shops at Mt. Olympus' 125
    'The Great Pool of Delphi' 125
    'The River Troy' 123
    'Tiki' 124
    'Triton's Challenge' 124
    'Triton's Fury' 124
    'Triton's Rage' 124
  'Parthenon' **122–3**, 125
    'Opa!' 123
    'Parthenon Arcade' 123, 125
    'Tea Cups' 123
  'Poseidon' 121
  'Rome' 118, 120
  'Santorini' 121
  'Zeus' (village) 121
  'Zeus' Playground' **126–8**
    'Almighty Hermes' 127
    'Apollo's Swing' 127
    'Artemis Apparel' 128
    'Athena Gifts and Apparel' 128
    'Catapult' 127
    'Cyclops' 120, 126
    'Delphi Funnel Cakes' 128
    'Get Shipwrecked' 128
    'Hades 360' 126–7
    'Hades BBQ Pit' 128
    'Helios' 126
    'Hermes' 126
    'Kiddie Balloon Ride' 127
    'Kiddie Biplane' 127
    'Kiddie Swing' 127
    'Kiddie Train' 127
    'Little Titans' 126
    'Manticore' 127
    'Orion' 126
    'Pan's Animal Farm' 127
    'Pegasus' 120, 126
    'Poseidon Go Karts' 126

'Tiny Heroes' 126
'Titans Track' 126
'Trojan Horse Go Karts' 126
'Zeus' 120, 126
Mulan (movie, 1998) 111
Mundomar, Benidorm, Spain 80–1
muses 98, 144–5, 186
museums, museology 4, 9, 13, 15, 19, 23–4, 46, 99, 130, 150, 153, 155, 198
My Big Fat Greek Wedding (2002) 108, 174
My Big Fat Greek Wedding 2 (2016) 108
Mycenae 34, 52–3, 85, 139
    Lion Gate 52, 85
Mycenaeans 34, 97–9, 112, 114, 143
Mykonos 29, 42–4, 47, 49–50, 58–9, 118, 121, 136, 152, 164, 190
    Agios Nikolaos 59–60
    Panagia Paraportiani 164, 190
Myron
    Discobolus 36, 43, 82, 95, 173, 184
mythology
    Chinese mythology 144
    German mythology 65
    Greek mythology 2, 31, 33–4, 36–7, 42–3, 47, 49–50, 52–4, 56, 59, 61, 63, 68, 70–3, 79, 88–91, 96, 99, 102–4, 111–12, 115, 117, 121, 129–30, 132, 135–7, 140–1, 143–5, 147, 149, 153, 155, 157, 161, 163, 165, 167, 172, 175, 177–81, 183, 188, 193–4, 206, 222
Mythos Park, Athens, Greece 193

Nanjing 132, 134
Naples 68
Napoleon I 30, 39, 152
Nashville 106
    Centennial Park 106
    Parthenon 106
National Socialism, *see* Nazism
Nationalism 11, 17, 39–40, 76, 151, 154, 168–9, 172–3, 192, 194, 207
Native Americans 9, 14–15, 62, 108, 115, 119, 124, 216
Naxos 98
Nazism 30–1, 40–1, 43, 106, 169–70, 216
Nekyia, *see* Homer
Nemea 90–1

Nemean lion 90–1, 186
Neoclassicism 125, 140, 152, 157, 159, 164–5, 168–9, 173, 183
Nero 83, 158–9
Netherlands 45, 47, 198
New Culture Movement 130
New England 45
New Orleans 108, 191
New Reoma World, Marugame, Japan 2
    'Oriental Trip' 2
New York 109, 111, 119
    Broadway 111
    Fifth Avenue 109
    'Hercules Electrical Parade' 111
    New Amsterdam Theatre 111
Nice 170, 177
Nike of Samothrace 169
Nile river 84–5, 149
Niobe 93
North Macedonia 194
nostalgia 5, 8, 20, 22–3, 33, 54, 57, 95, 154, 189
Numantia 76, 212

occidentalism 131, 134, 139, 219
ocean 56–8, 60, 62, 100, 133, 137, 142, 210
Odysseus 32–3, 49–50, 53, 60, 64–73, 89, 97, 99–102, 112, 115, 137, 139, 141–3, 145, 147, 158, 162–3, 180, 191
Odyssey, *see* Homer
Oenomaus 93
Oktoberfest 148
Olivier, Laurence 112
Olympia 19, 25, 29, 35, 50–1, 54, 86, 89, 92–94, 123, 137, 139, 144–8, 170, 173–4, 183–4, 186, 191, 194
    Bouleuterion 174
    Hellanodikeon 174
    Philippeion 184
    Prytaneon 174
    Temple of Zeus 19, 25, 51, 86, 89, 92–4, 96, 123, 139, 147, 173–4, 186
Olympia Aqua Park, Kyllini, Greece 194
Olympia – Fest der Völker (movie, 1938) 40, 43
Olympic flame 35, 40, 77, 146, 148, 185

Olympic Games 19, 35, 40, 43, 77, 79, 85, 87, 95, 106–7, 113, 135, 137, 139, 144, 146–9, 153, 161, 165, 170, 173, 176, 180, 183–4, 191, 193, 221–4
Olympus, Mount 2, 37–8, 49–50, 90, 93, 109, 115, 117–21, 123, 125–6, 128, 131, 148, 162, 165, 175–6, 185
orientalism 2, 29, 31, 43, 84, 131, 168–9, 173
Orion 126
Orlando 1–3, 6, 11, 56–7, 110–11, 113, 115–17, 197, 226
Ortega y Gasset, José 212
Orthodox Christianity 29, 49, 59, 108–9
Osaka 130
Otto of Greece 39
Ottoman empire 2, 29, 75, 84, 90, 168
Overseas Chinese Town Enterprise 132, 220

Paestum 88
Palenque 24
Pan 127
pan flute 2–3
Panathenaic Games 155
Pandora 58, 69, 97–8, 125, 157
panorama 27–8
Paramount theme parks 81
Parc Astérix, Plailly, France 7, 18, 37–8, 43, **177–88**
  'À travers le temps' 177–8
  'Bienvenue chez les Gaulois' 177–8
    'Lutèce Plage' 178
  'Egypte' 177–8
  'Grand Lac' 177
  'Grèce' 177–8, **179–88**
    'Au comptoir des mers' 180
    'Discobélix' 179, **183–5**
    'L'Hydre de Lerne' **182–3**
    'La Descente du Styx' 178–9
    'La Rivière d'Elis' **183**, 184
    'La Tonnerre de Zeus' 127, 184, **185–8**
    'Le Cheval de Troie' 179–81
    'Le Vol d'Icare' **181–2**
    'Les jeux d'Odous' 180
    'Pégase Express' 179, **181**
    'Taverne Dionysos' 180
    'Théâtre de Poseidon' 179–81
  'L'empire romain' 177–8, 181
    'Romus et Rapidus' 178
  'Les Vikings' 177–8
  'Square in Gergovia' 177
  'Via Romana' 177–8
Paris (mythological character) 89
Paris (city in France) 1–2, 44, 57, 79, 111, 150, 159, 169, 171, 177–8, 181, 184, 193, 223
  Eiffel Tower 1
  Gare Montparnasse 181
  Louvre Museum 72
  Montmartre 159
  Paris-Plage 178
Parnassus 181
Paros 43
Parque España, Shima-Isobe, Japan 212
Parthenon, *see* Athens, Greece
pastness 20, 24, 204
Patroclus 90
Pausanias 93
Pegasus 3, 49, 52–4, 60, 104, 113, 120, 126, 179, 181
Peloponnese 183
Pelops 93
Penelope 50, 100, 180
People's Republic of China, *see* China
Peplos Kore 98
Pergamon 54
  Altar of Pergamon 54
Pericles 30, 106, 186, 224
Persephone 101
Perseus 112
Persia 107, 127, 176
Persian Wars 31
Phaistos 98, 103
  Palace of Phaistos 103
  Phaistos Disc 98
Phantasialand, Brühl, Germany 24, 61
  'China Town' 24
  'Mexico' 24
  'Chiapas' 24
Pharos of Alexandria, *see* Alexandria
Phidias 25, 86, 93, 147, 186
Philadelphia 106
philhellenism 19, 28, 30, 39, 41, 43, 107, 130, 168, 170, 190–2, 207

Philip II of Macedon 184, 194
philosophy and philosophers 28, 30, 35, 39,
　　　　　44, 64, 71–2, 85, 110, 113,
　　　　　170, 173, 192, 194
Phinaeus 103
Phocaea 170
Phoenicians 28, 77, 80, 110
Phylakopi 97
　　Flying fish Fresco 97
Pinocchio 211
Pirates 84, 90, 104, 161, 199
Plailly, *see* Parc Astérix
Plato 35, 56–7, 81, 116, 139, 160, 210
Polykleitos 36
　　Diadumenos 87
　　Doryphoros 36, 87, 152, 206
Polynesia 124
Polynesian Cultural Center, Laie, USA 1 2
Polyphemus 50, 57, 68–9, 99–100, 162–3
　　see also Cyclopes
Pompeii 18, 26, 57, 71
Pontius Pilate 27
PortAventura World, Vila-Seca, Spain 80, 83
　　PortAventura Park 80
　　'Mediterránea' 80
Portofino 139
Portugal 45, 76, 117
Poseidon 36, 47–54, 56, 58–9, 68, 72–3, 82,
　　　　　94, 100, 102, 104, 115–16,
　　　　　121, 124–7, 132–3, 143, 152,
　　　　　162–3, 179–81, 215
　　Poseidon (or Zeus) of Cape Artemision 82
postmodernism 4, 8–9, 15, 20–2, 33, 54,
　　　　　132, 189, 193, 197, 199–200,
　　　　　202–3
Praxiteles 173
　　Hermes 173
presentification 10, 20–1, 194
Princeton 107
Prometheus 131
provence 169
Prussia 40, 106, 171, 223
Pylos 99
pyramid 24, 63, 66, 85, 95, 149
Pythagoras of Rhegion 72
Pythagoras of Samos 63–4, 110, 211

Qing dynasty 24

racism 173, 207, 224
Raffaello Sanzio 110
　　School of Athens 110
Rainbow Magic Land, Rome, Italy 26
re-mediatization 7, 37, 167, 179, 187
Remus 179
renaissance 45, 117
Republic of China, *see* Taiwan
Rhode, *see* Rosas
Rhodes 98, 145–6, 158, 174
Riefenstahl, Leni 40, 43
Rodin, Auguste 173
Roman empire 1, 11, 26–30, 32, 36, 43,
　　　　　54, 57–8, 72, 76–7, 79–85,
　　　　　87–8, 92, 95–6, 105–6, 111,
　　　　　114–15, 118–19, 123–32,
　　　　　134, 143, 148, 152, 159,
　　　　　169, 171–4, 176–84, 208,
　　　　　212, 219
Roman Vision, Nanjing, PRC 134
Rome (city) 26, 118, 120, 173, 178–9
　　Arch of Constantine 118
　　Circus Maximus 98
　　Musei Capitolini 72
　　Museo Nazionale Romano 43, 173
　　Piazza Navona 150
　　Trevi Fountain 219
Romulus 179
Rosas 77
ruins 2–3, 11–12, 23–5, 28–30, 32,
　　　　　34–6, 40, 44, 50, 52–4, 99,
　　　　　102, 104–5, 109–10, 112,
　　　　　115, 118, 121, 123, 126,
　　　　　135, 140, 144, 146, 152,
　　　　　160, 163–4, 168, 172, 181,
　　　　　193–4
Rushmore, Mount 194
Russia 2, 45–6, 193
rust, *see* Europa-Park

St. George 148
Saint Seiya (1986–1991) 136
Saint-Exupéry, Antoine de 133
Salento 70
Samos 87
Samothrace 169, 174

Santorini 29, 43–4, 56, 60, 121, 136, 146–7, 152, 155–6, 159–61, 165
    Fira 160
        Catholic Cathedral 160
    Oia 160–1
        Panagia Platsani 60, 146, 160
Sardinia 153
Satyrs 183
Savalas, Telly 108
Saxony 61
Scandinavia 45–6, 137
Schliemann, Heinrich 34, 52–4, 66, 86
Scio 168
Scotland 114
Scylla 65–6, 101, 162, 183, 211
Sea World parks 58, **116–17**
    Sea World Orlando, Orlando, USA 56, 116
        'Journey to Atlantis' 56, 116–17
    Sea World San Antonio, San Antonio, USA 116
        'Journey to Atlantis' 116–17
    Sea World San Diego, San Diego, USA 116, 202
        'Journey to Atlantis' 116–17
seasons 93
sedan 169
Sedaris, David 108
Seneca the Younger 76
Shanghai 132–4
Shanower, Eric 112
    Age of Bronze 112
Schengen Treaty 45
Shenzhen 130, 132–3
Shōdoshima 130
Sicily 65, 68
Simulacrum 9–10, 24, 191, 200
Sirens 60, 70, 101, 104, 117, 162, 176, 183, 212
Sirtaki 42, 63, 88
Six Flags over Texas, Arlington, USA 12
Skansen, Stockholm, Sweden 4
slavery, slaves 173
Smith, Maggie 112
Snake Goddess 173
Snoopy 180
Snow White 211
Socrates 44, 107
Solon 56

Sophocles 110
    Oedipus King 110
Sounion, Cape 98
South Africa 25
South Korea 131
Spa World, Osaka, Japan 130
Spain 15, 33, 37, 45, 47–8, **75–104**, 133, 139, 167, 171, 195, 212, 215
Sparta 31, 40–1, 79, 99, 106–7, 131, 136–8, 171–2, 205, 208, 216
Sphinx 93, 98, 142–3
Sphinx of Naxos 98, 142
Splendid China, Shenzhen, PRC 132
sports 6, 35–7, 40, 43, 50, 85, 87–8, 95, 113, 122, 135, 139, 147–9, 153–4, 165, 170, 172–4, 206
Stalingrad 41
Stagira 194
Star Wars 13
steampunk 6, 54, 57–8, 117, 124, 135, 156, 164
stereotypes 1, 6–7, 9–10, 17–18, 20–1, 28–9, 34–6, 42–3, 46–8, 63–5, 70, 84, 89, 106, 108, 114–15, 131, 136–7, 165, 167–8, 171–6, 179–80, 184, 187, 190, 195, 224–5
Stockholm 4
Strickland, William 106
Styx 100, 178–9
Sun god, *see* Helios
Sweden 4
Switzerland 3, 45–6, 49, 55
Sydney 135

Tableaux vivants 13
Taipei 154
Taiwan 37, **149–65**, 190, 195, 221–2
Taiwan Folk Village, Sanchun, RoC 151
Taman Mini Indonesia Indah, Jakarta, Indonesia 10, 198–9
Tantalus 101
Tarquinia 165
Tartaros 69
Tartessos 78, 213
Tauromachy Fresco, *see* Knossos, Greece
Teenage Mutant Ninja Turtles 190
Telemachus 99–102
Tennessee Centennial 106

Terra Mítica, Benidorm, Spain 15, 18–19, 24–5, 33, 37–8, 43, 76, **80–104**, 125, 141, 143, 174, 182, 184, 186, 191, 214
   'Atalaya' 81
   'Egípto' 81–2, 84, 96, 214
      'Cataratas del Nilo' 94
      'Obelisk Square' 85
   'Grand Luxor Hotel' 82
   'Grécia' 81–2, 84, **85–96**, 97, 99, 102–4
      'Acropolis' 86, 95
      'Alucinakis' 88, **95–6**
      'Arquéologos' 89
      'El Labirinto del Minotauro' 86, **90–1**, 100
      'El Sueño de las Nayades' 87
      'Fountain of Hera' 86, 89, 95
      'Hercules' **89–90**
      'Isla Golosina' 87
      'La Furia de Tritón' 86, **94**
      'Los Icaros' **95**, 96, 104
      'Olympic Exedra' 87, 95
      'Plaka' 88
      'Portico de Ágora' 87, 99
      'Synkope' 86, **94–5**, 104
      'Teatro de Olimpia' 92
      'Templo de Kinetos' 86, 89, **92–3**, 95
      'Titánide' 81, 86, **91–2**
      'Troya, la conquista' 87, **89**, 90, 143
   'Iberia' 81–3, 91, 96
      'Barbarroja' 84, 89–90
      'Jabato' 83
      'Tizona' 91–2
   'Las Islas' 81–4, 88, 94, **96–104**, 214
      'Auditorio de Pandora' 97
      'Corfú' 104
      'El rescate de Ulises' **99–102**, 214
      'El sueño de Pandora' 98
      'Isla Golosina' 99
      'La cólera de Akiles' 97, **103–4**
      'La sorpresa de los dioses' 98, 104
      'Los Rápidos de Argos' 99, **102–3**
      'Mithos' 97, **104**
      'Nintendopolis' 98
      'Numen' 98
      'Rodas' 98
      'Tarantela' 98
   'Mediterranean Village' 82–4, 92
   'Ocionía' 81–2
   'Roma' 81–4, 95–6
      'Espartaco' 83
      'Hispania' 83–4
      'Imperium' 83
      'Inferno' 82
      'Magnus Colossus' 95, 127
      'Nerón' 83
Texas 12
Thanksgiving 149
theatre 32, 49, 52, 63–4, 85, 97–8, 110–11, 137–8, 157, 179–81
theming 5–6, 17–18, 36, 49, 53, 55, 58, 63–4, 70–3, 80–1, 85, 87–8, 91–95, 102–4, 117, 119–28, 140–1, 143, 148, 150, 152, 155, 157, 159, 161–2, 164, 177, 179, 186, 202, 204, 209–10, 215
Theopompus 57
Thermae Romae (2008–2013) 130
Thermopylae 31, 40, 106–7, 131, 138
Theseus 28, 91
Thessaloniki 193
Third Reich, *see* Nazism
Thrace 52
Thucydides 31, 65, 68
Thurrakos el Celtibero 76
Tianjin 132
Tiber river 179
Tibet 135, 221
Tierra Santa, Buenos Aires, Argentina 27
Tiki 124
time travel 10, 12–13, 19, 22–4, 85, 201
Tiryns 97–8
   Palace of Tiryns 97
Titans 34, 92, 112, 126, 153, 158, 163
Tobu World Square, Kinugawa Onsen, Japan 130
Tokyo 1–2, 57, 111, 189, 197, 199
Trajan 76
Trapani 65
Treasure Island Resort, Wisconsin Dells, USA 120–1, 124
   'Bay of Dreams' 120–2
tritons 86, 94, 124
Troilus 165

Trojan Horse 33, 52, 65–6, 87, 89, 95, 99, 118–20, 126, 137, 140–3, 145, 152, 156, 161, 165, 179–81, 191, 195
Trojan War 33, 52, 89, 107, 112, 143
Troy (mythological city) 34, 50, 58, 60, 65–6, 87, 89–90, 99–100, 123, 137, 140–2, 145, 152, 164, 191
Troy (movie, 2004) 107
Turkey 48, 227
Turin 36
Tuscany 83
Tutankhamun 82
Twain, Mark 124
Tyrannicides 152
Tyrrhenian Sea 68

United States Military Academy 124
United States of America 1–2, 5, 8, 13–16, 28, 31, 37, 45, **105–28**, 131, 135, 137, 149, 153, 165, 194–5, 197, 217
Universal Studios theme parks 189
   Universal Orlando Resort 6
     Universal Studios Orlando 115
       'Poseidon's Fury' **115–16**
Utopia 5, 22, 57, 111, 133–4, 150, 210

Valencia 80
Valentine's Day 149
van Beethoven, Ludwig, *see* Beethoven, Ludwig van
Vatican 180
Vecchio Plazza, Beijing, PRC 133–4, 150
Venice 1, 114
Venus 176
   Capitoline Venus 152
   Venus de Milo 44, 60, 152, 169, 190, 223
   Venus of Arles 88
   see also Aphrodite

Vergil 130
Verne, Jules 57–8, 164
Vesuvius 71
Vicky the Viking 81
Victorian age 26, 133
victories 93
Video games 7, 13, 18, 32–3, 91, 186, 201–2
Vikings 81, 135, 177–8
Vila-Seca, *see PortAventura World*
Viriatus 76
Visigoths 75, 77, 212

Wagner, Richard 65
Walhalla, Donaustauf, Germany 39
Water World, Ayia Napa, Cyprus 227
Weddings 146–7, 159–60
Wild West 149
Winckelmann, Johann Joachim 39, 203
Windmill 48, 118, 139, 146, 160–1, 180, 195
Window of the World, Shenzhen, PRC 130, 132
Wisconsin Dells 117–20, 122, 125, 128
Wisconsin river 118
Wolf, Christa 59
World's Fair 4, 46, 197
Wrath of the Titans (2012) 112
Wuhan 132–3

Xenophon 40

Zeus 19, 25, 34–5, 51, 63, 69, 86–7, 89–90, 92–3, 96, 113, 120–3, 126–7, 132, 139, 147, 173–4, 184–7, 219, 224
Zhongshan 143
zodiac 136, 153, 157, 159, 164–5
zoo 4, 127
Zorba the Greek (novel, 1946) 41
Zorba the Greek (movie, 1964) 41
Zorba's Dance 41, 174

www.ingramcontent.com/pod-product-compliance
Lightning Source LLC
Chambersburg PA
CBHW070024010526
44117CB00011B/1705